The Cambridge Companion to Hip-Hop

It has been more than thirty-five years since the first commercial recordings of hip-hop music were made. This *Companion*, written by renowned scholars and industry professionals, reflects the passion and scholarly activity occurring in the new generation of hip-hop studies. It covers a diverse range of case studies from nerdcore hip-hop to instrumental hip-hop to the role of rappers in the Obama campaign and from countries including Senegal, Japan, Germany, Cuba, and the UK. Chapters provide an overview of the "four elements" of hip-hop – MCing, DJing, breakdancing (or breakin'), and graffiti – in addition to key topics such as religion, theater, film, gender, and politics. Intended for students, scholars, and the most serious of "hip-hop heads," this collection incorporates methods in studying hip-hop flow, as well as the music analysis of hip-hop and methods from linguistics, political science, gender and film studies to provide exciting new perspectives on this rapidly developing field.

JUSTIN A. WILLIAMS is Lecturer in Music at the University of Bristol, and the author of *Rhymin' and Stealin': Musical Borrowing in Hip-Hop* (2013). He has taught at Leeds College of Music, Lancaster University, and Anglia Ruskin University, and has been published in *Popular Music, Popular Music History*, and *The Journal of Musicology*. As a professional trumpet and piano player in California, he ran a successful jazz piano trio and played with the band Bucho! which won a number of Sacramento Area Music Awards and were signed to two record labels. He has co-written (with Ross Wilson) an article on digital crowd funding for *The Oxford Handbook to Music and Virtuality* and is currently co-editing (with Katherine Williams) *The Cambridge Companion to the Singer-Songwriter*.

The Cambridge Companion to

HIP-HOP

. . . .

EDITED BY
Justin A. Williams

CAMBRIDGE
UNIVERSITY PRESS

University Printing House, Cambridge CB2 8BS, United Kingdom

Cambridge University Press is part of the University of Cambridge.

It furthers the University's mission by disseminating knowledge in the pursuit of
education, learning and research at the highest international levels of excellence.

www.cambridge.org
Information on this title: www.cambridge.org/9781107643864

© Cambridge University Press 2015

First published 2015

A catalogue record for this publication is available from the British Library

Library of Congress Cataloguing in Publication data
The Cambridge companion to hip-hop / edited by Justin A. Williams.
    pages   cm
Includes bibliographical references and index.
ISBN 978-1-107-03746-5 (hardback : alk. paper)   1. Rap (Music) – History and criticism.
I. Williams, Justin A.
ML3531.C356   2015
782.421649–dc23   2014032226

ISBN 978-1-107-64386-4 Paperback

Dedicated to the memory of Professor Adam Krims

Contents

Figures

The author and publishers acknowledge the following sources of copyright material and are grateful for the permissions granted. While every effort has been made, it has not always been possible to identify the sources of all material used, or to trace all copyright holders. If any omissions are brought to our notice, we will be happy to include the appropriate acknowledgments on reprinting.

Music examples

Contributors

Kyle Adams is Associate Professor of Music Theory at Indiana University. He has published on the analysis of sixteenth-century music in *Theoria* and the *Journal of Music Theory*, and on the analysis of rap music in *Music Theory Online*.

Regina N. Bradley, Ph.D., researches African American culture, specifically twentieth- and twenty-first-century African American literature, the American South, and hip-hop. Bradley is the founder of Outkasted Conversations, a critically acclaimed dialogue series that discusses hip-hop duo Outkast's impact on popular culture. She can be reached at www.redclayscholar.com.

Richard Bramwell is a Research Associate at the University of Cambridge. He completed his Ph.D. at the London School of Economics and Political Science. His teaching and research are in the fields of postcolonial studies, contemporary literature and culture, and the sociology of culture, with a focus on Black British and African American literary and vernacular cultures.

Brenna Reinhart Byrd is an Assistant Professor of German at the University of Kentucky. Her research interests include Germanic linguistics, Turkish-German identity, hip-hop studies, style and sociolinguistic variation, second language acquisition, and the history of the German language.

Christopher Deis specializes in the study of race and the politics of popular culture. He has taught courses on hip-hop culture and politics at a number of institutions including the University of Chicago and DePaul University, and has presented at national conferences and colloquia on the politics of popular culture in the USA.

Mike D'Errico is a Ph.D. candidate in the UCLA Department of Musicology, and the Digital Humanities graduate program. His research focuses on sound, software, and interface design in digital audio production, from beatmaking in hip-hop and electronic dance music to haptic interfaces in video games, apps, and mobile media.

Sujatha Fernandes is an Associate Professor of Sociology at Queens College and the Graduate Center, City University of New York. She is the author of *Who Can Stop the Drums? Urban Social Movements in Chávez's Venezuela* (2010); *Cuba Represent! Cuban Arts, State Power, and the Making of New Revolutionary Cultures* (2006); and *Close to the Edge: In Search of the Global Hip Hop Generation* (2011).

Travis L. Gosa is Assistant Professor of Africana Studies at Cornell University, where he teaches courses on education, music, and popular culture. Gosa is editor of *Remixing Change: Hip Hop & Obama* (Oxford University Press, 2014). He serves on the advisory board of Cornell's hip-hop library archive.

Kjetil Falkenberg Hansen is affiliated with the Sound and Music Computing Group at KTH Royal Institute of Technology, Stockholm, where he was awarded his Ph.D. on analyzing and modeling scratch DJ performances. Current research interests are new interfaces for expressive performances, and rehabilitation and training through interacting with sound.

Geoff Harkness is Assistant Professor of Sociology at Morningside College. His book, *Chicago Hustle and Flow: Gangs, Gangsta Rap, and Social Class*, was published by University of Minnesota Press in 2014.

Anthony Kwame Harrison is the Gloria D. Smith Professor of Africana Studies at Virginia Polytechnic Institute and State University. He is author of *Hip Hop Underground: The Integrity and Ethics of Racial Identification* and has published widely in the fields of popular music studies and qualitative research methodology.

Adam Haupt is an Associate Professor in the Centre for Film and Media Studies at the University of Cape Town. Haupt is the author of *Stealing Empire: P2P, Intellectual Property and Hip-Hop Subversion* (Human Sciences Research Council Press, 2008) and *Static Race and Representation in Post-apartheid Music, Media and Film* (Human Sciences Research Council Press, 2012).

Michael P. Jeffries is Associate Professor of American Studies at Wellesley College. He is the author of *Paint the White House Black: Barack Obama and the Meaning of Race in America* (Stanford University Press, 2013), and *Thug Life: Race, Gender, and the Meaning of Hip-Hop* (University of Chicago Press, 2011).

Imani Kai Johnson is an interdisciplinary scholar, specializing in the African diaspora, global popular culture, hip-hop, and dance. She is an Assistant Professor of Dance Studies at University of California Riverside. Her manuscript, "Dark Matter in B-Boying Cyphers: Race and Global Connection in Hip Hop," examines invisible forces within the ritual dance circles of breakers.

Loren Kajikawa teaches in the University of Oregon's School of Music and Dance where he serves as Assistant Professor, Ethnomusicology and Musicology. His book *Sounding Race in Rap Songs* (University of California Press) explores the relationship between stylistic change and racial formation in rap's first two decades as a commercial genre.

Oliver Kautny is Assistant Professor of Musicology and Music Education at the University Wuppertal. He has published various articles about hip-hop and co-edited *Die Stimme im Hip-Hop* (2009, with Fernand Hörner) and *Sampling im Hip-Hop* (2010, with Adam Krims).

Noriko Manabe is Assistant Professor of Music at Princeton University. She has published articles on the antinuclear movement, Japanese rap, DJs, the mobile internet, and children's songs. Her monographs, *The Revolution Will Not Be Televised: Music and the Antinuclear Movement in Japan Post-Fukashima Daiichi* and *The Revolution Remixed: A Typology of Intertextuality in Protest Songs*, are forthcoming from Oxford University Press.

Ivor Miller is a cultural historian specializing in the African diaspora in the Caribbean and the Americas. His book *Aerosol Kingdom* (University Press of Mississippi, 2002, reprint 2010) documents and interprets the creation of hip-hop culture in New York City from its beginnings in the late 1960s until the present, focusing on the Afro-Caribbean and African American contributions resulting from twentieth-century migrations.

Ali Colleen Neff is a media anthropologist and Ph.D. Drawing from her dual ethnographic fields of urban Dakar, Senegal, and the Mississippi Delta, and her experience as a turntablist and film-maker, her work centers on the anthropology of media, music, and sound. These and other work can be found at her website, www.ethnolyrical.org.

Nicole Hodges Persley is an Assistant Professor of Theater at the University of Kansas. She is a professional actress and producer. Her forthcoming book, *Sampling Blackness: Performing African Americanness in Hip-hop Theater and Performance*, explores non-African American hip-hop theater, conceptual art, and dance artists from the United States, Korea, and the UK.

Alice Price-Styles is a freelance writer based in London. She earned her BA in English and Drama at Goldsmiths College, where her research interests became music and spoken word poetry. Since graduating she has traveled often, interviewed a range of musicians and artists, worked with record label Delicious Vinyl, and now regularly contributes to publications such as *Wax Poetics*, *Dazed & Confused*, and *NYLON Magazine*.

Amanda Sewell is a professional academic editor in Traverse City, Michigan. She holds a Ph.D. in musicology from Indiana University. Her scholarship has appeared in the *Journal of the Society for American Music* and the *Journal of Popular Music Studies*.

Chris Tabron is a multi-platinum record producer and mixer based in New York City who has worked with a wide array of artists including Beyoncé, Blondie, Flume and Mary J. Blige. A Ph.D. candidate at New York University, his doctoral work focuses on hip-hop production in New York from 1989 to 1999.

Justin A. Williams is Lecturer in Music at the University of Bristol, and the author of *Rhymin' and Stealin': Musical Borrowing in Hip-Hop* (2013) for University of Michigan Press's Tracking Pop series. In addition to editing this volume, he is co-editing (with Katherine Williams) *The Cambridge Companion to the Singer-Songwriter*.

Christina Zanfagna is an Assistant Professor of Ethnomusicology at Santa Clara University. She has published on subjects such as gospel rap, hip-hop "krump" dancing, and digital DJing practices. She is currently writing a book on holy hip-hop culture in Los Angeles.

Acknowledgments

This book was a nerdy dream of mine, the kind that young academics have when they get enthusiastic about an academic book series they "grew up" with. As a student, then as an educator, my copies of books such as *The Cambridge Companions to Jazz, Beethoven, Rock and Pop*, and *Schubert* are well worn, and used year on year for numerous purposes. Victoria Cooper helped make my nerdy dream a reality. Special thanks to her and to Fleur Jones and Emma Collison at the press for their patience and advice. I would also like to thank all the contributors to the volume and for their enthusiasm for the project. Many of the authors are scholars whom I met at conferences where we ended up having long and passionate discussions about hip-hop, and I thank them for always reinvigorating me with passion for the topic. I'd like to think we are the Wu-Tang Clan of hip-hop academics, a diverse collective with different skills that has created a force more powerful than the sum of its parts.

Many authors were able to use their personal interviews with a number of practitioners and scholars (Amiri Baraka, Doze Green, MC Lars, MC Frontalot, Compton Virtue, to name a few) and I want to thank all the interviewees and those who gave permission to use photos for the volume. Special thanks to Belinda Lawley for letting us use two of her photos from the Breakin' Convention in Sadler's Wells for both the front and back covers, and thanks to Dave Barros at Sadler's Wells for finding them in the archives. I would also like to thank my students at Bristol University who took my Hip-hop Music and Culture class in spring 2014. The class provided a useful forum to test and discuss many of the ideas that follow. Thanks to my wife Katherine for her support, as always.

A large debt, personally and professionally, is owed to my former Ph.D. supervisor. All who study hip-hop, but especially those who analyze hip-hop music, are indebted to the work of the late Adam Krims. As Kyle Adams rightly states in his chapter: "No one contributed quite as much to the analysis of hip-hop as Adam Krims; in fact, analytical approaches can productively be divided into 'Krims' and 'Other'." Professor Krims had agreed to contribute two chapters to this volume (one on Russian rap and another on geography), but passed away suddenly in September 2012. Professor Krims's work has touched everyone working on hip-hop scholarship and thus looms as an important presence and influence on this book and the entire field. He had an extremely important professional influence on me, and I am happy to say he was also a friend. The book is very much dedicated to his memory.

Introduction: the interdisciplinary world of hip-hop studies

JUSTIN A. WILLIAMS

It has been more than forty years since DJ Kool Herc threw his first party, the universally agreed "big bang" moment for the birth of hip-hop music (August 11, 1973). It has now been more than thirty-five years since the first commercial recordings of hip-hop. Hip-hop icons have now been inducted in the Rock and Roll Hall of Fame, including Grandmaster Flash and the Furious Five (2007), Run-D.M.C. (2009), Beastie Boys (2012), and Public Enemy (2013). Harvard and Cornell Universities have important and extensive hip-hop archives and hip-hop artists such as 9th Wonder and Afrika Bambaataa, respectively, are visiting professors for those institutions. 2Pac's "Dear Mama," Public Enemy's *Fear of a Black Planet*, De La Soul's *3 Feet High and Rising*, Sugarhill Gang's "Rapper's Delight" and Grandmaster Flash and the Furious Five's "The Message" have all been enshrined in the Library of Congress National Recording Registry. *The Grove Dictionary of American Music* now includes entries on "beat-making," "A Tribe Called Quest," "Dr. Dre," "Ruthless Records," and many other hip-hop artists and labels. The Smithsonian Institution holds a turntable used by Grandmaster Flash, a boombox used by Fab 5 Freddy and a customized jacket worn by breaker Crazy Legs among their collections. There are now graffiti museums, hip-hop tours of the Bronx, and most countries around the world have some, if not more than one form of hip-hop in their own vernacular and related dialects.

In light of all this (and more), I hope there is no need to convince readers that hip-hop has been a powerful force globally. More so, it has been a positive force for many, if at times a problematic force. Hip-hop has influenced other styles of music, grassroots movements, political campaigns, protests, and has become at best an inspiration and empowering force, and at worst a promotion and glorification of poisonous ideas and behavior within societies (e.g. gang crime, homophobia, misogyny). And while such interpretations are often up to the situatedness of the listener/viewer, hip-hop has acted as stump, lectern, pulpit, and site of debate in ways that other opportunities to discuss African American cultures have not (or have simply been nonexistent). Not to mention that hip-hop originally existed, and still exists, as a party accompaniment, a soundtrack to dance, and a force for pleasure. The twin pillars of the DJ and the producer have also innovated new styles, utilizing old sounds to new ends, and transforming previous influences in the delicate balance between novelty and tradition. Most countries around the world now include some indigenous hip-hop, and it is fascinating to see how the regional variants take the form in new directions.

I also hope I don't need to convince readers that hip-hop should be studied, written about, and celebrated in the academic sphere. It is safe to say that hip-hop scholarship is now entering a new and exciting generation of thought. Books like David Toop's *The Rap Attack* from 1984 were crucial to painting the picture of the new style emerging from New York beginning to captivate the mainstream. Tricia Rose's *Black Noise* took the conversation to another level, as did Adam Krims's *Rap Music and the Poetics of Identity* (2000). Murray Forman's *The 'Hood Comes First* (2002) emphasized the importance of space and place, and Jeff Chang's *Can't Stop Won't Stop: A History of the Hip-Hop Generation* (2005) revisited the early days of hip-hop with the attention to detail and passion that only a "hip-hop head" could offer and spoke to a broad audience. His history, and timeline of hip-hop, is still the definitive and authoritative account of the first thirty years. Joseph Schloss has written *the* books on sampling (*Making Beats*) and breakdancing (*Foundation*), Felicia Miyakawa has discussed Islamic elements in hip-hop (*Five Percenter Rap*), and most recently Mark Katz has written an important history of the hip-hop DJ (*Groove Music*). In terms of edited collections on hip-hop, one stands out above the rest: Murray Forman and Mark Anthony Neal's *That's the Joint!* now in its second edition (2011). This collection is intended to complement, rather than replace, the other. I hope that this volume continues and extends the conversation that both acknowledges the foundational ideas of hip-hop scholarship and takes it in new directions. Like many hip-hop practitioners do, hip-hop scholars acknowledge their roots, giving an important nod to those forefathers and foremothers while taking the form in new directions. The contributors to this volume are at the forefront of new ideas, new books, new ways of studying how hip-hop has intersected with the cultural practices and objects around us.

For a number of reasons, hip-hop studies has become one of the most interdisciplinary fields in existence. This volume alone has contributors working in ethnomusicology, music theory, sociology, political science, anthropology, theater studies, dance, visual arts, freelance journalism, film studies, African American studies ("on and on, till the break of dawn"). Despite our varied disciplinary backgrounds, hip-hop becomes our connecting point, and it then becomes a discussion point for matters like method and discipline – their perspective on hip-hop has helped me to question my own, defending some of the tenets of my discipline and in other cases becoming more open minded about them. Never wanting to exclude any voices, the book is intended as a multidisciplinary conversation which at once broadens hip-hop studies while making implicit statements about the disciplines and backgrounds we come from.

While the volume covers a wide range of topics and geographical regions, it cannot be comprehensive in terms of regions covered or in terms of disciplinary foci. Because of this, there will inevitably be omissions in the eyes of some readers, but I have intended many of the articles to be a starting point for wider discussions. Where appropriate, the chapters have a 'further reading' section to direct the reader to additional information about the topic. Hip-hop is a dialogue, a conversation, both with itself and outside forces, and this book is no different. I would recommend that any scholar interested in hip-hop consult the canonical literature I have previously mentioned, but that this book can be used as the starting point into hip-hop studies or can act as a fresh volume for those already immersed in the subject. For those looking for a comprehensive timeline of hip-hop history, one could do no better than the timeline compiled by Jeff Chang for Kugelberg's *Born in the Bronx* (2007), which is a primarily photographic collection of hip-hop's early history in the 1970s and early 1980s. Like a rapper's flow, this book is intended to be part of a wider conversation with the hip-hop nation, and an inclusive one at that.

Part I of the book is subtitled "Elements," a reference to the original "four elements" of hip-hop culture: MCing (Alice Price-Styles in Chapter 1), breakin' (Imani Kai Johnson in Chapter 2), graffiti (Ivor Miller in Chapter 3), and DJing (Kjetil Falkenberg Hansen in Chapter 4). There are multiple candidates for the "fifth element" of hip-hop. It seems appropriate here for Travis Gosa in Chapter 5 to select Afrika Bambaataa's candidate for the fifth element: knowledge (others have said fashion, beatboxing, or theater, or see Mike D'Errico's Chapter 22 for beatmaking as the fifth element). Two other elements remain in this section: religion and theater. Religion has been an ever-present element in hip-hop culture, and Christina Zanfagna's chapter (Chapter 6) discusses holy hip-hop as an important element part of the ever-present sacred and profane in arts of the Black diaspora. Groups like the Five Percenters have influenced hip-hop, and hip-hop has now influenced the style of worship, and is being used to perform religion. Nicole Hodges Persley's chapter (Chapter 7) acknowledges that hip-hop always has an element of theatricality, and proceeds to outline developments and innovations in hip-hop theater, including musical theater, contemporary dance, and hybrids such as "choreopoetry" (spoken word with hip-hop inflected contemporary dance).

The second part of the book looks at ways of studying various components to hip-hop music and culture. Oliver Kautny focuses on new ways of analyzing flow, by moving beyond a semantic analysis of the lyrics and engaging with rhythmic placement, syllabic emphasis, and pitch to create a more multidimensional analysis. Kyle Adams comes from a music theory background, and discusses the problems of hip-hop musical analysis. He provides a useful tool to analyze flow based on George List's "The Boundaries of Speech and Song," adapted to rap flow (y-axis: staccato and legato spectrum; x-axis: sharp to dull consonants spectrum) to show the connection between types of flow and affect. Chapters 8 and 9 adopt the terminology "beat" and "flow," where the flow includes the rap and its delivery and the beat includes all other elements on the track.

Chris Tabron's chapter (Chapter 10) investigates hip-hop production at a specific moment in time, 1989–1999. He uses Tony Maserati's work on Mary J. Blige's *My Life* as a primary case study, using ethnographic methods to investigate "how technology informs listening practices." It is not a potted history of hip-hop production (I'd look to Oliver Wang's article on "beat-making" on *Oxford Music Online* for that),[1] but a case study of a producer's work on a canonical album. Something that Tabron's chapter shows, among other things, about the process and politics of music production, is that R&B and hip-hop production in the 1990s were closer than their fan discourses would suggest.

Anthony Kwame Harrison's (mis)recognition as a member of the Hieroglyphics in the open mic scene of the Haight/Ashbury area of San Francisco provides a fascinating study of race and freestyle hip-hop (Chapter 11). The chapter marries the auto-ethnography of Harrison's fieldwork with theory from cultural anthropology, sociology, and hip-hop studies to create a fascinating case study of scenes and race.

Chapters 12 and 13 explore hip-hop archetypes from two different, but related spheres. Geoff Harkness's Chapter 12 discusses hip-hop film over the past thirty years, as a cinematic subgenre, and describes a number of stereotypical characters from such films (e.g. "Skilled Sincerists," "Wannabes," etc.). In Chapter 13, Regina Bradley discusses hip-hop and gender, extending some of the archetypes we encounter in the work of Cheryl Keyes ("fly girl," "sista with attitude," "queen mother," and "lesbian")[2] by adding male archetypes as well ("philosopher king," "playa/pimp," etc.). Outlining and extending the work of Mark Anthony Neal, Imani Perry, Tracy Sharpley-Whiting, and others, Bradley expounds on the complicated space of gender politics and sexuality in mainstream US rap.

In Chapter 14, political scientist Christopher Deis engages with a number of questions, including "How do we define politics?" If hip-hop is political, how does it fit in the broader contexts of politics and "the political?" In Chapter 15, I discuss the analytical and legal implications of digital sampling and other cases of musical borrowing. Through a close reading of Xzibit's "Symphony in X Major" (2002), I put the analytical tools discussed in the chapter to work and ask questions related to the implications of re-using sounds with previous cultural associations while firmly acknowledging that intertextuality is one of the most, if not *the* most, defining features of hip-hop music and culture.

Part III includes a number of case studies which discuss some of the previous themes in more detail. Chapter 16 investigates the subgenre of "nerdcore" hip-hop, including useful interviews with some of the defining names in the genre (MC Lars, MC Frontalot, mc chris). Here, Amanda Sewell discusses nerdcore as an outlet for non-stereotypical (i.e. US mainstream) rappers to boast and rap about topics important to them. The chapter looks at fandom, race, and homophobia through a nerdcore lens and puts the music on the academic map. In Chapter 17, Adam Haupt looks at competing representations of black masculinity in three US films of the 1990s (*Boyz N the Hood, Do the Right Thing,* and *Slam*), and how hip-hop music plays a crucial role in all three.

Given that much of Parts I and II focus on the US mainstream, I wanted to find a careful balance between US and non-US examples in Part III. In recruiting authors for Part III, it became clear to me that the number of scholars working on hip-hop around the world could fill more than one entire volume, but I resisted the temptation to separate the book as I rarely see US and non-US hip-hop sharing space in the same volume. It is interesting to see shared themes emerge from two seemingly disparate case studies: to use one example, the answer song "Roxanne, Roxanne" mentioned in my Chapter 15 could be compared with other answer songs in other locales, such as in Japanese hip-hop (Chapter 18). Or the bragging and boasting found in wider African American culture can be found in both Price-Styles's reading of Gang Starr (Chapter 1), Noriko Manabe's account of boasting in Japanese hip-hop (Chapter 18), and in Sewell's chapter on "nerdcore" hip-hop (Chapter 16). It is also fascinating to trace a concept which originated in Africa such as the griot or storyteller, as it follows a lineage down to the origins of the hip-hop MC (Chapter 1), explained in the context of Senegal and Senegalese hip-hop (Chapter 21) by Neff.

One of the running themes of the book is geography, and rather than devote its own chapter to the topic, the theme runs throughout the book. It is always worth asking "where is this happening?" or "wherefrom have these artists come?" The historiography of mainstream US hip-hop is intertwined with geography: born in the Bronx, followed by continued East Coast dominance in the 1980s, with a shift to the West Coast in the 1990s, followed by the South in the late 1990s.

Another shared theme within some of the case studies is the ethnic and racial mixing in postcolonial cultures that use hip-hop as a voice for the voiceless. Much has been written about this in the context of Palestinian hip-hop,[3] and in this volume authors discuss using hip-hop either for political purposes (against the Japanese nuclear reactor in Chapter 18), or as a resistant identity (Turkish-German hip-hop's use of the resistance vernaculars of stylized Turkish-German in Chapter 23).

The presence of an (often disenfranchised) minority is something that needs more cross-cultural academic attention: in addition to the Turkish-German case, there are South American immigrants practicing hip-hop in Italy, or North Africans in France who rap in a mix of Arabic and French, or those from Cape Verde who use the dialect in Lisbon hip-hop, or the use of Chiac in Canada (e.g. the group Radio Radio), or Mexican in Southern Californian hip-hop. One can observe the polyethnicity of global hip-hop groups in the front and back cover photos of this book – of the French b-boy crews Phase T (founded in 1998) and the Vagabond Crew, respectively, performing in London at the Breakin' Convention in 2010 and 2011.

As Deis acknowledges in his chapter on politics (Chapter 14), hip-hop is often discussed as giving voice to the voiceless, empowering marginalized communities "disadvantaged by unequal arrangements of power" (Deis, Chapter 14). But while at once themes emerge which start to create links or narratives which hinge on a reduced notion of identity ("marginal" vs "dominant," or an empowered community vs. a ghettoized one), the situation is often more complex at a closer look. A number of hip-hop groups are polyglot, multiracial, and polystylistic.[4] For example, Manabe cites those in the Japanese hip-hop scene who are Korean, quarter-Trinidadian, half-Finnish, half-Filipino, quarter-Chinese, half-Caucasian American, half-Ghanian, and half-African American. Such is the nature of a postcolonial globe.

The routes and immigration of groups of people have a direct effect on the sounds of the music, and while we should be careful not to overstate the case, hip-hop becomes a political voice for some groups, as well as an outlet to create new hybrids from local and more mainstream forms (and, as Manabe shows us in Chapter 18, the working classes outside of Tokyo are starting to emerge on the rap scene). Nowadays, I only have to look at the use of hip-hop among the youth in the Egyptian Revolution in 2011 or Turkish protests in 2013 to see how powerful hip-hop can be. As the late Biggie Smalls rapped in 1994, "You never thought that hip-hop would take it this far."

In addition to geographies of place, there are also geographies of space, as Chapter 19 points to a particular record store in London (Deal Real Records) which became an important venue for the interactions of MCs, DJs, and audiences in the UK hip-hop scene. In Chapter 21, Ali Colleen Neff discusses the hip-hop scene in Dakar, Senegal, at the intersections of African practices and the arts of the Black diaspora. In many ways, hip-hop in Africa becomes a homecoming of the diaspora, but she also acknowledges the 1980s' Senegalese immigration to New York City, and US artists like Akon who come from a Senegalese background.

While Tabron discussed the linkage of 1990s' rap producer and DJ in Chapter 10, D'Errico discusses the next decade's rejection of the title "DJ" for beatmakers of "experimental hip-hop" in Chapter 22. "Post-turntable" artists such as MF Doom, Madlib, J Dilla, and Flying Lotus are the subject of both criticism and praise as an "alternative" to more mainstream hip-hop forms. As jazz rap was given "alternative," high art status within hip-hop,[5] it seems as if these artists working within instrumental hip-hop have grasped the torch. Without feeling that they have to pay dues to the turntablist tradition, these experimentalist beatmakers are using the Akai MPC sampler as a musical instrument, Ableton on the iPad, or live coding at shows. D'Errico argues convincingly that "beatmaking" should be considered the fifth element of hip-hop.

In the spirit of Darius Brubeck's article "1959: the beginning of beyond" for *The Cambridge Companion to Jazz* which looked at the four seminal albums of that year (Dave Brubeck's *Time Out*, John Coltrane's *Giant Steps*, Miles Davis's *Kind of Blue*, Ornette Coleman's *The Shape of Jazz to Come*),[6] I asked Loren Kajikawa to choose what he saw as the most important year in hip-hop. He picked 1988, which is argued for extremely convincingly in Chapter 24, a year which heralds a "golden age" in the genre. The chapter also raises important questions about historiography, canon, and influence.

In the final case study, Chapter 25, Michael Jeffries discusses the intersection of Barack Obama, the hip-hop generation(s), Black masculinity, and US politics more broadly. One could point to the street artist Shepard Fairey's "hope" poster for the Obama 2008 presidential campaign, or the fact that two-thirds of 18–29-year-olds voted for Obama in 2008, or that a number of prominent hip-hop artists promoted his candidacy, and celebrated his election win. Not to mention Obama's strategic engagement with hip-hop which "established a new political location for hip-hop," according to Jeffries. What his chapter reminds us, as do the others, is how powerful hip-hop culture is. Yes, it's a party music. Yes, in certain instances it is used for commercial profit. Yes, it can be political, and religious, and offensive. It can be empowering. It can be exclusionary. It can be pleasurable. Something this big cannot be reduced to a single affect, or a single purpose, or subject to a single verdict.

In May 2014, when I was cooped up in my house and office finishing the editing for this book, I went to the Breakin' Convention as it toured through my locale of Bristol, England. Breakin' Convention is an annual festival of hip-hop dancing and theater hosted by Jonzi D (see Chapter 7) and Sadler's Wells Theatre. Numerous groups performed, from London, France,

Swindon, Bristol, and elsewhere. The most awe-inspiring group was ILL-Abilities, an international crew of breakdancers with various disabilities, and use breakdancing to express themselves. No one can put into words how powerful their show was, so I won't even try, but it reminded me what this book is about. The whole event blew me away, with impromptu breakdancing in the foyer of Bristol's Colston Hall (named after Edward Colston, as it was formerly the boys' school that he founded in 1707). Colston was heavily involved in the transatlantic slave trade, and it was extremely powerful to see such a positive product come from the forced migration of African-based people in a space named after a man associated with such atrocities. That's taking something abominable and turning it into something positive. That's hip-hop.

Notes

1 Oliver Wang, "Beat-making," in Charles Hiroshi Garrett (ed.), *Grove Dictionary of American Music*, 2nd edn. (Oxford University Press, 2013). Available at www.oxfordmusiconline.com/subscriber/article/grove/music/A2218626 (accessed June 1, 2014).

2 Cheryl L. Keyes, "Empowering Self, Making Choices, Creating Spaces: Black Female Identity via Rap Music Performance," *The Journal of American Folklore* 113 (2000): 255–269.

3 Amal Eqeig, "Louder than the Blue ID: Palestinian Hip-Hop in Israel," in Rhoda Kanaaneh and Isis Nusair (eds.), *Displaced at Home: Ethnicity and Gender among Palestinians in Israel* (New York: State University of New York Press, 2010), pp. 53–74; Ela Greenberg, "'The King of the Streets': Hip-Hop and the Reclaiming of Masculinity in Jerusalem's Shu'afat Refugee Camp," in Murray Forman and Mark Anthony Neal (eds.), *That's the Joint! The Hip-Hop Studies Reader*, 2nd edn. (New York and London: Routledge, 2011), pp. 370–381; David McDonald, "Imaginaries of Exile and Emergence in Israeli Jewish and Palestinian Hip Hop," *The Drama Review* 57/3 (2013): 69–87; Sunaina Maria and Magid Shihade, "Hip Hop from '48 Palestine: Youth,

Music, and the Present Absent," *Social Text* 30/3 (2012): 1–26; Joseph Massad, "Palestine Put to Music," in Rebecca Stein and Ted Swedenburg (eds.), *Palestine, Israel and the Politics of Popular Culture* (Durham, NC and London: Duke University Press, 2005), pp. 175–201. My sincere thanks to Polly Withers for her work which brought these references to my attention.

4 Curse Ov Dialect, for example, is a hip-hop band from Australia, which was formed in 1994. They use ethnic samples and sometimes sing in Turkish or Indian. They use folk costumes on stage and declaim a multiculturalist message; three of them from origins other than Australia. My thanks to Tony Mitchell for bringing this up on an International Association for the Study of Popular Music (IASPM) listserv discussion on global hip-hop.

5 See Justin A. Williams, "The Construction of Jazz Rap as High Art in Hip-Hop Music," *Journal of Musicology* 27/4 (2010): 435–459.

6 Darius Brubeck, "1959: the beginning of beyond," in Mervyn Cooke and David Horn (eds.), *The Cambridge Companion to Jazz* (Cambridge University Press, 2002), pp. 177–201.

PART I

Elements

1 MC origins: rap and spoken word poetry

ALICE PRICE-STYLES

The shared forms and tenets of spoken word poetry and rap are prominent and many. Just as the boundaries between genres of music ebb and flow, the lines and limits between rap and poetry are likewise fluid and open. It can be difficult attempting to fully separate the two when defining their relationship, as their function and history intertwine so.

Some see rap as one natural progression in African American oral forms, and strong cases can be made tracing the lineage between rap and forms such as the talking blues and oral storytelling. Amiri Baraka, marked figure of contemporary African American arts and founder of the Black Arts Movement (BAM), discusses what he terms as the "changing same" in his criticism of Black music and art forms, referring to the constant evolution of art that is necessary in order to keep the core spirit of expression consistent. Of contemporary rap he stated in 2010:

> Music changes because the people change . . . but the forms are more closely related than people think. Rap is nothing but a modern blues. You listen to old Lightnin' Hopkins or one of them old blues singers, the form is not too far from something say Tupac would use . . . There's no great difference between rap and talking blues. That's why rappers are always sampling people, because they can feel the continuity.[1]

Sarah Webster Fabio, another influential proponent of African American art and education, describes this intrinsic connection between African American art forms as "a lifeline which extends from the early slave/work songs and religious spirituals and folktales to James Brown's 'Staggolee' and Jimi Hendrix's 'Dolly Dagger.'"[2] Therefore, when tracing the lineage of rap and its forebears, it can be appreciated that this extends much further back into history than the immediately preceding forms, such as the blues or spoken word of the twentieth century.

To chart the history of modern spoken word and rap, it is crucial to recognize the age-old traditions of oral performance and storytelling in African culture. From oral folk tales to traveling griots, oral forms have long been an integral element of communication within African communities. And, despite historic attempts to suppress indigenous African culture in America, these forms remain a congenital part of African American expression. As Baraka stated: "Afro-American culture is strong, that's why

[11]

it still exists . . . You can remove people from a place, but they carry their culture with them . . . because that's shaped their way of thinking, that's the way they think."[3]

African-style orality in the form of spoken word poetry came to notable prominence in the American popular conscience in the twentieth century. Around the time of the Harlem Renaissance of the 1920s, jazz poetry became popular, as poets like Langston Hughes experimented with developing their writing in accordance with jazz rhythms, utilizing freestyle approaches and incorporating various subversions to form.

Free-form jazz poetry was then embraced in the 1950s by figures of the Beat Generation, such as Allan Ginsberg, William S. Burroughs, and Jack Kerouac, who were drawn to the style as an alternative to mainstream, nuclear America. The immediacy and spontaneity of live performance and creation also suited the Beat taste for hedonistic forms and pursuits.

Popular spoken word poetry became more overtly political in the 1960s as artists such as the Last Poets, Sonia Sanchez, the Watts Poets, and Amiri Baraka, among others, spoke out in accordance with the era's civil rights movement (see case study 1, on the BAM below). During this epoch, the direct nature of oral forms, coupled with the inherent Black aesthetic, served to carry pressing messages of racial inequality.

In the 1970s came the greatly influential poet and musician Gil Scott-Heron, whose political poems such as "Whitey on the Moon" (1970) and "B-Movie" (1981) remain pertinent examples of how rhythm and melody can perfectly offset uncomfortable truths and deep messages. In more recent times modern spoken word artists such as Saul Williams, Paul Beatty, and Ursula Rucker, to name just a select few, continue to create spoken word poetry and frequently collaborate with contemporary musicians.

Both African American music and literature have historically gravitated toward each other. Scholar Fahashima Patricia Brown has noted that "Both African American poets and musicians have recognized interrelationship between their arts . . . a continuum between music and literature."[4] Furthermore, African American forms of literature and music both tend to have ingrained speech-like rhythms. For instance on the use of rhythm and nuance in the blues, Baraka states that "Afro-American speech is itself close to the blues. It's the way people talk; the way they slur the words, the way they draw out the words and the meanings. You can give one word several different meanings just on emphasis of it."[5] The diverse array of sounds that can be used in order to play and communicate different meanings is reflective of the pastiche nature of African American speech that Brown describes:

> In the sacred and secular traditions of African American vernacular cultural expression, we can identify modes of language performance: sermon,

testimony, and prayer as performed in the traditional Black Church; public orator in the spheres of political and social life; children's games and jump-rope rhymes: "playin the dozens"; rappin' and signifyin'; tall tales, including toasts and boasts; and the lyrics of the spirituals, shouts, jubilees, gospel songs, field hollers, work songs, blues, jazz, and popular songs. In form, subject, and theme, all of these elements are present in African American poetry.[6]

Rap likewise incorporates a spectrum of aural styles and techniques, often mimicking the various modes that Brown outlines above. However, it is essential to recognize rap's unique quality of being an oral form that arose from hip-hop and that shares a certain sensibility and "cadence" with the genre, particularly in order to resolve the confusion that can arise when considering rap that is not poetry.[7] Many raps are formulated with no designs or intention for the poetic, often more for entertainment value. Styles of rap and lyrical content can vary greatly, but the unifying quality that, for better or for worse, links up the diverse array of rap is the signature hip-hop flow and aesthetic. Rap is not simply a type of spoken poetry, but a relation in the family tree of Black artistic expression. Rap can therefore take inspiration and borrow from preceding spoken word works and styles, while standing independently as an individual member of the family.

So while it is not quite so simple as to state that the spoken word poets such as Amiri Baraka and the Last Poets were somehow the original rappers, the influence and similarities between the poets that preceded rap and rap innovators are apparent.

When tracing the lineage of rap and poetry, active poet and MC of the Project Blowed movement in Los Angeles, Abstract Rude, clarifies that "poetry is old as dirt; rap is dated back to early '70s with roots out of funk/soul movements."[8] Credited with being the first MCs are the likes of Coke La Rock, Kool Herc, DJ Hollywood, and Kurtis Blow, who would "talk-over"[9] the DJ with the intention of encouraging people to dance and raise the energy levels of a crowd. DJ Eddie Cheeba, frequently touted as a "pioneer" of rap, says of the need for MCing over the music in nightclubs: "These people go to discos every week and they need more than music to motivate them . . . I not only play records, but I rap to them and they answer me."[10] The original intention of MCing was to engage with the audience and build a rapport, and in order to do so and maintain interest levels, the art of MCing expanded. Kurtis Blow says of DJ Hollywood's rhythm and how he inspired him to want to rap:

Before 1976, MCs would just work the crowd; introduce people and stuff. "You're rocking with the number one DJ, somebody say, 'Oh yeah'" type of stuff. But DJ Hollywood was a rapper too, and he was actually the first rhythmic rapper I ever encountered. . . . He'd do long, rhythmic verses and just moved the audience.[11]

Similarly credited with being the first "rhyme technicians" to advance their rapping by engaging poetic nuances and innovations in rhythm were DJ Kool Herc's MC Coke La Rock and the Furious Five's Kid Creole and Melle Mel. Forefather DJ Grandmaster Flash summarizes: "Kid Creole and Melle Mel were the first to really flow and have a poetic feel to their rhymes. They were the first rhyme technicians. They were the first to toss a sentence back and forth . . . Along with Coke La Rock with Herc, they were the root."[12]

Then, as the hip-hop movement gained ground and grew, with more artists taking inspiration and becoming involved, developments in styles of rap began to surface and push the form forward. Once innovation in rap began to perpetuate, the parallels between rap and spoken word poetry became more pronounced, and instances where the two cross over became plentiful. Many factors can be attributed to rap flourishing, as increased participation and a need to carve out one's own distinct voice or niche, coupled with hip-hop's intrinsic competitiveness, pushed the attention paid to form and creative intent. In exploring the possibilities of rap as a medium, rappers were able to experiment, channeling and taking cues from spoken word poets before them, and thus strengthening the connection between rap and spoken word.

For some, the influence of spoken word poetry on certain rappers is clear, whether through delivery style, explorations in poetic form, or through allusions to those poets and their work. For instance, on the classic hip-hop track "DWYCK" (1994) by Gang Starr and Nice & Smooth, Guru states, "Poet like Langston Hughes and can't lose when I cruise," which follows the tradition of boast rap by lining himself up alongside the highly influential and respectable figure Langston Hughes, who was a key proponent of jazz poetry. Earmarking an influence of his, he simultaneously partakes in the ancient African mode of "toasting" and "boasting" by comparing his status to that of Hughes and, like an African griot, educates his audience by dropping in the name of a seminal African American literary figure.[13]

Just as Baraka is keen to outline the influence of Black music and rhythm on the content and aesthetic feel to his poetry and writing, several MCs who are noted for dexterous lyrical composition and flow have been likened to preceding jazz artists for the similarities in their sound, including Nas, Busta Rhymes, and Big Daddy Kane, to name just a few. Frequently touted as one of the most accomplished and influential MCs, Rakim readily notes the influence of jazz artists on his rap style: "The thing about the way I styled my rap, drawing from Coltrane and Parker or James B., and building off the flow that they had, that was because that's the music that surrounded me."[14]

Similar ripples of inspiration can often be traced in the respective works of poets and rap artists who have been exposed to the same canon of music, as both take influence from those sources. In the case of twentieth-century poetry and rap, the history and times are close enough for rappers with an awareness and alertness of history to be reacting to shared, or at least partly shared, reference points to those who came before.

As well as being labeled a "poet" by key BAM figure and spoken word poet Sonia Sanchez, Rakim has been credited with raising the bar for rap by initiating the use of multi-syllable flows.[15] Noah Callahan-Bever, editor of *Complex Magazine*, says: "Before him people rhymed very simply, one syllable the last word of every line would rhyme, very much in the style of Run DMC. He came and brought the idea of variable multi-syllable flow, and that really set the tone for everything that would come after it."[16]

Within both underground and mainstream hip-hop, those who use such rhyme patterns are often regarded as lyrically adept at mastering dense and more complex multi-syllabic formations. The former Juice Crew member Masta Ace, for instance, utilizes very measured compound rhymes in his lyrics, serving his stylized and clean delivery. In "Born to Roll" (1994) he tells us how he: "Throws crazy blows and they knows I be plastering." The flow is unique and recognizably Ace's. Alongside this Ace also frequently uses repetition in his verses for flair, which lightens and makes his lines more catching. Later in "Born to Roll" he relays: "Drivin' down the block like what else should a brother do/ It's Saturday, it's Saturday, the heat might smother you."

Another prominent rapper to use dense multi-syllabic rhyme formations is the former Leaders of the New School member Busta Rhymes.[17] In contrast to Ace, Rhymes works with his own distinct style which is arresting and frenetic, though still tight and consistent. His flow has been likened to that of a "jazz trumpeter" by contemporary jazz musician and producer Robert Glasper: "He's an underrated rapper in general to me. Rhythmically? He phrases his rhymes like a jazz trumpeter; it's like listening to a jazz trumpet listening to Busta Rhymes. And you can understand everything he's saying."[18] On 1998's "Gimme Some More," Rhymes comes in on the second verse with "Flash with a rash gimme my cash, flickin' my ash/ Runnin' with my money son go out with a blast," squeezing four rhymes into the first line, and returning to the same half-rhyme at the end of the second line.

Just as the rhyme schemes and structures used by rappers vary greatly with regard to style, so does the level of complexity within the lyrics. When talking of Rakim, Bay area poet and writer D. Scot Miller says: "Lyrically I can't think of anybody who could even come close to him, still. Except one person: Q-Tip. When I find myself in intellectual or existential crisis, a lyric from him can actually pull me out of the doldrums."[19]

Native Tongues MC Q-Tip,[20] of the widely influential group A Tribe Called Quest, tends to rhyme in couplets, for instance the playful "I Left my Wallet in El Segundo" (1990) opens with the simple and straightforward: "My mother went away for a month-long trip/ Her and some friends on a ocean liner ship/ She made a big mistake by leaving me home/ I had to roam so I picked up the phone." And so the cult story of mischief and variable luck starts. The real complexity to Q-Tip's lines, however, lies within the layered meanings and strong metaphors that he conjures and implements to communicate his messages.

On the same album as "I Left my Wallet in El Segundo," *People's Instinctive Travels and the Paths of Rhythm*, is the prophetic track "Footprints." In this song Q-Tip draws parallels between creating new music and traversing the globe, as well as directly comparing the members of his "Tribe" to roamers exploring the world, charting new musical territory. "The valleys of time, are always on my feet/ At least the beat will combine/ The calluses and corns with the funky bassline." He plays on the idea of how success and wealth can alter what you create and leave behind, advocating organic formats: "If you're a megastar, worth will buy you a car/ I'd rather go barefooting, for prints I will be putting." Painting an image of himself and his fellow musicians as pilgrims on a mission he says: "Hand in hand 'cross the land as Muhammad cross the fade/ It's a Tribe who meanders, precious like a jade." He offers up wisdom on deviating from the beaten path, using wordplay on the double meaning of track as either song or path: "Catch the track, track to track, get a map to track a trail/ You will find yourself behind for a map does not prevail." Throughout "Footprints" the use of imagery and metaphor is consistent, cohesive, and multi-faceted.

The progression made in rap to incorporate innovative structural and stylistic form, as well as conscious and intelligent lyrical content, akin to spoken word poetry, follows a tradition in African American music and oral forms to have words and content alongside music and rhythms.

On this evolution, Fahashima Patricia Brown has noted: "Each generation brings its own vocabulary and its own set of issues to the mix that constitutes African American vernacular culture, including its poetry... generations mark the changes on the tradition of the vernacular 'same.'"[21] The sounds and content may differ, but the common thread of expressing and communicating topical issues alongside rhythm is present through to the hip-hop generation. With a multitude of similarities, shared influences, and also of marked differences, spoken word poetry and rap stand separately and complementarily alongside one another in the lineage of African American artistic forms.

Case study 1: the Black Arts Movement (BAM)

Following on from the Harlem Renaissance of the 1920s, which embraced and elevated African American modes and styles of expression, creating art *pour l'art*, the BAM was birthed in the mid 1960s and lived through until the mid 1970s. The BAM continued to advocate and celebrate distinctly Black aesthetics to the point of differentiation, but, blossoming around the same time as the Civil Rights movement in America, did so with very acute political prerogatives. As radical ideas about Black identity for the time were pushing forward, the BAM took a markedly confrontational and provocative approach.

Spearheaded by poet, playwright, and political activist Amiri Baraka (formerly LeRoi Jones), the movement sought to uphold and utilize distinctly Black modes of expression and empower the Black community. The BAM is often viewed in line with the Black Power and Black Panther movements, and it has been noted how "black poets, literary critics, and theorists achieved an exceptional level of national visibility . . . [and] produced a body of texts that exuded the spirit of Black Power self-determination and amplified the vibrant, versatile rhythms of African American expressive culture."[22]

The Black Arts Repertory Theater/School was established in Harlem in 1965. Fittingly, performance and oral forms were the favored modes used, and while not the only medium explored, spoken word poetry played a considerable role within the movement. The potential to play with and manipulate sound and words ignited the movement's deliberately provocative and revolutionary messages. The visceral element to spoken word also allowed the poetry to create an immediate impact upon listeners, in line with the movement's intentions. Baraka's iconic poem "Black Art," which calls for "poems that kill" and in delivery mimics bullet shots and war-planes, has been deemed a poetic manifesto of the Black Arts literary movement.[23]

While the movement garnered much criticism for its aggressive tone and violent imagery, the powerful example that it set has inspired, and continues to inspire, many. James Edward Smethurst writes on how this relates to the hip-hop generation:

> The Black Arts movement made a considerable impression on artists and intellectuals too young to remember its events first hand. Many of the more explicitly political hip-hop artists owe and acknowledge a large debt to the militancy, urgent tone, and multimedia aesthetics of the Black Arts movement and other forms of literary and artistic nationalism.[24]

As a result, interactions between BAM poets and contemporary hip-hop artists have tended to be potent, natural, and numerous. When Amiri Baraka collaborated with hip-hop group the Roots on the track "Something in the Way of Things (In Town)" (2002), his style of poetry was made relevant to modern, underground audiences through the juxtaposition of his distinctive voice and delivery against jazz and drum and bass inflected electronic production. Similarly, in the collaboration between Chuck D of Public Enemy and the Last Poets on *The Time Has Come*, the shared experiences and sensibilities between their respective generations is made clear, as is the likely influence of the Last Poets on key outspoken figures in hip-hop such as Chuck D.

Also reflective of the mutual respect that the spoken word and hip-hop scenes hold for one another, and how easily they can interplay, is Def Jam's Russell Simmons's HBO venture *Def Poetry* (also known as *Def Poetry Jam*). Hosted by Mos Def, the show has seen performances by Sonia Sanchez, Nikki Giovanni, and Amiri Baraka alongside contemporary artists such as Jamie Foxx, Erykah Badu, and Jill Scott, as well as up and coming young poets. In this set-up oral traditions once again provide a means for older generations to communicate and engage with the youth, and for the young to learn from and interact with those who came before them.

Case study 2: Project Blowed

> Like a cross between a church and a sports locker room. – Abstract Rude[25]

A family-run health food café in South Central, Los Angeles was the perfect setting for a unique movement that served up raw hip-hop: Project Blowed. In the documentary *This Is the Life*, Monalisa Murray astutely recalls, "If you are into organically grown, unmanufactured, unprocessed hip-hop, just raw hip-hop, that's where you go."[26]

The movement grew out of a hip-hop open-mic night which started in 1994, run by B. Hall and her son R. Kain Blaze at the Good Life Café. The weekly session ran each Thursday, and provided a space for young MCs, poets, producers, and dancers to perform and share their work. As Marcyliena Morgan writes in the introduction to *The Real Hiphop: Battling for Knowledge, Power, and Respect in the LA Underground*, "If you were a young person who loved hip-hop and could rhyme, dance, write, and draw, and you searched for *real* knowledge and wanted to be recognized and respected – and had respect for others – then the Good Life was a lyrical heaven on earth."[27] Many underground West Coast artists came up through the Good Life, including Freestyle Fellowship, Abstract Rude, and Jurassic 5, and, as the cult status of the open-mic night grew, many influential names in hip-hop, as well as celebrities, began to pass through.

The Good Life Café operated various rules, which contributed to the unique energy and output tremendously. B. Hall enforced a strictly no-cussing rule, which elevated the feeling that it was a serious arts workshop, and also made rapping and freestyling more challenging. Of the decision B. Hall says: "You can't move forward. And that's what we were trying to do, use culture, go back to our original culture, which is honoring the word. That is why you don't use profanity."[28] This boundary in particular encouraged MCs and poets to stretch their creativity, which in turn pushed the poetic quality to their rhyming and freestyling. Those who took part in the Good Life were challenged to experiment with form, concept, and delivery. As a result many prominent figures of the scene developed brilliantly original personas, such as NgaFsh, a part of the Chillin' Villian Empire (C.V.E.), whose output centered on aquatic imagery and allusions.

The atmosphere of the Good Life was notoriously honest and unforgiving to those who did perform. If the crowd were unimpressed, chants of "please pass the mic" would oust performers from the stage, humiliating them in the process. It was this harsh standard-setting, however, that encouraged those involved to push and hone their respective crafts further, and inspired those young artists to be the very best that they could. For this, the deep-voiced MC Chali 2na of Jurassic 5 states that it "became a mecca for skill."[29]

While the predominant form of expression at the Good Life was rap, when asked about the balance of spoken word and rap, Abstract Rude concedes that: "the best, most entertaining rappers had this element of spoken word to their flow. If the beat would stop they could keep going acapella or freestyle even, or, they would do a long acapella before or after their set. So it definitely had a strong spoken word undertone more so than an equal balance of the two."[30] Within this rap setting there is a strong reverence for spoken word freestyle.

Arguably one of the most crucial acts to arise from the Good Life Café was the Freestyle Fellowship. Consisting of MCs Aceyalone, Myka 9, P.E.A.C.E., and Self Jupiter, the quartet incorporated experimental jazz styles into their rap patterns and delivery. They were also adept at incorporating spoken word flows into their verses. Myka 9 talks of how he started out visiting coffee houses:

> I'd get sparked on the coffee and would kick my hip-hop lyrics in a spoken word cadence. At some point I'd start writing spoken word rhymes. It grows in a rap cadence when on a hip-hop beat. You might have a verse or a chorus or a bridge, and want to sacrifice or supplement that with a spoken word segment. It's another way to be creative with your approach to the arrangement of a song, the composition.[31]

Also in keeping with the spirit of the Good Life Café, and their group name, the members of Freestyle Fellowship are firm proponents of the merits of being able to freestyle as an artist. Myka 9 continues:

> You can freestyle as a ride to your approaches. Freestyle holds on to your skill and your cypher, and also helps break your own melody if you are writing a song. You can freestyle and then go back and re-transcribe your material. Also, you can do a "one-take-Jake" when you are so tapped in that it's like a song is flowing through you spontaneously. Those are bright moments indeed.[32]

Freestyle Fellowship's fluid and experimental approach to creating music blurs the boundaries between rap and spoken word, thus exemplifying how closely connected the two artistic forms are.

Conclusion

Both case studies serve to show the interplay between spoken word poetry and hip-hop, in light of their unique histories and shared lineage. When considering the BAM the impact and influence that political spoken word poetry of the movement has had on the hip-hop generation is clearly discerned. In highlighting Project Blowed of the Good Life Café it is possible to see how the experimental and progressive nature of rap as an oral form so closely relates to spoken word poetry, and how rap borrows from spoken word. In comparing the two forms of rap and spoken word, the merits and achievements of both are illuminated and the two can be appreciated as important and equal entities.

Notes

1 Amiri Baraka, interview with the author (London: Southbank Centre), December 20, 2010.
2 Sarah Webster Fabio, "Boss Soul Notes," in *Boss Soul* (New York: Folkways Records and Service Corp., 1972).
3 Baraka interview.
4 Fahashima Patricia Brown, "Song/Talk: African American Music and Song as Poetic References," in her *Performing the Word: African American Poetry as Vernacular Culture* (New Jersey: Rutgers University Press, 1999), p. 74.
5 Baraka interview.
6 Brown, *Performing the Word*, p. 8.
7 Myka 9, interview with the author (Los Angeles: The Vanguard), October 8, 2011.
8 Aaron Pointer, Abstract Rude, interview with the author (London–Los Angeles), June 10, 2013.

9 Similar behavior was occurring in the Jamaican music scene with a similar phenomenon of DJ "talk over" or "toasting" by DJs such as U-Roy and King Stitt in the 1960s and 1970s.
10 Robert Ford Jr., "Jive Talking N.Y. DJs Rapping Away in Black Discos," *Billboard*, May 5, 1979, p. 3, in Murray Forman and Mark Anthony Neal (eds.), *That's the Joint! The Hip-Hop Studies Reader* (New York: Routledge, 2004), p. 43.
11 David Ma, "Blessed the Mic: The Kurtis Blow Interview," *Wax Poetics*, August 13, 2012.
12 Nelson George, "Hip-Hop's Founding Fathers Speak the Truth," in Forman and Neal, *That's the Joint!*, pp. 51–52.
13 Tricia Rose, "Soul Sonic Forces: Technology, Orality, and Black Cultural Practice in Rap Music," in her *Black Noise: Rap Music and Black*

Culture in Contemporary America (Middletown, CT: Wesleyan University Press, 1994), p. 64.

14 Erika Blount Danis, "Dedicated: Microphone Fiend Rakim is Back," *Wax Poetics*, May 2, 2010. For more on Rakim, see Chapter 24 in this volume.

15 Rakim interview on BET. Available at www.youtube.com/watch?v=OLB3oLSzY5A (accessed October 13, 2013).

16 Rakim: The Definition of a Classic. Available at http://vimeo.com/45722608 (accessed October 13, 2013).

17 Leaders of the New School were a New York hip-hop group formed in 1989 and consisting of Busta Rhymes, Charlie Brown, Dinco D, and Cut Monitor Milo.

18 Robert Glasper, interview with the author (San Francisco: Yerba Buena Center of the Arts), September 29, 2011.

19 D. Scot Miller, interview with the author (Oakland, CA), October 13, 2011.

20 The Native Tongues were a hip-hop collective of like-minded groups, primarily based on the East Coast. Notable core members include the Jungle Brothers, A Tribe Called Quest, De La Soul, Black Sheep, and Monie Love, among others.

21 Brown, *Performing the Word*, p. 122.

22 James E. Smethurst and Howard Ramsby II, "Reform and Revolution, 1965–1976: The Black Aesthetic at Work," in *The Cambridge History of African American Literature* (Cambridge University Press, 2011), p. 405.

23 Sonny Murray, *Black Art (with LeRoi Jones reading)* (USA: Jihad Productions, 1965).

24 James Edward Smethurst, "Introduction," in *The Black Arts Movement: Literary Nationalism in the 1960s and 1970s* (University of North Carolina Press, 2005), p. 3.

25 Aaron Pointer, Abstract Rude interview.

26 *This Is the Life: How the West Was Won*, dir. Ava DuVernay (Forward Movement, 2009).

27 Marcyliena Morgan, "Introduction: I Am Hip-Hop," in her *The Real Hiphop: Battling for Knowledge, Power, and Respect in the LA Underground* (Durham, NC: Duke University Press, 2009), p. 3.

28 *This Is the Life.*

29 *Ibid.*

30 Pointer, Abstract Rude interview.

31 Myka 9, interview with the author.

32 *Ibid.*

2 Hip-hop dance

IMANI KAI JOHNSON

Hip-hop dance is not a single genre of dance, or even an accurate label for the dances for which it attempts to account. The term is more appropriately an umbrella that encompasses a range of genres, some that were born out of hip-hop, and a number that were adopted into the culture. "Hip-hop dance" thus refers to both adopted and invented genres, which overlap aesthetically, and are related to one another through hip-hop culture.

Unfortunately, in the growing field of hip-hop studies, dance is the least written about of the four elements. While a number of hip-hop scholars address dance in works that largely focus on rap music, only a handful of scholars have made dance their primary focus. They include Joseph G. Schloss (writing on breaking and uprocking in New York City), Carla Stalling Huntington (writing on the media marketing of hip-hop dance), Mary Fogarty (who covers a broad scope of work including international networks and the cultural tastes of breakers), and myself (with work on b-boying cyphers and their African diasporic influences). More extensive have been a growing number of documentaries made about hip-hop dances, their social contexts, and their histories. And of course, the practitioners themselves are the true experts in the field, and a few are publishing works that have academic import: b-boy Louis "Alien Ness" Roberto Martinez, b-boy Niels "Storm" Robitzky, popper Jorge "Popmaster Fabel" Pabon, and house dancer and locker Moncell "Ill Kosby" Durden are exceptions.[1] Ultimately, we must mine the expanse of information from all of the above to get a better understanding of hip-hop dance.

Historical overview

There is no singular place, time, or genre that constitutes "the beginnings" of hip-hop dance. Rather there was simultaneous activity across the USA that would collectively assert itself as a shared culture *after* hip-hop came into being. One of the shared qualities of these dances lies in their adaptation of traditional African diasporic aesthetic imperatives in new ways and for contemporary contexts. All of the genres discussed below play with polyrhythms, improvisation, call and response, spiritual communion, and a number of other elements that, though not exclusive to the African diaspora, are central to its aesthetics. They also frequently incorporate traditional buck, wing, and jig elements indicative of African American culture.[2] Beyond diasporic influences, these dances reflect urban American contexts among culturally diverse, working-class and working-poor communities of predominantly African diasporic peoples – including African Americans, West Indians, and Puerto Ricans – as well as small pockets of working-class whites, Mexican Americans, Dominicans, Pacific Islanders, and other ethnicities depending on location.

One among many "beginnings" is through the California-based "funkstyles" of locking and popping. Long before hip-hop began to congeal into a culture and prior to it even having a name, there was the funk. Noted for its syncopated bass lines, dynamic percussions, soulful or gospel-inspired singing, and the rhythmic build-up of energy as all of the instruments worked together toward an improvisational climax, funk music is just that: funky.[3] The term "funkstyles" is used to designate the range of social dances and genres generated out of their relationship to funk music and in counter-distinction to hip-hop. Locking and popping are the two most recognized genres. Most credit locking to Don "Campbellock" Campbell, a Los Angeles-based dancer who cites his inspiration from having stumbled onto the dance's titular move after a failed attempt at the Robot Shuffle (or the Funky Chicken some sources say), a popular social dance in the early 1970s. Locking exudes a vibrant and playful theatricality that found an audience via *Soul Train*, television's first nationally syndicated Black popular music and dance show hosted by its founder Don Cornelius. The show moved to Los Angeles from Chicago in 1971, and provided a platform for young Black teenagers to display their skills for a national audience. Interest in locking prompted its swift transition from a local style to staged entertainment on national television. The Lockers, a group formed by Campbellock, was the most recognized group in this genre, and featured a number of noteworthy dancers including Fred "The Penguin" Berry who would go on to play "Rerun" in the television show *What's Happening?*; Adolfo "Shabadoo" Quiñones who would play Ozone ten years later in the *Breakin'* franchise; and choreographer/singer Toni Basil. The Lockers creatively combined dance and storytelling, then staged it for diverse television and theater audiences.

Popping is not locking, though they are often mistakenly combined into "pop-locking" – an early 1980s misnomer frequently depicted as an aspect of "breakdancing," which combined all of the funkstyles. Where locking is presentational, bouncy, and playful, popping combines staccato-like movement with water-like flow for a more forceful and almost confrontational style that pushes at the limits of what it seems possible for the body to actually do. Inspired by the dynamic social dances that were part of the California Bay area club scene in the late 1960s and early 1970s, popping was a distinct style of dance where the muscle's contractions are pulsated rhythmically in sudden bursts or pops. Sam "Boogaloo Sam" Solomon is one of the originators of this genre. He would go on to form the Electric Boogaloos (originally the Electronic Boogaloo Lockers) in 1977 with Nate "Slide" Johnson and Joe "Slim" Thomas.[4] Popping too, quickly found an audience via *Soul Train.* The dance garnered so much attention that pop star Michael Jackson trained with Bruno "Pop N Taco" Falcón for over fifteen years, ultimately inspiring Jackson's signature dance style including the "moonwalk" – which was in fact a popping move called "the backslide." A number of other genres that fall under the "unauthorized umbrella" of popping include ticking, waving, tutting, strutting, roboting, and boogaloo – all of which developed in different parts of southern, central, and northern California.[5]

Another "beginning" to hip-hop dance is through the urban underground dance club scene, predominated by but not exclusive to Black and Brown gay men whose post-Stonewall social dance venues became legendary sites for a freedom of expression through dance in safe, welcoming environments. Their dancing styles helped to usher in an era where "collective performances" of "individual free-form dance" were acceptable in club environments.[6] Innovations in dances like lofting and house grew out of these types of venues in Chicago and New York (e.g. the Sanctuary, the Loft, Paradise Garage) – while dances like waacking grew out of similar venues in California. They were places that openly invited clientele who until then had been typically doubly discriminated against by race and sexuality. The underground dance club scene had its beginnings within venues created by a small handful of party promoters and DJs like David Mancuso, Larry Levan, and Francis Grasso. DJs (rather than a jukebox) "foreground[ed] the beat" of bass-heavy music, and the "loosened... matrix of social dance" no longer required male–female couples or couples dancing altogether.[7] This new standard helped to foster marathon dance sessions that became the signature of these social spaces. Though "underground," these networks of parties helped to generate chart hits that shaped a new genre of music: disco.[8] As the discotheque went mainstream and rapidly expanded, so did a formula for commercial disco music, both of which eventually overshadowed the underground club phenomenon. Disco became so big in fact that it sparked a profound backlash that for many also felt racist and homophobic. Yet the so-called "death" of disco did not mark the end of the underground dance music scene. The music diversified, newer generations of dancers entered, and times changed; but the fundamental call and response exchange with the DJ and a full-bodied collective communion on the dance floor would remain key features of the culture.[9]

Finally, the most familiar point of entry into hip-hop dance is the South Bronx phenomenon of b-boying/b-girling or breaking (popularly though again mistakenly referred to as "breakdancing"). B-boying is presentational, confrontational, and communal. It is a battle dance but not exclusively so. It constantly borrows from many genres yet maintains a distinct brand of bravado and style that has become its signature. Some mark this "borrowing" from cultural predecessors as breaking's own multiple beginning points. For example, while the dance draws inspiration from an incredible range of movement practices including but not limited to tap, kung fu, and mambo, one local dance in particular – called rocking or uprocking – is crucial to b-boying's aesthetic. Uprocking is a "battle dance in which two people . . . square off and simultaneously taunt each other through movement," while openly insulting each other with "burns" or pantomimed violence against an opponent.[10] Uprocking is identified as a Brooklyn style, though popper and dance history documentarian Jorge "Popmaster Fabel" Pabon argues in his documentary *Rock Dance History: The Untold Story of Up-Rockin'* that it too was born in the Bronx. Origins aside, variations on uprocking would become part of breaking's upright dance aesthetic.

Breaking began as a genre in the early 1970s when dancers basked in the "break" – a "brief percussion solo" typical in funk music – whose eventual repetition would extend their opportunities to dance for longer periods of time.[11] Extending or looping the break, and modifying its rhythms with scratching – made possible by new DJing techniques innovated by DJs Kool Herc, Grandmaster Flash, Grand Wizard Theodore, and Afrika Bambaataa – were the foundation to a burgeoning music-based culture that would eventually be named hip-hop. In the midst of basement parties and block parties in the South Bronx, the beginnings of b-boying predominantly formed by early-teenage boys (and a small handful of b-girls) of largely African American, West Indian, and Puerto Rican descent. In its earliest manifestations, it was an upright dance that was named "rocking," "going off," "the boiyoiyoing," and other names that attempted to describe its frenzied, sometimes bouncy, and explosive movement – a visual spectacle that matched the breakbeats of 1960s and 1970s rock, funk, disco, soul, and salsa music played by the DJs. As it began to form a distinct style and transitioned from an upright dance to the ground, breaking's rudimentary manifestation incorporated stylized footwork, shuffles, drops, spins of various kinds (e.g. butt spins, backspins), and freezes. It is a style with moves in constant revolutions, with the dancers pushing themselves to do something unprecedented. Groundbreaking for its time, this would be the foundation for the extraordinary dance we see today.

While the first generation of breakers who started in the early 1970s aged out within five years, newer generations in their early teens were coming up and seeking out others who kept the dance alive on their own blocks in New York City. This is the story of the Rock Steady Crew (R.S.C.), one of the most recognized crews in b-boying history. R.S.C. has been under the long-standing presidency of Richard "Crazy Legs" Colon, who got permission from the former R.S.C. president, Jo-Jo, to continue the then defunct crew among a new generation that would take it into the 1980s, and to the world.[12] As a result, R.S.C. were among the first faces of hip-hop culture to hit mainstream media. While songs like Sugarhill Gang's "Rapper's Delight" were already hits, the media had little sense of the expanse of the culture and its near-defunct dance until a *Village Voice* cover story in April of 1981 by dance critic Sally Banes, with photographs by Martha Cooper. The article featured R.S.C. vice president, the late Frosty Freeze – tall, slim, and afroed – on its cover. By 1983, members of R.S.C. were featured in a thirty-second clip in a summer blockbuster titled *Flashdance* (Crazy Legs would also body double for a portion of the dance finale). This clip showcased b-boying (and popping) to international audiences, in the case of the former for the first time, triggering a frenzied response by nascent breakers from around the world. For anyone not a teenager in the South Bronx, Harlem, and Brooklyn at the time, b-boys were the public's first introduction to hip-hop as a culture.

By 1984, b-boying was the hot new thing, though it was not the only dance captured in this moment of popular culture. Street dance in general became trendy, but with little understanding of what they were looking at media outlets labeled everything "breakdancing" whether it was breaking, popping, locking, or something else. "Breakdancing" was featured on the news, in movies, on sitcoms, commercials, music videos, and on tours with DJs, rappers, and the Fantastic Four Double Dutch Girls. Breakers were coupled with ballet dancers in showcases meant to juxtapose high and low culture. So intrigued was the public by these performances that b-boys were a featured segment on *Ripley's Believe It or Not* (1983), a popular television show dedicated to mystical natural wonders and freak show oddities. The New York City Breakers danced at the opening of the 1984 Olympics in front of President Reagan. And the extremely short-lived television show *Graffiti Rock* (1984), produced and hosted by Michael Holman, attempted to further package the culture and the dance for weekly national consumption (though the show only aired its pilot episode). By 1984, breaking was a hook for dozens of low-budget, teen-oriented movies that showcased street dance in their storyline, though very often they relegated actual practitioners to the background and foregrounded modern dancers who simply incorporated one or two breaking moves. The most popular of these films were *Beat Street*, *Breakin'*, and *Breakin' 2: Electric Boogaloo* (all released in 1984). Interestingly, there was very little actual b-boying in the *Breakin'* series, which featured locking and popping. More accurate representations were available in small, independent favorites like *Wild Style* (directed by Charlie Ahearn 1983) and *Style Wars* (directed by Tony Silver 1983), which featured a legendary battle between R.S.C. and Dynamic Rockers.

Though not as dramatic as the backlash against disco, the popularity of breaking and street dance quickly waned in the USA, and by 1986 it was considered passé. Clubs discouraged circles where breakers demonstrated their solo skills; patrons would throw drinks on the floor to make it difficult and dangerous to break. Young kids around the country were ticketed or arrested for public dance circles that were said to be disruptive to the flow of traffic and commerce, and gathering sites for criminals (a particularly classed and racialized reference to the kind of youth who gathered to break). One city ordinance in San Bernardino, California, attempted to ban "breakdancing" circles altogether, though they eventually simply passed a $100 fine.[13] The media began to depict "breakdancing" as dangerous and disruptive, featuring stories of untrained beginners injuring themselves in some way, the most notorious example being that of a man who broke his neck after attempting a head spin. Though injuries in any dance are common, breaking was ultimately depicted as a problem. Yet simultaneously, in the midst of this domestic backlash two things also took place: the innovation of new hip-hop social dances; and the growing interest in street dance outside of the USA.

The surge in hip-hop social dances reflected the music of the late 1980s and early 1990s. By then, rap music had supplanted breaking as hip-hop's representative cultural element. As rap began to flourish and influence other genres, especially R&B, a new expanse of hip-hop social dances reflected the stylistic shifts in music. These dances included moves such as the Running Man, the Roger Rabbit, the Smurf, the Wop, and many others along with them. The kinds of club spaces that welcomed the dancers schooled in circles were the very same underground dance clubs that originated in the early 1970s. Formerly called discos, these clubs branched off in multiple directions including electronic music (e.g. techno, drum 'n' bass, etc.), and house music. The house club space was where all of these different approaches to dance intermingled, influencing each other. Dance troupes also began to form, and were featured in music videos that had by the late 1980s become commonplace. Mop Top Crew was the most prominent, and its members were featured in two TV documentary shorts: *House of Trés* and *Reck'n Shop: Live from Brooklyn*.[14]

By the time breaking, popping, and locking peaked in US popular culture, they found new life internationally. Countries like the UK already had prominent breakers by 1984, with particular attention to the B-Boys of Wolverhampton – featuring b-girl Bubbles (now Hanifa Queen), the first recognized b-girl in Europe. Mary Fogarty's "Whatever Happened to Breakdancing?" is one of the few works to trace international b-boying networks through the 1990s. She argues that the street dance scene in Europe flourished, as a result of three channels of interactions: the tours that started in the early 1980s, underground videos, and competitions. Dance centered tours – including groups such as R.S.C., Rhythm Technicians, and Ghetto Original Dance Company – were comprised of breakers and poppers largely from New York who formed their own dance companies. Underground videos (first VHS tapes, later DVDs) featuring their shows, interviews, and club excursions after performances began to circulate. These networks fostered new communities that culturally identified with hip-hop, though their direct interactions with each other were greatly limited.[15] With technological advancements came new ways of learning how to break and connecting with others trying to do the same. Mediated images allowed beginners to play back videos in slow motion, to pause, rewind, and skip to the good part. Finally, large-scale competitions such as the International Battle of the Year in Germany (now France) beginning in 1990, and the Notorious International Breakdance Event in Rotterdam beginning in 1998, expanded international networks of street dancers. These competitions sought the return of early practitioners, fostered a flourishing international scene, and became venues for direct interaction with the resurgent US scene in the early 1990s.

In the new millennium, hip-hop social dances (like the Soulja Boy, the Chicken Noodle Soup, and too many others to cite) continue to impact the mainstream. New genres on the other hand have also come into prominent recognition. Los Angeles's krumping and Oakland's turfing are two examples of dances that were born out of a combination of hip-hop and the histories of street and social dances in California, where both hail from. Again, an overlap with hip-hop does not capture all aspects of those genres, especially as they begin to branch off in distinct directions, including music production and expressions of spiritual worship and memorial practices. Yet hip-hop offers an inroad to witnessing and understanding the unique contributions of these burgeoning dance cultures.

New directions in hip-hop dance research

Though the scope of the literature on hip-hop dances is limited, ongoing work indicates that this area of hip-hop studies will soon feature more prominently in the field. The twenty-first century ushered in a growing body of crucial analyses of hip-hop dance cultures and practices. Joseph G. Schloss's *Foundation* (2009) is the most recognized examination of b-boying culture and aesthetics and yet more work is on the horizon, whether it is from students, like Naomi Bragin, junior scholars such as Dr. Mary Fogarty and myself, or documentarian practitioners like Moncell Durden. These new works move in distinct directions, yet each contributes to a larger body of work that takes dance seriously as an area of inquiry.

New studies on hip-hop dances challenge hip-hop scholars to consider movement as central rather than peripheral to the culture, impacting how we understand hip-hop's roles around the world. Scholar and practitioner Dr. Mary Fogarty, for example, writes extensively on breaking, perhaps because she is also a b-girl known as Mary Jane out of Toronto. Rather than rehashing origin stories, a frequent topic in hip-hop dance discussions, she delves into the aesthetic and cultural politics of contemporary and global practices. Fogarty explores areas of research that foreground the pivotal moment in the early 1990s when b-boying resurfaced as a dance of interest in North America, and other underexplored areas including musical tastes and values, cross-cultural aesthetic transmission, improvisation, apprenticeship culture, careers in hip-hop dance, aging, hip-hop dance in the academy, and soundscapes in hip-hop dance movies. Her attention to dancers' concerns and investments is a prominent feature of her work.

In his forthcoming documentary, *Everything Remains Raw*, locker, house dancer, and choreographer Moncell "Ill Kosby" Durden draws together an incredible array of footage and interviews of dancers from different eras and genres to document both the aesthetic progenitors to hip-hop dances and the histories entailed in them. He firmly embeds the aesthetic foundations of hip-hop dance within the African diaspora, often foregrounding Latin American and Caribbean dimensions. What becomes clear in the film is that innovations in hip-hop dance are recontextualized forms of movement repeated over time, as with for example, the echoes of lindy hopper Al Minns in the 1920s that we see in Link of Mop Top Crew in the 1990s. Durden's work is a praisesong for the rich aesthetic depth of hip-hop dance.

Naomi Bragin's studies of popping, turfing, and waacking set a new precedent for critical analyses of streetdances precisely because she gives long overdue attention to both longstanding and burgeoning dance practices. Like Fogarty and Durden, she is a practitioner as well, studying the practices of those dances alongside their histories, discourses, and politics surrounding intersections of gender, race, class, and sexuality. The latter aspect of her work is largely absent from work on hip-hop dances, which reminds us that dance, like all forms of cultural production, is a political practice that allows people to literally perform their identities, showcasing their capacities to subvert or simply complicate powerful social processes enacted on the body.

In a similar vein, my own work on b-boying engages intersections of race, gender, class, and national difference, albeit through a relatively more focused approach.[16] My research on b-boying looks specifically at dance circles (called "cyphers") and those elements essential to its dynamics. The project's central focus explores the spiritual dimensions of cyphering, the cultural foundations born in conditions of socio-economic exclusion, the gendered politics of marginality, the dynamics of globalization evident in the transport of hip-hop culture, and the effect of social networking on cyphering dynamics. I use the physics concept of dark matter as a metaphor to emphasize that embodied understandings born in cyphering experiences are not visible to the naked eye, but remain nonetheless tangible elements of its practice.

Prominent across these new works is a focus on practitioners rather than representational analyses alone, and due attention to the global scope of hip-hop practices, building on current ethnographic and international approaches in hip-hop studies. Hip-hop dances and the scholarship on them force us to understand the broader culture differently. If we center movement and dance communities rather than the music, entirely new sets of question, dynamics, peoples, places, and histories come to the fore. The beauty and spectacle of dancing only adds to its potential and its power. What is at stake, and thus what can be gained from acknowledging and engaging the dancers and the scholars researching them, is a deeper and more accurate understanding of global hip-hop culture.

Further reading

Banes, Sally, *Writing Dance in the Age of Postmodernism* (Middletown, CT: University Press of New England, 1994).

Johnson, Imani Kai, "B-Boying and Battling in a Global Context: The Discursive Life of Difference in Hip Hop Dance," *Alif: Journal of Comparative Poetics* 31 (2011): 173–195.

Schloss, Joseph G., *Foundation: B-Boys, B-Girls, and Hip-Hop Culture in New York* (New York: Oxford University Press, 2009).

Spady, James G., H. Samy Alim, and Samir Meghelli, "Umum Dance Cipha: Streetdancing to B-Boying to Hip Hop Phenoms and G's," in James Spady, H. Samy Alim, and Samir Meghelli (eds.), *The Global Cipha: Hip Hop Culture and Consciousness* (Philadelphia: Black History Museum Publishers, 2006), pp. 318–333.

Notes

1 Many practitioners write extensively about hip-hop in popular forums online. Though they are not recognized as academic works, they do provide a highly valuable archive of hip-hop dance and culture.

2 Thomas DeFrantz, "Buck, Wing, and Jig." Available at www.youtube.com/watch?v=A34OD4eA17o (accessed June 1, 2013). Buck dances, wing dances, and jigs are a trilogy of dances that developed in the nineteenth and

early twentieth centuries that continue to resonate in African American social dances today. They are characterized by stomping, heavy-footed percussive footwork (buck), flapping motions of the arms and legs (wing), and high-energy and fast-paced dancing (jig).

3 Rickey Vincent, *Funk: the Music, the People, and the Rhythm of the One* (New York: St. Martin's Griffin, 1996), p. 13.

4 Jorge Pabon, "Physical Graffiti: the History of Hip-Hop Dance," in Jeff Chang (ed.), *Total Chaos: The Art and Aesthetics of Hip-Hop* (New York: Basic Civitas, 2006), p. 23.

5 *Ibid.*

6 Kai Fikentscher, *"You Better Work!" Underground Dance Music of New York City* (Middletown, CT: Wesleyan University Press, 2000), p. 111; Tim Lawrence, "Beyond the Hustle: 1970s Social Dancing, Discotheque Culture, and the Emergence of the Contemporary Club Dancer," in Julie Malnig (ed.), *Ballroom, Boogie, Shimmy Sham, Shake* (Champaign: University of Illinois Press, 2008), p. 201.

7 Lawrence, "Beyond the Hustle," p. 202.

8 *Ibid.*, p. 210; Walter Hughes, "In the Empire of the Beat: Discipline and Disco," in Andrew Ross and Tricia Rose (eds.), *Microphone Fiends* (London: Routledge, 1994), p. 149.

9 See Fikentscher, *"You Better Work!"*

10 Joseph G. Schloss, *Foundation: B-Boys, B-Girls, and Hip-Hop Culture in New York City* (New York: Oxford University Press, 2009), p. 132. The "b" in b-boying conventionally refers to "break," i.e. the break of a record that people dance to. First generation b-boy Trac2 says that when he first used it, the "b" meant "beat," because they were dancing to the beat rather than the "break" – a not yet common term. Finally, for some the "b" refers to "the Bronx," in reference to the dance's geographical roots. Ultimately, the "b" comes to represent a beginning point in the dance's culture that marks its first naming and thus its roots.

11 Mark Katz, *Groove Music: The Art and Culture of the Hip-Hop DJ* (New York: Oxford University Press, 2012), p. 14.

12 See *The Freshest Kids* (dir. Israel, QD3 Entertainment, 2002).

13 Rube Goldberg, "'All-American City' Puts the Freeze on Break Dancers," *The Wall Street Journal*, May 1, 1984.

14 Though sometimes written as *Wrecking Shop* or *Wreck'n Shop*, its official title is spelled "Reck'n."

15 Mary Fogarty, "Whatever Happened to Breakdancing? Transnational B-boy/B-girl Networks, Underground Video Magazines and Imagined *Affinities*" (Master's Thesis, Brook University, 2006).

16 Imani Kai Johnson, "Dark Matter in B-Boying Cyphers: Race and Global Connection in Hip Hop." Ph.D. dissertation, University of Southern California, 2009. See also Imani Kai Johnson, "From Blues Women to B-Girls: Performing Marginalized Femininities," *Women & Performance: A Journal of Feminist Theory*, special issue *All Hail the Queenz: A Queer Feminist Recalibration of Hip-hop Scholarship* 24/1 (2014); and Imani Kai Johnson, "B-Boying and Battling in a Global Context: The Discursive Life of Difference in Hip Hop Dance," *Alif: Journal of Comparative Poetics* 31 (2011): 173–195.

3 Hip-hop visual arts

IVOR MILLER

Outside observers used the Italian term *graffito*, commonly defined as a "crude scratching upon public surfaces," to define a grassroots art movement that emerged in New York City in the 1970s. Instead, practitioners commonly referred to their form as "aerosol art," "signaturing," "spray-can art," "writing," or simply "graff." This form of public painting became an important element of the urban cultural movement known as hip-hop.

Graffiti being an art form based upon writing or painting stylized letters, its creators developed unique categories to evaluate mastery. Founding artist PHASE 2 categorized writers as "bombers," "stylists," and "hard-core stylists": bombers aspire for the quantity of their signatures across the city's walls, stylists reassemble letters in aesthetic patterns including abstraction, while hard-core stylists work with letters and figurative forms to create thematic murals.

This movement emerged in the early 1970s in New York City when local painters used active subway cars as their canvases. While Norman Mailer and a handful of journalists and photographers celebrated the phenomenon, others who viewed it as an attack on society called the painters "graffiti vandals."[1]

By the late 1970s, New York City "writers" began to produce whole-car murals that became a tourist attraction for international visitors. The origins of a cultural phenomenon like New York City writing are multiple. Some link it to archaic human impulses reflected in the graffiti of the ancient city of Pompeii, or the "latrinalia" found in bathroom stalls. Others suggested origins with the ubiquitous "Kilroy was here" tags from World War II, or the phrase "Bird Lives!" chalked on buildings and subway walls of New York City's bohemian Greenwich Village after the demise of jazz musician Charlie Parker in 1955.

A 1971 *New York Times* article about TAKI 183, a bicycle messenger who wrote his tag throughout Manhattan, spread the idea of signaturing throughout the city. The movement, partly inspired by logos from advertising campaigns, became a media phenomenon itself – as writers aspired to see images of their "hits" in the newspapers, on TV, and in movies. The aesthetic "battles" took on David and Goliath proportions as some "pieces" covered advertisements on billboards and painters such as MICO rendered slogans deriding political leaders on the trains (e.g. "Hang Nixon!," 1973–1974).

The subway painting movement emerged in response to the conditions of New York City at the time. In the 1960s and 1970s, college students and adults began to hold mass rallies protesting the Vietnam War, as well as institutionalized poverty, racism, and sexism. The protesters did not ask for permission; they acted spontaneously in order to force the hand of authorities. The painters followed this strategy by presenting their views creatively in public, calling their collective actions of covert paintings on the subway "bombing," partially in critical response to the ongoing war in southeast Asia. They recognized the subway system as an ideal public gallery for their work. It was available because the system had fallen into disrepair under the administration of city planner Robert Moses (1934–1968), whose efforts went to building roads for private cars rather than maintaining public transportation. Painters were able to communicate with their peers through their work on the trains. Founding artist MICO recalled the relationship between society and his art of the era:

> At 15, 16, 17, 18 years of age the Vietnam war was going on. One of the themes I've always been preoccupied with is the current oppression of Puerto Rico by the US, so I mounted campaigns of writing "Free Puerto Rico" with the Puerto Rican and Black Power flags. I figured the least I could do to help the cause was to write, "Free Puerto Rico," "Free Nelson Mandela," "Free Carlos Feliciano," who was also a political prisoner. I did my "Hang Nixon" piece in 73, 74.[2]

After Mailer's book *The Faith of Graffiti* appeared in 1974, the next book on graffiti was Castleman's *Getting Up* (1982), based on interviews with major painters, describing what writers actually did, as well as their conceptualizations of their work. Chalfant and Cooper's *Subway Art* (1984) used photographs to document some of the best work in New York City of that era.

By the late 1970s and early 1980s, whole-car murals dominated public vistas of the subway system. Among the master painters of that era LEE, as well as DURO, were of Puerto Rican descent. In the early 1980s the subway painters, the majority from marginal barrios of the city, participated in highly publicized exhibitions in downtown galleries. With the release of the films *Wild Style* (1982), *Style Wars* (1983), and *Beat Street* (1984), their art and related music and dance forms became known throughout world urban centers as the basis for what some called the "hip-hop revolution." Soon afterwards, Chalfant and Prigoff's *Spraycan Art* (1987) documented visually how the art had become a worldwide phenomenon.

Graffiti origins and ethnic diversity

The ethnic influences in this art form are dynamic and complex. Twentieth-century New York has been identified as the first "Caribbean" city, where peoples from all islands and nations met for the first time in one place.[3]

Aerosol art was primarily produced by Blacks and Latinos in the early 1970s with some important exceptions (e.g. ALE, COMET, FUZZ 1, LSD OM, TAKI 183, *et al.*). Some writers came to New York as immigrants from South America, or the Caribbean, and others from the interior of the USA. Still others were born in New York City, often the children of immigrants with multiple ethnic identities. All found that by participating in aerosol culture they could explore vital parts of their identities as young adults, as artists, political beings, and New Yorkers.

Considered one of the few indigenous art forms of the USA, aerosol writing developed collectively through the rich tapestry of styles that each innovator brought to the form. Several painters asserted specific ethnic identities through their work. COCO 144 integrated Taino ritual images into his signature in order to forge an identity related to his ancestral homeland on the island of Puerto Rico:

> I incorporated the Taino petroglyphs into my signature. The continued use of writing my name in my paintings is important to me. Although the letters are now an abstract form, the name is still there. It's in the face of the embryo I painted in some of the Taino paintings I did.
>
> When I was painting the Taino works, I wanted to express myself and my culture in a certain way. I was in Puerto Rico, where these petroglyphs were created. And it was a new experience for Puerto Ricans to see urban, aerosol art. At the time I didn't make a conscious connection between the Taino paintings and aerosol as underground work, but it's funny that my work evolved from the underground subways, and then here I'm combining it with something that was done 700 years ago that was also done underground. It's like history repeating itself.[4]

The conversation among writers from diverse cultural backgrounds occurred at many levels. MARE 139 observed that even if writers lived in segregated neighborhoods, the subway lines themselves became "integrated" as writers from all regions communicated with each other through their paintings:

> Writers were always from a mixed cultural background. The Number One line had a lot of Latinos, Dominicans, white and black writers, because it went from downtown to uptown to the Bronx, through Harlem, Manhattan, so there was no line that was segregated. The misconception is that graff wasn't that integrated. I was in a lot of integrated crews.[5]

LADY PINK reported that writers' groups included artists from all backgrounds:

> Writers came from all ethnic backgrounds, all classes, and the police knew to look out for a group of kids who were racially diverse – those were the writers. If a group of kids was all black or white the police wouldn't bother them. Race wasn't an obstacle for a writer to join a crew, gender wasn't either. That set in later. Barriers break down quickly when you go down into the subways . . . After you come out, you have a link, a comradeship. Once you were a writer, you were respected, you could go anywhere in the city. You were known, you had friends and connections, even if you had never set eyes on them before. It was a family.[6]

Many of the early writers, including CRASH, insist that although many of the writers were Black and Latino, the form is collective and urban:

> Our art is multi-racial, multi-cultural, multi-lingual, and multi-dimensional. As a teenager, most of my friends were Hispanic, white, black, Chinese, Korean. I never saw color until I was an adult, and that was how my parents brought me up. So when people tell me that [graffiti] is a black thing, I'm like "where? where? That's a lie." Most of the writers I knew were Hispanic, black, Asian, and white.[7]

Because the writers' official identities, ethnic or otherwise, were not knowable from their work on the trains, they were intentionally mysterious.

Among the achievements of this community of urban artists is to have created a space for themselves in leading international galleries and museums. They have influenced mainstream artists like their contemporaries Jean-Michel Basquiat, Keith Haring, Frank Stella, James Rosenquist, and Roy Lichtenstein. They created a global aesthetic movement that continues to transform the very look of many cities, and inspired the emergence of a multibillion dollar music and fashion industry.

The fate of graffiti

To regain visual control of the subways, New York mayors Lindsay (1966–1973), Beame (1974–1977), and Koch (1978–1990) waged multimillion dollar campaigns to erase the paintings and arrest the painters. In the 1980s the great majority of paintings were "buffed" in a $150 million campaign that resulted in a "graffiti free" system in 1989. Although the murals were suppressed from New York's subways, the art form is currently practiced in virtually every major city around the globe.

As it became increasingly popular in the 1980s, the form was practiced by young people around the world who learned from movies, not from other writers. Therefore its meanings have changed dramatically in many cases as new artists continually invent new ways of developing the ideas of the early masters, or morphing into other forms of public art without spray-paint or stylish letters.

Coming of age

By the 1990s, many leading artists in this movement had transcended all practical and aesthetic links to "scrawling on a wall": they were sculpting in metals and wood; creating clothing fashions and websites; selling canvas paintings and writing songs. No matter their medium, their work remains connected to the idea of signaturing, calligraphic embellishment, and letter transformation. CRASH, of Puerto Rican descent, exhibits in major galleries worldwide; DASH 167, of Cuban descent, has participated in a "writers-team" that painted and lectured internationally; EZO, of Puerto Rican/German descent, paints and runs an art gallery in Manhattan; JONONE, originally from the Dominican Republic, exhibits his paintings in European art galleries; LADY PINK, born in Ecuador, paints commercially in New York City; MARE 139, of Puerto Rican descent, sculpts abstract letters in metal; NIC-ONE, of Cuban descent, ran Video Graf, a video program on the contemporary aerosol movement; SPAR, of Cape Verdian descent, runs a website (www.at149st.com) documenting the movement; TATS Cru, Inc., is a Bronx-based "graffiti-mural" company founded by Wilfredo Feliciano (BIO), Hector Nazario (NICER), and Sotero Ortiz (BG183) that paints murals internationally; TRACY 168, of Puerto Rican, Irish, and Italian descent, continues to paint in local public spaces throughout the city.

DOZE speaks

As many of the early subway painters have become prolific in the art world, they are establishing a body of work for future generations to contemplate. Among their towering achievements is to have negotiated their way through the class, race, and ethnic barriers of the art world while retaining the style, perspectives, and communal spirit of their earlier movement.

Among the many leaders of this movement, DOZE (aka Devious Doze) stands out as a globally recognized artist. His evolution was singular, as a founding member of the dance group Rock Steady Crew (R.S.C.), a DJ, and a painter who has incorporated elements of all these forms into his work. In an interview, DOZE expresses how the collective movement and some of its teachers propelled him into his current artistic career:

Figure 3.1 Painting of people by DOZE (early 2000s).

Graffiti is an art form based on communication; it was created by the unheard masses to communicate with the people. It was only natural that the communication expanded amongst other disadvantaged youth. My experiences began as a B-Boy growing up in NYC. Later, while under the tutelage of [painter] Dondi White, I began to understand the importance of the forms of numbers and letters; I learned that the letter – through the use of slanting and leaning to imply motion – could become a figurative character unto itself.

The continual evolution of the craft expanded my own palette, sparking my interest in metaphysics and the unconscious. Once these became merged into my process, I was able to grasp a harmony within sacred geometry that took me on a journey from being a neophyte, to become an initiate, and finally a master, only to return to being a neophyte. My process today navigates my paintings through a series of experiments that the late master-painter Rammellzee called Map-a-matics. Map-a-matics are formulas that transport me into self-discovery.

Figure 3.2 Painting of Ganesha by DOZE (early 2000s).

The twenty-one faces in this painting by DOZE from the first decade of the century have a relation to DOZE's views of "sacred geometry" and "map-a-matics," since this number is viewed as "sacred" in many world systems. For example, for the Yorùbá people of West Africa and their transatlantic diaspora, twenty-one is the number of Esu-Elegbara, the god who "opens the way" for the aspirations of devotees. The shaved heads as well as the white eyes on all the figures suggest that the people are in a trance state, or somehow manifesting their shared "sacred" status as ancient-futuristic beings. One has an eye on the forehead, as does the Ganesha figure in the next painting (Figure 3.2), to represent the faculty of prophecy possessed by the few. All are "interconnected" as a single community by the black line running through the work, suggesting a historical narrative of solidarity. These figures emerged from DOZE's understanding of how letters can transform into human forms:

As I see it, in the tradition of wild style graffiti, the deconstruction of the letter and then the re-juxtaposition of symbolic elements are translated into the cycle of "build-story." As we constantly build and destroy, the world presents two faces: the natural and the artificial, both of which are clouded by the enigmatic omnipresent fog of the mysteries of creation. That is, my work has a profound element of mysticism that connects the present generations with the ancient archetypes of humanity. In my work, the interconnectedness of ALL is revealed through layers of color forms and interesting line-work that move from the macrocosmic to the unseen.

Initially, I create a dark palette for the background; bold lines and drawings and ideas are the foundation or blueprint of the piece. Tags, thoughts, bold strokes of motion create a kinetic value to the composition, then comes balance and color ports, or windows where I create a warehouse of holding cells of ideas and notes. Then I apply the glazes, through which things that were in the foreground fall into the back, the horizon, like the past sealed in time with amber. The fact that I am using acrylic-based paints, gels and mediums adds to its durability. I'm trying to visualize vibration, sound and light. I'm attempting to encapsulate that journey in the lines and shapes of the composition. Playing with depth, shadow, (e.g., the lack of color represents the void), and inter-dimensional windows. These ideas have propelled me from learning letter forms in their abstraction, to formulating the cohesiveness of letter forms and figurative work. The composition then presents the viewer with a visual journey thru the intricate layering of transparencies, gel mediums and glazes. This technique creates a somewhat stained glass effect, where nestled between the layers of transparencies are figures that weave in and out of the circulatory system. They are intertwined and connect back to each other thru the cycles of time. The line work also represents circulation, the blood that moves throughout the body and back to the heart.

Some of the techniques DOZE mentions above are seen in this bright red painting that uses "bold strokes" in the background to add a sense of flow and movement. By adding layers of glaze and lighter paint, DOZE creates a sense of multidimensions that represent events in the past that are actualized in the present, in this case the central image of Ganesha, the god with the elephant head, who is among the most popular deities in the Hindu pantheon. Ganesha is revered as the "remover of obstacles," the patron of the arts, and the patron of letters and learning. The symbol of Ganesha as b-boy sitting on a boom box with sneakers, a kangol cap and a belt, is a brilliant pun that reverently elevates the status of contemporary b-boys, who as self-conscious artists are leaders of their generation who are aware of their "godly" nature. These urban artists, in the spirit of Ganesha, must remove many obstacles to succeed in their work. The OM sign above Ganesha's head, the small tree with lotus flower to the left, the trident and drum on the right are commonly used with Hindi representations of Ganesha. They indicate the artists' perception that the supposedly "secular" activities of hip-hop artists in fact emerged from ancient activities of music, dance, and visual arts that were performed in the process of worshiping gods. In DOZE's view, it is the responsibility of each artist to study and learn enough about the history and arts of great world civilizations to make these connections. In his work DOZE attempts to fuse ideas from both old religions and modern science to create statements about the "interconnectedness" of all life, as he sees it:

> I continually push boundaries by creating new vocabularies with the letter-form in an abstract figurative sense. I work both with the mathematical designs and the philosophical symbols of a lotus flower, the structure of trees, their systematic patterns, with the phi-ratio and its relation to the human body. Quantum physics, and the unified field theory have really struck a chord with me. I'm playing with ideas like sacred geometry, the propositions of Euclid, the platonic solids, the study of fractals, forms and their parallels in nature. I understand the basic structure of life to be a spiral. Energy contracts inwards and propels outwards to expand. I'm trying to express the inter-connectedness of life, developing a link between the ethereal and the abstract, the character and the letter, merging them into one, like in quantum physics everything is related in some shape or form. It's all connected to something greater than itself.

DOZE exemplifies the complex approach of any artist to their work. So-called "graffiti artists" are simply artists, whether working with traditional canvas, subway cars, or the street. The enthusiastic reception of their work in galleries and from fans around the globe is a recognition of their heroic struggle to make art in spite of the obstacles facing people of their race and class.

Notes

1 Norman Mailer wrote the first book on this form. Published in the USA as *The Faith of Graffiti* (1974) and in the UK as *Watching My Name Go By* (1974), Mailer appreciated the criminal and rebel aspects of writing; his view that their work was art was a radical one at the time.

2 LEE, tape-recorded public presentation, Brooklyn Museum, New York, November, 2000. Revised and authorized by LEE, December, 2000. Research materials from this essay are located in the Ivor Miller Collection, Amherst College Archives and Special Collections, Amherst College Library.

3 Winston James, *Holding Aloft the Banner of Ethiopia: Caribbean Radicalism in Early*

Twentieth-Century America (London: Verso, 1998), p. 12:

> The number of black people, and especially Caribbeans, who migrated to the United States increased dramatically, from a trickle of 411 in 1899 to a flood of 12,243 per year by 1924, the high point of the early black migration . . . During the peak years of migration, 1913 to 1924, the majority headed not only for the state of New York, but also for New York City. By 1930, almost a quarter of black Harlem was of Caribbean origin.

Joseph Harris also outlined this phenomenon:

> From the early years of the twentieth century, African American migration from Southern

states resulted in the gradual emergence of large segregated communities in Northern American cities . . . This pattern of migration increased significantly after World War I. In these cities African Americans found better educational and employment opportunities that also attracted Black immigrants from Caribbean countries, notably Jamaica, Barbados, Trinidad, and Panama. New York City became the principal recipient of this emerging international community of African Diasporans.

Joseph Harris, "The African Diaspora in World History and Politics," in Sheila Walker (ed.), *African Roots/American Cultures: Africa in the Creation of the Americas* (Lanham, MD: Rowman & Littlefield, 2001), pp. 104–117.

4 COCO 144, tape-recorded interview, New York, November, 1989.

5 MARE 139, tape-recorded interview, New York, November, 2000. Revised and authorized by MARE in February, 2001.

6 LADY PINK, tape-recorded interview, New York, May, 1988.

7 CRASH, tape-recorded interview, South Bronx, New York, January, 2001. Revised and authorized by CRASH, January, 2001.

4 DJs and turntablism

KJETIL FALKENBERG HANSEN

Introduction

The disc jockeys (or DJs) who founded hip-hop music created the sound-track for an entire cultural movement. A hip-hop DJ's roles can be multi-faceted: finding the music for dancing, playing the popular tracks, being the rapper's background band, having, maintaining, and providing the equipment, producing the beats, and not least improvising instrumental solos. To accomplish all this, DJs have creatively adopted and adapted the technology available, and have been less mindful of the intended use of that technology – from tape recorders, amplifiers, drum machines, samplers to, above all, record players. But this has not been a one-way relationship: when hip-hop music has evolved, music technology has changed along with it.

This chapter investigates how the turntable has become a musical instru-ment, investigating the different DJ roles, some of the conditions for per-forming with turntables, the impact DJs have had on the outside world, and examples of scholarly interest in DJ practices.

A history of the DJ

In 2012, Mark Katz published *Groove Music*, a truly comprehensive study of the hip-hop DJ.[1] Although not the first of its kind, the book explores in depth the myths and legends which characterize the more than forty years of DJ history.[2] With the ambition to once and for all get the story straight, Katz accepts that the DJ history remains convoluted: "Although I would've liked to establish the facts definitively, the existence of competing claims turns out to be more interesting than a simple answer, for it reveals the high value DJs place on innovation and the differing roles of the individual and the community in the world of the hip-hop DJ."[3] Katz succeeds in unraveling the origins of playing techniques, musical styles, and technical advances, exposing the creative processes along the way.

The terms "DJ" and "disc jockey" were established long before hip-hop. Arising from the radio broadcast industry, the notion "disc jockey" first appeared in print in *Variety* in 1941 and was used inconsistently and with varied meaning in the following decades.[4] Katz and other scholars date the birth of hip-hop to August 11, 1973, when DJ Kool Herc held his party, the "Back to School Jam."[5]

A handwritten party invitation flyer had the text "a DJ Kool Herc party," so unquestionably the meaning of "DJ" was generally known and already connected to what was to be hip-hop. The music that was played at this party, however, was soul, funk, and rock, without breakdancing, rapping, or turntable tricks. Now within hip-hop, the terms "DJ" and "disc jockey" have been firmly settled, along with derivations like DJing and deejay (and for music video, the VJ).

DJing today is a sophisticated art of mixing different music styles. It is well known that the Jamaican dance scene influenced hip-hop DJs like Kool Herc, but Katz claims that this connection is somewhat overrated and simplified. For instance, arguments suggest that it was primarily the massive sound systems from Jamaica, not the music, that found their way to the Bronx.[6] The Latin music influence is arguably more important, for instance music from DJ Disco Wiz, Grandmaster Caz and Charlie Chase, who could mix in salsa records during their sets. Disco and hip-hop evolved in parallel and with mutual impact on each other. Disco records were played at hip-hop parties, and both genres used breaks to a large extent,[7] while the most notable difference was how hip-hop DJs physically manipulated the records (using them as musical instruments) instead of just letting them play.

One of the most important landmarks in DJ history – it is the hip-hop DJ's most canonical myth – is how and when the most widespread playing style called "scratching" was "invented." Generally the DJ community acknowledges Grandmaster Flash's student and collaborator Grand Wizzard Theodore for creating this around 1976. Theodore's story has been accounted for in detail, but after reviewing it thoroughly, Katz found it to be *mostly* correct, although inconclusive. Like many other innovations in our society, it seems reasonable to assume that the discovery was accidental, originating from systematically compensating for artifacts of the technology in use, and will also most realistically be the product of a confluence of factors and individuals rather than the entire invention of one person.[8]

In 1981, Grandmaster Flash released *The Adventures of Grandmaster Flash on the Wheels of Steel*, the single most important DJ composition which set the course for the subsequent turntablist movement.[9] Performed live using three turntables, it firmly demonstrated what a DJ was capable of. But at the same time the MC (rapper) was the one who caught the limelight as rap music entered the popular music hit lists, moving the DJ into the background.[10] The growing popularity of the MC led partly to the proliferation of hip-hop music, partly to a clearer definition of role for the DJ, and partly to a desire to perform hip-hop music even without rapping.

This was showcased with another momentous release; the MTV video hit for *Rockit* by Herbie Hancock, which featured DJ Grandmixer D.ST as a solo musician.[11]

From the second half of the 1970s, DJ performances had become progressively more intricate. Hip-hop jams where the winner was the one with the loudest sound system now turned into battles of skill, and those battles evolved into ruled-based competitions. The three most important battles were the N.M.S., D.M.C., and I.T.F. international competitions.[12] The D.M.C. competition (founded in 1985 in London), which soon became known as the D.M.C. World DJ Championships, is the most influential.

The D.M.C. Championships have had an enormous impact on the development of playing skills. The six-minute long routines performed in the competition need to be perfectly executed and technically advanced for the competitor to stand a chance. The D.M.C.'s impact on the music itself is less straightforward, but the quintessential battle aesthetics are clearly noticeable in conventional album releases as well.[13] In recent years the D.M.C. has expanded from individual six-minute battle performances to include a head-to-head style battle and a team performance category.

While rap music continued to grow in the pop charts, many rock, jazz, and experimental musicians collaborated with DJs. Especially in jazz, the curiosity about the new instrument led to recordings that exposed the DJ as a musician.[14] Through artists such as Sugar Ray, Beck, Portishead, Ozomatli, Buckshot LeFonque, and John Zorn, the hip-hop DJ found new ground; for the most part the DJ got to play a short scratch solo to contribute with the cool "wicky-wicky" sounds.

It was only in 1995, almost two decades after DJs began to use their turntables as instruments, that DJ Babu pronounced the terms turntablist to describe what kind of DJ he had become and turntablism about where the art form was going.[15] Many feel that turntablism as a movement peaked around ten years later; even the use of the word "turntablism" seems to have decreased. Not incidentally, the fiercest development in new technology for DJs coincided with this popularity peak with innovational digital devices tailor-made for the DJ market. This can partly explain why the word got outdated somehow: it was paradoxical to talk about "turntablism," the word a derivation of the vinyl record player, while the DJ set-up was changing more and more toward using CD players and laptops.

Since 2011, the D.M.C. Championships have allowed digital vinyl systems (DVS).[16] The acceptance of DVS signals that being a DJ is no longer a privileged occupation only for dedicated record collectors. Moreover, this advance in technology has made every recording instantly available to DJs without it even being pressed on vinyl; it has effectively lowered the threshold for starting to play, both in terms of costs and equipment, and the addition of visual feedback in the form of waveform representations has made mixing a great deal easier. Assisted by technology, today's DJs have the potential to reach a critical skill level faster. The field has thus opened up for a blooming number of not-quite-professional performers, but it has also given new possibilities for innovative artists to advance even further.[17]

The role of the DJ in hip-hop

The overview above suggests that we can categorize different kinds of DJs rather than simply defining a monolithic DJ archetype. At the one end of a continuum is the practice of mixing tracks together either to create a seamless set of songs or to combine two tracks to form a new piece of music.[18] In the middle is the practice of backing up a rapper by creating beats and laying a musical foundation. At the other end lies turntablism with improvisational playing styles – solo or with other musicians. This is the practice most would consider as using the turntable exclusively as an instrument.

The DJ has always had the role of being a record collector and having the knowhow to select music to play, for instance the original radio disc jockey who recreated the ballroom feeling, the Jamaican DJ who was often called the "selector," and the early hip-hop DJs like Afrika Bambaataa who were famous for their massive (and eclectic) record collections. Unlike in other elements of hip-hop, a substantial capital investment was needed in order to build up and maintain a sound system and music library.

The turntable as a musical instrument

Katz argues that although turntables were common in households, they were not necessarily available or usable for the aspiring DJ: the equipment could be kept out of bounds, or was of too low quality for DJing. Instead he sees – comparable in many ways to punk music aesthetics – that the driving forces behind turntables becoming hip-hop's main instrument are partly the power they embody, and partly how you break the rules by misusing the delicate vinyl.[19]

There have been different proposals for how to classify turntables as musical instruments. Miles White regarded the turntable as a manual analogue sampler, coded 521.21 in the generators and modifiers of electronic sound extension to the Sachs-Hornbostel classification system.[20] By "manual," White referred to the possibility of manipulating the playback of the sampled sound, and he divided this manipulation into six different "performance techniques": on a single turntable backspinning, scratching, and cutting, and on two turntables mixing, blending, and punch-phrasing. I have written elsewhere that it is mainly scratching and beat juggling that defined the turntables as instruments.[21]

Charles Mudede expressed a different point of view.[22] Based on ideas from Walter Benjamin, he argues that the turntable is a "repurposed object" for creating "meta-music" and thus not a musical instrument.[23] Now, more than a decade later, few argue against classifying turntables as instruments, either if used as a solo instrument, as a backing instrument, or in general for creating new music from existing recordings.

Playing styles: scratching and beat juggling

It is difficult to discuss playing styles without having described the equipment in detail yet, but the two main ones, scratching and beat juggling, are so important in defining the instrument that they must at least briefly be introduced at this point. Scratching has become a layman term because it is a distinct sound and a very strong metaphor. Many will doubtless make a scratching gesture with their hand waving in the air when asked how a DJ plays. While the meaning of the word and the experience of how turntables work suggest that the needle is dragged across the record to make a scratching sound, in reality the sound comes from the speeding up, slowing down and reversing the platter's rotation speed by hand. As such, scratching can be achieved with playback devices other than turntables, for instance cassette tapes, but the simplicity of adjusting the speed, as well as the tactile sensation and sensory feedback of handling the vinyl, made turntables perfect for this task.

Scratching can be compared to how, for instance, a violin is played where each hand controls different parameters of the sound. The left hand of the violinist adjusts the pitch, or tone height, but no sound comes until the bow, controlled by the right hand, touches the string. Similarly for scratching, one hand is on the record and controls the playback speed, or in other words the pitch (or tone height). The other hand controls the volume slider on the mixer to turn the sound on and off.

The beat juggling playing style has no parallel in other musical instruments. Here, the DJ controls two turntables and the volume slider to alternately play from each of two records. Katz gives an example from DJ Steve Dee, one of the originators of the playing style, where two copies of an Erik B and Rakim track with the lyrics "This is how it should be done" are played in alternation to create a new composition (see Table 4.1).[24]

Table 4.1 *DJ Steve Dee beat juggling routine*

Turntable A	Turntable B
This is how it should be	
	This is how it should be
This is how it should be	
	This is
how	
	how it sh
shou	
	should be done

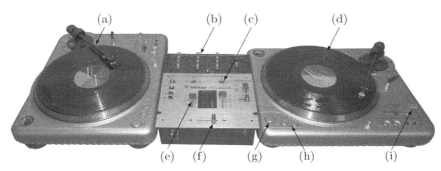

Figure 4.1 The DJ instrument set-up optimized for scratching and beat juggling with the mixer (Vestax PMC-5 ProIII) placed between the turntables (Vestax PDX-2000 MkII), and the left turntable rotated to keep the tone-arm away. The controllers are: (a) the tone-arm, pick-up, cartridge, and stylus; (b) EQ tone controls; (c) line switch; (d) skip-proof battle record with repeating grooves; (e) channel volume fader; (f) crossfader; (g) start–stop switch; (h) 33 or 45 rpm speed selector; and (i) pitch control.

The equipment

While a DJ only needs one turntable, strictly speaking, it is customary to use two turntables with an audio mixer placed in between to control the sound levels. Figure 4.1 shows a typical set-up with the most important controllers labeled. The turntables have pick-ups with a stylus (a) that converts the movement in the reel into an electrical signal. The design of the stylus or needle is crucial for allowing the record to move backwards (a hifi stylus tip is elliptical while a DJ stylus tip is spherical in shape). The other features that separate a purpose-made turntable in this context from a home hifi one are the strong direct-driven (as compared to belt-driven) motor and a slip-mat that reduces friction between the vinyl and the platter. Manufacturers have whole product lines aimed at DJs, but at the same time the turntable has remained largely unchanged since the Technics SL1200 model was released,[25] using pick-ups and needles made for radio DJs.

In contradiction, the audio mixer, which may seem to be of less importance, has undergone great changes, often based on ad hoc solutions by electronics-savvy DJs who needed new features. The mixer has very few controllers: most important is the crossfader (f) for gradually lowering the sound volume from one turntable (channel) while increasing the sound from the other. Next, used to somewhat lesser extent are for each channel the line switches (c), the volume faders (e), and the tone controls (b). Because playing techniques depend increasingly on switching the sound rapidly on and off, the crossfader has been made almost frictionless, and it is possible to set the distance needed to travel for turning the sound from on to off (fading curve). In scratching it is preferable to have the fading curve very steep, making the travel from sound-off to sound-on only around 1 mm. There is also an option to reverse the direction of the fading, useful for certain techniques.[26]

Although most DJs would concur that the vinyl record is the very soul of turntablism, the format is not always convenient. Records are heavy, prone to wear and physical damage, and they can be hard to find. As mentioned above, the DVS have therefore set a new standard for DJs. Rotating discs such as a record player with a time-coded vinyl or a CD player with a jog wheel are used to control the playback of sound files on a computer. In this way, the whole music library can be stored and accessed digitally with many additional benefits: quick changes of tracks, loading the same track on both decks, no reduction of sound quality due to wear, visual representation of the track on a computer screen, setting cue points to find specific parts of a track, and much more. But in the end the DVS and the standard turntable are quite similar from the instrument perspective.

Sound production and sound material

To produce sound with an acoustic instrument, the player must input some energy and cause movement in the system (an air jet stream; a vibrating string; scraping two objects against each other). The turntable is not so different as sound is created when the needle follows the notched groove of the record, which generates a vibration that is amplified by the pick-up. By changing the rotational speed, the pitch of the sound (or tone) changes as it is played faster or slower. A fast movement means a high pitch and a slow movement means a low pitch. The audio mixer does not produce any sounds, but it modifies the amplitude and timbre of the signal from the record player.

Some sounds, or recordings, are more suitable than others to play with. For scratching, the most popular sounds (samples) to manipulate are "ah" and "fresh" from the sentence "ah this stuff is really fresh,"[27] and "scratching" from "all that scratching is making me itch."[28] These are very short spoken utterances located on iconic records.[29] In general, any short sound will do just fine, and apart from the classics such as those just mentioned, various hard-to-trace drum beats, instrument tones, and special sound effects, for instance from games, and not least other vocal phrases are frequently used. From an acoustic understanding, there are some common characteristics: sounds often have a strong noise component, a sharp onset, and quite seldom tones with a distinct harmonic quality.

In beat juggling the sound material comes from two records, either two identical copies or two different records. The origin of beat juggling lies in mixing the break of a song: the part where all the vocals and instruments pause and the drum beat continues. With precise techniques, the records are played alternately from several bars down to very short durations. A few beat juggling routines have become renowned for the choice of sound material, such as performances using *Rock the Bells* (LL Cool J) or *Tom Sawyer* (Rush), but just like for scratching, almost any sound is applicable. For playing purposes it is an advantage that the recording has a distinct rhythm with gaps between each onset, and that the sounds can be matched in tonality.

The "ah" and "fresh" samples come from one 12″ single, released by the small company Celluloid Records.[30] How is it possible that each and every DJ uses these samples when there are not even remotely enough pressed copies of the vinyl? Before the DVS made playing digital files an option, desirable samples and breaks were collected on break collections and battle records.[31] One battle record alone can have hundreds of scratch-friendly sounds (with little respect for copyright clearance). This made life easier and cheaper for the DJ, but at the same time many still complain that it removed the mystery of the art and even compare it to cheating. Time-coded vinyl and DVS took this controversy to its extreme as it is no longer even necessary to change the record.

Interaction and playing gestures

On a basic level, all that is needed to perform the turntable is to change record speed, the playing position of the needle, and the output volume of each turntable. It is, however, almost impossible to create steady tones as on a traditional instrument, to play a scale for instance. Nonetheless, pitch variations are a crucial component of performances, and changing the pitch means varying the playback speed of the record. The connection between physical movement and sound is immediately comprehended.[32] As a result, and quite uniquely for this instrument, performers have individual hand positions and gestures.

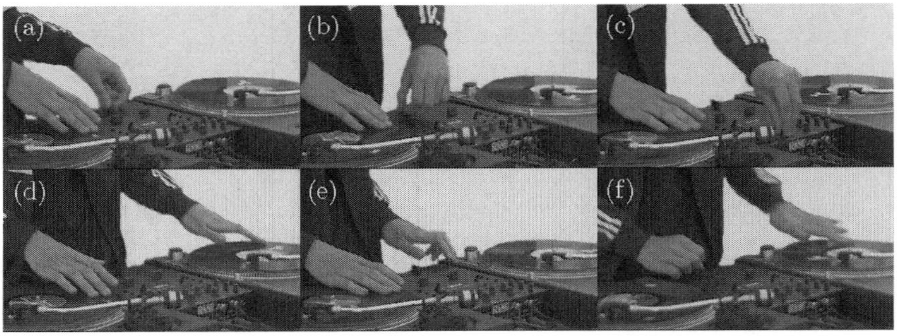

Figure 4.2 Images showing a short sequence of typical gestures from a DJ performance. The DJ uses both hands to control the two turntables and the mixer. In the top row, the right hand is on the record, and the left hand goes to (a) the crossfader, (b) the channel fader, (c) the tone controls, and in the bottom row to (d) the other turntable and (e) its stop button. In (f) the hands are switched so that the left goes to the vinyl and the right to the crossfader.

Figure 4.2 shows a DJ performing with different hand positions: in Figure 4.2(a)–(e) the right hand is always occupied with controlling the vinyl, while the left hand moves between faders and performs other gestures. Arguably, DJs become much more ambidexterous than other musicians because it is an advantage to master all techniques with the left hand on the fader and the right on the vinyl and vice versa; this is shown in figures 4.2(a) and 4.2(f).

Any musician's gestures can be divided into two groups: sound-producing and sound-modifying gestures, and ancillary, sound-accompanying, and communicative gestures.[33] The last group contains all gestures and movements that do not directly affect the sound, for instance when a pianist expressively moves the upper torso. As discussed earlier, such movements have become a fundamental ingredient in the DJ performance in the form of body tricks. Playing two records in quick alternation and backspinning them to the starting point (to create loops) requires remarkable arm and hand control, and this spectacular playing style quickly became distinctive for performers and popular with the audience. Backspinning evolved into an elaborate practice of body tricks on its own, with arms behind the back, moving the vinyl with the forehead or with strange objects, and climaxing with DJ David doing handstands on the turntable in the D.M.C. Championships.[34] Another example of ancillary playing gestures found in battles is the (mainly rude) gestures used to accentuate the "disses" that humiliate the opponent.

Even at the lowest level of sound production when creating only one tone the turntable is surprisingly complex. Consider moving the vinyl forwards and then backwards in a simple hand gesture. How many onsets are produced and how will it sound?[35] That depends on several factors:

the sample, the starting position, the place of returning the record, the extent of the movement, and the crossfader movement. The frequency of onsets is higher in scratching than compared with other instruments, and if the sample has more than one onset, a gesture will trigger each onset (e.g. moving the record forward and back over the word "scratching" will produce *four* onsets). Because every movement comprises an acceleration and deceleration, the pitch of each tone is also much less stable than for other instruments; furthermore, such pitch changes are performed on a sample whose own pitch in turn can be unstable as well.

In contradiction to the complexity described above, the relationship between the gestures we see and sounds we hear is apparent. The transfer of energy from the body of the performer to the instrument directly affects pitch and tone quality: a speeding movement results in a rising tone. In other words, the mapping between control parameters (what the DJ does) and the sound parameters (how the instrument sounds) are technically complex, but to the audience it appears simple.[36]

DJ performances

Turntablist performances can take place either in the classic solo DJ hip-hop setting, or in situations involving other musicians. As discussed above, the turntable instrument has many limitations. For instance, to produce defined pitches ("play the note C") is a great challenge, and playing sustained tones is almost impossible. Regardless of the impracticalities for playing melodies, scratching is often successfully performed in different settings involving a harmony-based musical background. In contrast, beat juggling has developed into a style of building complex compositions that leave no room for other musicians.

DJ battles have been the primary outlet for artistic creativity, where skills, originality, and showmanship are judged. In the typical battle, a perfectly prepared and rehearsed set is performed live. The sets normally include scratching, beat juggling, and other elements like body tricks and dissing opponents with word play from records. Musically, the sets are perhaps mainly appreciated by initiated listeners, but have had great impact on all aspects of the art form. Typically, new techniques, playing styles and tricks are first shown in battles (such as beat juggling, the crab scratch, transforming, most body tricks, and even team routines).

While the task of being a backing musician to the rapper is unquestionably one of the most essential to the DJ, this is not where the composition has had its main focus. Instead the (sometimes elongated) DJ introductions offered the opportunity to expose a bigger public to more than hit songs and beats. Rapping partners complement the performances by calling out the DJ's name, proclaiming the techniques, praising the skills, and not least reassuring that the music is made using two turntables.[37]

After the Invisibl Skratch Piklz entered the D.M.C. competition in 1992 as a synergetic turntable group, so-called DJ teams started to adopt the form of a typical band consisting of drums, bass, and solo instruments. One would play scratching solos, while the others created the background from single drum beats and instrumental samples. This playing style requires meticulously composed pieces and carefully synchronized movements.[38] As a result, team performances have a musical appeal and complexity that can hardly be achieved in individual performances, and this explains why competitions for many years have included a team discipline.

The team composition style – which basically aimed to create drums, bass lines, melody, and vocal phrases from short samples – worked very well also in conventional album recordings as compared to improvisation- or mix-based tapes. Full-length turntable albums started to appear during the 1990s, either by groups (the X-Executioners, the Invisibl Skratch Piklz), or by single DJs composing in a similar style (Rob Swift, DJ Q-Bert, Mix Master Mike).

The cultural impact of the scratching hip-hop DJ is remarkable, comparable to the way in which graffiti has influenced contemporary art, typography, and design, and how breakdancing has influenced modern dance, fitness exercise classes, and even clothing. While newspapers uncritically and repeatedly connect graffiti to vandalism and rap music to violence, the DJ is generally portrayed as more harmless and nerdy. DJs were also allowed to blend in with other musicians in a different, more autonomous way than rappers, graffiti artists, breakdancers, or beatboxers seemed to do within their respective areas.

It is also noteworthy that the scratch metaphor is so strong that the sounds even are imitated by other instruments, for instance in Tom Morello's guitar playing with the band Rage Against the Machine.[39] And this completes the circle: turntables developed into a musical instrument within a small musical genre by imitating and replacing other instruments – now they are inspiring new interfaces and playing styles performed by non-DJs far beyond the hip-hop community.

Further reading

For those interested in the history of the DJ, turntablism, and the turntable, the book *Groove Music* by Mark Katz that has been cited throughout this chapter is a wonderful read, providing an unparalleled overview and links to sound and video examples. Katz covers the ground from the early days of hip-hop to the recent-day transition from turntables to new technology.

Katz also included a chapter on the main DJ battles. The battle culture is one of the most interesting areas for further studies of turntable-made music. Although not further reading as such, the documentation and available material from these battles (on YouTube, for example) are either good or excellent. Most of the events feature world-leading musicians filmed by professional production companies. DJ battle material could be applied for studies and analyses in musicology, performance studies, interaction design, culture studies, and music technology, to name just a few.

In Kjetil Falkenberg Hansen's thesis,[40] a number of academic studies involving DJs are presented and it gives a thorough review of scratching and related technology with a scientific approach up until early 2010. The topics include expressive performances in scratching, the contribution of the sample in performances, modeling of scratch techniques, experimental interfaces, and more. The text is augmented with links to sound and video examples.

A different scholarly and musicological take on turntablism can be found in Alexander Sonnenfeld's dissertation *Bewegungslehre*.[41] Here he proposes a complete notation system for turntablism, called S-notation. This system has recently been employed in teaching at the respected QBert Skratch University.[42]

Justin A. Williams recently published a book covering the sampling tradition in hip-hop, in both the narrow sense of digital sampling and the broader sense of musical borrowing.[43] Here, the DJ has played a major role, both adding cultural references from other genres and areas, and also establishing within-genre citations as a musical mannerism.

In *Vinyl: A History of the Analogue Record*, Richard Osborne closely examines the development of the vinyl record, including the reasons behind the surprising and uplifting trends in record sales since 2000.[44] Although there is little about hip-hop specifically, the book is still an essential read for everyone with an interest in the DJ world.

Readers who want to stay updated on new technology for DJs are encouraged to browse the contents of the major scientific conferences in the sound and music computing area. These include the New Interfaces for Musical Expression,[45] the Sound and Music Computing Conference,[46] the International Computer Music Conference,[47] the CHI Conference,[48] and Advances in Computer Entertainment Technology.[49] The proceedings of papers from these conferences are often free for download.

Notes

1 Mark Katz, *Groove Music: The Art and Culture of the Hip-Hop DJ* (New York: Oxford University Press, 2012).

2 Katz uses multiple sources, often primary, to check and more reliably confirm the many historical accounts that have been presented

previously, for instance in such pioneering works as Bill Brewster and Frank Broughton, *Last Night a DJ Saved My Life: The History of the Disc Jockey* (New York: Headline Publishing, 2006); Jim Fricke and Charlie Ahearn (eds.), *Yes Yes Y'all: The Experience Music Project Oral History of Hip-Hop's First Decade* (Cambridge, MA: Da Capo Press, 2002); Steven Hager, *Hip-hop: The Illustrated History of Breakdancing, Rap Music, and Graffiti* (New York: St. Martin's Press, 1984); Ulf Poschardt, *DJ Culture*, trans. Shaun Whiteside (Hamburg: Rogner & Bernhard GmbH & Co. Verlags KG, 1998); David Toop, *Rap Attack 3*, 3rd edn. (London: Serpent's Tail, 2000); and also in films like *Wild Style*, dir. Charlie Ahern (First Run Features, 1983), and *Scratch*, dir. Doug Pray (Palm Pictures, 2001).

3 Katz, *Groove Music*, p. 8.

4 Marc Fisher, *Something in the Air: Radio, Rock, and the Revolution that Shaped a Generation* (New York: Random House, 2007), p. 13. See also Poschardt, *DJ Culture*.

5 Katz, *Groove Music*, p. 17.

6 *Ibid.*, p. 26.

7 "Breaks" refer to what was later called breakbeats, and referred to the instrumental break of a record, looped by the earliest hip-hop DJs for b-boys and b-girls to dance to, and became the fundamental building block of hip-hop beats. See also Chapter 2 in this volume.

8 For the full story see Katz, *Groove Music*, p. 59 and Steven Hager's interview with Grand Wizzard Theodore, available at youtu.be/4-JBa6w0OHI (accessed December 10, 2013). Indeed, several DJs have come up with the idea of scratching during the forming years of hip-hop, either accidentally or as a creative way to deal with noise from backspinning the record caused by imprecise crossfader control. Earlier experiments by the *musique concrète* pioneer Pierre Schaeffer could have had some impact, but this seems unlikely. See Kjetil Falkenberg Hansen, "The Acoustics and Performance of DJ scratching: Analysis and Modeling" (Ph.D. dissertation, KTH Royal Institute of Technology, 2010), p. 40.

9 Grandmaster Flash, *The Adventures of Grandmaster Flash on the Wheels of Steel* (Englewood, NJ: Sugar Hill Records, SH-557, 1981). Available at youtu.be/gXNzMVLqIHg (accessed December 10, 2013).

10 Katz, *Groove Music*, p. 73.

11 Herbie Hancock, *Future Shock* (New York: Columbia: FC 38814, LP, 1983). Available at youtu.be/GHhD4PD75zY (accessed December 10, 2013).

12 The N.M.S. (New Music Seminar) was held between 1981 and 1994, the I.T.F. (International Turntablist Federation) between 1996 and 2005, and the D.M.C. from 1985 until the present. See www.dmcdjchamps.com and Katz, *Groove Music*, p. 108.

13 Compare, for instance, the *X-Ecutioners* showcase from the 1999 D.M.C. in typical battle style with the 2008 album release from the related all-turntable band Ill Insanity. Available at youtu.be/5YuteDF7Tig and youtu.be/ukwbx4rONRQ (accessed December 10, 2013).

14 Jazz has always had a big influence on hip-hop music, and vice versa the vocal style of rapping and the unconventional sounds made by turntables has attracted jazz musicians; see, for instance, Justin A. Williams, "The Construction of Jazz Rap as High Art in Hip-Hop Music," *The Journal of Musicology* 27/4 (2010): 435–459.

15 DJ Babu was probably not the first to use these terms, but they were widely accepted after his usage. See Katz, *Groove Music*, p. 280, n. 3.

16 In DVS, time-coded records played on the turntable are used to control the playback of a sound file located on a computer. DVS also allow other types of controllers, such as CD players and computer input devices.

17 An example of how to take advantage of new technology can be seen in the 2011 D.M.C. showcase by the five-time Team Champions, Kireek. During the whole performance, they never change the records as these only control the music on the laptops placed on the sides, and they play with techniques impossible to accomplish using traditional equipment. Available at youtu.be/XNpiwZHv1KY (accessed December 10, 2013).

18 Consider here the performance practice and playing styles being scaled from having a low to high level of virtuosity, although this is a simplification.

19 Katz, *Groove Music*, p. 62. The concept of turntablism is more important than the actual medium, the vinyl record, and we can acknowledge that such music can be performed not only on turntables but on other devices too (e.g. iPads).

20 Miles White, "The Phonographic Turntable and Performance Practice in Hip Hop Music," *Ethnomusicology OnLine* 2 (1999): 1–6; see also Michael B. Bakan *et al.*, "Demystifying and Classifying Electronic Music Instruments," *Selected Reports in Ethnomusicology* 8 (1990): 37–57.

21 See Kjetil Falkenberg Hansen, "The Basics of Scratching," *Journal of New Music Research* 31/4

(2002): 357–365. The two latter terms cover White's techniques for, respectively, one and two turntables. This list of playing styles is nevertheless inconclusive: for instance, DJs can do drumming, needle drop, no-input fading and physical vinyl manipulation, to name but a few techniques.

22 Charles Mudede, "The Turntable," *CTheory* 4 (2003): 1–8.

23 Walter Benjamin, "The Work of Art in the Age of Mechanical Reproduction," in *Illuminations*, trans. H. Zohn (New York: Schocken Books, 1968), pp. 217–251.

24 Katz, *Groove Music*, p. 188.

25 The SL1200 was introduced in 1972, while the SL1200 Mk2 that became the definitive standard turntable for scratching was produced (with some design updates) from 1979 until 2010.

26 This set-up was first called hamster style by DJ Quest, who had connected his mixer incorrectly. This is another example of an accidental use of technology that changed music technology: the hamster style became so widespread that from then on the mixer manufacturers included a reverse switch.

27 Fab 5 Freddie, *Change The Beat* (New York: Celluloid Records, CEL 156, 12″ EP, 1982).

28 Malcolm McLaren and the World's Famous Supreme Team, *Buffalo Gals* (Island Records, 0–99950, 12″ EP, 1982).

29 The history of the different samples is covered in Katz, *Groove Music*, p. 89.

30 See www.celluloidrecords.net (accessed December 10, 2013).

31 Available at youtu.be/gVE-mbdzeDc (accessed December 10, 2013). This example also includes a skip-proof section starting from 11:20 where a one-rotation-long sample is repeated for several grooves.

32 Specifically, a fast movement produces a higher pitch than a slow movement; grabbing the vinyl toward the center or toward the edge determines how long the part of the sample is that is played in one gesture; a gesture performed close to the center produces a higher

pitch than the same gesture performed close to the edge.

33 Marcelo M. Wanderley *et al.*, "The Musical Significance of Clarinetists' Ancillary Gestures: An Exploration of the Field," *Journal of New Music Research* 34/1 (2005): 97–113; see also Rolf Inge Godøy and Marc Leman (eds.), *Musical Gestures: Sound, Movement, and Meaning* (New York: Routledge, 2010).

34 Available at youtu.be/49hlyhkFLGI (accessed December 10, 2013).

35 The start of a tone is called an onset.

36 See Tellef Kvifte and Alexander Jensenius, "Towards a Coherent Terminology and Model of Instrument Description and Design," in *Proceedings of the Conference on New Interfaces for Musical Expression* (Paris, 2006), pp. 220–225.

37 See, for instance, Katz, *Groove Music*, p. 70.

38 For more on DJ teams, see Sophy Smith, *Hip-Hop Turntablism, Creativity and Collaboration* (Aldershot: Ashgate, 2013).

39 Tom Morello MTV Interview, available at youtu.be/ESVDU5BViA8 (accessed December 10, 2013).

40 Hansen, "The Acoustics and Performance of DJ Scratching." Available at bit.ly/KFH-thesis.

41 Alexander Sonnenfeld, *Bewegungslehre* (Berlin: Alexander Sonnenfeld, 2011).

42 Available at www.qbertskratchuniversity. com (accessed December 10, 2013).

43 Justin A. Williams, *Rhymin' and Stealin': Musical Borrowing in Hip-Hop* (Ann Arbor: University of Michigan Press, 2013).

44 Richard Osborne, *Vinyl: A History of the Analogue Record* (Aldershot: Ashgate, 2012).

45 Available at www.nime.org (accessed December 10, 2013).

46 Available at www.smcnetwork.org (accessed December 10, 2013).

47 Available at www.computermusic.org (accessed December 10, 2013).

48 Available at www.sigchi.org/conferences/chi/ (accessed December 10, 2013).

49 Available at www.ace-conf.org (accessed December 10, 2013).

5 The fifth element: knowledge

TRAVIS L. GOSA

Introduction: doggs, lions, and neo-liberalism

Calvin Broadus Jr.'s career as Snoop (Doggy) Dogg[1] gestures to the death of socially conscious hip-hop[2] and the birth of the 1990s gangsta rap era in which gun-play, violence against women, and political nihilism were branded as ghetto authenticity.[3] Indeed, the years 1992 and 1993 – marked by Snoop Dogg's appearance on Dr. Dre's *The Chronic* and his solo debut album *DoggyStyle* – delineate what scholars now call the "neo-liberal turn" in hip-hop: the corporate consolidation of independent music labels, the silencing of Black Nationalist politics, and the commodification of human suffering as one of America's most profitable global exports.[4] "The extraordinary commercial penetration of hip-hop," Tricia Rose argues, has destroyed a "Black cultural form designed to liberate and to create critical consciousness and turned it into the cultural arm of predatory capitalism."[5] As historian and hip-hop activist Kevin Powell laments, Snoop Dogg helped "destroy a culture and art created to save lives, pointed it toward death, and marketed it to the children and grandchildren of its originators."[6]

Twenty years ago, the skinny gangsta rapper from Long Beach, California, helped engineer hip-hop's cross-over from "Black music" to an all-encompassing media lifestyle.[7] Long before 50 Cent used his nine bullet wounds to brand a "get rich or die trying" music, video game, clothing, and film franchise, Snoop Dogg brilliantly used his murder trial to market his debut album *DoggyStyle*. *DoggyStyle*'s dense mix of Parliament Funkadelic, Isaac Hayes, and Curtis Mayfield funky samples – combined with Snoop Dogg's melodic lyrical flow – ushered in the "G-Funk" (Gangsta Funk) subgenre of West Coast rap.[8] Unfortunately, as Eithne Quinn observes, the album also "captures in vigorous terms the values of an increasingly non-politicized generation" and "a new brand of Black economic empowerment: the ruthless gangsta or enterprising 'nigga'."[9] Snoop Dogg rebranded rap songs and music videos as infomercials for 40 oz St. Ides malt liquor and Tanqueray Gin, paving the way for artists like Jay-Z and Rick Ross to peddle black Mercedes Benz Maybachs and black American Express "Centurion" cards as the new vision of Black Power politics.[10]

Beyond rhyming that "bitches ain't shit, but hoes and tricks," Snoop Dogg formalized the connections between hip-hop and the pornography industry with his *Hustler*-produced film *Snoop Dogg's Doggystyle* (2000).[11] His music videos and live performances often promoted and glamorized the pimp lifestyle (i.e. *Boss N' Up* [2005]), encouraged sexual tourism in Brazil (e.g. "Beautiful"), and at the 2003 MTV music awards, he walked two Black "bitches" (women) around on dog leashes to promote his animated cartoon series, "Where's My Dogs At?" While sonically pleasurable, Snoop Dogg's performances symbolize the crisis of hegemonic masculinity and the betrayal of African American oral and literary traditions.[12] Historically, rappers have disguised critiques of white supremacy and state-sanctioned violence in subversive racial performances known as "badman" and "trickster" tales.[13] Snoop Dogg, however, was an early adopter of "keeping it real," the reenactment of racial caricature without the satirical or political edge. He used his Crips Street gang membership and real-life legal troubles, including multiple federal charges for illegal firearms and drugs, to fetishize predatory Black masculinity as all-American entertainment. The result has been global fame and infamy. Over the years, the UK, Australia, and Norway have issued temporary travel bans on Snoop Dogg and his entourage.

Yet, after a three-week trip to Jamaica in 2012, Snoop Dogg has been reborn as "Snoop Lion," a hip-hop, reggae-infused advocate of Black consciousness, peace, and universal love. The documentary film *Reincarnated* (2012) chronicles his spiritual journey in Jamaica. Under the tutelage of Rastafarian priests – and under the influence of a copious amount of marijuana – he learns about the histories of Ethiopian emperor Haile Selassie, the great kingdoms of Africa, and other "truths" not taught in American public schools. Reconnecting with the African diaspora opens his "third eye" to alternative images of Black manhood beyond the streets. By the end of the film, he is renamed after the Lion of Judah, the most sacred symbol of Rastafari culture. Snoop Lion's *Reincarnated* (2012) album oozes positivity, with tracks about love, unity, non-violence, and even the healthiness of drinking natural fruit juice without the Tanqueray Gin. Over dancehall beats and Miley Cyrus vocals, he apologizes for selling death to kids and vows to use his music to heal the world.

Snoop's journey for the truth echoes what Afrika Bambaataa (Figure 5.1) coined the fifth element of hip-hop: knowledge. "Knowledge of self" refers to the Afro-diasporic mix of spiritual and political consciousness designed to empower members of oppressed groups. The performance arts of MCing ("rapping"), DJing ("spinning"), breakdancing ("b-girling"), and graffiti ("writing") are often identified as the "four core elements" of hip-hop, but less attention has been given to the central role of knowledge in the cultural formation of hip-hop culture. This chapter provides a revisionist historiography of hip-hop knowledge, specifically its early normative development within the socio-economic realities of the 1970s' South Bronx. Building on

Figure 5.1 Afrika Bambaataa and Charlie Chase at the Kips Bay Boys Club, Bronx, New York, 1981.

the spatial theories of Murray Forman and Cheryl Keyes, special attention is given to how Afrika Bambaataa attempted to move hip-hop from street consciousness to Afrocentric empowerment.[14] Woven throughout the narrative of this chapter is the theme of tension between knowledge and the commercial impetus of hip-hop. Money, whether from the streets and/or multinational corporations, has helped spread hip-hop culture, but has also served as a major roadblock to making hip-hop part of an emancipatory politic.

Afrika Bambaataa's reincarnation

Snoop Dogg's reincarnation is reminiscent of the improbable birth of hip-hop culture forty years ago. In the early 1970s, Kevin Donovan, a warlord of the notorious South Bronx Black Spades gang, saw the movie *Zulu* (1964) on television, won a trip to Africa, and changed his name to Afrika Bambaataa Aasim, an Afro-Islamic name that means "affectionate leader" or "protector." As Bambaataa (Figure 5.2), Donovan co-opted the Black Spades into the Universal Zulu Nation, and created a global organization dedicated to knowledge, non-violence, and healthy living.[15] Bambaataa's most important contribution to hip-hop culture, beyond coining the phrase "hip-hop" and introducing electronic-funk music into DJing, is his insistence that "knowledge of self" be considered the official fifth element of hip-hop culture.[16] Pioneering hip-hop groups of the late 1970s and early 1980s occasionally espoused sociopolitical messages. Brother D and the

Figure 5.2 Afrika Bambaataa at Bronx River Projects, February 2, 1982.

Collective Effort's "How We Gonna Make the Black Nation Rise?" (1981) and the Treacherous Three's "Yes We Can Can" (1982) are two early examples of recorded songs that advocated knowledge of self. However, according to Bambaataa, a coherent ideological movement of beats, rhymes, dance, art, and politics could empower oppressed people around the world.

Romanticized retellings of hip-hop history tend to describe block parties as mini-revolutions spontaneously born out of the ashes of the failing Civil Rights and Black Power eras. Hip-hop's "original myth," as H. Samy Alim calls the narrative of hip-hop's genesis in the 1970s' New York ghettos, involves some truth, nostalgia, and wishful thinking. A serious, revisionist hip-hop history, Alim continues, should acknowledge "the immense cultural labor that hip-hop heads engage in as they make a 'culture' with a 'history' and 'traditions,' and of course, 'an origin.'"[17]

Afrika Bambaataa, the "Amen-Ra" and "Godfather" of hip-hop culture, has spent a lifetime (re)inventing hip-hop as a coherent, social movement.[18] In America, Bambaataa was the chief architect who merged DJs, b-boys, graffiti artists, and rappers into a unified community culture. As breakdance pioneer Jorge "Popmaster Fabel" Pabon recounts, before Bambaataa and the Zulu Nation brought these various art forms together, "each element in this culture had its own history and terminology contributing to the development of a cultural movement."[19]

Amid post-industrial destruction of labor market opportunities for young Black and Latino males, middle-class flight from inner cities, and

Figure 5.3 Party Flyer, "The Message: Don't Waste Your Mind on Dust or Any Drugs That Harm Your Body," Bronx, New York, 1981.

an unsuccessful war on drugs, few social supports were available for urban youth.[20] Based on the belief that social problems were caused by the moral irresponsibility of teenage mothers ("welfare queens") and violent youth ("street thugs"), the neo-liberal social policies of presidents Richard Nixon and Ronald Reagan cut domestic spending on healthcare, aid for needy families, and funding for public education programs. Amid the violence and joblessness, the streets became the primary social structure for youth. As Jeff Chang writes:

> Gangs structured the chaos. For immigrant latchkey kids, foster children outside the system, girls running away from abusive environments, and thousands of others, the gangs provided shelter, comfort, and protection. They channeled energies and provided enemies. They warded off boredom and gave meaning to the hours. They turned the wasteland into a playground.[21]

Bambaataa believed that unifying the four core elements under the same cultural tent would provide a sense of identity and purpose for a new generation. His idea to combat the chaos of urban life with music came from watching the film *Zulu* (1964). In the movie, a small group of Zulu warriors use the sound of beating shields and song to terrify, and then defeat, the powerful British army in pre-colonial South Africa. In the same way,

Bambaataa envisioned that music, dance, and a renewed sense of African pride could defeat drug dealers and hopelessness in the South Bronx.

One irony, though, is that gang warfare was the necessary basis of the hip-hop revolution. In order to overthrow the psychological chains of ghetto colonization, Bambaataa had to first merge opposing gangs into a unified Zulu Nation. Inspired perhaps by the early rhetoric of Malcolm X, the answer was the intelligent use of violence. As an early member of the Zulu Nation recalls, Bambaataa systematically grew his movement through "peace treaties" which forced rival gangs and crews to join: "if you resisted, sometimes peace came to you *violently*. We *demanded* peace."[22] The reputation of the Black Spades gang kept the drug dealers at bay and the violence to a minimum. The newfound peace allowed former enemies, breakdance crews, DJs, and graffiti writers to congregate at the same park jams and house parties (see Figure 5.3).

Street consciousness and the music hustle

The early hip-hop "jams" provided reprieve from gang wars, and good times for those who could not afford entry into the relatively expensive funk-disco scene.[23] However, the first hip-hop parties were not venues for raising consciousness or examining African identity. Oral history interviews with the "founding fathers," such as Grandmaster Flash, the Cold Crush Brothers, Crazy Legs (of the R.S.C.), Kool Herc, and Chief Rocker Busy Bee provide a realistic portrayal of hip-hop's formative years. Sex with "fly girls," drugs, and alcohol and, of course, music and dancing, were part of the early parties. But so too were gunshots, armed robberies, and fights.[24] Most pioneers were focused on throwing parties to make quick money, not educating the masses. The party culture primarily offered an alternative revenue stream for (former) street gangsters, a way to turn skills learned on the streets into a legal music hustle.

The South Bronx was no "Garden of Eden," untouched by the impetus of capital. The same economic forces that created poverty created hip-hop. As Jeff Chang describes, the Bronx was "blood and fire with *occasional* music," a war zone overrun with gangs and thugs who were marginally better than the slumlords, corrupt cops, and politicians.[25] One of the greatest ironies is that the crisis in capitalism created *both* the street hustler *and* global communications and technology – such as the influx of less expensive Japanese-made turntables, cassette decks, and equalizers – that would eventually give rise to the hip-hop generation.[26] If not for the collapse of the industrial economy and shift to service-sector production in the 1970s, hip-hop pioneers would have been at work instead of b-boying in the park or tagging subway cars. In the vacuum of sustainable job opportunities, kids merged street savvy with music to create a grassroots music economy.

In her exhaustive study of hip-hop, *Rap Music and Street Consciousness*, Cheryl Keyes argues that the streets are key to understanding the aesthetics and performances of rap music. She writes:

> The streets nurture, shape, and embody the hip-hop music aesthetic, creating a genre distinct from other forms of black popular music that evolved after World War II. Through a critical assessment of this tradition from within the culture of its birth, we can begin to adequately analyze rap's performance and aesthetic qualities, interpret its lyrics, and define its height of style.[27]

Street consciousness, including how corporate moguls reimagine the 'hood, has shaped the historical development of hip-hop culture.[28] Beginning with the street economies of the late 1970s, hip-hop refashioned the marketing, branding, and monetizing strategies of organized gang-life, numbers racketeering (illegal lotteries), and drug dealing into a profitable party culture.

Thinking back on the start of his DJing career, Afrika Bambaataa recalls that the early pioneers were "young entrepreneurs, when we didn't even know we was entrepreneurs."[29] It was the allure of getting money through the relatively safer music scene that attracted the early spinners. Kool Herc (Clive Campbell), considered the father of DJing, explains how he created the "music hustle" in 1974–1975:

> I was giving parties to make money, to better my sound system. I was never a DJ for hire. I was the guy who rent the place. I was the guy who got flyers made. I was the guy who went out there in the streets and promoted it. You know? Some nights it'd be packed . . . less money; some nights it'd be more people . . . more money. And after that they would say, "Kool Herc and Coke La Rock [his partner and MC] is makin' money with that music, up in the Bronx." We was recognized for hustlin' with music.[30]

Organizing and marketing these volatile events became an important part of the hustle in the emerging hip-hop business. While there were occasional free block parties and community center jams in the summer, the Bronx's northeastern climate meant breaking into high school gymnasiums and staging illegal jams. In the late 1970s and early 1980s, as hip-hop became more established, the party scene merged with established discotheque culture at clubs like the Ecstasy Garage and the Black Door.

The music hustlers of the "bombed out" Bronx established a multi-faceted economic structure around music, dance, fashion, and art. The flyer designers of the early and late 1970s, such as "Flyer King" Buddy Esquire, were paid street graffiti artists hired to publicize the weekend parties. Cash incentives for performers and partygoers were commonplace. Importantly, none of this was separate from the street economy. Local criminals provided the prize money for DJ/MC battles and best-dressed contests. Gang members and stick-up kids freelanced as security guards at the door and protected the talent and their equipment from harm. MC El Bee (Larry Boatright), a forgotten pioneer of 1970s' hip-hop (and childhood friend of members of Public Enemy), argues that the hustlers who funded the early jams, provided physical protection for artists, and paid for the iconic gear should be regarded as the "invisible legends" of hip-hop.

The hustler's mantra of getting money "by any means necessary," as KRS-One argues while alluding to the famous Malcolm X slogan, might be considered the sixth element of hip-hop culture. He defines the street entrepreneur as:

> *Street trade, having game, the natural salesman,* or the smooth *diplomat.* It is the readiness in the creation of a business venture that brings about grassroots business practices . . . Its practitioners are known as *hustlers* and *self-starters. Entrepreneur – a self-motivated creative person who undertakes a commercial venture.*[31]

Few seem to espouse their love of hip-hop more than KRS-One, yet he acknowledges that money is a core component of the culture. This should not be surprising: "smooth hustling," "running game," and "getting over" are compulsory survival adaptations on the margins of society where gainful employment opportunities and safety are scarce. In terms of abstract values, street entrepreneurs demonstrate the Protestant work ethic and spirit of capitalism. On the streets, the hustler grinds through sleepless nights with a stubborn-against-all-odds fortitude to make money. Marketing research firms have attempted to replicate this "get rich or die trying" approach that former street hustlers use to mass-produce hip-hop coolness.[32] The problem, though, is that the quest for liberation is rarely popular, profitable, or cool.

Edutainment for knowledge of self

In its first decade (1973–1982), hip-hop was primarily a party culture. The early MC specialized in making announcements, bragging-boasting-and-toasting on the microphone, and performing dirty versions of nursery rhymes. DJs looped and transformed breakbeats, the instrumental or drum section of a song, to keep the b-boys and b-girls dancing to the break of dawn. At best, these parties were successful in making money and redirecting real violence and crime into scripted dance floor performances of the streets.

Grey-haired hip-hoppers should recall that rappers of the pre-crack 1980s era appropriated the alter egos of local cocaine dealers. Kurtis Blow, Lovebug Starkski, J-Ski, and Kool Rock-ski (of the Fat Boys) are a few examples.[33] Sugar Hill's "Rapper's Delight" (1979) invokes the same trite narratives about luxury cars (e.g. "a Lincoln Continental and a sunroof Cadillac"), money (e.g. Big Bank Hank), and pimping "fly girls" (e.g. "hotel, motel, Holiday Inn/If your girl starts actin' up/then you take her friend") found in contemporary rap. Taking women from the club, to the limo, to the hotel for a champagne orgy is a prominent scene in Charlie Ahern's *Wild Style* (1982), perhaps the most acclaimed film on early hip-hop.

Bambaataa redesigned the hip-hop party scene as "edutainment,"[34] a mix of fun and socially conscious music and discourse. Unique was Bambaataa's attempt to educate partygoers with a pro-Black soundtrack of James Brown (i.e. "I'm Black and I'm proud"), Sly & The Family Stone ("Everyday People"), and Earth, Wind, & Fire ("Keep Your Head to the Sky"). During one of his signature jams, Bambaataa would bait partygoers with the familiar dance tracks, then once the dance floor was full, switch to the German electropop of Kraftwerk and the Nigerian Afro-beats of Fela Kuti. "During long music segments when Bam was deejaying," his official biography recalls, "he would sometimes mix in recorded speeches from Malcolm X, Martin Luther King, Jr., and, later, Louis Farrakhan."[35] Back then the freshest b-boys emulated the expensive athletic gear and leather jumpsuits worn by corner dealers. To combat the street culture, Bambaataa and the Zulus would rock parties dressed as ancient Egyptian pharaohs, indigenous Native Americans, or Afro-futuristic space aliens inspired by Parliament Funkadelic. Borrowing from the strategies of pan-African leader Marcus Garvey, Bambaataa bestowed partygoers with African-inspired titles of royalty. "Fly girls" were to be called "queens," and treated as such, while b-boys became reformed "kings."

Through his jams, Bambaataa slowly converted paying partygoers into loyal followers, and eventually, into the world's first and largest hip-hop political organization known as the Universal Zulu Nation. The Zulu Nation appropriated snippets of the political youth movements of the 1960s and 1970s, including the anti-Vietnam War movement, the hippie-infused flower power movement, and the Muslim teachings of the Nation of Islam and the Nation of Gods and Earths (the "Five Percenters"; see Chapter 6).[36] Rather than focusing on a specific political agenda, Bambaataa's notion of hip-hop knowledge involves "factology," an all-inclusive hodgepodge of any and all spiritual beliefs, metaphysics, science and mathematics, world history, and hidden insights from alien conspiracy theories and Hollywood movies.[37] Knowledge of self, according to the Zulu Nation's literature, can be derived from the critical and self-reflective study of anything in the universe, as long as knowledge is deployed toward peace, unity, love, and having fun. "The Infinity Lessons," the basic teachings of the Zulu Nation, emphasize a lack of substantive and methodological limits to knowledge. As Aine McGlynn writes:

> One of the most beautiful and appealing aspects of the lessons is that they are never complete. They can always, at any time, by any member, be added to . . . Hip-hop at its best is about the creativity that can happen within a specific moment; this is the legacy of the street corner ciphers, freestyle sessions where the beatboxer provided the rhythm and the rapper came up with rhymes right on the spot. In its purest form, hip-hop is dynamic and constantly morphing in the same way as the Infinity Lessons do.[38]

The all-inclusive universalism of the group is inherently anti-race and anti-racist, as it focuses on the commonality of humanity. "We believe in truth whatever it is. If the truth or idea you bring us is backed by facts, then we as Amazulu [Zulus] bare witness to this truth. Truth is Truth."[39] Still, the group's primary website on factology shows the influence of Black Nationalist ideology and the explicit rejection of the Western, "white supremacist" knowledge found in schools and official textbooks:

> We believe that through white supremacy many of the history books which are used to teach around the world in schools, colleges and other places of learning have been distorted, are full of lies and foster hate when teaching about other races in the human family. We believe that all history books that contain falsehoods should be destroyed and that there should be history books based on true facts of what every race has contributed to the civilization of Human Beings. Teach true history, not falsehood, only then can all races, and nationalities respect, like or maybe love each other for what our people did for the human race as a whole.[40]

Bambaataa's Universal Zulu Nation has created a global movement dedicated to peace, healthy eating, spirituality, and environmentalism. In the last forty years, the Zulu Nation has forcibly removed drug dealers from neighborhoods, rallied around political prisoners, and recently, warned WorldStarHipHop.com to stop pandering violent and sexual images to youth. Bambaataa was nominated to the Rock and Roll Hall of Fame in 2007, and his song "Planet Rock" is considered one of *Rolling Stone*'s greatest 500 songs of all time. However, commercial success and wealth have both evaded Bambaataa. His last chart-topping hits (in the USA and UK), "Planet Rock" (1982), "Looking for the Perfect Beat" (1983), and "Renegades of Funk" (1984), are now three decades old. A renegade of funk, to be sure, Bambaataa became marginalized by eschewing what Watkins calls hip-hop's Faustian bargain: "In exchange for global celebrity, pop prestige, and cultural influence hip-hop's top performers had to immerse themselves into a world of urban villainy."[41] Bambaataa refused, settling instead for a career as a working-class DJ and spiritual leader.

Conclusion: hip-hop knowledge beyond the beats and streets

The notion of a fifth element of hip-hop was briefly made popular (and profitable) in the late 1980s and early 1990s. Acts like Public Enemy and KRS-One, and hip-hop's "Native Tongues" movement including A Tribe Called Quest, De La Soul, and the Jungle Brothers reintroduced Afro-centric edutainment into mainstream hip-hop.[42] However, in the USA, conscious hip-hop continues to be segregated in niche, "underground" markets. Jay-Z has offered these classic lines on the relationship between knowledge and the hip-hop industry: "If skills sold, truth be told, I'd probably be/Lyrically Talib Kweli/Truthfully I wanna rhyme like Common Sense/But I did 5 mill' – I ain't been rhyming like Common since."[43] The influx of neo-liberal logic makes it difficult for commercial rap music to nurture intellectual or spiritual growth. The current journeys of Snoop Lion and Afrika Bambaataa speak to the surmounting difficulties of commerce, and the potential of hip-hop knowledge outside of music.

Mr. Broadus's reincarnation from Dogg to Lion encapsulates the chapter's overall assertion that commercial entertainment and emancipatory politics make uncomfortable bedfellows. Music critics lambasted his *Reincarnated* album and film, labeling his Jamaican trip a misguided "cultural safari" and elaborate moneymaking scam.[44] Bunny Wailer, an original member of Bob Marley and the Wailers, along with the Ethio-Africa Diaspora Union Millennium Council, issued a cease-and-desist letter to Snoop Lion, claiming that his Rastafarian conversion was an attempt to cash in on their religion. "Smoking weed and loving Bob Marley and reggae music," according to the group, "is not what defines the Rastafari Indigenous Culture."[45] In response to Bunny Wailer, Snoop Lion fired back, "Fuck that nigga. Bitch-ass nigga. I'm still a gangsta don't get it fucked up. I'm growing to a man, so as a man, do I wanna revert back to my old ways and fuck this nigga up, or move forward, shine with the light?"[46]

To fully complete his transformation from gangster to spiritual leader, Snoop Lion may have to focus on community service initiatives and philanthropy outside of the music industry. In a partnership with the League of Young Voters, Snoop Lion now uses his celebrity to speak out against gun violence, while his "Snoop Youth Football League" teaches inner-city youth the "values of teamwork, good sportsmanship, discipline, and self-respect, while also stressing the importance of academics."[47]

DJ Afrika Bambaataa has added "professor" to his many designations, after being appointed as a visiting scholar at my home institution Cornell University. Years ago, the former Black Spades warlord transformed ghetto street entertainment and entrepreneurship into a social movement. Now, as Ivy League professor, he is at the center, remaking elite educational spaces. College students have been reading hip-hop textbooks since the early 1990s, and Arizona University students can now earn a minor in hip-hop studies. However, Bambaataa is pioneering a new phase of the artist-centered hip-hop studies movement, in which hip-hop knowledge is created and transmitted through the unmediated collision of instrumentation, lyricism, and experience.[48] He joins artists like Bun-B of UGK (Rice University), M-1 of dead prez (Haverford College), Wyclef Jean (Brown University), 9th Wonder (Harvard University), and the Roots's ?uestlove (New York University) in this new phase of hip-hop knowledge.

Hip-hop knowledge, the fifth element of the culture, has migrated from dislocated ghettos, to corporate boardrooms, to the corridors of the ivy towers. While this is an exciting innovation in formal education, this move is likely to antagonize the integrity of hip-hop knowledge.[49] What place, if any, will radical, counter-hegemonic thought, Afrocentricism, or street knowledge have in spaces that operate primarily for the reproduction of race-gender-social class advantage? What does "knowledge of self" mean for students training to become future owners of Wall Street hedge funds? Timely is Houston Baker's early declaration that the ultimate goal of hip-hop studies should be to disrupt the "fundamental whiteness and harmonious Westerness of higher education" concerned only with "tweed-jacketed white men."[50] Likewise, time will tell how hip-hop's fifth element will adapt to the increasing corporatization and privatization of American education. The college and university hustle may prove to be more vicious than the streets or music industry.

Further reading

Allah, Supreme Understanding, *Knowledge of Self: A Collection of Wisdom on The Science of Everything In Life* (Atlanta, GA: Supreme Design Publishing, 2009).

Collins, Patricia Hill, *From Black Power to Hip-Hop: Racism, Nationalism, and Feminism* (Philadelphia, PA: Temple University Press, 2006).

Eure, Joseph D., and James G. Spady, *Nation Conscious Rap* (New York: PC International Press, 1991).

Harris, Mark, "Edutainment: The Rise and Fall of Hip-Hop's Intelligentsia," *PopMatters*, March 31, 2005. Available at www.popmatters.com/feature/050401-edutainment/ (accessed July 10, 2013).

Hill, Marc Lamont, *Beats, Rhymes, and Classroom Life: Hip-Hop Pedagogy and the Politics of Identity* (New York: Teachers College Press, 2009).

Knight, Michael Muhammad, *The Five Percenters: Islam, Hip-Hop and the Gods of New York* (Oxford: One World Books, 2007).

RZA, *The Tao of Wu* (New York: Riverhead Books, 2009).

Stover, A. Shahid, *Hip-Hop Intellectual Resistance* (Bloomington, IN: Xlibris, 2009).

Notes

1 Due to contractual agreements, Snoop Doggy Dogg shortened his name to "Snoop Dogg" in 1998 after leaving Death Row Records for Master P's No Limit Records.

2 In this chapter, I use the words "rap" and "hip-hop" interchangeably. Rap music and hip-hop are the same thing in colloquial, everyday speech. But for hardcore aficionados and fans (known as "hip-hop heads," "true-schoolers," and "purists") the rap–hip-hop conflation is tantamount to blasphemy. In what H. Samy Alim has coined "hip-hop linguistics," the politics of language surrounding the rather synonymous words involve a complex battle over race–gender–social class, authenticity, identity, cultural ownership, and belonging. I acknowledge these debates as sociologically interesting. See H. Samy Alim, *Roc the Mic Right: The Language of Hip-Hop Culture* (London: Routledge, 2006).

3 Tayannah Lee McQuillar and J. Brother, *When Rap Music Had a Conscience: The Artists, Organizations, and Historic Events That Inspired and Influenced the "Golden Age" of Hip-Hop from 1987 to 1996* (New York: Thunder's Mouth Press, 2007); Eithne Quinn, *Nuthin' but a "G" Thang: The Culture and Commerce of Gangsta Rap (Popular Cultures, Everyday Lives)* (New York: Columbia University Press, 2005); Greg Tate, *Everything but the Burden: What White People are Taking from Black Culture* (New York: Broadway Books, 2003).

4 Jared A. Ball, *I Mix What I Like! A Mixtape Manifesto* (Oakland, CA: AK Press, 2011); Lester K. Spence, *Stare in the Darkness: The Limits of Hip-Hop and Black Politics* (Minneapolis: University of Minnesota Press, 2011). Cultural critic Greg Tate poetically describes hip-hop's neo-liberal turn as "the marriage of heaven and hell, of New World African ingenuity and that trick of the devil known as global hyper-capitalism." See Greg Tate, "Hiphop Turns 30: Whatcha Celebratin' For?," *Village Voice*, December 8, 2004. Available at www.villagevoice.com/2004-12-28/news/hiphop-turns-30/ (accessed June 28, 2013).

5 Tricia Rose, "Hip-Hop on Trial: Hip-Hop Doesn't Enhance Society, It Degrades it," *Intelligence Squared and Google+ "Versus Liberating Opinion" Debate Series*, June 27, 2012. Available at www.youtube.com/watch?v=r3-7Y0xG89Q (accessed May 13, 2013).

6 On the hip-hop industry and Snoop Dogg, Kevin Powell writes, "Hip-hop culture has been assassinated by the hip-hop industry's desire to make money by any means necessary. It's the record and radio execs, the network producers, the publicists, the handlers, and the magazine writers and editors, of all persuasions, who push these images with no conscience whatsoever." See Powell, "Hip-Hop Culture Has Been Murdered," *Ebony*, June 2007, p. 61.

7 Craig S. Watkins, "The Hip-hop Lifestyle: Exploring the Perils and Possibilities of Black Youth's Media Environment," paper presented at Getting Real: The Future of Hip-Hop Scholarship, University of Wisconsin-Madison, September 21, 2009.

8 Justin Williams provides an in-depth analysis of the sonic and geographical significance of Dr. Dre's "G-Funk" production during the early 1990s, including the layering of electro-funk and synthesizers. See Justin A. Williams, "'You Never Been on a Ride Like this Befo': Los Angeles, Automotive Listening, and Dr. Dre's 'G-Funk,'" *Popular Music History* 4/2 (2009): 160–176.

9 Quinn, *Nuthin' but a "G" Thang*, pp. 15–16.

10 James Peterson, "All Black Everything: Exceptionalism and Suffering," TedX Lehigh University, April 23, 2013. Available at www.youtube.com/watch?v=ay0tKg9DyEw (accessed May 10, 2013). While the original "merchants of cool" Run-D.M.C. (backed by Russell Simmons and Rick Rubin) had teens everywhere pulling the laces out of Adidas shell-toes in the mid-1980s, their sneaker endorsement paled in comparison to the corporatization of Snoop Dogg's music and image. The Run-D.M.C. lyrics "Calvin Klein's no friend of mine/Don't want nobody's name on my behind" captures their limited willingness to use music to sell products.

11 In the USA, *Hustler* magazine is known for its explicit pictures of sexual intercourse, and in recent years the Hustler branding has extended to strip clubs, sex toys, and film.

12 Snoop Dogg's lyrics, Robin D. G. Kelley writes, "represent nothing but senseless, banal nihilism. The misogyny is so dense that it sounds more like little kids discovering nasty words for the first time than full-blown male pathos. It is pure profanity bereft of the rich story telling and use of metaphor and simile that have been cornerstones of rap music since its origins." Kelley, "Kickin' Reality, Kickin' Ballistics," in William Eric Perkins (ed.), *Droppin' Science: Critical Essays on Rap Music and Hip-Hop Culture* (Philadelphia: Temple University Press, 1996), p. 147.

13 William Jelani Cobb, *To the Break of Dawn: A Freestyle on the Hip Hop Aesthetic* (New York: New York University Press, 2007); Imani Perry, *Prophets of the Hood: Politics and Poetics in Hip Hop* (Durham, NC: Duke University Press, 2004).

14 Murray Forman, *The 'Hood Comes First: Race, Space, and Place in Rap and Hip-Hop* (Middletown, CT: Wesleyan University Press, 2002); Cheryl L. Keyes, *Rap Music and Street Consciousness: Music in American Life* (Chicago: University of Illinois Press, 2002).

15 Jeff Chang, *Can't Stop Won't Stop: A History of the Hip-Hop Generation* (New York: St. Martin's Press, 2005), pp. 89–166.

16 In 1982, a reporter for the *Village Voice* newspaper asked Afrika Bambaataa to name the party culture that was starting to become big business outside of New York. As Bam recounts, his choice of the word "hip-hop" was arbitrary. He chose "hip-hop" because it was a cool phrase that some of his favorite MCs would use on the mic. "I could have easily picked 'boing boing,' 'going off' or any other nonsensical word." The incident speaks to a fascinating aspect of hip-hop's first decade. Until then, no one had bothered to name the music or culture. Afrika Bambaataa, "Hip Hop: Unbound from the Underground," Ithaca, NY: Cornell University, April 5, 2013.

17 H. Samy Alim, "Straight Outta Compton, Straight aus Munchen: Global Linguistic Flows, Identities, and the Politics of Language in a Global Hip-Hop Nation," in Awad Ibrahim, H. Samy Alim, and Alastair Pennycook (eds.), *Global Linguistic Flows: Hip Hop Cultures, Youth Identities, and the Politics of Language* (New York: Routledge, 2009), p. 7.

18 The locomotion of hip-hop history cannot be reduced to the actions of great Black men, and the discussion of Afrika Bambaataa is not meant to marginalize the contributions of women. See Kyra Danielle Gaunt, *The Games Black Girls Play: Learning the Ropes from Double-Dutch to Hip-Hop* (New York University Press, 2006). Likewise, hip-hop's fundamental "Blackness" has become a major point of contention, as some argue that the emphasis on Blackness devalues the contributions of Latinos, especially Puerto Ricans. See Raquel Z. Rivera, *New York Ricans from the Hip Hop Zone* (New York: Palgrave Macmillan, 2003).

19 Jorge "Popmaster Fabel" Pabon, "Physical Graffiti: The History of Hip Hop Dance," in Jeff Chang (ed.), *Total Chaos: The Art and Aesthetics of Hip-Hop* (New York: Basic Civitas, 2006), p. 19.

20 Bakari Kitwana, *The Hip Hop Generation: Young Blacks and the Crisis in African American Culture* (New York: Basic Civitas, 2002).

21 Chang, *Can't Stop*, p. 49.

22 Emphasis added, as quoted in Jeffrey Ogbar, *Hip-Hop Revolution: The Culture and Politics of Rap Oybonna Green* (Lawrence, KS: University Press of Kansas, 2007), p. 4.

23 Johan Kugelberg, Joe Conzo, and Afrika Bambaataa, *Born in the Bronx: A Visual Record of the Early Days of Hip-Hop* (New York: Rizzoli, 2007).

24 Jim Fricke and Charlie Ahearn (eds.), *Yes Yes Y'all: The Experience Music Project Oral History of Hip-Hop's First Decade* (Cambridge, MA: Da Capo Press, 2002).

25 Chang, *Can't Stop*, pp. 41–65. Chang's study of the early 1970s' ghettoscape chronicles the creation of hip-hop by gangs. The streets provided socialization for youth – family, education, and entertainment – when traditional social structures failed or were destroyed by social policies.

26 Kelley, "Kickin' Reality, Kickin' Ballistics"; Quinn, *Nuthin' but a "G" Thang*.

27 Keyes, *Rap Music and Street Consciousness*, p. 122.

28 Forman, *The 'Hood Comes First*.

29 Fricke and Ahearn, *Yes Yes Y'all*, p. 45.

30 *Ibid.*, pp. 28–29.

31 KRS-One, *The Gospel of Hip-Hop: First Instrument* (Brooklyn, NY: powerHouse Books, 2009), pp. 122–123, emphasis in the original.

32 Steve Stoute and Mim Eichler Rivas, *The Tanning of America: How Hip-Hop Created a Culture That Rewrote the Rules of the New Economy* (New York: Gotham Books, 2011).

33 The "ski" moniker is an allusion to having so much cocaine that one could ski on the white powder.

34 *Edutainment* is also the title of an album by Boogie Down Productions released in 1990.

35 Universal Zulu Nation, "UZN Beliefs," available at Zulunation.com.

36 Known as the "Five Percenters," the Nation of Gods and Earths is an offshoot of the Nation of Islam that recruits heavily in prisons and on street corners. Core to the belief system is that 85 percent of the world is ignorant, 10 percent knows the truth, but uses it to exploit others, while the other 5 percent uses "knowledge of self" to teach others how to live peaceful, spiritual lives.

37 Travis L. Gosa, "Counterknowledge, Racial Paranoia, and the Cultic Milieu: Decoding Hip-hop Conspiracy Theory," *Poetics* 39/3 (2011): 187–204.

38 Aine McGlynn, "The Native Tongues," in Mickey Hess (ed.), *Icons of Hip-Hop: An Encyclopedia of the Movement, Music, and Culture*, vol. 1 (Santa Barbara, CA: ABC-CLO, 2007), pp. 269–270.

39 Zulunation.com, "UZN Beliefs."

40 *Ibid.*

41 S. Craig Watkins, *Hip Hop Matters: Politics, Pop Culture, and the Struggle for the Soul of a Movement* (Boston: Beacon Press, 2005), p. 2.

42 McGlynn, "The Native Tongues."

43 Jay-Z, "Moment of Clarity," *The Black Album*.

44 Craig Jenkins, "Snoop Lion Reincarnated Review," *Pitchfork*, April 24, 2013. Available at http://pitchfork.com/reviews/albums/17920-snoop-lion-reincarnated/ (accessed June 28, 2013). Likewise, music critic Derek Staples advises that listeners embrace the new Snoop Lion with a healthy skepticism. "Before falling into Snoop's Rastafari renaissance, remember that this is also the man who claimed to be a member of the Nation of Islam in 2009 and tried reaching into the R&B world with his project Nine Inch Dicks in '06." See Staples, "Album Review: Snoop Lion – Reincarnated," *Consequence of Sound*, April 25, 2013. Available at http://consequenceofsound.net/2013/04/album-review-snoop-lion-reincarnated/ (accessed June 28, 2013).

45 Ian Burrell, "Snoop Lion: Old Dogg, New Tricks from the World's Most Recognisable Gangsta Rapper," *The Independent*, April 19, 2013. Available at www.independent.co.uk/news/people/profiles/snoop-lion-old-dogg-new-tricks-from-the-worlds-most-recognisable-gangsta-rapper-8580837.html (accessed July 10, 2013).

46 As quoted in Jonah Weiner, "Q&A: Snoop Lion Strikes Back at 'Reincarnated' Collaborator Bunny Wailer," *Rolling Stone*, April 24, 2013. Available at www.rollingstone.com/music/news/q-a-snoop-lion-strikes-back-at-reincarnated-collaborator-bunny-wailer-20130424 (accessed July 9, 2013).

47 Snoop Football League, "About Us," Snoopfl.net, retrieved July 19, 2013 from http://snoopyfl.net/page.php?page_id=39811 (accessed July 19, 2013).

48 Travis L. Gosa, "Love and Hip Hop: (Re)Gendering the Debate over Hip Hop Studies," *Sounding Out!* Available at http://soundstudiesblog.com/2013/04/01/love-and-hip-hop-regendering-the-debate-over-hip-hop-studies/ (accessed July 10, 2013).

49 Travis L. Gosa and Tristan Fields, "Is Hip-Hop Education Another Hustle? The (Ir)Responsible Use of Hip-Hop as Pedagogy," in Brad J. Porfilio and Michael Viola (eds.), *Hip-Hop(e): The Cultural Practice and Critical Pedagogy of International Hip-Hop* (New York: Peter Lang, 2012), pp. 195–210.

50 Houston A. Baker, *Black Studies, Rap, and the Academy* (University of Chicago Press, 1993), p. 8.

6 Hip-hop and religion: from the mosque to the church

CHRISTINA ZANFAGNA

On September 5, 2001, *The Onion* published an article entitled, "God Finally Gives Shout-Out Back to All His Niggaz." The piece reported satirically that the Lord Almighty had finally reciprocated his gratitude for the many proclamations of "praise" and "props" he had received from hip-hop artists in their liner notes and acceptance speeches at award ceremonies. Based on the sheer amount of hip-hop "thank yous" aimed at God over the past few decades, *The Onion* estimated that "the historic shout-out" was likely to last an entire week. While the article subtly mocked the commonplace (almost mandatory) practice of rappers thanking God, it did point toward a significant element within hip-hop history and culture: hip-hop has and continues to exhibit powerful and diverse religious phenomena, from Islam to Christianity, Judaism to the Rastafarian movement, and Hinduism to Buddhism.

In spite of the music industry's ostensibly homogenizing, dehumanizing force, both hip-hop artists and mainstream media often turn consumer culture into a space of religious exploration and rumination. From MC names such as U-God and Killapriest, to religious iconography on album covers, explicit references to religious concepts such as sin, suffering, and salvation, or the incorporation of sacred music genres, hip-hop artists have developed provocative, and at times controversial, expressions that intertwine profane realities with pious ideas.[1] These contradictory expressions are not surprising given the complicated identities of hip-hop's creators and listeners as well as the complex religious architecture of America's major cities. How do rap artists engage with religious and spiritual beliefs? How are religious concerns worked out, thought through, and ultimately performed through hip-hop music? How does hip-hop extend or change the legacy of spirit-seeking in African American music and culture? In attempting to answer these questions, it becomes apparent that hip-hop's postmodern mix of spirituality cannot be known in its totality. While Islam has historically been the prevailing religious inclination in hip-hop culture, this chapter deals predominantly with hip-hop's relationship to Christianity – a religion that has become increasingly

popular in mainstream hip-hop in part due to the rise of Prosperity Theology and holy hip-hop (aka Christian rap).[2] I will briefly outline hip-
hop's mélange of spiritual forces, highlight mainstream rap artists who
espouse religious beliefs, and present an overview of the subgenre of holy
hip-hop.

Spiritual sampling: religious sensibilities in mainstream hip-hop

While pop culture industries and religious authorities have tried to establish
discursive and aesthetic borders as well as divisive market labels, between
"secular" and "religious" hip-hop, hip-hop culture has been in syncopated
lock-step with religion from the beginning – an infrequently examined
relationship that complicates reductionist notions of Islam, Christianity, and the Rastafarian Movement as completely coherent, distinct, and
separate entities.[3] As a scholar of religion, Josef Sorett has noted that
hip-hop has never aligned itself with one particular religious orthodoxy,
but instead has been a vessel for "heterodox spiritual musings."[4] Drawing on the work of Paul Gilroy and Stuart Hall, Sorett claims that these
multifarious religious significations are bound together by the "cultural
repertories of the African Diaspora."[5] With a long vision of the historical
trajectory of Black religions, he notes that looking at hip-hop's spiritual
matrix affirms that religion is always historically contingent and connects
to what's happening "on the ground" not only in Black communities but
also around the world.[6] What constitutes "Black religion" in Black popular
music has always been something very hybrid, creatively mixed, and profoundly relevant to the lived realities and geographies and Black and Brown
peoples.

Furthermore, hip-hop's spiritual sampling may reflect a need for greater
ideological pluralism and recognition of Black diversity in the public sphere.
Like the sampled music they rap over, MCs and DJs express their religious
views through a Sonic collage: clips of fiery sermons and civil rights speeches
sit beside Jamaican-styled Black Nationalist rhetoric, shout-outs to Jesus,
and the subtle oratory of the Nation of Islam, all frequently interspersed
with explicit lyrics.[7] It follows that rap music embodies the pluralism of
current religious energies as well as the spiritual touchstones of hip-hop's
exalted predecessors – the sweet testifyings of Marvin Gaye, Stevie Wonder's
politicized preaching, the extraterrestrial transcendence of George Clinton's
P-Funk, the meditative bedroom lamentations of Al Green, and Prince's
performances of erotic deliverance. But it was James Brown's shrieks for

Black Power and hard-hitting funk grooves that would become the musical bedrock for early hip-hop in the late 1970s and early 1980s, bringing with it a strong Black Nationalist current informed by Nation of Islam doctrines and rhetorical practices.

Hip-hop, Islam, and the Five Percent Nation

Hip-hop culture's early penchant for both funk music and the iconography of Malcolm X reveals the way in which hip-hop practitioners in post-Civil Rights America identified with and nurtured a militant separatist politics as well as an alignment with the Islamic faith. In addition to hip-hop's nostalgia for generations past and obsession with posthumous leaders, Malcolm's articulation of a Black racial identity and concern for Black consciousness resonated with a generation of Black and Brown youth suffering through the postindustrial transformations of urban renewal in the Bronx and other boroughs. From Afrika Bambaataa's Zulu Nation to the Native Tongues collective to Public Enemy's Black Nationalist rhetoric, Islam – in its various forms and guises – provided a means of self-definition while Malcolm X offered an example of talking back and talking Black to white America. Tracing the sonic and political lineages of some of hip-hop's most commercially successful acts unveils how Islam has been a potent yet less explicit thread in the development of Black cultural expression in the late twentieth century, from Black Power to Black Arts to *Black Noise* – a moniker Tricia Rose bestowed on rap music in her seminal 1994 monograph.[8] Like jazz and the Black Arts Movement, Sohail Daulatzai states that hip-hop culture also "became a space in which Black radicalism, Islam, and the politics of the Muslim Third World had a powerful impact on the lyrical imaginations, sonic landscapes, and political visions" expressed by artists.[9] New York in particular was an important site of incubation for Muslim MCs in the 1980s and was "rechristened via Islam's holiest sites, with Harlem becoming Mecca and Brooklyn becoming Medina."[10] This new spiritual geography of New York would set the stage for the continued coevolution of Black Islam and hip-hop culture.

The brand of Islam that became the most widespread among early hip-hop MCs was the Five Percent Nation, an offshoot of the Nation of Islam founded by Clarence 13X.[11] Hip-hop icons such as Rakim (the first to openly claim membership in the Five Percent Nation in 1987), Poor Righteous Teachers, Brand Nubian, AZ, Guru, Queen Latifah, and members of the Wu-Tang Clan were among the early adherents, lacing their lyrics with both subtle and blatant references to their Five Percenter beliefs and practices, and immortalizing common idioms such as "Droppin Science," "Word," and "What up, G?" within the hip-hop lexicon. These Five Percenter MCs saw themselves (namely Black men) as "Gods" – teachers, leaders, and bearers of a unique and critical self-knowledge.[12] Felicia Miyakawa states:

> The Five Percent Nation may be unknown to most Americans, yet within hip-hop culture, Five Percenters have long been an active presence. Any "old-school hip-hop head" (long-time fan of hip-hop music and culture) will speak knowingly of the "God" and may even have passing familiarity with basic Five Percenter doctrines, yet the details of Five Percenter theology – an idiosyncratic mix of black nationalist rhetoric, Kemetic (ancient Egyptian) symbolism, Gnosticism, Masonic mysticism, and esoteric numerology – are not widely understood.[13]

For many young Black men, Clarence 13X's teachings provided structure in the midst of the chaos associated with everyday life on the streets. Furthermore, young Five Percenters are renowned for their tremendous oral skills, gained through intensive drilling in the lessons and through street preaching. This skill set meshed well with the verbal dexterity and performative charisma required in hip-hop MCing.

Despite these areas of mutual aesthetic enhancement as well as the positive messages of self-determination often expressed through Five Percenter lyrics, the Five Percent Nation has been criticized for its patriarchal and homophobic beliefs. Some Sunni Muslims claim that the Five Percent Nation has hurt Islam because of its inability to hold on to any theological concept consistently and its prolific references to violence, drugs, and misogyny.[14] AZ the Visualiza speaks of his inconsistent relationship to religion on Nas's 1994 release *Illmatic*:

> Yeah, we were beginners in the hood as five percenters
>
> But something must of got in us cause all of us turned to sinners

The chorus follows with an air of chilling detachment:

> Life's a bitch and then you die; that's why we get high
>
> Cause you never know when you're gonna go

The rising intonation of AZ's voice leaves something unresolved. For AZ and his fellow "sinners," salvation must be attained here on earth, before an unpredictable death strikes. Rebuking the possibility of an afterlife, he must take his pleasures in the material world and get "high" before he goes below.[15] Some may view the lives and lyrics of Five Percenter rappers as hypocritical. On the other hand, these hip-hop artists embody a desire to make music that accurately expresses the contradictions and complexities of African American experiences in America.

From Islam to Christianity

Thus, for most of hip-hop's life span, Islam and its various sects and offshoots (e.g. Five Percent Nation, Nation of Islam, Sunni, etc.) have comprised the main religious currents within hip-hop. Despite the huge popularity of Five Percenters within hip-hop in the 1980s and 1990s, some MCs managed to integrate Christian ideas and concepts into their lyrics as well. Sorett states, "Alongside Islam, Christianity was a fixture in hip-hop as far back as 1987 when MC Hammer's first record included 'Son of the King', a track that showed up again on his second and more popular album, *Let's Get it Started*."[16] Just as Islam within hip-hop has taken on many different faces, so rap artists have explored aspects of Christianity in a variety of ways, be it through lyrics, digital sampling, album art and iconography, music videos, or hip-hop apparel. Oftentimes, Christian imagery and concepts are irreverently paired with deeply profane lyrics and narratives. Christian rapper Ron T. (aka Get Wizdom) believes that "entertainers spend more time confusing their audience about their core beliefs than any other people (except possibly some ministers)."[17] He continues, "Saying a prayer on your CD before you verbally rip your ex-girlfriend to shreds speaks of conflicted spirituality."[18] Compton Virtue, a Christian poet/MC from Compton, California, made a similar comment regarding mainstream rap star Kanye West's diamond cross in his video entitled "Jesus Walks" (2004). In an interview from June 2004, she stated, "A cross that costs $190,000 is a contradiction to me."[19] Furthermore, in commercial rap (or rap that is specifically made with the intent of financial profit), where material wealth supplants the "promised land" as the new locus of freedom, artists struggle to reconcile the almighty dollar with their almighty God and join together who they are with what they buy.

Other rappers, such as 2Pac and DMX, utilize hip-hop as a space to question and wrestle with religious ideas. In the song "Prayer," DMX raps, "I'm ready to meet him cause where I'm livin' ain't right." But his conclusion is ultimately inconclusive as he finishes on a selfless and sacrificial note:

> Lord why is it that I go through so much pain
> All I saw was black, all I felt was the rain
> If it takes for me to suffer, for my brother to see the light
> Give me pain till I die, but Lord treat him right

As DMX illustrates, suffering is a catalyst for spiritual questioning, a way to come to terms with deep-soul anxiety or alienation, and a possible route to freedom. In his 2006 release, DMX asks, "Lord Give Me a Sign," as the song becomes a prayer and testimonial offering to the Lord. While he doesn't identify as a Christian rapper or holy hip-hop artist, DMX clearly articulates his belief in Jesus.

Other rap artists, such as Mase, Reverend Run (of Run-D.M.C.), and Kurtis Blow have publicly spoken about their conversion to Christianity. This may be part of what Sorett calls a gradual shift from Islam to Christianity in terms of hip-hop's central religious consciousness, especially as Creflo Dollar (perhaps the most popular Black Prosperity preacher of the day) has become a fixture in certain commercial hip-hop circles.[20] Sorett argues that for rap artists, "To invoke Christianity, whether or not one expresses an exclusive allegiance to its theological tenets, has been to avail oneself of rhetorical, cultural and financial capital,"[21] revealing the ways in which popular culture and religion are enmeshed in broader fields of power. Beyond the various forms of capital that come with Christianity (e.g. religious and commercial networks, resources, social acceptance, etc.), Islam within hip-hop has not disappeared or diminished. Daulatzai argues that "Mos Def uses hip-hop culture to explore the overlapping influences of Islam, Black internationalism, and Pan-Africanism within the realms of arts and politics."[22] Islam continues to be a critical component of global hip-hop cultures and soundscapes, but the Five Percent Nation does not have the stronghold it once had within commercially successful hip-hop. This is in part due to the rise of hip-hop cultures and markets located outside the New York City and East Coast milieu – namely the West Coast and Southern hip-hop scenes, which include more Christian members. Further, Miyakawa points toward September 11 and the articulation of "Islam as terror" as precipitating a major shift in the *visibility* of Islam within hip-hop. Muslim artists have found new ways to encode and submerge their religious commitments in an environment that is often skeptical of and hostile toward Islam, whereas explicit references to Christianity have found a home in the steadily growing culture of holy hip-hop.

Hip-hop and the Church

Through the 1970s, the Black Christian Church, in its various denominations, maintained a central and influential role in African American communities, even among those who did not attend services on Sundays. During the 1980s, however, postindustrial formations under the Reagan and Bush administrations adversely impacted American inner cities. The African American urban community was acutely affected by these geopolitical and economic shifts. Weakened by the Black middle-class flight from urban "ghettos" to the suburbs[23] and the loss of Black youth to the crack cocaine epidemic, gang violence, and prison, the Black urban church – the bedrock of the African American community – suffered significantly as its membership waned. Furthermore, as unemployment and high school drop-out rates soared and poverty increased, African American inner city youth became more vulnerable to a variety of social ills, including a "generalized demoralization" and nonconformist behaviors associated with the "culture of poverty."[24] Domestic violence, increased and unchecked police brutality and corruption, and homicides involving innocent bystanders or victims of mistaken identity, all led to increased generational poverty and urban decay. The HIV/AIDS epidemic was also silently yet insidiously moving into African American communities via intravenous drug use and prostitution during the 1980s and 1990s. In addition, communities of African American Muslims, Jews, Buddhists, Scientologists, and those practicing other Eastern and African-derived spiritualities, offered viable alternatives for those seeking God and religion yet dissatisfied with the church.

Some Black Churches have evolved to address the myriad social issues affecting African American communities in the late twentieth and early twenty-first centuries, including issues of gentrification, intergenerational disconnection, incarceration rates among Black males, economic instability, physical and sexual abuse, and concerns regarding classism. Those churches that have not been able to address these issues have often waned in membership, especially among youth and young adults. Bakari Kitwana writes, "according to the National Opinion Research Center at the University of Chicago, attendance for eighteen to thirty-five year olds dropped 5.6% from 1995 to 2000."[25] In an effort to steer its young members from these vices of street culture, some church elders and clergy vilified their own offspring as "criminals." When the renowned Reverend Calvin O. Butts of Abyssinian Baptist Church, New York, defended, "We're not against rap. We're not against rappers, but we are against those 'thugs,'"[26] he failed to recognize that he was denouncing the very people who created the music he supposedly accepted. Furthermore, he was turning a blind eye to the real issue affecting Black inner-city communities – that the violent and criminal behaviors of "thugs" was in part due to the lack of moral and spiritual guidance that young people were receiving from their elders and the culture at large.

As Christian MC and poet Compton Virtue states,

> The church is dying. The congregation is forty and above. Where is the church of tomorrow? Where are the young people? It's not tangible for

young people. Don't talk over them; talk to them. How do you talk to them? You have to speak their language.[27]

Or as Tupac Shakur (who recorded under the name 2Pac), a Los Angeles-based MC who was known for exploring Christian themes in his unique brand of gangsta rap, states on "Black Jesuz" (1999): "Went to church but don't understand it, they underhanded." Both quotes elucidate how some African American youth felt alienated from the church for its inability to preach uplifting messages that addressed the harsh realities of street life in vernaculars and musical styles that they understood.

While some hip-hop heads sought guidance and insight from a variety of religious teachings, most notably with the Nation of Islam and an Islamic sect known as the Five Percenters, a number of hip-hoppers ultimately decided to convert to Christianity. These newly converted hip-hoppers sought to merge their musical tastes with their faith in Jesus, creating a new brand of religious hip-hop.

Hip-hop and Christianity

Emerging in the mid 1980s and 1990s, holy hip-hop is a unique response to a specific current social conjuncture. It celebrates the worldview of many young people who grew up during the post-Civil Rights years and who comprise what Bakari Kitwana calls the "Hip-Hop Generation."[28] Members who profess a holy hip-hop identity define a diverse subculture of youth that self-identify as both Christian and hip-hop. As they explore Christianity, they in turn bring hip-hop worldviews and aesthetics to their worship practices. Holy hip-hop, sometimes called Christian rap, Christ hop, Gospel rap, or hip-hope, broadly defines a musical genre, culture, and ministry opportunity that glorifies Jesus Christ to those who are living in and influenced by hip-hop culture.[29] Moreover, holy hip-hop is enmeshed in a genealogy of the lived struggles and victories of African American artists who have blurred the lines between the "sacred" and the "secular" (usually expressed in terms of binaries such as spirituals/blues, gospel/soul, urban gospel/hip-hop) within the polyvalent power relations of the church, the nightclub, and the music industry.[30] Every time holy hip-hoppers *perform* religion through hip-hop and *represent* hip-hop through Christ, they engage in processes that rearticulate and transform transgenerational histories and discourses.

As a cultural practice used to articulate both a spiritual and social conception of self, holy hip-hop music enables multiple fields of identification using biblically informed, Christ-centered, and morally instructive lyrics over gospel singing, DJ scratching, and hip-hop beats of all flavors.

Ironically, while the lyrics often rebuke the "worldly" and demonize "secular" hip-hop and its indulgent displays of material wealth, Christian rap has been known to sample commercially successful hip-hop tracks.[31] If one did not listen closely to the rhymed lyrics, there would be no way to distinguish holy hip-hop from so-called "secular" hip-hop. And yet, despite all this musical, cultural, and ideological overlap, holy hip-hop continues to be forged in opposition to mainstream hip-hop.

Some members of an older generation as well as more traditional adherents of Black Christian worship, expressing an aesthetic aversion to the "noise" and iconography of hip-hop, see hip-hop as an unorthodox presence in the church. For them, holy hip-hop literally brings a street sensibility of the block parties and schoolyard battles associated with early hip-hop into the sanctuary. Craige Lewis, holy hip-hop's number one public enemy, preaches his anti-hip-hop gospel to congregations of one to two thousand people every weekend. When Lewis finishes his sermons, he calls those in the audience who have purchased hip-hop CDs to pile them on the altar, where they will be smashed to pieces, sometimes with sledgehammers. Those with tattoos – what Lewis calls "marks of Cain" and "emblems of the occult religion of hip-hop" – are called to kneel before the altar so that Lewis can pray for God to save their souls before it is too late. Duce, a Christian rapper with one of the more commercially successful holy hip-hop acts, the Cross Movement, said that an owner of a Christian bookstore in Detroit told him that Lewis's DVDs outsell gospel rap titles combined at a rate of three to one, while churches boasting congregations of ten thousand have canceled Christian rap shows after listening to Lewis speak.

One assumes, given the cyclical return to debates about the use of popular music in worship, that holy hip-hop will some day be perceived as completely acceptable church music. Already, certain open-minded pastors and churchgoing parents have recognized the power of hip-hop to initiate conversations about God with the youth of their communities and see rap music as an invigorating presence in Black churches – a presence which is calling traditional churches into a more meaningful and relevant relationship with the realities and challenges of coming of age in urban America.

From gospel rap to holy hip-hop

Stephen Wiley is recognized as the first artist to record commercially and distribute a gospel rap cassette with his 1985 release *Bible Break*, a fact which was acknowledged by Christian rapper T-Bone in his song "Our History" on his own album, entitled *GospelAlphaMegaFunkyBoogieDiscoMusic* (2002). Hailing from Oklahoma, he is often referred to as the "Godfather of Gospel

Rap." While the title track of Wiley's album reached the no. 14 spot on Christian radio in 1986, many gospel rappers have called his style "soft" or "homogenous." New York's Michael Peace followed in 1987 with *Rock it Right* as well as the late Danny D-Boy Rodriguez with his 1989 album, *Plantin' A Seed*. He was murdered a year later in Dallas, Texas, for unknown reasons. Rodriguez saw rap music as a vehicle to reach inner-city youth in Dallas, Texas through the Street Church Academy, a ministry founded in the Buckner Terrace area in 1983 by his parents, former drug addicts Demi and Irma "Cookie" Rodriguez. The ministry focused on anti-gang activities as well as fighting drug addiction. Danny had been the Academy's first graduate and was one of the first Christian rappers to make extensive use of sampling.

While mainstream media and press generally focused on these few artists as the forerunners of holy hip-hop, artists in Los Angeles were also producing gospel rap as early as 1986. Despite Los Angeles's key role in the emergence of Christian hip-hop, producing some of the early well-known artists such as Gospel Gangstaz, L.A. Symphony, and the Dynamic Twins, Sup the Chemist (originally known as Super C when he was a secular rapper) has generally not been acknowledged among the likes of Wiley, Peace, and Rodriguez. In 1987, he produced his first gospel rap cassette, *Fully Armed*. As Sup began gaining local notoriety among churches throughout Los Angeles, he and his DJ, DJ Dove, struggled to find a suitable name for the kind of music they were making. Sup recalled that DJ Dove came up with the name holy hip-hop in 1990. "We started it right there in West Covina. Victory Outreach presents Friday Night Holy Hip Hop."[32] Sup and other gospel rap acts in Los Angeles would go on to perform alongside the likes of Ice Cube.

Christian rap acts like DC Talk, I.D.O.L. King, S.F.C. (Soldiers For Christ), and P.I.D. (Preachas in Disguise), and eventually Cross Movement, led the way in the early days of gospel rap. While many of these holy hip-hoppers tell a gangbanger-turned-churchgoer narrative, other young people have grown up simultaneously in the Church *and* hip-hop – attending hip-hop events and parties with their friends and attending church with their parents on Sunday. In some cases, parents themselves are fans of hip-hop, having grown up around the sounds of early rap music.[33]

Other industry developments have also paved the way for the growing presence and popularity of holy hip-hop. The increasing number of FM, Internet, and satellite gospel radio stations have been critical in exposing gospel music audiences to holy hip-hop. Many gospel rap artists remember first hearing Christian rap during these radio programs. Affordable computer software has also made it easier for amateur rappers and holy hip-hop artists to produce their own music. Categories for gospel music have been expanded to include Christian rap by the National Academy of the Recording Arts and Sciences (the Grammy Awards), the Stellar Awards, and the Gospel Music Awards.

Chicago, Harlem, the Bronx, Philadelphia, Atlanta, Tampa, and Minneapolis, among other cities, all boast their own hip-hop ministries. Christian rap is performed throughout these services, utilizing turntables, pre-recorded beats, and rapping (sometimes with the addition of piano, organ, drums, and a gospel choir). Many Christian rappers conceive of hip-hop as a tool, instrument, or medium of reaching the masses – the unsaved hip-hop youth. For many of them, hip-hop acts as the *outer* mouthpiece, Christianity as the *inner* message. The Tonic, another member of the Cross Movement, speaks of this inner/outer dichotomy (a dichotomy that needs to be complicated to really understand how the sacred works in Christian rap):

> We were in the church and they were like "why you dressed like that?" Then
> we were in the streets and they were like "why you carrying a bible?" So it
> was hard to find somebody to identify with both our outer and our new
> inner that we were all attached to in Jesus.[34]

The Cross Movement struggles to negotiate and find "breathing room" within these projected scripts based on appearance. This is the double pressure of holy hip-hop culture: the push and pull to "keep it real" with the streets and "keep it clean" with the Church. Holy hip-hop occupies a delimited grey area both in and out of the Church, walking a narrowly policed, tightly scripted line between expectations of "hardness" and "realness" in hip-hop and norms of devotional behavior and worship in Christianity. Holy hip-hoppers' relationship to the Church continues to be inconsistent and contested despite significant efforts by some pastors and Church leaders to incorporate both hip-hop youth and hip-hop music, language, street codes, and aesthetics into worship services and events. In light of this, many holy hip-hop practitioners have created alternative sites to perform Christian rap, such as community centers, open-mics, parks, and street corners. This impulse to practice hip-hop in open urban spaces is of course a part of hip-hop's original ethos, when Bronx-bred Black and Brown youth in the 1970s and 1980s hooked up turntables, speakers, and microphones to street lampposts to party and purge on public grounds.[35] Years later, young Five Percenters would also form cyphers on corners to drill their lessons and rhyme about the realities of Black urban existence.

Conclusion

In this chapter, I have touched upon a few of the myriad instances in which hip-hop artists interact with religious ideas and practices, but many questions remain. What happens when spiritual practice meets the politics of the entertainment industry? In what ways can the celebrity power of hip-hop music and religious institutions positively influence each other while maintaining the integrity of both enterprises? What does hip-hop's polycultural,[36] polyvocal, polyrhythmic nature have to offer modern religious practices? How are hip-hop religious identities marked by both fixity and flow?

How do hip-hop artists reconcile the search for pleasure and the divine? How do material success and the promise of comfort pose challenges to utilizing hip-hop as a mode of religious expression? For fans and listeners, how do musical consumption practices function as an articulation of religious identity? What kinds of religious experiences are fans undergoing as they listen to hip-hop in cars, on earphones, or at concerts? Addressing these questions will require rigorous ethnographic studies of local hip-hop cultures and scenes – studies that focus on how hip-hop and religion intersect in the everyday lives of hip-hop artists, professionals, and fans.

From Muslim-inspired hip-hop to Christian rap, hip-hop artists continue to illuminate the synergistic ties between popular music, religion, race, and place in dynamic and varied ways. Notably, the hip-hop nation readily absorbs many different kinds of religious identities, affiliations, and practices, allowing diverse spiritual communities to live in contiguous relations with one another. On the level of the nation state, however, such relations are often antagonistic and religious identities are understood as separate and fundamentalist. To talk about hip-hop's religious mixture is to talk about sampling not only an aesthetic but also an ethic – a digital technology and a cultural mythology that rethinks power in terms of a merging of discourses/horizons as opposed to common vision of power over and against. Furthermore, hip-hop expressions of Islam and Christianity also articulate the transnational nature of these religious practices. When a Christian rapper invokes the common hip-hop colloquialism "Word" (a term from Five Percenter rhetoric, which also has resonances in Christianity) as they rap over a Rastafarian-inspired dancehall beat, we are reminded of an important truth: that Black religion has always been diasporic in nature, characterized by mixture and heterogeneity.

On a final note, music provides people a way to creatively pose questions of meaning, offering an expressive locus in which to live and wrestle with the difficult and sometimes unanswerable questions themselves – questions with great existential and ontological weight. Hip-hop, despite its blasphemous wrap, continues to provide such a locus for those seeking spirit and liberation, be it in churches or mosques, studios or the streets.

Notes

1 For further examination of the sacred and profane in African American music and culture, see Amiri Baraka, *Blues People: Negro Music in White America* (New York: William Morrow, 1963); James Cone, *The Spirituals and the Blues* (New York: Orbis Books, 1972); Anthony Pinn, "Making a World With a Beat: Musical Expression's Relationship to Religious Identity and Experience," in Anthony Pinn (ed.), *Noise and Spirit: The Religious and Spiritual Sensibilities of Rap Music* (New York University Press, 2003), pp. 1–26; Guthrie Ramsey, *Race Music: Black Cultures from Bebop to Hip-Hop* (Berkeley and Los Angeles: University of California Press, 2003); Teresa L. Reed, *The Holy Profane: Religion in Black Popular Music* (Lexington, KY: The University Press of Kentucky, 2003); Efrem Smith and Phil Jackson, *The Hip Hop Church: Connecting with the Movement Shaping our Culture* (Downers Grove, IL: InterVarsity Press, 2006); Jon Michael Spencer, *Theological Music: Introduction to Theomusicology* (New York: Greenwood Press, 1991); Jon Michael Spencer, *Blues and Evil* (Knoxville, TN: University of Tennessee Press, 1993); Robin Sylvan, *Traces of the Spirit: The Religious Dimensions of Popular Music* (New York and London: New York University Press, 2002).

2 See Josef Sorett, "'Believe Me, This Pimp Game is Very Religious': Toward a Religious History of Hip Hop," *Culture and Religion* 10/1 (2009): 11–22 for a discussion on Prosperity Theology preacher Creflo Dollar and his relationship to hip-hop artists.

3 For discussions on hip-hop and spirituality see Michael Eric Dyson, "Rap Culture, the Church, and American Society," *Black Sacred Music: A Journal of Theomusicology* 6/1 (1992): 268–273; Michael Eric Dyson, *Between God and Gangsta Rap* (New York and London: Oxford University Press, 1997); Michael Eric Dyson, *Holler If You Hear Me: Searching for Tupac Shakur* (New York: Basic Civitas, 2001); Michael Eric Dyson, *Open Mic: Reflections on Philosophy, Race, Sex, Culture and Religion* (New York: Basic Civitas, 2003); Cheryl L. Keyes, "At the Crossroads: Rap Music and Its African Nexus," *Ethnomusicology* 40/2 (1996): 223–248; Imani Perry, *Prophets of the Hood: Politics and Poetics in Hip Hop* (Durham, NC: Duke University Press, 2004); Pinn, *Noise and Spirit*, 2003; Philip M. Royster, "The Rapper as Shaman for a Band of Dancers of the Spirit: 'U Can't Touch This,'" *Black Sacred Music: A Journal of Theomusicology* 5/1 (1991): 61–67;

James Spady, *Nation Conscious Rap: The Hip-Hop Vision* (PC International Press, 1991). Other scholars have examined the complicated connections between discourses on hip-hop and Islam; see H. Samy Alim, *Roc the Mic Right: The Language of Hip-Hop Culture* (London: Routledge, 2006) and Felicia Miyakawa, *Five Percenter Rap: God Hop's Music, Message, and Black Muslim Mission* (Bloomington, IN: Indiana University Press, 2005); as well as hip-hop and Christianity, see Garth Kasimu Baker-Fletcher, "African American Christian Rap: Facing 'Truth' and Resisting It," in Pinn (ed.), *Noise and Spirit*, pp. 29–48; Cheryl R. Gooch, "Rappin' for the Lord: The Uses of Gospel Rap and Contemporary Music in Black Religious Communities," in D. A. Stout and Judith M. Buddenbaum (eds.), *Religion and Mass Media: Audiences and Adaptations* (Thousand Oaks, CA: Sage Publications, 1996); Deborah Smith Pollard, *When the Church Becomes Your Party: Contemporary Gospel Music* (Wayne State University Press, 2008); Smith and Jackson, *The Hip Hop Church*; Sorett, "Believe Me," 2009; Ralph C. Watkins, *The Gospel Remix: Reaching the Hip-Hop Generation* (Valley Forge, PA: Judson Press, 2007).

4 Sorett, "Believe Me," p. 11.

5 *Ibid.*, p. 12.

6 *Ibid.*, p. 19.

7 For hip-hop songs that contain these juxtapositions and mixtures, see Nas and Damian Marley's "Road to Zion," Public Enemy's "Fight the Power," Lupe Fiasco's "BMF (Building Minds Faster)," will.i.am and Common's "A Dream."

8 See Tricia Rose, *Black Noise: Rap Music and Black Culture in Contemporary America* (Middletown, CT: Wesleyan University Press, 1994).

9 Sohail Daulatzai, *Black Star, Crescent Moon: The Muslim International and Black Freedom beyond America* (Minneapolis: University of Minnesota Press, 2012), p. 91.

10 *Ibid.*, p. 89.

11 See Miyakawa, *Five Percenter Rap*, 2005.

12 *Ibid.*, p. 3.

13 *Ibid.*, p. 23.

14 Hisham Aidi, "Jihadis in the Hood: Race, Urban Islam and the War on Terror," *MERIP* 223 (2002): 36–43.

15 Christina Zanfagna, "Under the Blasphemous W(RAP): Locating the 'Spirit' in Hip-Hop," *Pacific Review of Ethnomusicology* 12 (2006): 1–12.

16 Sorett, "Believe Me," p. 12.

17 Ron T. (aka Get Wizdom), "Even Rappers Know His Name!" Available at www.crossmovement.com (accessed May 1, 2002).

18 *Ibid.*

19 Compton Virtue, interview with the author, June 2004.

20 See Ludacris and Jermaine Dupri's track, "Welcome to Atlanta."

21 Sorett, "Believe Me," p. 16.

22 Daulatzai, *Black Star*, p. 135.

23 Black professionals and families who could afford to buy houses elsewhere began leaving south Los Angeles. Some moved into racially integrated neighborhoods in Leimert Park, West Adams, Baldwin Hills, and Hyde Park, among others.

24 Elijah Anderson, *Streetwise: Race, Class, and Change in an Urban Community* (University of Chicago Press, 1992), p. 4. For further discussion see Lee Rainwater, *Behind Ghetto Walls: Black Family Life in a Federal Slum* (Chicago: Aldine, 1970); William Julius Wilson, *The Truly Disadvantaged: The Inner City, the Underclass, and Public Policy* (University of Chicago Press, 1987); and William Julius Wilson, *When Work Disappears: The World of the New Urban Poor* (New York: Vintage, 1996).

25 Bakari Kitwana, *The Hip-Hop Generation: Young Blacks and the Crisis in African American Culture* (New York: Basic Civitas, 2002), p. 22.

26 Bone Thugs n Harmony feature a clip of Reverend Butts delivering this exact quote on their 1998 track "Thuggish Ruggish Bone."

27 Compton Virtue, interview with the author, Los Angeles, June 2004.

28 Bakari Kitwana narrowly defines the hip-hop generation as African Americans born between 1965 and 1984, whereas Jeff Chang says the generation begins with DJ Kool Herc and Afrika Bambaataa, includes "anyone who is down" and ends "when the next generation tells us it's over." Kitwana, *The Hip-Hop Generation*; Jeff Chang, *Can't Stop Won't Stop: A History of the Hip-Hop Generation* (New York: St. Martins Press, 2005), p. 2.

29 Smith and Jackson, *The Hip Hop Church*, p. 131.

30 For example, Thomas Dorsey, Andrae Crouch, the Edwin Hawkins' Singers, and Kirk Franklin have all incorporated "secular" forms into "sacred" worship, whereas Sister Rosetta Tharp and Ray Charles took church music to the nightclub. Sam Cooke, Al Green, Aretha Franklin, Stevie Wonder, Donny Hathaway, and the Staple Singers, among others, have also blurred these boundaries in their music.

31 Christian MC and poet Compton Virtue explained to me in an interview in Los Angeles: "I realized that if you're going to be a fisher, you gotta have some bait. So, I would take urban hip-hop beats that are popular on the radio that young people are listening to, because that is what is infectious." Interview with the author, 2004.

32 From there, other holy hip-hop groups formed in the Los Angeles area, some under the guidance and mentorship of Sup and DJ Dove. These early groups, such as JC and the Boys, the Dynamic Twins, Freedom of Soul, Gospel Gangsterz, and I.D.O.L. King, often performed together, shared resources, and supported each other on the road of faith and in the midst of external temptations.

33 It is important to note that holy hip-hop thrives in cities such as Inglewood, California, Harlem, and Atlanta, where there is a strong black middle class.

34 Tonic, quotes in the documentary *Holy Hip Hop* (Amen Films, 2006).

35 See Christina Zanfagna, "Building 'Zyon' in Babylon: Holy Hip Hop and Geographies of Conversion," *Black Music Research Journal* 31/2 (2010): 145–162.

36 Robin Kelley talks about the concept of "polyculturalism" in, among other places, "Polycultural Me," *ColorLines*, September-October 1999, in the *Utne Reader*. Available at www.utne.com/politics/the-people-in-me.aspx#axzz33n7BXYak (accessed June 1, 2014).

7 Hip-hop theater and performance

NICOLE HODGES PERSLEY

Hip-hop is an act of storytelling that is inherently theatrical. The first hip-hop theater stage was not in a traditional proscenium. Imagine simple stages created by passersby gathered round to watch local MCs in the Bronx spit rhymes as breakers danced in a cypher. Picture graffiti artists creating beautiful backdrops that framed these impromptu street stages, as a DJ provided sound using power from a streetlight to animate her turntables. Iconic breakers, such as the R.S.C., would perform in these types of improvised street theaters drawing crowds around them. This legendary dance crew would later become some of the first documented hip-hop theater artists. Jorge "Popmaster Fabel" Pabon and Steffan "Mr. Wiggles" Clemente of the R.S.C. are credited with writing and choreographing two of the first hip-hop musicals: *So What Happens Now?* (1991) and *Jam on the Groove* (1997); the latter is documented as one of the first hip-hop theater pieces to play off-Broadway.[1]

As the vignette above suggests, hip-hop's theatricality has always been a part of the music and culture. Varieties of performance styles reflect the varied modes of artistic expression under the rubric of hip-hop theater, such as dance theater, spoken word, solo performance, performance art, and ensemble theater. In its early stages, hip-hop theater attempted to incorporate the sounds and practices of the hip-hop generation that were literally connected to the four core elements of hip-hop: DJing, MCing, breaking, and graffiti. As the theater practice has evolved over almost twenty years, the musical and cultural deposits contain both literal and abstract acknowledgments of the practices, concerns, and politics of an ever-expanding group of artists inspired by hip-hop around the world. Some pieces have more direct references such as Joe Hernandez-Kolski's *You Wanna Piece of Me?* (2006). This solo play uses a live DJ and music in a call and response with the solo performer to present his autobiography. An abstract use of the DJ element is found in Rickerby Hinds's *Dreamscape* (2012), a two-person play based on the real-life killing of Tyisha Miller by Riverside police. Hinds's DJ and his turntables stand in for a coroner and his examination table. The main character, Myeisha, tells her story as the DJ/coroner examines the bullet wounds in her body as sites of memory. These creative expressions of hip-hop's elements result in innovative approaches to theater making, that not only challenge performance styles, but how theater is made around the world.

Hip-hop is simultaneously an arts practice and cultural movement that reflects contradictory and controversial representations of its practitioners and audience.[2] Like hip-hop music, not every play or performance in hip-hop theater has an original story or a deliberate sociopolitical message. Some artists are just in it for the fun, fame, or money. Others are committed to using theater as a platform to speak about the diversity of American experiences, institutional inequality, and social injustice. Some artists do it all. The tension between social justice and status quo, pleasure and profit, are part of the paradoxical nature of hip-hop music and culture around the world. The majority of hip-hop theater artists reconcile their desire to be successful with creating thought-provoking work committed to social change.

The purpose of this chapter is to provide an overview of hip-hop theater that narrates an aesthetic and practice of hip-hop performance. This sketch is by no means exhaustive as the innovation in hip-hop theater is constant. Hip-hop theater is influenced by a wide array of sonic, linguistic, and embodied exchanges that draw inspiration from people and music from around the globe. As I have written elsewhere, hip-hop theater artists "have a connection, both profound and superficial, to hip-hop's capacity to connect diverse racial and ethnic audiences who identify with Hip Hop as a space to resist the status quo and to re-imagine racial, social, and cultural identifications."[3] One could argue that all of hip-hop culture involves theatrical practice.[4] I begin with a brief history of hip-hop theater and then discuss various theatrical forms in the genre from dance and spoken word, to solo performance and straight-play ensemble productions. I conclude with a discussion of the existing archive of hip-hop theater published in critical anthologies and play scripts.

A hip-hop theater history

Hip-hop's theater history is strongly linked to the culture's core elements of breaking, graffiti, MCing, and DJing (see Chapters 1–4).[5] Hip-hop's hybrid aesthetic influences are an amalgamation of these elements that are always already connected to "race, place, and polyculturalism, hot beats and hybridity."[6] Akin to the predominantly African American jazz music scene that emerged in New Orleans in the 1900s and revealed the points of contact between diverse ethnic groups living in the city, hip-hop's historic connections to the African and Latino diasporas are reflected in the aesthetic practice of sampling and remixing that occur throughout hip-hop cultural production. Jazz's layered aesthetic would later influence the theatrical practices of theater artists across racial lines as Adrienne Kennedy, Amiri Baraka (formerly Leroi Jones), Ed Bullins, Edward Albee, and Sam Shepard all identified with the music's improvisational base and social message. Today, hip-hop music has influenced a new generation of playwrights and performers from Danny Hoch and Toni Blackmon to Jonzi D and Joe Hernandez-Kolski, who sample sounds, ideas, experiences, images, etc. from the past and remix them in the present to shape their aesthetic and artistic practice.

We can see a direct connection between hip-hop theater and early African American theater practices. African American theater scholar Harry Elam identifies the syncretism of American and European theater practices that are rearticulated in hip-hop inspired theater and performance:

> While hip-hop theatre is a new form of cultural expression, it still retains,
> repeats, and revises the past as it pushes into the future. With its celebration
> of language, meter, poetic strictures, verbal play and display, it hearkens
> back to earlier traditions of oral expression in African-American culture,
> such as the spoken word of Gil Scott-Heron and The Last Poets, and even to
> classical theatrical conventions and the productive wordplay of William
> Shakespeare. Hip-hop theatre's inclusion of actual, live rap music and DJ
> scratching and sampling, its allowance for freestyle improvisation, its
> embrace of non-linearity and presentational direct address to the audience,
> breaks with conventional theatrical realism and reflects contemporary
> artistic directions.[7]

Hip-hop theater pioneer Danny Hoch's early commentaries on hip-hop aesthetics also cite Black theater aesthetics: "Hip-hop theater must fit into the realm of theatrical performance, and it must be by, about, for and near the hip-hop generation, participants in hip-hop culture, or both."[8] By revisiting the theater practices practiced by W. E. B. Dubois with his Krigwa Players, Hoch asks us to consider who is doing the writing of history and the possibilities of revision and repetition:

> the notion that hip-hop is solely an African-American art form is erroneous.
> It is part of the African continuum, and if it were not for African Americans
> there would be no hip-hop, but neither would hip-hop exist if not for the
> polycultural social construct of New York in the 1970s.[9]

Elam's and Hoch's discussions of hip-hop music and theater in the early 2000s create a frame that allows us to see that hip-hop theater is influenced by African American cultural practices and equally dependent upon the multiple racial and ethnic groups that contributed to hip-hop's creation in New York in the early 1970s. The early theatrical hip-hop scenes captured by the multiracial R.S.C. in their musicals in the early 1990s build upon the grassroots theater of resistance of the past of the Black and Chicano arts movements of the 1960s. As hip-hop theater pushes well into the twenty-first century, it continues to repeat and revise the past as it shifts its modes of representation in response to the diverse variables of the music, people, and culture that inspire it.

Daniel Banks observes that hip-hop theater "addresses ethnicity, class, culture, gender, sexuality, and generation – it is the theater of the issues that address not just young people, but the whole world."[10] Banks contends that artists across racial lines engage in call and response traditions gleaned from the Black Church, African griot storytelling traditions, and the ritual practices of hip-hop culture. Hip-hop theater performers challenge the established boundaries of theater by pushing audiences to interact with them as members of a shared community. As they write, produce, direct, and promote their works with entrepreneurial savvy and aplomb, hip-hop generation theater artists speak truth to power in order to challenge social and cultural stereotypes.[11] The fourth wall barrier between performer and audience is broken by hip-hop theater artists because they want to create a dialogue between artist and audience in order to address how social change is supposed to happen. Before any regional theater included the word "hip-hop" as an adjective in its theater season descriptions, hip-hop theater artists were bringing theater arts to prisons, women's shelters, youth organizations, schools, hospitals, and progressive performance spaces.[12] For almost twenty years, hip-hop theater has unsettled the definitions of what theater is, was, and can become as it incites community dialogues about institutional inequality and social justice.

Dance based hip-hop theater

Dance based hip-hop theater is one of the foundational languages of hip-hop.[13] Dancers use their bodies and the common language of hip-hop to speak across socially imposed boundaries of difference. Early examples of dance based theater inspired by hip-hop include African American theater artist and producer Rhodessa Jones's *The Medea Project* (1989), a theater piece that uses dance and autobiographical narrative as a hybrid vehicle to address the life experiences of incarcerated women of diverse racial and ethnic groups. Savion Glover and George C. Wolfe's collaboration, *Bring in Da Noise, Bring in Da Funk* (1996), is a musical that deploys tap dance, documentary film, and live music to present a chronology of African American music genres including hip-hop. The show premiered at the New York Shakespeare Festival in 1995 and later moved on to Broadway. American choreographer Rennie Harris[14] founded *Puremovement*, a dance collective in Philadelphia, Pennsylvania, dedicated to teaching and performing hip-hop dance. Harris's choreography and teaching are based in kinaesthetic learning practices where feeling the gestures of hip-hop is linked to cultural experiences. Harris's ensemble work opened the doors for other street dancers to influence dance-training practices. Harris's groundbreaking work in documenting how hip-hop artists create, and his outspokenness about the fact that hip-hop artists never needed a dance studio or theater to legitimize their work, have positioned him as a pioneer of hip-hop dance theater. In the late 1990s in London, Jonzi D and Benji Reid[15] followed Harris to develop the hip-hop theater scene in Britain in the early 2000s. Today, they continue to create a theater practice that synthesizes hip-hop dance and spoken word. Benji Reid's *13 Mics* (2005) incorporates dance, spoken word, and theatrical monologues.[16] Jonzi D began to combine breaking and spoken word, and was one of the first artists to use the term hip-hop theater abroad. He has used the term "Lyrical Fearta," a play on the term "physical theater," as an umbrella term to describe his choreopoetry. Two examples include *Broken Lineage,* a duet that deals with the tensions between the older and younger hip-hop generations, and *The Letter,* a solo piece surrounding Jonzi D's decision to refuse an MBE (Member of the British Empire) Order of the Queen.[17]

Other early representations of hip-hop theater's hybrid aesthetic are also reflected in the work of the late Iranian born Reza Abdoh's *Hip-hop Waltz of Eurydice* (1991). This performance piece borrowed from American radio shows, music, dance, video and classical theater texts to expose the intersections of race, ethnicity, gender, and sexuality. Other important international hip-hop theater companies that focus on hip-hop dance as communal theatrical language are Compagnie Käfig in France and Brazil. Their critically acclaimed show *Boxe Boxe* fuses martial arts, classical music, dance, and hip-hop. The Rubberband Dance Group is a hip-hop inspired repertory company in Montreal, Canada. Their piece *sHip sHop Shape Shifting* was commissioned by the Hip-hop Theater Festival in 2005. Gerard Veltre and the Phunktional dance company in Australia fuse hip-hop dance with flamenco, African, Capoeira, and contemporary indigenous dance to problem solve and educate in youth communities in Australia. The Project Soul Collective in Korea is a troupe of b-boys who are considered some of the best dancers and teachers of b-boying in the world. The transnational reach of hip-hop dance theater is not limited to these few mentions. The language of hip-hop dance has influenced and continues to influence dance vocabularies and people around the world. World-renowned American b-boy, Kwikstep, argues in a 2006 *American Theater* article written by Roberta Uno that hip-hop dance is the "Classic Hip-hop Theater." Kwikstep (born Gabriel Dionisio) began touring in some of the earliest hip-hop dance theater pieces in the country, including *Jam on the Groove,* in 1997.

Spoken word

A surge of spoken word style hip-hop performance began to rise across the USA in the 1990s. Not all spoken word artists are involved with hip-hop theater or accept the label, yet many played an integral part in giving visibility to hip-hop theater as a genre of performance that continues well into the twenty-first century. Progressive arts venues across the nation such as the Nuyorican Poets Café and P.S. 122 in New York, the Kirk Douglass Theater and Mark Taper Forum in Los Angeles, and the New World Theater in Amherst, Massachusetts, recognized the value of spoken word artists whose labor built the ground floor of the hip-hop theater movement. These venues began to feature many artists who were simultaneously poets, singers, actors, writers, and directors. Performing in non-traditional performance spaces such as coffee houses,[18] impromptu street theaters, lofts and people's living rooms across the nation, many artists such as Sarah Jones, Hanifah Walidah, Aya De Leon, Will Power, and Danny Hoch began to mesh dance, spoken word, music, theater, performance art, and autobiography to challenge the traditional ways in which theater could be made and received by audiences. Hip-hop theater was so new to theater communities that producers did not know what to call it or how to include it in traditional regional theater line-ups. Hollywood began to capitalize on the youth audience's love for hip-hop by offering hip-hop inspired works on stage, TV, and film. *Russell Simmons Def Poetry Jam* (see Chapter 1), an HBO series that ran from 2002 to 2007,[19] was the first hip-hop television show to be adapted into a Broadway play of the same name on Broadway in 2002. The play is considered one of the first mainstream hip-hop inspired works to be featured on Broadway.

A survey of spoken word based hip-hop theater pieces includes Matt Sax's *Clay* (2007), which remixes Shakespeare, hip-hop, and family drama to chronicle the journey to stardom of a suburban rap artist. Poet Rha Godess's *Low* (2007) addresses mental illness and its debilitating effects on communities, families, and love relationships. *Goddess City* (2008), by Abiola Abrams and Antoy Grant, uses ritual and myth in the form of a choreopoem[20] to explore violence against women, self-love, and female unity. *Word Begins* (2011) is a two-person play written and performed by Steve Connell and Sekou Andrews that speaks to race, social injustice, war, and love from white and Black American perspectives. *How to Break* (2013) by Aaron Jefferies mixed freestyling, breaking, and monologues to explore the experiences of youth with chronic illness. Bryonn Bain's *Lyrics from Lockdown* (2013) weaves autobiographic events of the author/performer's arrest by New York City Police Department in 2002 against a backdrop of Black male racial profiling in the USA. Together, these works reflect the broad range of topics hip-hop artists engaged with spoken word explore and the social justice message embedded in many hip-hop theater performances.

Solo performance

The early performances of hip-hop theater were not only dance and spoken word based, but also directly tied to solo performance. Many solo performance artists are also writers, directors, and producers. Solo artist, director, and producer Danny Hoch partnered with playwright/director Kamilah Forbes and pioneering theater producer Clyde Valentin to create the Hip-hop Theater Festival in 2000 in New York. This festival launched the careers of many hip-hop theater pioneers such as Will Power, Sara Jones, Mark Bamuthi Joseph, and Eisa Davis in the USA, and Benji Reid and Jonzi D in the UK. Many artists discussed in this chapter have been connected to the festival over its tenure. As of 2013, the festival was renamed Hi-Arts and has expanded to become an interdisciplinary hip-hop arts foundation in New York.

Several important solo works mark the rise of hip-hop theater practice in the 1990s in plays such as Danny Hoch's *Some People* (1998) and *Jails, Hospitals and Hip-hop* (1998) which opened opportunities for artists and audiences to address the institutionalization and commodification of hip-hop by artists and consumers. Hoch's works challenge hip-hop artists to examine their motives and mission in calling themselves hip-hop across racial and class lines. The call and response aesthetic that is connected to many solo hip-hop performances suggests that these artists are not simply breaking the fourth wall to be aesthetically provocative, but more so to engage institutional and social inequality. Sarah Jones's spoken word letter to hip-hop, "Your Revolution" (1997), critiques inequality of women and misogyny in hip-hop music.[21] Jones resists the hip-hop theater label, yet her history on the spoken word scene and solo plays connect her historically to hip-hop theater. Her Tony award-winning solo play *Bridge and Tunnel* (2006) uses a hip-hop inspired spoken word open-mic night to weave the stories of immigrants who want to make claims to the American dream. Jones's solo works challenge racial, ethnic, and class stereotypes in American popular culture using hip-hop as a thematic device.

Another artist who challenges negative images of women in hip-hop is solo Washington, DC based artist/writer Holly Bass.[22] Bass was one of the first performers to use the term "hip-hop theater" in a 1999 *American Theater* article entitled "Blowing Up the Set: What Happens When the Pulse of Hip-hop Shakes Up the Traditional Stage?" In her performance *Moneymaker* (2012), featured at the Corcoran Gallery in Washington, DC,

Bass danced for seven hours in a glass box to explore the objectification of women in hip-hop music videos.[23] Similarly, West Coast solo artist Aya de Leon[24] has been an integral part of the hip-hop theater movement. Her prolific critique of misogyny in hip-hop, *Thieves in the Temple* (2004), addresses heteronormativity, gender bias, and physical violence. Hanifah Walidah's *Straight Folks' Guide to Gay Black Folks* (2003), challenges homophobia and racial stereotypes in African American communities that are also prevalent in hip-hop. Her multi-character solo performance was commissioned by the Hip-hop Theater Festival in 2004.

Matt Sax's *Clay* (2007) references Shakespeare, beat boxing, and deft MCing to recount an aspiring rapper's rise to fame. Sax's classical acting training is remixed with his prowess as an MC to offer a compelling story of ambition triumphing over family dysfunction. Baba Israel's[25] *Boom Bap Meditations* (2008) chronicles Baba Israel's autobiographical journey as a hip-hopper journeying to his mother's homeland of Australia. Playing several characters, Israel makes transnational connections to hip-hop's capacity to reach across racial and national borders to affect social change. Other solo hip-hop theater pieces are Marc Bamuthi Joseph's *The Break/s: A Mixtape for the Stage* (2009) and *Word Becomes Flesh* (2010). Joseph uses the metaphor of the mix tape in his aesthetic practice to create sonic, theatrical, and physical mashups of hip-hop inspired theater.

Kilusan Bautista's *Universal Self* (2011) is a unique multimedia solo performance that blends spoken word poetry, hip-hop, dance, martial arts, music, and animation to weave stories of immigration, indigenous spiritual influences, national identification, and belonging from a Filipino American perspective. Across the Atlantic, hip-hop solo performance works such as Benji Reid's *13 Mics* (2004) use rap, dance, and poetry to trace the circulating routes of American music from bebop to hip-hop using a DJ and diverse characters to demonstrate the influence of Black American music on African diasporic populations. Hip-hop theater and performance has more to do with proving your "authentic" relationship to hip-hop culture than your racial, class, or gender identification. However, unlike hip-hop music, where men still dominate the genre of performance, women in hip-hop theater have been integral parts in realizing the aesthetic. From performing and writing works for the stage or producing and directing them, women in hip-hop theater have been involved in establishing diversity across gender, racial, class, and national lines. As Stuart Hall argues, popular culture is not necessarily a place where we find truth, but it is a place where "we play with the identifications of ourselves, where we are imagined, where we are represented not only to the audiences out there who do not get the message, but to ourselves for the first time."[26]

Ensemble plays

Ensemble hip-hop theater productions that follow a "straight-play"[27] form more closely than solo and spoken word works began to surface in American theater spaces in the late 1980s. Regional theaters around the USA and abroad now feature hip-hop inspired works as part of their seasons. One of the first full-length plays to label itself "hip-hop theater" is Rickerby Hinds's *Daze to Come* (1989).[28] This play was one of the first to use the elements of hip-hop and the language of the culture to establish the given circumstances of a play. Hinds started the Cali hip-hop Fest in 2005, an annual festival that continues to showcase artists who are inspired by hip-hop to create works for the stage. Robert Alexander's *A Preface to the Alien Garden* (1996) takes place in Kansas City and addresses issues of violence, poverty, and gang life which all figure prevalently in many early hip-hop narratives. Kamilah Forbes's *Rhyme Deferred* (1998) remixes African American playwright/poet Langston Hughes's poem "A Dream Deferred" and the biblical story of Cain and Abel[29] to address the intersection of community building, materialism, misogyny, and violence. *In the Heights* (2005), by Lin-Manuel Miranda, highlights the intersection of African American and Latino culture in hip-hop culture to articulate Latino perspectives and quests for the American dream in Washington Heights, New York. The musical was presented in workshop at the Hip-hop Theater Festival in 2006. After a successful off-Broadway run, the show moved to Broadway in 2008 and was nominated for thirteen Tony Awards, winning four of the nominations.[30] Miranda's exploration of the intersection of hip-hop with other Afro-Latino inspired music forms speaks to the syncretism of hip-hop and the already hybrid process of sampling.[31] Zakiyyah Alexander's *Blurring Shine* (2003) is a compelling play about two long-lost African American brothers whose relationship reflects the tensions of "keeping it real" and commodification of hip-hop. The dialogue driven play offers a deft critique of commodification, notions of black authenticity, and masculinity. Will Power's[32] *Flow* (2003) is a multi-character solo performance constructed as a series of overlapping monologues featuring an MC and a DJ who challenge audiences to speak and write their history on their own terms or risk cultural erasure. Power's most recent show, *Fetch Clay, Make Man* (2013), is an ensemble show that explores the friendship between boxer Mohammed Ali and the late actor Stepin Fetchit.

In Case you Forget (2001), by Ben Snyder, explores the legacy of graffiti writers and the contradictions at play between the desire to use aerosol art as an artistic outlet for expressing frustrations with urban blight by black and brown men. *Slanguage* (2002) by the multiracial ensemble Universes remixes spoken word poetry with African oral griot traditions of storytelling. Borrowing influences from hip-hop, blues gospel, and Spanish boleros, *Slanguage* uses the subway as a metaphor to explore exchanges of culture in New York. Danny Hoch's *Till the Break of Dawn* (2007) also explores cross-cultural exchanges and addresses the different meanings that hip-hop and activism take across national and racial borders, pushing American hip-hop artists to look at themselves as transnational subjects and hip-hop itself as a site of cross-cultural exchange and influence. He describes the play as a

> hip-hop play. There is no rapping in it. No break dancing choreography, no graffiti and no DJ scoring it live. It is simply a play that is about a maturing hip-hop generation and how it is desperately struggling with contradictions, politics, identity, sense of responsibility and what community means.[33]

Hoch's description marks the ways that production values and topics of hip-hop theater have matured and reflect the hip-hop generation's coming of age.

Eisa Davis is a Pulitzer Prize nominated playwright, actress, and activist.[34] She is the niece of activist Angela Davis. Her ensemble play *Angela's Mixtape* (2009) explores generational responsibility for social justice and the power of women to affect social change. *Welcome To Arroyo's* by Kristoffer Diaz (2010) was also a Pulitzer Prize finalist, in 2010. The play explores the lives of a brother and sister who try to make sense of their lives after the death of their mother, and the rich contributions of female Latina graffiti artists[35] that have been ignored in hip-hop's history. Matt Sax and Eric Rosen's musical performance collaboration *Venice* (2010) is a musical that remixes R&B, hip-hop, punk, and rock to create a hip-hop inspired dystopia that considers hip-hop's relationship to postracialism in the age of Barack Obama. The Broadway musical *Holler if You Hear Me* (2014), with a book by Todd Kreidler and music by Tupac Shakur, is inspired by the life of the late rapper (and stars Saul Williams as Shakur). The musical chronicles the lives of "two childhood friends, John and Vertus, and their extended families as they struggle to reconcile the challenges and realities of their daily lives with their hopes, dreams and ambitions."[36] Marc Bamuthi Joseph's *Red, Black, and Green: A Blues* (2013) is an ensemble spoken word piece that "combines dance, poetry, music, and visual art in a new mode of hybrid performance."[37] Joseph uses theater as a site for society to bear witness to the intimate details of racism as he challenges his audience to consider racism as an environmental and ecological concern. Joseph also moves hip-hop theater forward to claim a new mode of "hybrid performance." Hip-hop theater's newness, self-reflexivity, and ambition allows it to be conscious of when it needs to move forward as it pays homage and respect to its rich past.

The multiple hip-hop theater approaches discussed here, from dance and spoken word, to solo performance and ensemble works, suggest some of the ways that hip-hop theater can be created. However, like hip-hop music, the genre is always open to new approaches to theater and performance making. All of these works become collective manifestos that subvert mainstream conventions of theater and performance as they create openings for intersectional explorations of race, ethnicity, gender, sexuality, and/or class to become central to American and global theater history. The contributions of these artists, and many others not mentioned here, suggest that hip-hop music inspires a global movement of interdisciplinary creativity. Hip-hop theater challenges us to reclaim past uses of theater as an alternative public sphere in innovative new ways that can help us foster dialogues about social justice and equality within and outside of hip-hop culture.

Conclusion

The increased interest in hip-hop theater and performance in global popular culture is reflected in the surge of live hip-hop inspired performances in mainstream theaters and performance venues around the world. Despite this growing interest, many hip-hop theater texts are not always available in print. Seeing this void in the archive, many theater scholars have begun to include these works in anthologies. Kim Euell and Robert Alexander's edited volume, *Plays from the Boom Box Galaxy: Theater from the Hip-hop Generation* (2009), marks the first anthology of plays inspired by hip-hop and features work from many of the theater artists discussed here. Daniel Banks's landmark anthology *Say Word! Voices from Hip Hop Theater* (2011)[38] is a comprehensive volume by hip-hop playwrights and contains a glossary of terms and weblinks to artist statements and production histories. Earlier theater publications such as Harry Elam's *The Fire This Time: African American Plays for the 21st Century* (2009) include works by hip-hop theater playwrights. As many hip-hop artists, practitioners, scholars, and fans have confirmed, the fifth element of hip-hop is knowledge. Hip-hop theater and performance produces new knowledge by flipping margins, bending them, twisting them, and remixing them in new and innovative ways that challenge how we understand the world. Hip-hop theater practitioners are no longer just local to the United States, but exist around the world. Now is the time to publish, perform, teach, and create more of these works so that we can reclaim the stage as a place to perform our shared humanity in stories that reflect the connectedness of our experiences.

Further reading

Banks, Daniel, *Say Word! Voices from Hip Hop Theater* (Ann Arbor: University of Michigan Press, 2011).

Chang, Jeff (ed.), *Total Chaos: The Art and Aesthetics of Hip-Hop* (New York: Basic Civitas, 2006).

Persley, Nicole Hodges, *Remixing Blackness: Sampling Race and Gender in Hip-hop Theater and Performance* (Ann Arbor: University of Michigan Press, forthcoming).

Notes

1 See Jeff Chang, "Profile 7: Dancing on the Through-Line: Rennie Harris and the Past and Future of Hip-Hop Dance" (2002), Democratic Vistas Profiles, Book 7, available at http://digitalcommons.colum.edu/cap_vistas/7. See also Jeff Chang, *Can't Stop Won't Stop: A History of the Hip-Hop Generation* (New York: St. Martin's Press, 2005). Chang provides a more in-depth discussion about the R.S.C. and their important contributions to hip-hop history.

2 See Danny Hoch's prolific hip-hop arts manifesto "Here We Go Yo! A Hip-hop Arts Manifesto," *American Theater* 21/10 (2004): 97–102.

3 Nicole Hodges Persley, *Remixing Blackness: Sampling Race and Gender in Hip-hop Theater and Performance* (Ann Arbor: University of Michigan Press, forthcoming).

4 Joseph Schloss, "Culture, Ethnicity and the Theater of Hip-Hop," in Chinua Akimaro Thelwell (ed.), *Of Unimagined Spaces: The Legacy of New WORLD Theater* (forthcoming).

5 See the documentary *Scratch: The History of Turntablism*, dir. Doug Pray (2001).

6 Chang, *Can't Stop Won't Stop*.

7 Harry Elam, "Revising the Past, Pushing Into the Future," *American Theater* (2004).

8 Hoch, "Here We Go Yo!".

9 *Ibid.*

10 Daniel Banks, "Introduction: Hip Hop's Ethic of Inclusion," in *Say Word! Voices from Hip Hop Theater* (Ann Arbor: University of Michigan Press, 2011), p. 9.

11 For an excellent introduction to the hip-hop generation's coming of age, see Nelson George's classic text *Hip Hop America*, 2nd edn. (New York: Penguin Books, 2005).

12 Artists such as Jorge "Fabel" Pabon, Danny Hoch, Stephan "Mr. Wiggles" Clemente, Rennie Harris, Will Power, Aya de Leon, Baba Israel, Holly Bass, Marc Bamuthi Joseph, Benji Reid, Jonzi D and many others not mentioned here are considered pioneers of hip-hop theater and dance in the USA and Britain. These artists have dedicated their careers to bringing theater to underserved audiences in schools, prisons, women's shelters, and homeless shelters in order to bring social awareness about hip-hop to community members across racial and class lines.

13 For more on hip-hop dance language, specifically as it pertains to breaking, see Joseph Schloss, *Foundation: B-Boys, B-Girls, and Hip-hop Culture in New York* (New York: Oxford University Press, 2009).

14 In 2001, Rennie Harris created an adaptation of Shakespeare's *Romeo and Juliet*, entitled *Rome and Jewels*, which addressed African American gang violence. He continues to explore the ways that the body can translate across cultural experiences using hip-hop dance as a space to challenge social and discursive boundaries. Available at www.rhpm.org.

15 Jonzi D established a resident hip-hop dance company and an annual Hip-hop Dance Theater Festival called The Breakin' Convention at Sadler's Wells Theatre in London in 2000. Benji Reid's company Breaking Cycles, also located in London, is dedicated to using physical theater and hip-hop dance to break down barriers of inequality.

16 For more conversation about the collaboration between Wolfe and Glover see interview with George C. Wolfe and Savion Glover: *Charlie Rose*, PBS, New York, April 11, 1996.

17 ItsOnCardiff, "Jonzi D – Lyrical Fearta: Interview," *ItsOnCardiff*. Available at www.itsoncardiff.co.uk/Interview/Interviews.aspx?FCID=29685 (accessed May 29, 2014).

18 See Anthony Kwame Harrison's work on hip-hop performance in underground clubs in Oakland, California. Anthony Kwame Harrison, *Hip Hop Underground: The Integrity and Ethics of Racial Identification* (Philadelphia: Temple University Press, 2009).

19 Russell Simmons's *Def Poetry Jam on Broadway* was produced by hip-hop mogul Russell Simmons and his partner, director Stan Lathan. The show featured spoken word

vignettes performed by nine "slam poets" of
diverse racial, ethnic, and sexual orientations
and premiered at the Longacre Theater and ran
from November 14, 2002 to May 4, 2003.
20 Ntozake Shange used the term
"choreopoem" to describe her spoken
word-dance piece *For Colored Girls Who Have
Considered Suicide when the Rainbow Was Enuff*
(1975). Artists around the world have used the
phrase to describe dance-based theater that
incorporates poetry or other spoken text. The
fact that this term is appropriated by a new
generation of female identified hip-hop theater
artists suggests the ways that sampling is also
used to bring historic texts from the Black
political archive into the present of hip-hop
aesthetic practices.
21 Sarah Jones was frequently labeled a hip-hop
poet and theater artist early in her career, yet she
resists such labels because her desire is to situate
her work more broadly.
22 Holly Bass is a dancer, actress, singer,
journalist, and producer. She speaks at academic
conferences on hip-hop theater and
performance and has created hip-hop inspired
works for regional theaters, museums, and
performance spaces cross the USA.
23 Holly Bass's intertextual performance
included documentary clips referencing Sarah
"Saartjie" Bartmaan, sound files from Malcolm
X speeches, hip-hop music, and music samples
from James Brown. More information is
available at www.getinvolved.corcoran.org/
moneymaker (accessed August 21, 2013).
24 Aya de Leon lives and works in Oakland,
California where she is a writer, performer, arts
activist, and mother dedicated to teaching
poetry and theater to provide a bridge between
the academy and the community. She is director
of Poetry for the People at UC Berkeley. See
http://ayadeleon.wordpress.com/about/
(accessed August 21, 2013).
25 Baba Israel is a hip-hop theater pioneer who
has a self-published volume on hip-hop theater
and ritual entitled *Remixing the Ritual: Hip Hop
Theater Aesthetics and Practice* (Baruch Baba
Israel Press, 2010).
26 Stuart Hall, "Cultural Identity and
Diaspora," in Patrick Williams and Laura
Chrisman (eds.), *Colonial Discourse and
Post-Colonial Theory: A Reader* (London:
Harvester Wheatsheaf, 1994), p. 474.
27 A straight play is a theatrical production that
is non-musical but relies on dialogue to tell the
story, not song and/or dance.
28 Rickerby Hinds immigrated to the USA
from Honduras at the age of thirteen and began
to share his style of theater-making in London

in the late 1980s and early 1990s. Hinds moved
to South Central Los Angeles and became
immersed in hip-hop culture.
29 Kamilah Forbes is one of the founders of the
Hip-hop Theater Festival in New York. The
festival is now called Hi-Arts. See www.
hi-artsnyc.org (accessed August 30, 2013).
Forbes is also a director and producer. More
information available at www.kamilahforbes.
com (accessed August 30, 2013).
30 *In The Heights* won Tony awards for best
musical, best musical score, best choreography,
and best orchestrations in 2010. It was
nominated for the Pulitzer Prize in 2009.
31 See Paul Carter Harrison, Victor Leo Walker,
and Gus Edwards (eds.), *Black Theater: Ritual
Performance in the African Diaspora*
(Philadelphia: Temple University Press, 2002).
Harrison *et al.* link Black American theater
practices to Africa and African ritual. The
scholars analyze African American theater
practices as part of a larger expression of Black
Theater practices in Africa and the African
diaspora. For Harrison, Black theater and
performance are mutually constitutive and
should incorporate both traditional conceptions
of theater as well as more improvisational styles
that include spoken word, hip-hop music, and
African oral traditions.
32 Will Power is an African American artist
born in California. He is bi-coastal and has
been commissioned to create theater across the
United States. He is also a community activist
who shares his work with schools, prisons, and
women's groups. More information available
at www.willpower.tv (accessed August 30, 2013).
33 Nicole Hodges Persley, personal
correspondence with Danny Hoch, February 17,
2006.
34 Eisa Davis's landmark article "Hip-hop
Theater: The New Underground," published in
the *Source* in March 2000, was one of the first
commentaries that named the influence of
hip-hop music and culture in the USA on a
new generation of theater artists who grew up
with the music, helped create the culture, and
continue to live its interdisciplinary practice.
35 Female graffiti artists such as LADY PINK,
MUK, and CLAW are important parts of
hip-hop culture and have translated their work
into gallery and commercial spaces. See Jessica
Pabòn, "Be About It: Graffiteras Performing
Feminist Community," *TDR/The Drama Review*
57/3 (2013): 88–116.
36 *Holler if You Hear Me* has been in workshop
for several years. According to Broadway.com,
August Wilson was approached to write the
book for the Tupac inspired musical before his

death. Kenny Leon directed the workshops
in New York and has been directly involved
in developing the musical along with August
Wilson protégé, Todd Kreidler, who wrote
the current book. Hollywood manager
and producer Eric Gold is executive
producer on the project. Available at
www.digitaljournal.com/article/320484#
ixzz2etk9zCSt (accessed September 1, 2013).
37 See maps international productions.
Available at www.mappinternational.org/
programs/view/214/ (accessed September 14,
2013).
38 See Daniel Banks's anthology *Say Word!*

PART II

Methods and concepts

8 Lyrics and flow in rap music

OLIVER KAUTNY

Introduction

Somebody who grew up outside of hip-hop culture reading the lyrics of a rap song might be astonished by their length compared to those of an average pop or rock song. The fact that many MCs need more words per minute than an average singer of a pop song has a lot to do with their specific rhythmical approach to lyrics, using the vowels and consonants to form a mostly rapid and rhythmical highly organized flow of syllables. Looking closely at the music, rapping combines a stylized form of *Sprechgesang* (speech song) with vocal percussion, which explains its vast "consumption" of words. This musical function of the lyrics is so essential to rap music that Kyle Adams argued that the meanings of many rap lyrics are far less important than their pure sonorities.[1] This argument might be striking when contrasting non-narrative, self-referential boasting songs like "Scenario" (1992) by A Tribe Called Quest featuring Leaders of the New School, to storytelling songs like "The Message" (1982) by Grandmaster Flash and the Furious Five, or "Stan" by Eminem (2000). But the semantics of rap lyrics cannot be reduced to mere storytelling. Even those songs which seem to be incomprehensible and self-referential at first glance may be understood as statements about identity, e.g. representing politics, gender, or geography. And what rap songs actually mean depends strongly on aspects of the subgenre and the overall aesthetic preferences of the listeners.

From a methodological point of view, I therefore recommend not making a preliminary decision to examine the semantics or the musical elements of MCing. It may be that we can relate the semantic devices of a song to the musical ones, which might in turn improve our close readings. This could broaden our analytical perspective toward both the sociocultural context and the intermedial fabric of the song, established by its vocal delivery over (often times sampled) beats, mostly related to music videos as well as other media. Although the main interest of this chapter is the rhythm of rapping, which is called flow, I will first give a very brief overview of some common lyrical aspects, with respect to the MC's use of rhetorical means and rhyme.

All the transcriptions are made by the author unless otherwise stated.

This will lead to the examination of the musical quality of lyrics, to their rhythmical organization as flow.

Rhetorical means and rhyme

It is impossible to provide a general overview of the content of rap songs given the variety of subgenres in rap music that have been created and diffused globally since the 1980s. Rap lyrics have incorporated numerous themes, from political storytelling to self-referential braggadocio, strongly depending on the individual approaches of the rap artist and the socio-cultural, historical, and generic context in which his or her work originates. Therefore I will focus on exemplifying some general rhetorical devices and semantic references. Of crucial importance to rap lyrics are the kinds of content and rhetorical devices which refer to the symbolic world of hip-hop culture. This indirect communication is often intended exclusively for members of that culture.

Rap lyrics are linked to all genres of rap (reality rap, party rap, etc.) and hip-hop culture (graffiti, hip-hop dance, etc.), but the lyrics are also tied to African American culture in general. Given the fact that hip-hop emerged in the USA, many scholars interpret this practice of indirect comment as a special form of African American rhetorical gesture, called Signifyin(g).[2] This can be realized, for example, by irony, simile ("But like Sly for the fam I still stand" from "I Am Music" by Common, 2002), metaphors ("Life's A Bitch" by Nas featuring AZ, 1994), allusions or quotations (e.g. of political speeches as in "Fight the Power" by Public Enemy, 1989). This practice, certainly transformed in many ways by the global diffusion of hip-hop, strengthens the cultural identities of those who are capable of denoting the semantics of hip-hop and willing to share the values of its culture.

As hip-hop culture is strongly characterized by competition, it has generated various aesthetic forms of dueling, and the verbal strategies of rap-battling are the most prominent of them. The lyrical genre of battle rap provides the possibility both to praise one's own qualities (boastin') and to weaken the reputation of the opponent, e.g. by questioning his/her technical skills, his/her sexual power, and the personal integrity of the rapper or his/her mother's personal integrity (dissin'). Although sociolinguists discovered that this kind of verbal ritual can be found in many folk traditions all around the globe,[3] the context of rap asks one to consider the African American tradition of verbal dueling, called the Dozens, as the model of rap-battling.[4] "MC's can only battle with rhymes that got punchlines," raps KRS-One, well-known New York-based battle MC in his song "MC's Act Like They Don't Know" (1995). Punchlines are the most funny and insulting lines of battle rap mocking at other personas. This can be illustrated by a verse performed by New York's gangsta rap legend, the Notorious B.I.G.: "Take them rhymes back to the factory / I see, the gimmicks – the wack lyrics / The shit is depressing – pathetic – please forget it" (Craig Mack featuring the Notorious B.I.G.: "Flava in Ya Ear," 1994). Compared to the misogynistic and homophobic standards of many battle songs, this punchline is a rather modest one.

The B.I.G. example also illustrates one of the most important features of rap lyrics: the quality of the rhymes and their ability to provide the lyrics with a "musical" quality, which varies based on how many rhymes and which types of rhymes are used and where they are placed within the lyrical structure. Rhyme is the repetition of the same (perfect rhyme) or similar (half or slant rhyme) sounds between two words, locating these segments mostly at the end of the words, whereas alliteration places them at their beginning. From the musicological point of view, this linguistic differentiation between rhyme and alliteration can be neglected, as we are basically interested in the play of sounds, with less regard for the sounds' position within the word. Of utmost importance is the MC's repetition, transformation, and restructuring of the same or similar speech-sounds in a heteronomous soundscape of non-rhyming speech. This provides MCing with a basic musical quality, characterized by the dialectics between identity and difference of sound. Rhymes are like instruments, arranged by rhyme scheme and musical delivery. Furthermore, we distinguish between monosyllabic and polysyllabic rhymes. The latter especially contribute to the density of rhyme speech and the rhymed rhythm of MCing. Finally, it is important to note the position of the rhymes, which can be placed as common couplets (at the end of two paired lines) and/or as internal rhymes. Obviously the latter have a strong impact on both the density and rhythmic structure of rhymes. But we have to keep in mind that we are not dealing with written poems but with rhymed lyrics rapped to a beat. Thus nothing can be said about the position of rhymes without considering their overall rhythmic context as given by the beat. It is therefore necessary to think about the rhymed rhythm of rapping.

"Rhyme flow" to a beat

The rhythmic delivery of MCing is called flow. I distinguish three different aspects of flow, all of which are discussed by rappers as well as rap fans.[5] The first aspect describes the process of the rhythm's production, the air flowing out of the lungs, formed into a flow of sound. The second part of flow describes the musical result of the airflow synchronized to a musical arrangement called beat. A third aspect of the term flow reminds us – like the term groove – of the feel of music while perceiving it. Does the rapper's

Example 8.1 A Tribe Called Quest, "Push It Along" (1990), 1:18–1:20 (first verse).

1	x	y	z	2	x	y	z	3	x	y	z	4	x	y	z
Q-	Tip	is	my	tit-	le			I	don't	think	that	it's	vi-	tal	

flow make the audience's heads nod with her/his delivery? Is he perhaps able to astonish us with his rhythmical mastery?

Thus in "MC's Act Like They Don't Know" (1995) KRS-One calls on his audience to "(f)low with the master rhymer, that's to leave behind the video rapper, you know, the chart climber." This hints to the fact that not only producing, but even perceiving and judging the MC's delivery, requires a lot of training. Flow is the result of learning, informed by listening to and comparing a huge number of songs and considering the negotiations fans, artists, and critics have about "good flow."

According to these three dimensions of flow – production, texture, and reception – the ideal analysis should consider all of them, which is not always possible, of course. But even though we will not manage to ful-fil this ideal, defining rhythm by its perceptual dimension as well has an overall methodological consequence: if the phenomenon "flow" is something which is co-constructed by rappers and their audiences with their heteronomous concepts of flow, we should always be capable of critically rethinking our choices of "objects" and our judgments about the structure, values, and impacts of flow.[6] We always run the risk of choosing musical examples which fit well into our scholarly tools and concepts (e.g. of complexity, unity, etc.). But do they have the same significance to the artists and fans?

Fortunately, the research on flow has intensified over the last decades with scholars such as Cheryl Keyes, Adam Krims, Kyle Adams, and Oliver Kautny providing models for analysis. Thus, I will exemplify some of the most important methods and results below, though we are still at the beginning and we know little about this complex rhythmic phenomenon, especially when compared to the state of research in fields such as jazz.[7] The rhythmical and metrical styles of flow I will now exemplify are meant as an approximation of significant styles in flow.

Styles of flow

Example 8.1 illustrates a measure of "Push It Along" delivered by the rapper Q-Tip, in an excerpt of a notation produced by Kyle Adams.[8] Each beat is subdivided into sixteenth notes, symbolized by the beats (e.g. "1") and the letters x, y, and z.

This is perhaps the most "regular" style of MCing in existence. The rapper Q-Tip flows in even sixteenth notes, landing predictably on the downbeats and backbeats. The hits of the snare on measure two and four coincide precisely with the on-beat end-rhymes of the couplet – a structure which is mechanically repeated in the next measures. Q-Tip synchronizes his flow both with snare accents on the backbeats and with pauses within the musical arrangement on the "ands" of beats two and four.[9] On-beat flows are commonly associated with "old school" US rap, which was replaced by a new generation of MCs with new and more complex styles of flow at the end of the 1980s and the beginning of the 1990s.[10] Thus, "Push It Along" can be called "old school," although it is associated with the later "golden age" of hip-hop.

When we compare Q-Tip's MCing with two old school classics, Melle Mel's "The Message" (1982) and Kurtis Blow's "The Breaks" (1980), we will find out that the vocal attacks of all three MCs can be relatively precisely mapped within the metrical grid, as they fit within the four-beat meter and its subdivisions into an eighth-note or a sixteenth-note pulsation, the norm of rap beat production.[11] Moreover, Blow and Mel, as many rap artists of that time, preferred simple rhyme couplets, as did Q-Tip in "Push It Along." Melle Mel and Q-Tip share the same preference for on-beat rhymes; the former places them mostly on beat four of each measure, which is called a feature of old school flow.[12] But the crucial difference between Q-Tip and the other two MCs is that the latter make use of syncopation. Melle Mel sometimes places unrhymed words off-beat ("Broken glass"), whereas Kurtis Blow very often advances the rhymed and accented word so that off-beat rhymes fall on weak parts between beats three and four. Of most importance, however, is the vocal quality of flow. As illustrated by Cheryl L. Keyes,[13] Melle Mel notably stresses rhymed and unrhymed words with a sing-songy intonation typical of MCing until the middle of the 1980s. Whereas Run-D.M.C. and the Beastie Boys still syncopate the rhyme couplets in a way similar to Kurtis Blow, the "melodic quality" has changed into a shouting style.[14] This stands in contrast to Q-Tip's relaxed delivery with almost no rhythmical variation. Perhaps this is the musical expression fitting best to the Native Tongues' relaxed lyrical understatement ("a brother who ain't dissin'"), which contrasts sharply to the often angry MCing of reality rap of that time.

Example 8.2, an excerpt from KRS-One's "MC's Act Like They Don't Know" (1995), illustrates another step in the evolution of flow, which began in the 1980s thanks to MCs like Rakim, and then became dominant during the 1990s: the song starts with a historical flashback by imitating the syncopated sung style of Kurtis Blow, alluding to "The Breaks" in the first

Example 8.2(a) KRS-One, "MC's Act Like They Don't Know" (1995), 3:43–3:54, third verse (*pronounced: run'n/ runnin'), lyrical chart.

Measure	Lyrics and rhymes
1	A A You dope, you <u>lied</u>, I re<u>side</u> like artef-
2	B A B A -<u>acts on</u> the wrong <u>side</u> of the <u>tracks</u>, electri<u>fied.</u>
3	C D D C A <u>Comin'</u> ar<u>ound</u> the <u>mountain</u>, you <u>run and*</u> <u>hide.</u> Hopin' your de-
4	E [E] fence mecha<u>nism</u> can divert my heat-seeking lyri-/ [next measure:] <u>cism</u>

Example 8.2(b) KRS-One, "MC's Act Like They Don't Know" (1995), 3:43–3:54, third verse, rhythmic analysis.

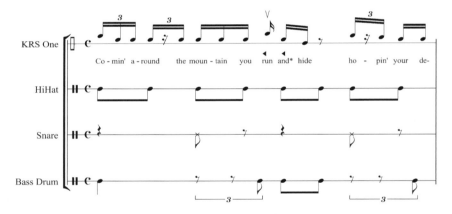

lines. But then the vocal delivery soon shifts to a more complex, modern flow.[15] The lyrical chart (Example 8.2(a)) illustrates the incomplete sentences overflowing the lines of the couplet ("enjambments"). Also note the syncopated internal rhymes contributing to a metrical rhyme structure far more complex than the former on-beat end-rhyme schemes. This is what Adam Krims calls an "effusive" style of MCing.

Note the rhythmic delivery in measure three (Example 8.2(b)), with its tight and fast rhythmic triplets, the binary sixteenth notes precisely "riding" on the snare and the hi-hat eighths and the well-timed off-beat accent on the word "run," which begins slightly earlier than the kick drum attack. The articulation is percussive and pitch is at least partly relatively fixed, being used in this measure as a device for rhythmic grouping. This delivery resembles drumming or scat-singing and contrasts sharply with metrically more irregular natural speech. It is in fact DJ Premier's sampled arrangement which provides the song with additional rhythmic and metric irregularities. Note, for example, the attacks of the bass drum on measure two and four (see Example 8.2(b)) notated as triplets, which are actually played neither exactly within a ternary nor in a binary pulsation, as both attacks are slightly pushed microtemporally out of the metric grid. Or note the bass, which is not notated in the figure, playing whole passages slightly out of time compared to the steady hi-hat pulsation. These microtemporal shifts and metric divergences both intensify the groove of Premier's beat. And it is possible that we experience KRS-One's very tight, powerful MCing as even more intense and vivid since it benefits from these temporal tensions, which can hardly be placed in the notation, but are nevertheless at work. This shows that almost nothing can be said about flow without examining its interplay with the beat.

Some scholars believe that microtiming and metrical divergences are crucial for an effective (and pleasurable) perception of rhythm. The interplay of deviation and norm seems to correspond very often with the dialectic perception of tension and resolution, variety and stasis, excitement, and predictability.[16] We also know that many MCs use these devices, even if they do not do so consciously. Example 8.3 shows an excerpt of "Hammerhart" (1998) by the German group Absolute Beginner, one of the most acclaimed songs in Germany's rap history, illustrating a style of flow contributing to polyrhythm in a rap song.

Denyo is rapping in seamless chains of tight, rapid sixteenth notes, making hardly any use of microtiming. At first glance, it seems like the MC accentuates the flow of unchopped note-rows only by heavily using internal rhymes, which contribute to a "rhythmic effect of rhymed syllables on their own," as shown by Adams in Blackalicious's "Blazing Arrow" (2002).[17] But is this dense internal rhyme structure solely important for the rhythmic gestalt of "Hammerhart"? In fact, considering the even structure of accentuation within each measure, which partly does not depend on its rhymes, is also of crucial importance. For example, the first measure contains five accents within the vocal layer: three of them are rhymes, two of them are non-rhymed accents. All accents contribute to a 4–3–3–3–3 pattern, establishing first a quaternary pulse, then switching into a ternary subdivision of the beats two, three, and four. Moreover the accents are highlighted by pitch and dynamics in an almost Jamaican toasting style, melodically alternating between three pitches, which are however very close to each other. The rapping in "threes" conflicts with the steady binary

Example 8.3 Absolute Beginner, "Hammerhart" (1998), 0:42–0:53, first verse.

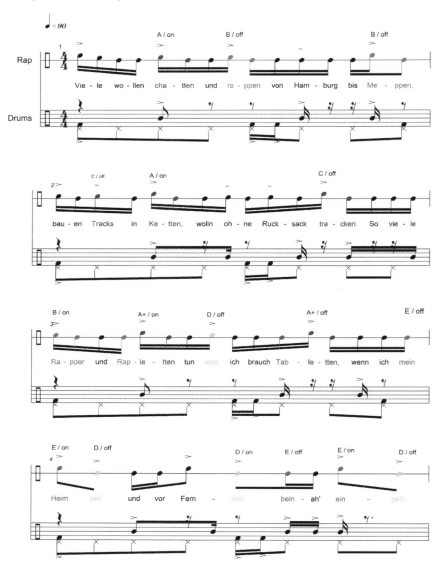

pulsation of the hi-hats. The first three measures are all structured like this and the fourth measure reproduces the same cross-pulsation half speed. It is noteworthy to mention that this phenomenon, which can be called a metric dissonance,[18] is already pre-established in the syncopated beat produced by Jan Delay. But Denyo even intensifies this effect by adding metrically important off-beats to the arrangement, e.g. in the first and third measures. This polyrhythm results from the interplay of vocal and instrumental layers, enriched by a dense sonic grid of rhymes. Well-known US MCs who make

Example 8.4(a) Eminem, "'Till I Collapse" (2002), 0:55–1:07, first verse (*pronounced: fill'em), analysis of rhymes.

Measure	Lyrics and rhymes
1	A **B/on** A+/off B/off A++/off A/off C/off 'Till I col-/**lapse** I'm <u>spillin</u> these <u>raps</u> long as you <u>feel'em</u>*. '<u>Till</u> the <u>day</u>/
2	D/off C/off D/off **A+++/on** (d)<u>ay</u> that I <u>drop</u> you'll never <u>say</u> that I'm <u>not</u> **killin'em**./
3	<u>E/off</u> D/off E/off D/off A++++/off E/off Cause <u>when</u> I'm <u>not,</u> <u>then</u> I'ma <u>stop pinnin'em</u>. <u>And</u>/
4	D/off D/off E/off D/off **A+++++/on** I am <u>not</u> hip-<u>hop</u> and I'm just <u>not</u> **Eminem**.

use of crossing pulses include Busta Rhymes, Chuck D, and Dr. Dre. Chuck D's complex flow in Public Enemy's "Fight The Power" (1989) is additionally characterized by microtiming and Dr. Dre's MCing in N.W.A.'s "100 Miles and Runnin'" (1990) is more percussive than Denyo's, sometimes interrupting the flow with sustained notes. Denyo's MCing illustrates that MCs can contribute to metrically divergent passages without varying their flow microtemporally.

Something very different occurs in Eminem's "'Till I Collapse" (2002), where Eminem plays microtemporally around very steady rock beats. He phrases his flow by framing a series of internal off-beat rhymes with two on-beat rhymes. The one falls on the downbeat of the first measure ("collapse"), the other on beat four of the second (killin'em), which is the typically end-rhyme position in rap music (Example 8.4(a)). It is striking that this two-measure structure established by rhyme and vocal phrasing corresponds to the beat and its two-measure melodic theme in C sharp minor played by a guitar. This frames the rhythmically flexible, highly syncopated delivery within its boundaries, which is notated in Example 8.4(b).

For the analysis of this complex flow I used software which allows one to slow down the speed of the music sample (Sonic Visualizer, magix music maker). This facilitated the location of the vocal attacks (rap: marked with "X"), especially when relating them to the even downbeat/backbeat structure of the drums (Bd = bass drum; Sn = snare). This microscopic timestretch reveals that many onsets are not fully precise within the grid, which is the reason why I placed them slightly irregularly in the chart. Not all of them can necessarily be perceived listening to the song at the original tempo (85 bpm). Of crucial importance to me are passages characterized

Example 8.4(b) Eminem, "Till I Collapse" (2002), 0:55–1:07, first verse, notation of delivery.

Last measure of the Intro | **Beginning of the new 4-measure pattern**

Measure 1

	Last measure of the Intro	Measure 1			
Beats	4	1	2	3	4
Drums		Bd	Bd / Sn	Bd	Bd / Sn
rap	X X X X X	X X X X X X	X	X X X X X X X
lyrics	'Till I col- la-	pse I'm spi- llin these ra-	ps long	as you fee - lem. 'Till the day-
rhymes	A/off B/on	A+/off B/off		A++/off A/off C/off

Measure 2

	1	2	3	4
Beats				
Drums	Bd / Bd	Sn	Bd / Bd	Sn
Rap	XX X X X	X XX	X X X X	X X X
lyrics	(d)ay that I dro -	pyou'll ne - ver	say	that I'm no - t kil - li - nem
rhymes	(C/off) D/off	C/off		D/off A+++/on

Example 8.4(b) (cont.)

Measure 3

beats	1		2		3		4	
drums	Bd	Bd	Sn		Bd	Bd	Sn	
rap	X	XX	X̲		X X	X̲	X X X X	
lyrics	'Cause	when I'm no –		t, then I'ma s -	to –	(p)pi - mi - nem.	And	
rhymes		E/off	D/off		E/off	D/off	A++++/on	E/off

Measure 4

Beats	1		2		3		4	
drums	Bd	Bd	Sn		Bd	Bd	Sn	
Rap	X	X	X̲	X	X X X X	X̲	X X X	
lyrics	I	am	no –	t hip - hop	and I'm just	no -	t E - mi - nem.	
rhymes	(E/off)	D/off		D/off	E/off	D/off	A+++++/on	

Example 8.4(c) Eminem, "'Till I Collapse" (2002), 0:55–1:07, first verse, schema of rhymes.

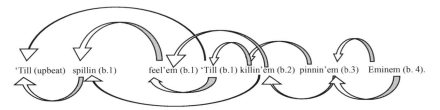

'Till (upbeat)   spillin (b.1)   feel'em (b.1) 'Till (b.1) killin'em (b.2) pinnin'em (b.3)   Eminem (b. 4).

by strong microtiming (underlined) and the many microtemporally mod-
ulated syncopations marked by arrows in Example 8.4(b). In the first two
measures, four of the eight off-beat rhymes are slightly advanced. Only the
last off-beat rhyme, located before the on-beat rhyme "killinem" is deleted.
It seems as if Eminem wants to savor the last syncopation by delaying it,
finally highlighting the following on-beat conclusion of the two-measure
phrase. The second phrase (measures three and four) reveals much more
laid back off-beat accents concluding in same way as the first one. The main
accents (marked with **X** in bold) in this example are stretched, throaty, and
raised in pitch, except for the last rhyme at the end of each phrase, which
is lowered, highlighting the phrases' caesura. The pitched and stretched
accents play around the beat and interrupt the fast flow of syllables, which
results in a permanent and quick alternation between accelerating and slowing down, like a rider modulating the tempo of his horse, speeding over a
course, slowing down before jumping over a fence and speeding up afterwards again, etc. The temporal shifts correspond to the effect of advanced
and deleted syncopations.

It is important to note that the rhymes are not only a means of highlighting accents. They also provide the vocal layer with additional coherence, following their own phonetic and temporal logic, which is exemplified by the phonetic "generation" of the word "Eminem" at the end
of the fourth measure, which is derived from the word "'till," which
appears in the upbeat of measure one for the first time. Eminem over
and over permutates, adds, and subtracts segments of words (till > *spillin*)
until his own name emerges out of the flow of rhymes. This enables the
listener to memorize (at least parts of) a track of rhymes, which over-
flows the boundaries of all four measures (see Example 8.4(c)). Moreover
this vocal track is crossed by additional internal rhyme structures (see
Example 8.4(a)).

MF Doom's MCing in "All Caps" (2004) by Madvillain has at least two
properties in common with Eminem's flow. First, it uses the fourth beat
of each measure as a metrical anchor, and second, it makes heavy use of

internal rhymes. But MF Doom's use of microtiming differs enormously from Eminem's, because his flow seems to be derived much more from natural speech with regard both to melody and rhythm. Apart from the anchored beats, where voice and meter are strictly synchronized, many passages tend to almost leave the grid of steady pulsation without playing strategically around the beats as Eminem did in the previous example. This ambivalence of staying inside and outside the meter makes it even more difficult to notate than Eminem's delivery. When reading Kyle Adams's analysis of MF Doom's flow (2009) we have to take into consideration that many regular binary, quaternary, or quintuple subdivisions of the proposed notation actually sound slightly different, leaving the frame of a pulsation many times. If MF Doom's a cappella track were copied to a metrically even beat, as used in Eminem's production, it would cause strong metrical divergences. In fact, ambivalent pulses also characterize Madlib's arrangement of Madvillain's song, providing the whole track with an experimental texture.[19]

This kind of locally unsteady delivery, which is typical of natural speech, is very common in rap music. The following example shows that speech effusiveness need not to be complex. Note the irregularly placed notes mirroring the microtemporal shifts of Samy Deluxe, one of Germany's finest MCs, while rapping (Example 8.5).[20]

Further directions for flow studies

Further research on flow still has several problems to resolve. In order to cope with microtiming, we need to engage with alternative methods of notating rap music. In rhythm research, it is quite common to work with software for visualizing sound. My first attempts with the software Sonic Visualizer and Praat created a new question: which and where is the perceptible beginning of syllables and – in the case of a consonantal beginning – what contributes most to its accent? Certainly the vowel is of great importance, especially in languages generating stress mainly by pitch like English or German. But of course the consonants cannot be neglected, at least in styles of flow with a crisp, percussive articulation. Besides, questions concerning the measurement of speech rhythms cause controversial discussions for phoneticians and phonologists too. Perhaps we need to differentiate between several types of articulation and consonants, e.g. softer and longer ones vs. shorter and crisper ones, which would afford different types of notation for different types of stress (see Chapter 9 for examples). On the one hand, we probably have to adjust our microconcepts of rhymed and temporally organized syllables with regard to notation, measurement,

Example 8.5 Dynamite Deluxe, "Wie jetzt" (2000), 0:49–0:59, first verse.

and articulatory categorization. On the other hand, we need more close readings of flow, especially with regard to larger entities such as verses or whole songs. This would help us to discuss several interesting issues:

(a) Are certain languages (e.g. those counting syllables, like Spanish, vs. those which count accents, like English) more suitable for certain styles of flow than others? I assume that those languages tending more to isochrony, like Spanish, are better suited for steady styles with crossing pulses. Less isochronous languages, like English, are perhaps more appropriate for speech-effusive rhythms.

(b) Adam Krims proposed a generic model of rap music, which included the classification of flow. With regard both to the globalization of hip-hop cultures and to the impact of languages on flow, we possibly need a more "regionalized" view on hip-hop cultures and their poetics.

(c) Walser, Krims, and Adams have already proposed some detailed examinations of the semantics of rap, focusing on the interrelations of beats, lyrics, and flow.

In this field there is still a lot of research to do, as the close reading of sampling is a desideratum of hip-hop studies, too.[21] Another interesting object of further research are the semantics of onomatopeia, which is used both by early party rap with its scatlike imitations of instruments (Sugar Hill Gang: "Rapper's Delight," 1979) or by reality rappers like Dr. Dre and his featured male and female MCs on "The Chronic" (1992), who strikingly often imitate the sound of gun fire. Moreover, flow and function of a song can coincide, for example in Eminem's "'Till I Collapse," which in many ways is a "letter of application" for inclusion into hip-hop's elite canon of rappers, lyrically praising and musically exemplifying his own extraordinary skills.[22]

(d) The rhythm of rap music seems to me one of the most fascinating aspects of popular music, which could however seduce academics into focusing on aspects which fit their values best. It is easy to fall into the "trap of complexity," overlooking the fact that complex flows are not appreciated by all members of the hip-hop community. Thus, the study of flow needs a corrective. According to three dimensions of flow – production, texture, and reception – it is therefore of utmost importance that we stay in contact with hip-hop artists and fans. Because they are producing the textures and negotiating the concepts of flow we are dealing with.

Flow discography

Absolute Beginner, "Hammerhart," from *Bambule* (Buback/Universal, 1998).
A Tribe Called Quest, "Push It Along," from *People's Instinctive Travels and the Paths of Rhythm* (Jive, 1990).
A Tribe Called Quest feat. Leaders of the New School, *Scenario* (Jive, 1992).
Common, "I Am Music," from *Electric Circus* (MCA, 2002).
Craig Mack feat. the Notorious B.I.G. *et al.*, "Flava in Ya Ear (Remix)," from *Flava in Ya Ear* (Bad Boy Entertainment, 1994).
Dr. Dre, *The Chronic* (Death Row, 1992).
Dynamite Deluxe, "Wie jetzt," from *Deluxe Soundsystem* (Buback/EMI, 2000).
Eminem, "Stan," from *The Marshall Mathers LP* (Aftermath Entertainment/ Interscope, 2000).
    "'Till I Collapse," from *The Eminem Show* (Aftermath Entertainment/Interscope, 2002).
    "Underground," from *Relapse* (Aftermath Entertainment/Interscope, 2009).
Grandmaster Flash and the Furious Five, *The Message* (Sugar Hill, 1982).
IAM, "Le 7," from *Ombre Est Lumiere I* (Delabel, 1993).
KRS-One, "MC's Act Like They Don't Know," from *KRS-One* (Jive, 1995).
Kurtis Blow, *The Breaks* (Mercury, 1982).
Madvillain, "All Caps," from *Madvillainy* (Stones Throw, 2004).
Nas feat. AZ, "Life's A Bitch," from *Illmatic* (Columbia, 1994).
N.W.A., *100 Miles and Runnin'* (Ruthless, 1990).
Public Enemy, *Fight The Power* (Motown, 1989).
Sugar Hill Gang, *Rapper's Delight* (Sugar Hill, 1979).

Further reading

Adams, Kyle, "Aspects of the Music/Text Relationship in Rap," *Music Theory Online* 14/2 (2008). Available at www.mtosmt.org/issues/mto.08.14.2/mto.08.14.2. adams.html.
"On the Metrical Techniques of Flow in Rap Music," *Music Theory Online* 15/5 (2009). Available at www.mtosmt.org/issues/mto.09.15.5/mto.09.15.5.adams. html.
Kautny, Oliver, "Ridin' the Beat. Annäherungen an das Phänomen Flow," in Fernand Hörner and Oliver Kautny (eds.), *Die Stimme im HipHop. Untersuchungen eines intermedialen Phänomens* (Bielefeld: Transcript, 2009), pp. 141–169.
Krims, Adam, *Rap Music and the Poetics of Identity* (Cambridge University Press, 2000).
Williams, Justin A., "Beats and Flows: A Response to Kyle Adams, 'Aspects of the Music/Text Relationship in Rap,'" *Music Theory Online* 15/2 (2009). Available at www.mtosmt.org/issues/mto.09.15.2/mto.09.15.2.williams.html.

Notes

1 Kyle Adams, "Aspects of the Music/Text Relationship in Rap," *Music Theory Online* 14/2 (2008). Available at www.mtosmt.org/issues/ mto.08.14.2/mto.08.14.2.adams.html, paras. 3–5, 42 (accessed June 1, 2014).

2 Cheryl L. Keyes, *Rap Music and Street Consciousness: Music in American Life* (Chicago: University of Illinois Press, 2002), p. 132.

3 Monika Sokol, "Verbal Duelling. Ein universeller Sprachspieltypus und seine Metamorphosen im US-amerikanischen, französischen und deutschen Rap," in Eva Kimminich (ed.), *Rap: More than Words* (Frankfurt: Peter Lang, 2004), pp. 113–160.

4 Elijah Wald, *The Dozens: A History of Rap's Mama* (New York: Oxford University Press, 2012), pp. 183–200. See also Cheryl L. Keyes, "Verbal Art Performance in Rap Music: The Conversation of the 80's," *Folklore Forum* 17/2 (1984): 147.

5 See Oliver Kautny, "Ridin' the Beat. Annäherungen an das Phänomen Flow," in Fernand Hörner and Oliver Kautny (eds.), *No Time for Losers. Charts, Listen und andere Kanonisierungen in der populären Musik* (Bielefeld: Transcript, 2009).

6 See Martin Pfleiderer, *Rhythmus. Psychologische, theoretische und stilanalytische Aspekte populärer Musik* (Bielefeld: Transcript, 2006).

7 See *ibid.* for a broader overview about studies examining rhythm in popular music in general, dealing with research on rhythm in jazz, too.

There is a huge amount of interesting case studies in jazz research examining different aspects of rhythm and meter. See, for example, Matthew W. Butterfield, "Variant Timekeeping Patterns and their Effects in Jazz Drumming," *Music Theory Online* 16 (2010). Available at www.mtosmt.org/issues/mto.10.16.4/mto.10.16. 4.butterfield.html (accessed May 29, 2014).

8 Adams, "Aspects."

9 *Ibid.* In the article, Adams states that the beats are normally produced before the MC flows over it (para. 5), so that "rappers incorporate elements of the sampled drumbeat into the lyrical delivery" (para. 14). This probably occurs very often; nevertheless we have to be aware of the fact, e.g. that at least some rappers deliver the flow to sketches of the beat. Thus, the MC's track is sometimes recorded before other instrumental layers are added to the arrangement; this is how Eminem's productions work. See Paul Tingen, "Eminem & Mike Strange: Not Afraid," *Sound & Recording* 5/12 (2010): 22–26. Given the varied nature of hip-hop compositional process, it is sometimes difficult to judge whether the flow incorporates structures of the beat or vice versa.

10 Adam Krims, *Rap Music and the Poetics of Identity* (Cambridge University Press, 2000), pp. 49–52.

11 Rare metrical variants are the five-beat meter in Eminem's "Underground" (2009) or the seven-beat meter in "Le 7" by the French group IAM (1993).

12 Krims, *Rap Music*, p. 49.

13 Keyes, *Rap Music*, p. 131.
14 *Ibid.*, 127.
15 Krims, *Rap Music*, pp. 58–62.
16 Butterfield, "Variant Timekeeping Patterns," and Pfleiderer, *Rhythmus*, p. 330.
17 As discussed in Kyle Adams, "On the Metrical Techniques of Flow in Rap Music," *Music Theory Online* 15/5 (2009). Available at www.mtosmt.org/issues/mto.09.15.5/ mto.09.15.5.adams.html (accessed May 29, 2014).
18 Pfleiderer, *Rhythmus*, pp. 129–134.
19 Adams, "On the Metrical Techniques."
20 See also Kautny, "Ridin' the Beat."
21 Oliver Kautny and Adam Krims (eds.), "Sampling im HipHop," in *Samples* 9 (2010). Available at http://aspm.ni.lo-net2.de/samples/ 9Inhalt.html (accessed May 29, 2014).
22 Kautny, "Ridin' the Beat."

9 The musical analysis of hip-hop

KYLE ADAMS

The problems of hip-hop analysis

Hip-hop music resists traditional modes of musical analysis more than almost any other genre. The techniques developed for the analysis of Western art music, even when they can provide accurate descriptions of some of hip-hop's surface phenomena, often leave the analyst without a deeper sense of how hip-hop operates and why it seems to communicate so effectively with such a broad audience. And yet there is no question that hip-hop *does* operate according to some set of musical principles: clearly, hip-hop is not a jumble of random sounds, but a collection of sounds and words organized in some deliberate fashion. The organizational principle ought to be knowable, just as it is with more traditional Western repertoires, but none of the current analytical tools seems to be equal to the task.

The reasons for this are directly related to the primary difference between the natures of Western art music and of hip-hop. Music of the eighteenth and nineteenth centuries (and some of the twentieth) is primarily linear: it follows a tonal and emotional trajectory that builds up throughout the work, culminating in either a single climactic moment or a series thereof. If the music is texted, the musical trajectory usually follows that of the poetry.[1] Instrumental music, by contrast, creates expressive trajectories through the employment of well-known harmonic, contrapuntal, and timbral devices.[2] Consequently, most of the techniques developed to analyze Western music were designed to track these sorts of expressive trajectories and to show the ways in which individual musical elements work together to form a coherent whole. These techniques can be placed into four categories:

1   the identification of sonorities, and descriptions of their interactions, often using Roman numerals, pcsets, schemas, or transformational labels;
2   the identification of large-scale structures based on quasi-recursive voice-leading principles, as practiced in Schenkerian analysis;
3   the unlocking of musical meaning via text/music analyses or semiotic approaches;
4   the description of either small- or large-scale formal structures.[3]

Each of these tools allows music analysts to grasp the deeper levels of tonal structure that undergird the musical surface. And they do so because they were designed explicitly to model music that is goal oriented.[4]

The music of hip-hop, by contrast, is cyclical.[5] In a typical hip-hop song, a core drum pattern repeats every measure. Over this, pitched elements of the beat also repeat every measure, or every two or four bars.[6] Other elements – scratches, sampled sounds, synthesizers, and so forth – might come and go throughout the song, but they are dispensable; the character of the song would remain intact even if they were removed.[7] The repetitive beat stays relatively unchanged, at least throughout the verse of a song. If there are changes to the musical layers in the chorus, then the verses and chorus form a larger repetitive cycle, as they do in many other song genres.

Thus, while many rap songs contain familiar harmonies as part of their underlying beats, those harmonies rarely participate in harmonic "progressions." If such progressions are found in the song's beat, they are likely to repeat every one, two, or four bars, which renders them incapable of creating the long-range teleologies for which musical analysts typically search.[8] With hip-hop, analytical techniques such as Roman numeral analysis and Schenkerian voice-leading graphs are therefore unable to do the job they were designed for: to reveal the inner workings of a large-scale pitch structure as it develops over the course of an entire work. Likewise, text/music and semiotic approaches, which depend on showing how text and music work together to create directed narratives, also often find themselves unable to uncover meaningful correspondences in hip-hop. Although such narratives are often present in the lyrics, the fact that they unfold over a circular beat makes it difficult to establish any but the most superficial expressive connections between beat and lyrics. Rappers and producers may work together to ensure a certain amount of affective conformity between the two elements, but the cyclical nature of the beat renders it incapable of mirroring long-range changes in the affective state of the lyrics.[9]

But the problems with applying traditional analysis to hip-hop run even deeper. From the early 1980s through the "golden age" of hip-hop (which ended around 1993), hip-hop beats were created from samples of preexisting recordings.[10] The fact that most of the parameters of the beat were recorded by other artists for other expressive purposes makes it difficult to argue for analytical significance in any affective correspondences among elements of the beat, or between beat and lyrics.[11] For example, consider the beat for "Say No Go" by De La Soul, from their début album *3 Feet High and Rising* (1989), which was produced by Prince Paul (Paul Huston). Among the five sample sources for the song's beat are "I Can't Go For That" by Hall and Oates, which provides the drum and bass elements of the beat (in addition to the titular lyric sample), and "Baby Let Me Take You in My Arms" by the Detroit Emeralds, which provides the recurring guitar riff given in Example 9.1.[12]

Example 9.1 Sampled guitar riff from De La Soul, "Say No Go," recorded on *3 Feet High and Rising*.

The primary harmonic support for this riff in its original setting is a bold, brassy, D major chord, which makes the F naturals of the riff sound like witty, playful blues inflections. But the bass line sample used in "Say No Go" centers on D without being identifiably major or minor. The F naturals in the riff therefore provide a definitive minor-mode context for the bass line (and, thus, the song itself), which robs the riff of most of its formerly light-hearted character. The fact that a sampled sound can take on such dissimilar expressive states depending on its context undermines the idea that expressive musical states somehow inhere in musical figures themselves. Moreover, the guitar riff and the drum and bass patterns come from songs with contradictory lyrics. "I Can't Go for That" warns the song's addressee that the singer is shying away from commitment, while the singer of "Baby Let Me Take You in My Arms" wants to draw his lover in closer. Huston combined these two samples to form the beat for a song warning listeners about the dangers of drug use. That music from two songs with opposing messages can be sampled in a third song with yet another message challenges the notion that specific types of musical figures naturally support specific types of lyrics.

Even after the sample-based aesthetic waned in favor of studio-produced beats, the drum and bass portions of the beat were often replications of typical funk, soul, or R&B patterns; thus, although these beats were not literally sampled, they were borrowed from pre-existing styles (in some cases, even from pre-existing songs).[13] Moreover, hip-hop lyrics themselves are often created independently of the beat; they are composed after or alongside a newly created beat.[14] So the idea of a hip-hop track as a unified artwork, in which beat and lyrics work toward a singular expressive purpose, is undercut by the collage-like production of a typical hip-hop track, in which a patchwork beat supports lyrics that may or may not have been composed for it.

Finally, most Western musical analysis depends in large part on musical notation. That hip-hop is unnotated is not a problem *per se*; many jazz solos and rock songs are unnotated, but their pitch content is easy enough to transcribe. For hip-hop, though, there is as yet no form of transcription that captures both the linear nature of the lyrics and the cyclical nature of the beat.[15] The beat can be notated conventionally, provided we disregard the problems inherent in the transcription of sampled music.[16] But the analyst must choose between notating one iteration of the beat, with instructions to repeat *ad infinitum,* in which case it is difficult to represent the various additions to the beat that happen inconsistently throughout the song, or notating it as we would notate any other musical layer, which obscures its fundamentally repetitive nature.

Hip-hop lyrics are also much more difficult to transcribe than they might seem: at first blush, it would seem easy enough to transcribe them just as one would any other kind of rhythmic chant, perhaps using a percussion-style single staff or a normal five-line staff with x's instead of noteheads (see Example 8.1). But the transcriber is confronted with the surprising amount of subtlety in the rhythmic flow of most rappers. A flow that at first seems to be a steady stream of eighth and sixteenth notes, upon close listening reveals itself to be a complex array of syncopations, "swung" notes, and so forth.[17] Furthermore, although rap lyrics are spoken, rappers still manipulate pitch for expressive purposes, sometimes within single words (Eminem is a prime example of this). The analyst must therefore make certain choices: in the rhythmic domain, he/she must either transcribe the rhythms faithfully, leading to a dense stream of sixty-fourth and even one-hundred-twenty-eighth notes (and tuplet variations thereof), or decide to quantize the rhythm to some degree, thereby gaining clarity of notation but sacrificing the rhythmic intricacy that energizes so much of the music. In the pitch domain, the analyst must likewise choose between a faithful, *Sprechstimme*-style representation of the lyrics, or choose to ignore variations in pitch at the expense of an accurate representation of the flow.[18]

All of the problems outlined above confront any analyst, and as of this writing, none of them has been completely solved; that is, there is not yet a universal analytical method for hip-hop music. Perhaps because of these methodological obstacles, published analytical work on hip-hop remains rather scarce, despite the explosion in the past two decades of musicological and ethnographic approaches.[19] Analytical approaches to hip-hop have therefore been developed in the same ad hoc way that approaches to Western art music were: an analyst wishes to illuminate some aspect of the music, and fashions an analytical apparatus that will allow him/her to do so. I will discuss a few such approaches and conclude with a sample analysis of my own.

Overview of previous approaches

No one has contributed as much to the analysis of hip-hop as Adam Krims; in fact, analytical approaches can productively be divided into "Krims" and "other." His 2000 book *Rap Music and the Poetics of Identity,* a tour de force of hip-hop scholarship, was the first music-theoretical work devoted solely to hip-hop, and it remains central to hip-hop studies. Krims not only developed an analytical approach to hip-hop, but also presented impassioned arguments for a close reading of hip-hop texts, for a reimagining of "music theory" as "musical poetics," and for the importance of attention to the specific times and places in which individual rappers and their works developed.

After laying out his analytical philosophy, Krims explained his genre system for rap music of the 1990s and identified three major categories of flow in rapping. All of this set the stage for a chapter dedicated to a close reading of "The Nigga Ya Love to Hate" by Ice Cube, from the 1990 album *AmeriKKKa's Most Wanted*. This chapter, more than any other, laid the groundwork for future scholarship. Krims analyzed the construction of the song's beat, separating the beat's most fundamental layers from those that were added to it at various points throughout the song. He then coupled this close reading of the beat with a close reading of the lyrics, highlighting both general and specific ways in which the two supported each other.[20]

Krims's work was influential in several respects. First, he established the viability of text/music readings of hip-hop tracks, provided they paid respect to the unique relationship between words and music in the genre. Second, he showed that an analysis of the beat was a necessary precursor to the search for correspondences between beat and flow, given that the beat was often developed independently. Finally, he demonstrated the importance of attention to differences in styles of flow in determining stylistic differences both among rappers and within single songs. Along the way, he hit upon the convention of notating the lyrics in chart form, allowing him both to display them as poetry and to indicate their rhythm.[21]

Other approaches to hip-hop have much in common with Krims's work, examining the relationship of the lyrical flow to the underlying beat. Felicia Miyakawa, in a study that intersects with music theory, musicology, and ethnomusicology, analyzes beat and flow to show how each parameter manifests the "five percent" philosophy shared by many rap artists.[22] Robert Walser and Jeff Greenwald, in musicological and ethnomusicological studies respectively, begin from the premise that the rhythmic, pitch, and expressive content of the beat play at least as big a role in the overall affect of a hip-hop song as do the lyrics.[23] This approach informed my own 2008 article, in which I argued that it was possible to make sense of seemingly impenetrable lyrics by examining their rhythmic, grouping, and motivic correspondences with the beat.[24]

Additionally, many scholars have examined either the beat or the flow independently. Monographs by Joseph Schloss, Mark Katz, and Justin Williams have been devoted to exploring the ramifications of sampling in the creation of hip-hop beats.[25] In particular, they have explored the ways in which the aesthetics of sampling and borrowing demand non-traditional approaches to understanding the musical layers of hip-hop. Recent studies by Amanda Sewell and Christine Boone also provide typologies of sampled sounds and of mashups respectively.[26] All of these studies are, broadly speaking, analytical, although they lie at varying degrees of distance from the narrow construal of "analysis" that I used earlier.[27]

Finally, scholars have also analyzed flow on its own. I will not survey those approaches here, since they form the bulk of Chapter 8. Suffice it to say that scholars have recognized the inherent complexity in the rhyme schemes, rhythmic organization, pitch contours, and articulation of rap lyrics. This last feature has been analyzed least, and the second part of this chapter will therefore provide a heuristic for studying articulation and its effect on the overall expressive state of a rap song. In the spirit of the types of ad hoc analysis I have already described, and having noted the methodological obstacles that hinder attempts at using traditional analytical methods, I present the next section of this chapter in order to demonstrate both a fruitful analysis of rap lyrics and the inherent difference between an analytical approach to hip-hop and other musical genres.

Analysis: articulation and affect

In hip-hop, the sound object and the composition are one: songs exist as recordings, rarely transcribed into musical notation and even more rarely performed from musical notation. As in other popular-music genres, song composition consists of a collaborative process between artists and producers, resulting in a recorded sound product that becomes something like an authoritative text. Listeners usually refer to this as the "original" song, as opposed to any of the various remixes, covers, or live versions that are created from it (although as Theodore Gracyk has pointed out, even the "definitive" recorded version is just one of many instantiations of a song).[28] For listeners, this often means that the timbral properties of both voices and instruments are as fundamental to the composition as the pitches and rhythms they perform. This, too, lies in sharp contrast to Western art music, where the pitches and rhythms themselves, composed prior to performance, form the "real" artwork – Schubert lieder, for example, exist as abstract pieces of music distinct from any one performance. But in popular music, artists' voices are integral to their songs, so that any acculturated listener would immediately recognize a cover performance of a song by Eminem (or Led Zeppelin, or Madonna) and consider it derivative. In hip-hop, which does not employ melody, articulation is one of the defining features of an artist's voice, and as such plays a key role in conveying expressive meaning.

In my 2009 article on flow, I divided the techniques of flow in rap into "metrical" and "articulative" categories.[29] I identified three articulative techniques: the amount of legato or staccato used, the degree of articulation of consonants, and the extent to which the onset of any syllable is before or after the beat. What follows is an attempt to analyze the ways in which the first two of these techniques contribute to the affective state of a rap song.

The focus of this study is on the articulation of English consonants. I will largely ignore vowels, and will also disregard what phonologists refer to as "suprasegmentals," aspects of sounds that belong to larger units like syllables or entire words (these include pitch, speed, stress, intonation, and nasality). I will consider only the way that words are articulated in the finished song, not the reasons for which they might be articulated that way. I will therefore disregard regional dialects, as well as studio techniques used to manipulate the perceived amount of articulation, including microphone placement, level adjustment, and so forth. I take it as given that the articulation of words in the primary recorded version of a song is intentional, regardless of whether it was a natural outgrowth of the rapper's speech or was digitally manipulated.

Articulation alone cannot shoulder the entire burden of creating affective states in hip-hop songs, but can augment the existing affect in two ways. First, vocal articulation can mimic certain types of instrumental articulation that listeners already associate with specific affective states. For example, a *scherzando* instrumental style is associated with a light touch and crisp, staccato articulation, so a rapper who wanted to come across as playful or lighthearted might use a similarly light but crisp vocal articulation. Second, different types of articulation can suggest states of being that lead to those types of articulation. A song about drinking, for instance, might be delivered in the type of slurred, slack-jawed articulation typical of intoxication. But this technique manifests itself in ways more subtle than that, as I will discuss below.

Articulative effects are also independent of the natural articulation of the words. As the following examples will show, dull or voiced consonants, or even vowels, can be articulated staccato, and sharp, voiceless consonants can be articulated legato. Rappers also manipulate the amount and type of articulation by using glottal stops, aspiration, and voicing of consonant sounds.

In order to map out articulative techniques, I have developed a methodology based on Figure 9.1, which was taken from George List's seminal article "The Boundaries of Speech and Song."[30] List's graph measures the amount of pitch stability against the amount of inflection to locate various vocal genres on a set of coordinates defined by *Sprechstimme*, speech, monotone, and song. He then uses the coordinate system to plot vocal forms from around the world. Hip-hop did not exist when List's article was written, but he describes a tobacco auctioneer's delivery as "monotonic chant displaying an increasing number of auxiliary tones," which is also a fairly accurate description of rapping.[31] He locates auctioneering in the southeast quadrant, along the diagonal leading from "monotone" to "song."

Figure 9.2 presents a similar graph for measuring types of articulation in rap. The oppositions measured on the graph are between what I have

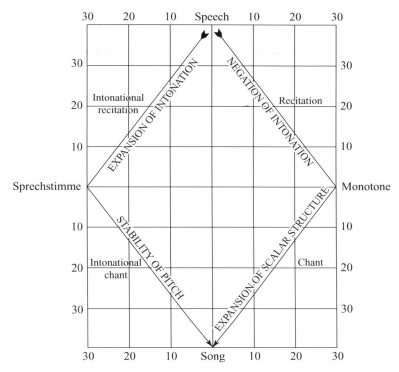

Figure 9.1 George List, diagram from "The Boundaries of Speech and Song," *Ethnomusicology* 7/1 (1963): 1–16.

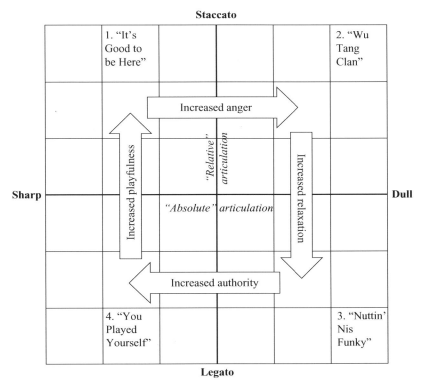

Figure 9.2 Graph of articulation and affective states in rap.

termed "sharp" and "dull" consonant sounds, measured on the x-axis, and the amount of staccato or legato, as measured on the y-axis. I have characterized the difference between the two axes as "absolute" articulation versus "relative" articulation. Absolute articulation refers to how much aspiration is behind the consonant, the extent to which air builds up in the oral cavity before the consonant is articulated. The "sharp" side of this axis has a high degree of emphasis on "stop" consonants, which involve complete closure of whatever articulators are involved – the lips, the tongue and teeth, the tongue and palate, etc. – so that air cannot escape, and a small burst of sound when the consonant is articulated. They are the bilabial /b/ and /p/, dental /d/ and /t/, and the velar (back of the palate) /g/ and /k/.[32] Additionally, on the "sharp" side there is an emphasis on voiceless consonants, and a tendency to change voiced consonants into voiceless ones where possible; a rapper might change a /g/ sound into a /k/ to give his flow an even more clipped, disjunct feel. Finally, sharp articulation includes the use of initial glottal stops, especially before nasal stop consonants like /m/ and /n/, and before initial vowel sounds.[33] The "dull" side of the x-axis comprises the opposite sorts of sounds. Rather than an emphasis on stop consonants, dull articulation emphasizes fricatives, sounds in which air escapes through the lips or teeth. Rappers mostly emphasize labiodental fricatives /f/ and /v/, dental fricatives /th/ (both voiceless ("three") and voiced ("thy")), and the alveolar (part of the palate directly behind the teeth) /s/ and /z/. Also in opposition to sharp articulation, dull articulation tends to emphasize voiced consonants over voiceless ones; this voicing of consonant sounds has the effect of lengthening them.[34]

Relative articulation, on the y-axis, encompasses the extent to which final sounds are held and the ways in which individual phonemes are connected to one another within syllables. It therefore describes the positions of consonant sounds relative to one another and to the vowel sounds. Staccato articulation, at the top, comprises a high degree of alignment between consonant sounds and beats, and a high degree of separation of sounds within and between words. Legato articulation, at the bottom, comprises a fuzzier relationship between syllables and beats, with consonant sounds themselves – especially voiced consonants – elongated so that they are articulated across the beat.

The purpose of this coordinate system is to locate the expressive characteristics of rap songs or verses that arise from different types of articulation. The shaded arrows on the graph indicate the ways in which affective states change with increased usage of various types of articulation. The following section will examine rap verses that typify the types of articulation used in each quadrant, using examples located in each corner to provide the greatest degree of contrast.[35]

The upper-left quadrant combines a high degree of emphasis on sharp consonant sounds with a high degree of staccato. Songs employing this type of articulation tend toward a jocular, playful affect. A typical example is the first verse by Ladybug Mecca (Mary Ann Vieira) from "It's Good to Be Here" by jazz-rappers Digable Planets, from their 1993 debut album *Reachin' (A New Refutation of Time and Space)*. Ladybug does not, by herself, create the playful affect of the song: the verses, which tell a fanciful story of the rappers traveling from outer space to bring "the funk" to earth, are delivered over a leisurely major-mode sample that lays the foundation for her buoyant delivery:

> …and it's good to be here **ge**tt̲in' fly with the ra*ps*
>
> we love it where we from, but we *kick* it where we a̲t
>
> **b**umpin' out with somethin' that *pops* and transcends
>
> *D.P.*'s baby it's sli**m** but not thi**n**
>
> i̲n amongst the *p*ebbles we ro*ck*s on your blo*ck*s
>
> soa*k*in' in the **g**hetto for *k*ids that have not
>
> slappin' on some s*k*in when we slam che*ck* the cheers
>
> so we **g**reet their virgin ears with a *k*iss

> (**bold**=voiced consonant made voiceless, u̲nderline=glottal stop, *italics*=aspirated stop consonant)

Figure 9.3 "Playful" articulation: Digable Planets, "It's Good to Be Here," Ladybug Mecca's verse (1:40–2:00), recorded on *Reachin' (A New Refutation of Time and Space)*. Pendulum Records, 1993. 9 61414–2.

Ladybug Mecca employs several "sharp" techniques to reinforce the cheerful nature of the beat and lyrics. She emphasizes aspirated stop consonants, italicized in the example. These consonants are emphasized at both the beginnings and endings of words, detaching them from one another. Also, she either de-emphasizes voiced consonants or turns them into voiceless ones. Some examples of this are in boldface in the example. The /b/ in "bumpin'" and the /g/ in "ghetto" are turned into a staccato /p/ and /k/ respectively. When she employs voiced consonants in which it is impossible to make this change, like /m/ and /n/ of "slim" and "thin" in the fourth line, she clips them off quickly to achieve the same staccato articulation. Finally, she also employs glottal stops to create breaks either within or before words. The most notable examples are underlined; these include the two /t/ sounds in "gettin'" and the initial vowels of "in" and "at."

Moving rightward on Figure 9.2, rappers use the same degree of detachment between words, but with an emphasis on voiced and fricative consonant sounds. This type of flow, which features a series of long, voiced sounds separated from one another at unpredictable intervals, is unsettling for the listener, and as a result the playfulness of the upper-left quadrant disappears in favor of a more chaotic flow suitable for angry lyrics. A classic example is the verse by the RZA (Robert Diggs) from "Wu-Tang Clan Ain't Nuttin' ta Fuck Wit'," from the Wu-Tang Clan's 1993 album *Enter the Wu-Tang (36 Chambers)*. Even without hearing the "dirty" beat and thumping minor-mode sample, a quick scan of the lyrics reveals a much different expressive state than that of Ladybug Mecca's verse:

> Give up, there's
> no pla**c**e to hi*de* as I **s**tep in**s**i*de* the
> room. Dr. Doom – prepare for the boom.
> BAM! Aw—man! I
> SLAM, jam, and scream like Tarzan! I be
> tos**s**in', enforcin', my **s**tyle is awesome. I'm
> causin' more Family Feu*ds* than Richard Dawson
> and the **s**urvey **s**ai*d*—you're *d*ea*d*
> Fatal Flying Guillotine chop**s** off your fuckin' hea*d*
> MZA who was that? Hey yo, the Wu is back
> makin' niggas go BO BO!, like on Super Cat
> Me fear no one, oh no, here come the
> Wu-Tang **sh**ogun, killer to the ear**dru**m[i]

> (**bold**=fricative sound, underline=voiced consonant, *italics*=suppressed final consonant)

---

[i] With this verse and all the others in this chapter, I have transcribed the lyrics so that each line matches one measure of music. In the RZA's verse, this leads to some odd-looking semantic breaks, such as the break between "the" and "room" from line 2 to line 3.

Figure 9.4 "Angry" articulation: "Wu Tang Clan Ain't Nuttin' ta Fuck Wit'," The RZA's verse (0:14–0:43), recorded on *Enter the Wu-Tang (36 Chambers)*. Loud Records, 1993. 07863–66336–4.

The RZA often raps with a lisp in order to foreground the fricative sounds that typify dull articulation, highlighted in bold in the example. Also in opposition to Ladybug Mecca's sharp articulation is RZA's emphasis on voiced sounds like the /b/ of "Bo! Bo!," underlined in the example. He often obliterates final consonants altogether, essentially ending a word with its last vowel and expecting the listener to mentally fill in the rest. This technique, italicized in the example, is used throughout the verse, but appears most obviously in the second line, on the words "hide" and "inside."

RZA creates an artificial staccato despite the use of so many dull sounds. For example, in the fourth line the natural articulation of the words "Bam aw man I slam" would be legato. A rapper who wanted to make this line staccato would do so with glottal stops and aspiration, which would enable him/her to keep the pitch relatively stable, but still to articulate each word independently. The RZA, who avoids those kinds of "sharp" techniques, instead detaches the words by suppressing initial and final consonants, and inserting silence between successive words. This gives most of his syllables and monosyllabic words a swell up to the vowel sound, followed by a drop-off after it. The only way to achieve this kind of flow – a staccato flow that de-emphasizes stop consonants – is to push the air out forcibly from the diaphragm. Such a manner of speaking accents individual syllables and produces an extreme amount of pitch variability, and also typifies angry speech or shouting, which explains the RZA's use of this type of flow here.

Continuing to the lower-right quadrant of Figure 9.2 increases the level of relaxation in the lyrics. It does so by employing the types of facial movements typical of a state of extreme relaxation: slack jaw, relaxed lips and tongue, and slow, deep breaths. A typical verse in this quadrant is the first verse by Big Money Odis (Odis Brackens III) from "Nuttin' Nis Funky" by Digital Underground, on their 1991 EP release *This is an EP Release*. Even the title of the song, with its intentional misspelling of "this," has the same exaggerated degree of legato that saturates each of the verses:

> You ain't heard
> nuttin' ni**s funky** *b*rother, it'**s** like no other
> you feel the *b*a**ss** *b*ouncin' off the wall**s** like ru*b*ber
> the real McCoy thi**s** ain't no toy or ano**th**er
> how *d*o we *d*o it? [Yo go ask your mother]. The
> freak needers, the beat leaders, let me tell you
> **s**ome**th**ing, you ain't heard nuttin' thi**s f**unky Peter
> so li**s**ten up as we *b*egin. Hey yo,
> **F**uze, ru*b* the record in. 'Cause you ain't heard
> nuttin' nis funky

> (**bold**=fricative sound, *italics*= voiced stop consonant de-emphasized/ turned into a fricative)

Figure 9.5 "Relaxed" articulation: Digital Underground, "Nuttin' Nis Funky," Big Money Odis's verse (1:01–1:24), recorded on *This is an EP Release*. Tommy Boy Records, 1991. TBEP 964.

Like the RZA, Big Money Odis emphasizes fricative sounds, highlighted here in bold. But although he shows no preference for voiced or voiceless fricatives – or rather, articulates them all the same way – he seems to relish the voiced stop consonants, nearly turning them into fricatives wherever possible. These are italicized in the example. This is clearest in the words "bass bouncin'" in the third line, where Odis relaxes his lips and cheeks to the point where they barely stop the airflow at all. A rapper aiming for a more playful affect would probably aspirate these /b/ sounds or change each one into a /p/, but as Odis articulates them, they become minor interruptions in an almost continuous flow of air. As with the RZA's verse, all of the techniques that Odis uses conjure up certain facial or bodily awarenesses in the listener: the only way to articulate them as he does is with an extreme degree of relaxation in the facial muscles.

Lastly, moving into the lower-left quadrant of Figure 9.2 finds a legato but sharp articulation, used for authoritative, lecturing, or preachy lyrics. This is found in the last verse of "You Played Yourself" by Ice-T (Tracy Marrow), from his 1990 album *Freedom of Speech . . . Just Watch What You Say*:

> You got problems, you *c*laim you need a <u>b</u>rea*k*,
> but every dollar you get you <u>t</u>a*ke*
> straight to the <u>d</u>opeman, trying to get a <u>b</u>eam u*p*
> Your idle time is <u>s</u>pent tryin' to scheme u*p*
> another way to <u>g</u>et money for a jumbo
> When you go to sleep, you *c*ount five-ohs
> Lyin' and cheati*n'*, every<u>b</u>ody you're beati*n'*, dirty
> clothes and you're <u>s</u>kinny, '*c*ause you haven't <u>b</u>een eati*n'*
> You ripped off all your family and your friends,
> nowhere does your larceny e**n**d
> And then you <u>g</u>et an idea for **a** big mo*ve*,
> An armed robbery, smoo*th*.
> <u>B</u>ut everything went wrong, somebody <u>g</u>ot shot
> You couldn't <u>g</u>et away, the cops roll you're <u>popp</u>ed
> and now you're locked, yo, lampin' on death row
> Society's fault? No.
> Nobody <u>p</u>ut the crack into the <u>pi</u>*pe*
> Nobody made you smo<u>k</u>e off your li*fe*
> You thought that you <u>c</u>ould <u>d</u>o <u>d</u>ope and still stay <u>c</u>ool?
> <u>F</u>ool.

> (**bold**=glottal stop, <u>underline</u>=aspirated consonant,
> *italics*=suppression of final consonant)

Figure 9.6 "Authoritative" articulation: Ice-T, "You Played Yourself," last verse (3:14–4:02), recorded on *The Iceberg: Freedom of Speech . . . Just Watch What You Say.* Sire/Warner Bros., 1989. 9 26028–2.

A legato flow would seem incompatible with the emphasis on stop consonants that characterizes sharp articulation. But Ice-T achieves a synthesis of the two by drawing out vowels and other voiced sounds until he reaches a stop consonant, which he aspirates sharply. The result is a fairly constant stream of sound punctuated by aspirations, which are underlined in the example. Ice-T also tends to change voiced consonants, especially b's, into voiceless ones, although not quite to the extent that Ladybug Mecca does. Note that the /f/ in the final word "Fool" is also italicized as a stop consonant, despite the fact that, phonologically speaking, this is incorrect. But Ice-T closes his lips and teeth so tightly in articulating the /f/ that the result is a stop-consonant-like burst when he releases the pressure off his lower lip, and the sound becomes a *de facto* stop consonant. Additionally, he employs initial glottal stops on vowel sounds, which further creates the effect of every word beginning with a sharp burst of air. The most significant of these are highlighted in bold.

Even with this emphasis on stop consonants, Ice-T still creates a legato flow by drawing out the ends of words as long as possible; to that end, he often obliterates final consonant sounds, or lets final voiced sounds trail off as long as possible. I have italicized instances of this technique, which is especially prevalent at the ends of lines. Whereas the RZA de-emphasized both initial and final consonants, giving each word an unsettling "hairpin" dynamic, Ice-T explodes the initial consonant and de-emphasizes the final one. Many of these final underlined consonants are in fact completely inaudible (e.g. the nonexistent /p/ sounds in "beam up" and "scheme up" at the ends of lines 3 and 4). Like other kinds of articulative techniques, Ice-T's flow contributes to the affective state of the verse by recalling, in the listener's mind, when that sort of articulation is often used. I characterize this as "authoritative" articulation, since the sharp initial sound followed by a decrescendo into the final sound is commonly heard in oration and preaching.[36]

The system presented in Figure 9.2 is only a first step in formalizing the relationship between articulation and affect in rap. It is intended not as a fully worked-out system for analyzing the articulative techniques of flow, but rather as a framework for developing such a system – and more importantly, as an illustration of an analytical model drawn from musical phenomena inherent in rap music, rather than one imported from another repertoire. The figure only has four songs on it, but by providing extreme examples of each type, I hope to have facilitated the reader's ability to plot other songs and styles, which will naturally lead to greater refinement of both the figure and of the concepts that inform it. Ideally, a third dimension to the graph would plot pitch, which necessarily forms a crucial part of any study of articulation. Studies of affective states always involve subjective judgments, of course, and judgments about vocal articulation can also depend on individual perception. But correlating one with the other will begin to bridge the gap between subjective and objective phenomena, and more importantly, will help incorporate the analysis of recorded sound into music analysis in general.

The musical analysis of hip-hop, like any other repertoire, depends on the identification of the salient features of that repertoire and the development of an appropriate methodology for exploring and explaining those features. The methodological obstacles presented in the first part of this chapter are only obstacles if one insists on analyzing hip-hop using pre-existing techniques. I would not claim to have surmounted all of those obstacles, but rather to have circumvented them. Our analytical goals remain the same as ever: to understand something about the inner workings of a musical repertoire, and to understand how that repertoire communicates to listeners. For hip-hop music, the identification of vocal articulation as a key element of that communication helped to unlock an analytical approach that parsed the various kinds of articulation and the types of expression they communicated. Given enough time and critical distance, it will no doubt be possible to use analyses of articulation in conjunction with others to work toward a coherent picture of the genre as a whole. I look forward to a time when such a unified analytical approach to hip-hop music will render the first part of this chapter obsolete.

Notes

1 One could name virtually any non-strophic art song as an example, but Richard Strauss's celebrated Lied "Allerseelen" is a particularly clear case.
2 All of these are at work, for example, in the last movement of Mozart's Jupiter symphony.
3 Although theories of form typically describe events on the musical surface, they often have an aspect of goal orientation to them as well, with analysts speaking of the fulfillment or achievement of a certain formal goal. For example, regarding sonata form, Hepokoski and Darcy describe the essential structural closure as "the goal toward which the entire sonata-trajectory has been aimed" and describe the movement itself as "driv[ing] through vectored sequences of energized events toward a clearly determined, graspable goal." See James Hepokoski and Warren Darcy, *Elements of Sonata Theory: Norms, Types, and Deformations in the Late-Eighteenth-Century Sonata* (Oxford University Press, 2006), pp. 232 and 242.
4 This is not to say that Western art music does not employ repetition; quite the contrary. But such repetition serves a much different purpose than it does in hip-hop. Ostinato patterns, the closest analogue to hip-hop beats, typically serve to highlight improvisational (or quasi-improvisational) flights of fancy. The point of the ostinato, however, is always to provide a backdrop for the solo music. Hip-hop is unique

in that the repetitive, cyclical beat is itself a locus of musical expression, for some listeners at least as important as the lyrics.
5 The cyclical beat patterns underlying many West African musics have been amply noted in the scholarly literature, and the repetitive beat of hip-hop songs is commonly thought to originate in these patterns. Olly Wilson describes these musical practices in a description of an Ewe social dance: "As is customary in West African music, the ensemble is divided into . . . a fixed rhythmic section consisting of instruments whose basic rhythmic patterns are maintained essentially unchanged throughout the duration of the piece and a variable rhythmic section consisting of instruments whose rhythmic patterns change in the course of a piece." See Olly Wilson, "The Significance of the Relationship between Afro-American Music and West African Music," *The Black Perspective in Music* 2/1 (1974): 9. Keyes connects rap practices even more explicitly to West African bardic traditions; see Cheryl L. Keyes, *Rap Music and Street Consciousness: Music in American Life* (Chicago: University of Illinois Press, 2002), pp. 20–21.
6 I use the term "beat" in the way that hip-hop practitioners do, to indicate all non-vocal layers of the song.
7 Krims, in his discussion of the Bomb Squad's production techniques, was the first to

differentiate between essential and non-essential layers of the beat, calling the former "configurations" and dividing the latter category into "upbeats" and "adjuncts." See Adam Krims, *Rap Music and the Poetics of Identity* (Cambridge University Press, 2000), pp. 98ff.

8 As Schloss pointed out, "the looping aesthetic . . . creat[ed] a radically new way of making music. As breaks are torn from their original context and repeated, they are reconceived . . . as circular, even if their original harmonic or melodic purposes were linear. The end of a phrase is juxtaposed with the beginning in such a way that the listener begins to anticipate the return of the beginning as the end approaches." See Joseph Schloss, *Making Beats: The Art of Sample-Based Hip-Hop* (Middletown, CT: Wesleyan University Press, 2004), p. 33.

9 Manabe discussed the collaborative nature of beat production at length in a paper presented at the 2010 meeting of the Society for Music Theory (Noriko Manabe, "The Role of the Producer in Hip-Hop: An Ethnographic and Analytical Study of Remixes," paper presented at the Annual Meeting of the Society for Music Theory, November 4–7, 2010, Indianapolis, IN).

10 Justin A. Williams, in his monograph on borrowing in hip-hop, put it best: "[T]he fundamental element of hip-hop culture and aesthetics is the overt use of pre-existing material to new ends." See Justin A. Williams, *Rhymin' and Stealin': Musical Borrowing in Hip-Hop* (Ann Arbor: University of Michigan Press, 2013), p. 1. Williams's central thesis is that borrowing manifests itself not just in the use of sampled music to create new beats, but in all aspects of word, sound, and image used by rappers.

11 Sinnreich notes the difficulty that musicians, music executives, and scholars have in understanding what sort of activity sampling is, let alone how it transforms the expressive states of the sampled works into that of the new work: "Sampling isn't 'taking,' because the source material is still available, intact, in its original form. It's not 'borrowing,' because the sampler doesn't ever return the work, except in a holistic sense. It's not 'quoting,' because (a) it's the mediated expression itself, not merely the ideas behind it, that's being used, and (b) the output often bears little or no resemblance to the input." See Aram Sinnreich, *Mashed Up: Music, Technology, and the Rise of Configurable Culture* (Amherst and Boston: University of Massachusetts Press, 2010), p. 124.

12 The other three samples are "I'm Chief Kamanawanalea (We're the Macadamia Nuts)" by the Turtles (drum beat), "Crossword Puzzle"

by Sly Stone (brass), and "Best of My Love" by the Emotions ("ah" vocals).

13 Williams cites Dr. Dre in particular for his use of session musicians to replicate funk sounds in his production. See *Rhymin' and Stealin'*, pp. 87ff.

14 The order in which hip-hop tracks are composed has been the subject of much scholarly discussion; in particular, the question of whether the lyrics are composed before, after, or independently of the beat. The most common model – as described in Manabe, "The Role of the Producer," and confirmed in my own discussions with rappers Freddie Gibbs, Josh Martinez, and Das Racist – is for some version of the basic beat to be composed first, at which point the rapper either writes suitable lyrics to it or uses pre-existing ones that seem to fit well, whereupon the producer may add additional layers to complement the lyrics. See Kyle Adams, "Aspects of the Music/Text Relationship in Rap," *Music Theory Online* 14/2 (2008). Available at www.mtosmt.org/issues/mto.08.14.2/mto.08.14.2.adams.html (accessed March 15, 2014); Manabe, "The Role of the Producer," and Justin A. Williams, "Beats and Flows: A Response to Kyle Adams," *Music Theory Online* 15/2 (2009). Available at www.mtosmt.org/issues/mto.09.15.2/mto.09.15.2.williams.html (accessed March 15, 2014).

15 The previous chapter demonstrated many different styles of notation that have been developed for hip-hop analysis.

16 For an excellent discussion of the pitfalls of transcription with regard to hip-hop analysis, see Schloss, *Making Beats*, pp. 12–15.

17 To date, the most detailed examination of the subtleties of syllable placement within beat subdivisions has been done by Mitchell Ohriner in a 2013 paper presentation: Mitchell Ohriner, "Groove, Variety, and Disjuncture in the Rap of Eminem, André 3000, and Big Boi," paper presented at the Annual Meeting of the Society for Music Theory, October 31 to November 3, 2013, Charlotte, NC.

18 To my knowledge, the only scholar to attempt a *Sprechstimme*-style notation was Christopher Segall, in 2009 (Christopher Segall, "Rap and Sprechstimme: Analyzing the Pitch Content of Hip-Hop," paper presented at the Annual Meeting of Music Theory Midwest, May 15–16, 2009, Minneapolis, MN). All other hip-hop analysts that I know of essentially ignore subtle fluctuations in pitch.

19 I am construing "analysis" narrowly here, in the usual music-theoretical sense of manipulating notes, rhythms, and so forth, in order to reveal something about the inner

workings of a piece of music. I realize that musicological, ethnomusicological, and sociocultural studies represent other types of analysis, but I believe that readers will understand the sense in which I use the word here.

20 Krims characterized his analysis as "an attempt to observe . . . a 'patterned context' in action, creating Ice Cube's black revolutionary identity" (*Rap Music*, p. 97). After an analysis of the lyrics and a close reading of the beat, he spends the bulk of the chapter demonstrating the ways in which the Bomb Squad's production projects this identity (see pp. 111–122).

21 Krims first writes out the lyrics as lines of verse, then draws a four-beat grid in which individual syllables appear as X's. In my own work, I have adapted Krims's notation by showing the actual syllables in the grid.

22 Felicia Miyakawa, *Five Percenter Rap: God Hop's Music, Message, and Black Muslim Mission* (Bloomington, IN: Indiana University Press, 2005). The Five Percent Nation is a breakaway group from the Nation of Islam, whose theology, as Miyakawa describes it, comprises "an idiosyncratic mix of black nationalist rhetoric, Kemetic (ancient Egyptian) symbolism, Gnosticism, Masonic mysticism, and esoteric numerology" (p. 23).

23 Robert Walser, "Rhythm, Rhyme, and Rhetoric in the Music of Public Enemy," *Ethnomusicology* 39/2 (1995): 193–217; Jeff Greenwald, "Hip-Hop Drumming: The Rhyme May Define, but the Groove Makes You Move," *Black Music Research Journal* 22/2 (2002): 259–271.

24 Adams, "Aspects."

25 See Schloss, *Making Beats*; Williams, *Rhymin' and Stealin'*; and Mark Katz, *Capturing Sound: How Technology Has Changed Music* (Berkeley: University of California Press, 2010).

26 See Amanda Sewell, "A Typology of Sampling in Hip-Hop" (Ph.D. dissertation, Indiana University, 2013); and Christine Boone, "Mashing: Toward a Typology of Recycled Music," *Music Theory Online* 19/3 (2013). Available at www.mtosmt.org/issues/mto.13.19.3/mto.13.19.3.boone.php (accessed March 15, 2014).

27 See n. 19.

28 Gracyk argues that there is in fact no such thing as the "actual" rock song, only different recorded or live representations of the song's quasi-platonic form (Theodore Gracyk, *Rhythm and Noise: An Aesthetics of Rock* (Durham, NC: Duke University Press, 1996) p. 17. Thomas Robinson, having come to the same conclusion, proposes a methodology by which one can arrive at some idealized version of a song by "averaging" out its various performances. Thomas Robinson, "Singer and Song: Core Components in Jimmy Webb's 'Didn't We,'" *Popular Music* 33/2 (2014): 315–336.

29 Kyle Adams, "On the Metrical Techniques of Flow in Rap Music," *Music Theory Online* 15/5 (2009). Available at www.mtosmt.org/issues/mto.09.15.5/mto.09.15.5.adams.html (accessed March 15, 2014).

30 List, "The Boundaries of Speech and Song."

31 *Ibid.*, p. 11.

32 I have adopted IPA notation when referring to sounds rather than letters, thus, I will refer to "the letter b" but "the sound /b/" (as in the first sound of "button").

33 One of the clearest examples of a glottal stop is in the way most Americans pronounce the word "button": the two "t"s are articulated by using the glottis to close off the throat, rather than by touching the tongue to the palate.

34 All of the phonological terminology in this article was taken from Peter Ladefoged, *A Course in Phonetics*, 3rd edn. (New York: Harcourt Brace Jovanovich, 1993). My great thanks to Rachael Frush Holt for her guidance in this area.

35 As of this writing, the four songs discussed in this section are all available on Youtube and at Grooveshark. Youtube links are as follows: "It's Good to Be Here," www.youtube.com/watch?v=lyGy0ODCutE; "Wu-Tang Clan Ain't Nuttin' ta Fuck Wit'," www.youtube.com/watch?v=88jr9QUxbcs; "Nuttin' Nis Funkey," www.youtube.com/watch?v=wvBZEp4HTmY; "You Played Yourself," www.youtube.com/watch?v=v7djYYE63Ug. The timings given in the examples are for the official album versions of each song; these may differ slightly from those found online.

36 Another example, familiar to rap audiences, is the sample of Thomas "TNT" Todd's speech used at the beginning of Public Enemy's "Fight the Power" (1989).

10 The glass: hip-hop production

CHRIS TABRON

Mary's *magic*... that's just the genius of what she is. With someone like that, you're just trying to let her do her thing. And stay the hell out of the way. (TONY MASERATI ON MARY J. BLIGE'S *MY LIFE* (1994))[1]

There was a time when you had to dig. Dig in, dig it, or just plain *dig* to earn your chops. Among hip-hop DJs, digging meant paying dues by plowing through the used stacks and dollar-bins at secondhand stores – "looking for the perfect beat" as Afrika Bambaataa would put it. A generation prior, "to dig" had a more euphemistic meaning in Black American vernacular: to have a deep, perhaps even unspoken and empathetic understanding.[2] Both euphemistic and literal expressions of digging resonate deeply within modes of Black musical kinship, or to put it colloquially: real heads know the deal.

Yet the current historical moment has taught us that digging now happens in quicker bursts. One can become conversant in a niche subculture in an afternoon of internet research, and the time it takes to learn a new piece of technology can often outweigh the time it takes to engineer its replacement. Modes of music distribution have evolved with new technologies, and what was once the mainstream can now be better understood as a polystream. As many twentieth-century science fiction writers once imagined, technology has led the charge in decentralizing old modes of education, production, and dissemination. Real heads, it would seem, abound.

So too goes the arc of the modern recording process. Around the time hip-hop musicians started using recording studios to make their music, digital technology was in its initial stages. Digital samplers, synthesizers, and MIDI were first being used with analogue multi-track tape machines and "state of the art" meant merely a few seconds of sampling capability. Now, computers dominate the recording and production process, and fully operable "virtual studios" have been condensed into laptop size only occasionally to find their perch on top of a vintage recording console – new cities built upon the bones of the old. Yet, as the trajectory of technological advancement has shown, even this cutting-edge image will one day seem like an archaic approach to music-making. Consequently, any quantitative study of hip-hop production – particularly one confined to the pages of a book – is destined to be outdated by the very subject of its analysis. At best, these studies can seem prophetic, and though we may try, these pages will never really turn fast enough.

Thus, this chapter seeks to provide a cursory outline of hip-hop production techniques, predominantly their foundations and trajectories, and to provide a more qualitative look at how such techniques influenced social, cultural, and physical spaces both inside and outside of the recording studio. To this end, I will investigate how various modes of listening engage one another in the recording studio, and focus on the innovative ways in which music producers have correlated sound with sentiment, converging upon the intersection of Black performance, aurality, and technology. These auralities will be used as an interpretive key for understanding how sounds and discourses are enmeshed in the social uses to which music has been applied. That is to say, the task at hand shifts focus from what hip-hop production is toward a better understanding of what hip-hop production does. I will more specifically use an analysis of Mary J. Blige's *My Life* as an exemplary work that emerges from the 1990s' hip-hop/R&B tradition, and examine how the work of the album's engineer, Tony Maserati, was congruent with its sonic and social viability.

The present work focuses particularly upon New York City as a central point of analysis, as well as the decade of 1989 to 1999, to argue that the repertoire of hip-hop music has been shaped by the discursive role of technology and by the listening practices of audio engineers, producers, DJs, and audiences. Hip-hop music during the period in question is particularly suited for an examination of how technology informs listening practices. It is a genre that has been enabled by the exponential growth in music technologies during the 1980s and 1990s. Aided by advances in digital sampling and drum machines, hip-hop and music technology grew in parallel to one another. New technology enabled different approaches to performing "liveness" in a studio, and artists and their needs also influenced new technical advances. For example, Akai's MIDI Production Center (MPC) sampler had just been released in 1988,[3] enabling playback of any sampled sound triggered by rubberized pads; musicians/producers could now manipulate and play an entire drum kit with their fingertips. Furthermore, sounds could be played chromatically across the pads, allowing for the pitch of a sample to be manipulated as well.

Advances in technology such as the MPC were originally inspired by the live performances that DJs gave in public spaces. A dexterous musician, the DJ performed the convergence of two sonic events (using two turntables) that would move crowds to the beat (see Chapter 4 in this volume). These performing technicians engineered – and often *reverse* engineered – what Black music signified, becoming performers of space, and place, cultivating a sound that became an aural imprint of irrefutable presence. They listened to records and audiences and publicly defined their listening practices at the convergence of both. Because of their beginnings in repurposing extant recordings into new ones – in reanimating the object into a subject – hip-hop records distill listening practices (and the intricate human emotions associated with them) into morsels of stored affect. Hip-hop records are a chronicle to the relationships and technical virtuosity of DJs, producers, and audio engineers creating side by side in studios where – for the first time – all of the musical choices were made in the control room "behind the glass."

I will focus on the period 1989 to 1999 for several reasons. First, it was a decade in which an enormous body of seminal hip-hop records were produced. Second, many current practices of hip-hop and of music production closely parody what happened two decades ago.[4] In 1989, technological advances in musical equipment redefined what could be achieved both inside and outside of a studio setting, and redefined what liveness meant. As Joseph Schloss discusses in *Making Beats*, the implementation of the digital sampler also facilitated the transfer of a live hip-hop performance's aural effects to recorded music:

> although playing a popular funk record at a hip-hop show made sense, playing a popular funk record *on a record* did not. It seemed strange (not to mention illegal) to release recordings that consisted primarily of other records. Early hip-hop labels, such as Sugar Hill, therefore relied on live bands and drum machines to reproduce the sounds that were heard in Bronx parks and Harlem recreation centers.[5]

Third, the decade of the 1990s was a time when the CD was at the height of its salability, with million-selling CDs by rock artists like Dire Straits and David Bowie creating so much revenue for record companies that they were inclined to invest in hip-hop.[6] Finally, 1989 saw the release of albums by De La Soul, Ice-T, and DJ Jazzy Jeff and the Fresh Prince that were a sonic departure from the dance-oriented hip-hop of the early 1980s.

The process of making records has always been one steeped in technological intervention, particularly with the advent of electrical and magnetic tape recording in the latter half of the twentieth century. The technology used in recording at professional studios serves to animate artistic vision, to actualize the abstract. At a lexical level, the terminologies used by engineers and creative professionals in the recording studio have evolved into an amalgam of esoteric electrical jargon and synaesthetic descriptors. At a social level, the most technologically advanced studios were often the most expensive, and thus the most exclusive. For artists to have access to a New York studio like Green Streets, the Hit Factory, Chung King, or any other large facility, they usually had to go through a record label for funding.

In light of all this, it is crucial to engage technology in two ways: (1) as a touchstone of access, and (2) as creative device. Despite the increasing affordability of technology, there are nonetheless lines drawn between who has access to certain technology, and who has access to the training/education necessary to learn how to operate it. The audio engineering world was traditionally a closely guarded fraternity, predominantly populated by white men, who usually came from middle-class backgrounds.[7] Furthermore, audio engineers are taught – and often perpetuate – strong tendencies to follow tradition. Tasks as complicated as placing microphones around an orchestra, or as mundane as storing boxes of magnetic tape, all emerge from a traditional sense of pragmatism that many engineers possess. Unless apprentices or interns had been properly initiated into the bookkeeping, cleaning, daily maintenance, client relations, and running of errands that are required to run a studio, they were traditionally not permitted access to the recording equipment. This is a process that discourages far more potential engineers than it promotes.

It has also been tradition among engineers, especially the more successful ones, to break with tradition altogether. An engineer like Atlantic Records' Tom Dowd is cited by many present-day engineers as a seminal figure because of the many ways he utilized multi-track recording, developed what would become the modern level fader on a mixing desk, and established mixing as a *separate* part of the recording process.[8] Yet for all of his accomplishments, Tom Dowd's biggest achievement was a paradigmatic one: he refused to be an invisible engineer sitting stoically behind a mixing console. By the end of the 1960s, recording technology had emerged in a way that allowed the recording process to happen a lot faster than before. Engineers now had *time* to experiment with different sounds, to make mistakes in doing so, and to begin to move their bodies around this cavernous and intricate instrument called the recording studio. The introduction of hip-hop music into the recording studio is grounded in this paradigm shift, and this historical moment framed engineers as performers and artists themselves, and a generative theory of technology, aurality, and identity will necessarily emerge from the complications that arise from considering them as such.[9]

Any analysis of hip-hop engineering practice should acknowledge the contribution of the DJ in shaping the genre. Numerous authors have previously discussed the central role of the hip-hop DJ as a musical tastemaker.[10] However, I would like to extend this long-established notion and consider the DJ as a model for subsequent hip-hop engineering techniques as well as a figure who conveyed affect through the manipulation of sounds. As we will see, the abilities that were needed to be a good hip-hop engineer or producer in the 1990s were quite similar to the criteria by which effective DJs were defined.

At a general level, what a good DJ (of any genre) is able to do is control mood and/or vibe. Radio DJs do so with theme-based playlists, deliberate use of elocution during their air breaks, and playing a combination of records that are classics, not-yet-released singles, or obscure and oft-forgotten album cuts. The radio DJ's reach is enhanced by the ability to contribute to the shared experiential listening of a large number of people. Thus, the technology of broadcasting itself facilitates the experience of hearing your favorite song on the radio, and feeling a shared sense of memory with the few hundred thousand people listening to that same song at the same time. The party DJ – the most direct ancestor of the hip-hop DJ – has a smaller domain of influence, but also a more direct relationship with his constituents. To control the vibe of a room, hip-hop and other dance music DJs need to be able to instantly translate the intangible feeling of a room into knowing what record to put on or that it's time to acknowledge the crowd over the microphone. Sometimes a good DJ enhances the feeling, at other times he changes it altogether.

As Brewster and Broughton's *Last Night a DJ Saved My Life* has pointed out, the hip-hop DJ is indebted to the disco DJ who was particularly adept at keeping people dancing.[11] Hip-hop's musical presence in the social spaces of the Bronx was largely a response to the ways in which disco clubs operated. Combined with an influence from Jamaican dub tradition led by DJ Kool Herc, hip-hop DJs worked to keep people dancing as well as to create a feeling of excitement by playing the extended rhythm section breaks of records through massive speakers. Herc can be thought of as a seminal engineer of the hip-hop sound because he focused on both the massiveness of his sound as well as the clarity. Thus, audiences were able to hear their favorite recordings in a new way, as DJ Grand Wizzard Theodore says:

> It made you listen to a record and made you appreciate the record even more. He would play a record that you listened to every day and you would be like "Wow, that record has *bells* in it?" It's like you heard instruments in the record that you never thought the record even had. And the bass was like WHUMM!, incredible![12]

From this vantage point it's easy to see what a producer like Puffy[13] does as similar to the work of a good DJ. His instinct for the vibe (and thus salability) of a record makes him particularly good at knowing what types of songs will be hits. Track by track, Puffy DJs his way through other artists' tracks, maintaining the flow or vibe throughout an album, schedule of released singles, or even across a label's entire roster of artists. The technical implementation of this instinct, and the attention to audio fidelity that a

DJ like Kool Herc possessed, also finds its correlate in a lot of the ways that Maserati has been a successful engineer.[14] Both made a name for themselves by having a bigger sound than their contemporaries, and both were aware of how harnessing the power of low-end frequencies was crucial to achieving this goal.

Tony Maserati is an uncommon amalgam of traits. He has the ability to fill a room with his personality, to be the center of attention among his peers and associates, and he is often heard laughing the loudest when an off-color joke is told. Tony's deep and unbridled way of laughing betrays a boyish sense of humor, and uncontrived sincerity. Sometimes he's so accessible that one can almost forget the sheer mass of hit records to which he has contributed.

But there's also this other side of Tony – one I've seen in equal parts in the decade we've known each other – that enables him to disappear in a room. I've seen this side manifest in a number of ways: when he's intently focused on the mixing task at hand, eyes squinting through absurdly thick-rimmed glasses, whenever he's in the room with an artist/client, and when he's staring at you unflinchingly while you ask him a question. I remember finding the latter quite disorienting when I first met Tony at his room at the Hit Factory in New York. A mutual friend in the music industry introduced him to me and Tony immediately asked, "What do you want to do? Who do you want to work with?" What I actually said is a blur to me now, but being all of twenty years old at the time, I must have offered a string of presumptuous blather that included *at least* Radiohead, half of the current Billboard hot 100, and most likely Björk, for good measure. What I do remember clearly about that moment is that Tony never opened his mouth to interject the entire time I was speaking, which alarmed me into listening to myself while talking. After what felt like a ten-minute soliloquy, I hit the wall, and sheepishly concluded, "So, I guess I don't know." "Hmm," he said.

And that was it. Tony had known me for all of thirty seconds, and had already reduced my ambitions to an existential quandary. And all he had to do was listen to me a little bit longer than I was used to people listening to me. Looking back, it makes a lot of sense to me that Tony would be so properly equipped to disarm a person while listening to him. He made a career out of listening to artists, coaching them, challenging them, consoling them, or pissing them off enough to get them to reveal something about themselves that he could capture. Yet it is not this connection between the ability to listen in conversation and in a recording studio that makes this a compelling memory, but rather what he is able to achieve with the act of listening.

To consider listening as something that one might be able to do something with, it is important to first consider listening as a process. For recording engineers, it is a vocation as well as a means of survival in a competitive and crowded market with room for only one artist and one song at the top. Some of the best engineers are able to listen and react to sonic cues instantaneously, translating a musical passage into a technical equivalent or vice versa. Others are able to react through inaction, providing space for an artist to dictate the tempo of the sonic encounter. It is a negotiation of instincts, and of knowing when to allow the technology to become an aesthetic catalyst, and when to allow it to dissolve away, yielding to the elegance of simplicity.

Nearly a decade after our first encounter, I would have the opportunity to ask Tony a pressing question of my own: "What is a record you've worked on that you felt you were the *only* person who could have done it justice?" He answered without hesitation:

> *My Life* – Mary J. Blige. That record really culminated a period in my career and in my relationship with Puff and Mary, Uptown, and Bad Boy . . . I was part of a team at that point. And they would bring me the tough ones, and they would bring me the ones that really meant something. Certainly this record was one of those. It was imperative – well really – it was *unspoken* that Mary was the center of it all . . . There's one track, from that album "I Never Wanna Live Without You," where she's singing and it's a seriously emotional moment in all three of our lives. We're rolling tape, and she's in tears in the booth singing and neither Puff nor I could hit stop on the tape machine. It was a seven-minute track, and I'm not hitting stop there's no way in *Hell* I'm hitting stop. And Puff is like "I'm not hitting stop!" Even if she's in tears or not . . . something is gonna' come out of her that we're gonna' want.[15]

I'd like to consider this relationship as an illuminating account of how the hip-hop artist, producer, and engineer are able to make an affective connection with one another, and in turn, transmit this affect to the listener. To "manufacture stored affect" is to create a form of music that conveys the emotions of the artist and evokes an emotional response from the listener regardless of the temporal, spatial, circumstantial, or sociological distance that might separate the two. Of course, the emotional effect that music has on the listener is nearly as common as music itself; it would be a much more difficult task to find songs that did *not* elicit an affective response than to recount any loosely related string of songs that made someone at some time feel something. My purpose here is not to assemble a comprehensive "best of hip-hop affect" list, but rather to investigate the underlying methodologies, relationships, and genealogies behind a select number of songs and albums engineered by Maserati. Rather than giving a full analysis of *My Life* (1994), my interest is in drawing upon this moment, as well as a number of other productions that feature Maserati's work, to ask more general questions about how temporal disjuncture, mutual absences, and sonic memory are essential aspects to the creation of affectively remarkable records during the second-wave period of hip-hop music.

Here we can trace the situational, technical, and emotional origins of records that have inspired powerful affective connections from listeners.[16] Of particular interest is the way that the structural layout of the recording studio serves to facilitate and impede this process, and what hip-hop producers and engineers have done in order to enhance or mitigate this effect, respectively. The engineer/producer/artist relationship is one of collaborative listening, and their respective roles in negotiating this relationship directly impact the production process through an aural paradigm. At the center of this is an inquiry into how the notions of temporal disjuncture, mutual absences, and social memory are immanent in the recording process, and furthermore, how they point to a fundamental ideology of recorded sound that is still in the process of being realized.

When preparations were being made to record *My Life*, Uptown Records was on the ascent from the success of Blige's debut *What's the 411?*, and Puffy (who was A&R at Uptown Records at the time) chose Maserati to be the "lead guy to implement Puffy and [Uptown founder] Andre Harrell's sonic vision for the record."[17] Producer and songwriter Cory Rooney, who had worked with Maserati on Blige's 1992 single "Real Love," recommended Maserati's sound for the new project, and together with engineers Bob Brockman, Rich Travali, Rob Paustian, and producer Chucky Thompson a veritable dream team of personnel were assembled to support Blige's album.[18] Blige's work in the 1990s, particularly *My Life*, was a turning point for the world of hip-hop that represented a new phase for what hip-hop records could sound like; as Maserati says, "we were making hip-hop records with singing on them, and that was something that hadn't really ever been conceived before that on a big scale."[19]

The 1994 album *My Life* was a milestone in Mary J. Blige's career. It was her second studio album, and Blige took nearly a year to complete what would be widely regarded as a breakthrough. *My Life*, an album that was largely about Blige's struggles at the time, debuted at number one on the Billboard Top R&B/Hip-hop albums chart. Clinical depression, an abusive relationship, and substance abuse were among the themes covered. The album resonated with her audience, as it would go on to become the best-selling R&B album of 1995. Billboard noted that "Blige has clearly stretched out musically, emotionally, and creatively . . . Hip-hop? Blige has redefined the term."[20] From the beginning of her career with the 1992 album *What's the 411?*, Mary J. Blige had – as Billboard suggests – redefined the sound and image of hip-hop music. Under the production oversight of Sean "Puffy" Combs, Blige's work – particularly her first two albums – forged a new set of sounds into the hip-hop soundscape; dusty samples and driving drum patterns underneath Blige's melismatic delivery came to define the amalgam genre of what would come to be known as "hip-hop/soul."[21]

The notion of placing Uptown's youngest and first female artist at the forefront of the hip-hop/soul movement was an ingenious collaborative idea between Harrell and Puffy. The instrumental tracks on *What's the 411?* sounded like straight hip-hop records of the day. Yet, with Blige's vocal at the center, there was a striking juxtaposition between timbres and themes that appealed to the diehard hip-hop fans and nostalgic R&B audiences alike. *My Life* was a maturation of Blige's sound, and highlighted another powerful combination in Blige's vocal ability and her unparalleled talent for tapping into the essence of a song: "[Mary] can take a lyric written by her – or not written by her – and make it sound like she just lived it. It doesn't even have to be a deep lyric when she sings it; it *becomes* deep when she's delivering it."[22]

The ways that these moments are delivered are influenced by the record-making process, the manufacture of stored affect, insofar as they are multi-layered mediations. The notion of the mediated listening experience is nothing new, and has previously been explored by many others at length.[23] Yet mediated listening experiences also occur during the process of creating media. For instance, while it is true that, generally speaking, Maserati and Puffy were moved by the power of Blige's performance while watching her perform live in the studio, it is crucial to acknowledge that theirs was not a listening experience devoid of mediation. First, listening in the control room of the studio is mediated by the acoustics of the room. Typically, if properly acoustically treated, a control room is an environment where the reflections of sound waves bouncing off of walls is strictly managed, and the walls, ceiling, and floor are constructed in a manner that isolates it from the load-bearing structures of the building. Simply put, it is an airtight room within a room, virtually immune to the breach of unwanted sound. Second, the control room glass that provides visual communication to the live room creates a dynamic of surveillance for the artist performing in the live room or vocal booth. Even the "talkback" system evokes a "Wizard of Oz" paradigm on studio communications: the artist is always heard by the engineer in the control room, who, in turn, can only be heard by the artist once a button is depressed. As Maserati's story elaborates, neither he nor the producer could even see Blige as she sang into the microphone during the vocal session. To some artists, this relationship lends itself to discomfort, but the most seasoned recording artists can use this dynamic as a creative device.

Third, the microphone, microphone preamp, equalizer, compressor, mixing desk, reverb, type of tape machine, and formula of tape used all influence the sound in ways that highly mediate the listening experience of those on the control room side of the glass. Finally, as Maserati indicated that the aesthetic goal of the album was to have it be "all about Mary," it was a rare occurrence that she would come into the studio during the recording of *My Life* without the backing track already mixed to a point where it resembled the final sound of the record. At the very least, it was customary for a rough mix of the recording to have been done and given to the artist on CD or cassette to listen to while she worked out her vocal parts on her own. This allowed an artist of Blige's caliber to be inspired by the sonic nuances of the track, and perform accordingly. Such was the case with "I Never Wanna Live Without You," but the virtuosic performance that happened in the studio was unexpected by both Puffy and Maserati:

> Axis studio had this little booth . . . some people even used it as a lounge
> sometimes, so when we set up Mary in there, I think we were only supposed
> to do some ad-libs. So I was mixing at that point for six or seven hours, and
> Puff says "Let's see what Mary does and we'll edit from there." And she
> comes in and she takes the track all the way to the end. The shocking and
> dramatic part of it is that we couldn't even see her in the booth. There was a
> window in the booth, but the blinds were closed and she went into her own
> space at that moment. So this thing is going on for six-plus minutes . . . and
> we can't see her so we don't know if she even wants us to stop the tape, or if
> she's even on the microphone. And there comes a point when you're just
> wondering are you torturing this poor girl making her do this? But without
> that session, the song you hear on the record would have been much shorter
> than it ended up. There was something in there that happened – maybe a
> catharsis – that needed to happen over the entire course of the track.[24]

One particularly interesting aspect to Maserati's story is that in telling it, he does not mention sonic quality once. This is not to say that sonic quality was not a factor in his mind at the time – clearly his ability to produce an ideal sound is why he was hired in the first place – but rather that the sonic quality was *incidental* to the experience itself. It is a story about recording, about what the recording process is like, but it is also an important commentary on how emotional impact configures the recording process. Microphones capture a performance, but they also capture their own noise. A vocalist sings for/into the microphone, but *for* herself or an imagined other. She hears her voice inside of the track, inside of her head, and in the empty vocal booth. Meanwhile, the technical staff hear the full mix in the control room, through loudspeakers, where they are hearing the acoustic effects of the room and the vocal booth simultaneously. The vocal is also perhaps accompanied by an artificial space created by a reverberation unit, separate from the microphone, the vocalist, and the pre-recorded tracks on tape, but designed to synthesize a coherent space around all three. The affective transduction that occurs is framed by repetition, loops, and recursivity between techne and flesh.

While there are many ways that the control room serves to mediate the listening experience of its occupants, it is also a locus where technology enhances the affective listening experience. The most important character in this story (and in any story in popular music) is the voice, and its accomplice, the microphone. As Jonathan Sterne has said, recording technologies allowed the voice to become "a little more unmoored from the body, and people's ears could take them into the past or across vast distances."[25] If, as Sterne says, the voice can take us away from our bodies, then our ears must also be capable of such a feat. Perhaps this is why we place such a weight on the recorded voice unequaled to any other instrument. It is capable of conveying intimacy, power, wisdom, empathy, and desire in ways unparalleled by entire ensembles. The glass that separates a vocalist from the engineer and producer serves two very different roles at the same time. At once it creates isolation – both physical and emotional – around the artist. Yet, the isolation that the glass creates also affords an intimacy in the recording process. The artist is alone, the lights dim, only the silvery hue of a microphone and her reflected glare on the glass offer solace.

Ian Penman takes this notion further, articulating the way we as listeners project ourselves onto the person singing into the microphone:

> When the singer first starts to sing into – and more crucially *for* – the microphone, it was assumed that what was being captured were moments of immortal truth: the record of a performance which would exist whether the microphone had been there or not. But the microphone is like a syringe, which can put in as much as it takes out, filling the singer's head with hallucinatory notions. Outsiders slip through now, because the microphone is a short cut (like the telephone) which repays a more economical delivery, honouring the whisper as much as a holler . . . The "intimacy" of microphonic singing is also the distanced "take" of recording and, thereby, transmission and reception at a distance. Intimacy is also the first step toward the promiscuous impersonality of a record buying public; of both the homogeneous "they" of popular reception and the Song's pivotal and ambiguous "you."[26]

This points to the relationship of the recording process that can be thought of as mutual absence. The recording artist is performing for an audience who is not there; the audience hears a recording of an artist who is also absent. In the case of the many virtuosic emotional performances captured in the twentieth century, vocalists utilized this relationship to achieve an affective connection with the audience. They needed us so much, that they had to forget about us.

The amplification that a microphone provides for the recording artist has become a pre-condition of modern vocal techniques and aesthetics. Frank Sinatra was known for his impeccable "mic technique," the ability to utilize the sonic characteristics of a particular microphone to achieve the desired euphonic effect. Billie Holiday made a career out of capturing her melismatic delivery in a dire strain amplified by the microphone. The "proximity effect" that vocalists used to their benefit during vocal performances provides both a technical grounding for the reason why we hear what we do in vocalists since the postwar period, as well as a useful entendre to our own perspectives as listener. In order for such an effect to be achieved, the vocalist is close to the microphone – closer to us, in effect, with the enhanced lower frequencies perceived as "warmth" to our ears and the higher frequencies pushed toward yearning or urgency. The inhale. The damp creak of saliva. The intimacy. The vulnerability. The breath. We strain to hear them individually, yet simultaneously. But it is too much for our ears to process at once, and so we shift focus at intervals from the vibrato to the timbre, then back to the pitch. Recording a vocal is unlike recording any other instrument precisely because listening to a vocal is unlike listening to any other instrument. Its unique power is equal parts Ray Charles's yearning falsetto and Glenn Gould's daedal coaxing.[27] We listen to a compelling vocal performance, and we cannot help but listen to ourselves.

The effect is exemplified in what Don Ihde has called a "phenomenology of the voice,"[28] and what Angela Davis has pointed to specifically in the musical and social complicities of Billie Holiday's technique: "One way to explore Billie Holiday's awesome ability to transmute musical and lyrical meaning in the popular songs she performed is to think about her relationship to her musical material as analogous to African Americans' historical appropriation of the English language."[29] What Davis engages as Holiday's mastery of linguistics to produce multiple – and often veiled – meanings of words can also be applied to the multivalence of a recorded vocal performance itself.[30] Variances of intonation, timbre, cadence, and phrasing all serve to articulate (or obfuscate)[31] meaning in vocal deliveries. The best vocalists use these variances to compel under the guise of effortlessness. Furthermore, because the personal nature of the voice is unparalleled, the recordings of voices we hear are construed through the understanding we have of our own voices, and vice versa. In other words, part of what makes listening to a recorded voice so different than listening to anything else, is that we decipher what we hear through ourselves, and we are thus deciphered through what we hear.[32]

These factors that converge upon performance, recording, and audition of the recorded voice can be understood as technologies of the voice, and thus, technologies of the body. I would argue that Mary J. Blige has the same effectiveness as Billie Holiday. Though it is difficult to quantify their vocal abilities, both artists had a way with using style over mere technical ability. Neither Blige nor Holiday has the technical ability of Whitney Houston or Ella Fitzgerald, but their voices created a new narrative of powerful vocal performance. Blige's first two records have a grit and sincerity that was not a part of the musical landscape at that historical moment, and their impact on the historical moment in which they were released is pervasive.

"I Never Wanna Live Without You" comes right in the middle of *My Life*, and it serves as a fulcrum that changes the thematic balance of the entire record. At over six minutes in length, it is at least a minute longer than every other track on the album, which in terms of popular music recording is typically considered quite long. The groove of the song comes from the interplay between the bass and the electronic percussion, particularly the reverse snare sound that wipes a brief flash of white noise before each hit twice in the measure. The intro where Blige sings "can't live without you," is already a lush and full arrangement less than 20 seconds into the song, and the interplay between her main vocal and the response of her emotive ad-libs sets up the song as a contemplative catharsis. On its surface, this is a song about love that transcends life and living, one that is so powerful that it makes the narrator unable to eat or sleep at the mere thought of losing it. Despite the quite repetitive sentiment of "let's stay together," there is a powerful melancholy that is enhanced by Blige's delivery from the bridge to the end of the song. The bridge begins, "I don't wanna be alone, so baby let's stay together," and the listener can interpret the true nuance of the song: it is a union that is designed to keep solitude at bay, and Blige is not singing about the joys of love, but rather trying to keep a failing relationship alive.[33] The outro lasts about another 90 seconds, and it becomes clear that these were the emotional ad-libs that Maserati was talking about in the Axis Studio overdub session. Her sorrow is palpable, chilling, and it reaches its apex as her voice devolves into a melismatic plea that is equal parts style and vulnerability. The song's title and refrain might be rethought of as "I Never Wanna Live Without You (but I know that I will eventually have to)."

The sound of Maserati's mix is congruous with his estimation in the epigraph of this chapter: he's "staying out of her way" sonically in a manner that creates a warm musical bed for her voice to perform to the best of its capacity. The electric piano and strings that occupy a similar frequency range to Blige's voice are tucked in tightly behind her vocal, and during the choruses they serve to fill out the track rather than provide any leading melodic information. The "drops," where the rhythm section is muted abruptly, happen in the measure immediately preceding each verse, and this technique serves to accentuate that Blige is at the center of the story that is being told. Additionally, this effect is often used to give the sense of dynamics in a programmed (as opposed to live) production, in much the way that a live band would follow a vocalist's cues during a live performance.

"I'm Going Down" is Blige's interpretation of a Rose Royce track, written by Norman Whitfield. Musically, it is a faithful copy of the original song, although the drums and bass are more prevalent in the mix in the 1994 version, which was likely a decision made to keep the timbre of *My Life* consistent throughout the album. It is a quintessential torch song, and Blige's vocals have never sounded better. Even though "Down" is one of two songs that Blige did not have a hand in writing on this album, her vocal performance is unparalleled and her work on the song made it decidedly hers. By the time the three major-chord hits of A, B, and C have abruptly stopped, Blige can already be heard taking a deep breath preparing for her performance. It is a slight and mundane moment that is enhanced by her close proximity to the microphone, Maserati's decision to leave the breath in during the mixdown, and the natural intimacy with which Blige sings. Once the first line is sung, "Time on my hands, since you been away boy/I ain't got no plans, no no no," the sonic palette has been firmly established. The listener is being told a story about unrequited love, but also one in which a singer can do nothing to soothe her pain but belt out her sorrows in the room with a band. Unlike the album's previous track, "I Never Wanna Live Without You," the sound of "I'm Going Down" is made to convey a narrative of Blige singing in the room with a live ensemble to support her. The reverb that surrounds her voice is not unlike the one on Gwen Dickey's voice in the Rose Royce version, but its effect is more diffuse and the decay time slightly longer. The producers wanted to capture the success and poignancy of the original track, but Puffy undoubtedly wanted to go a step further and surpass the original. Thus, the effect is of Blige singing with a more aggressive band, in a larger space (with greater reverberation), and with a modern relevance. Her reworking is more than a cover of a popular song, it is an interpretation that is embodied and, as Maserati says, as if "she just lived it." Through her deciphering of the extant sounds of the past, her repurposing of a song that existed in the collective conscious and her forging of a new affective connection with a new audience two decades later, Blige has indeed lived it.

This deciphering is particularly relevant to hip-hop music. Artists of the second wave of hip-hop trained regularly in the repetition of listening to their forefathers. It was common for an aspiring rapper to listen to records and cassettes of preeminent artists from the early 1980s and learn styles of flow, breath control, cadence, and idiomatic structures. Of course, this is nothing new within black cultural traditions: "Whereas Bessie Smith had needed to go on the road with Ma Rainey in order to learn from her, Victoria Spivey and Billie Holiday and Mahalia Jackson could learn from Bessie Smith by staying put . . . and playing her records."[34] What is unique to hip-hop as a black cultural form, however, is that where the blues and R&B had live instrumentation, hip-hop producers had instrumentals comprised of extant sonic texts, sampled and reconstituted morsels from the past. Also, hip-hop is a genre that emerged through the traditions of DJ culture, and the tastemakers of the day balanced crowd favorites with obscure gems. Recontextualization occurred in the producer's ingenuity to rework the sample into something else, but the hip-hop song as a viable form only truly took shape once a performance from the rapper or vocalist was in place. Any commentary, or what Henry Louis Gates calls "Signifyin(g),"[35] was a task that rested largely upon the shoulders of the vocalist. For example, Mary J. Blige's "Don't Go" (1994) features an instrumental sample from Guy's "Goodbye Love" (1988), but during the intro, Blige sings a rendition of DeBarge's "Stay with Me" (1983).[36] It is a vocal melody that is immediately recognizable, and Blige's rendition elicits the nostalgia an early 1990s listener might feel when listening to that recording. Blige is not seeking to eclipse the original, but rather to evoke the experience of singing a popular song to a loved one. The effect is a sincere reappropriation of a love song that is resignified with contemporary relevance.

But how has technology influenced the experiential act of listening, and thus the connection between the aural and the affective? The aural relationships between engineers and musicians (and engineers-as-listeners and musicians-as-listeners) are as old as modern recording itself. As with all music, hip-hop is dependent upon the skilled listening practices of its cultural producers. What sets hip-hop apart, is that this generation of skilled listeners manipulated tangible extant traces of the past (i.e. samples) and presented them with an aesthetic sensibility toward the promise of the new. Perhaps the allure of hip-hop productions is how readily they accept our listening – our straining – toward an audible past adorned with the artifacts of our impermanence. Hip-hop provides fleeting moments of musical virtuosity layered to recreate newer ones, replayable ad infinitum to our eager ears. All the while, we yearn to find a sonic correlate that speaks to our own sense of self. And in identifying the story of another, our own story so resonates.

Notes

1 Tony Maserati, interview with the author, Canaan, NY, February 4, 2011.
2 For further reading on how musical identity correlates to cultural and social currency, see

Phil Ford, *Dig* (New York: Oxford University Press, 2013).
3 The MPC's introduction was prefaced by the introduction of the SP-12 drum machine in

1986, which provided sampling capabilities, but which did not feature an interface that was especially conducive to playing live.

4 I argue that the last three decades of hip-hop can be roughly separated into three movements each lasting about a decade: (1) 1979–1989: the beginning and becoming dance music; (2) 1989–1999: movement from dance music to a highly commodified subcultural form of political music; and (3) 1999–2009: popular music and dance music again.

5 Joseph Schloss, *Making Beats: The Art of Sample-Based Hip-Hop* (Middletown, CT: Wesleyan University Press, 2004), p. 34.

6 Dire Straits's album *Brothers in Arms* (1985) was the first CD to sell a million copies.

7 There are certainly exceptions to this generalized demographic of engineers. Yet it is my argument that the traditional apprenticeship programs followed by many large studios contributed to the type of labor force who entered the audio engineering field. Many studios require apprentices to work long hours for little or no pay for months (sometimes years) before being promoted to a paying position at a studio, making it impractical for someone without financial resources to live while working as an intern. Furthermore, the long hours and late-night hours made it a job that was particularly taboo for aspiring women engineers in the middle and latter half of the twentieth century.

8 Tom Dowd, Mark Moorman, and Palm Pictures, *Tom Dowd and the Language of Music*, (video recording) (New York: Palm Pictures, 2004); Ahmet M. Ertegun *et al.*, *Atlantic Records: The House that Ahmet built* (video recording) (Burbank, CA: Rhino Entertainment, 2007).

9 This concept is closely related to the origin of the word "technology" from the Greek *tekhne* meaning an art or craft, and it was used in the seventeenth century to describe a systematic study of the arts. See Raymond Williams, *Keywords: A Vocabulary of Culture and Society* (Oxford University Press, 1985), p. 315.

10 Frank Brewster and Bill Broughton, *Last Night a DJ Saved My Life: The History of the Disc Jockey* (London: Headline Publishing, 2000). See also David Toop, *Rap Attack 2: African Rap to Global Hip-Hop*, 2nd edn. (London: Serpent's Tail, 1991); Jeff Chang, *Can't Stop Won't Stop: A History of the Hip-Hop Generation* (London: St. Martin's Press, 2005); William Eric Perkins (ed.), *Droppin' Science* (Philadelphia: Temple University Press, 1996); and Tricia Rose, *Black Noise: Rap Music and Black Culture in Contemporary America* (Middletown, CT: Wesleyan University Press, 1994).

11 Brewster and Broughton, *Last Night a DJ Saved My Life*, pp. 204–209.

12 *Ibid.*, p. 212.

13 Born Sean John Combs, the founder of Bad Boy Records has gone by numerous stage names, including P. Diddy, Puff Daddy, Diddy, and Puffy. For the sake of clarity, I will refer to him by the latter as that is what he was referred to as during the period in question as well as how he is referred to in the interviews I conducted.

14 The term fidelity, specifically when coupled into the term "hi-fidelity," typically means a pure or faithful representation of an audio signal. My usage of the term does not presuppose that fidelity means a clean or transparent reproduction of a signal, though this is often the case (i.e. DJ Kool Herc's usage of McIntosh audiophile amplifiers, and Maserati's meticulously clean vocal sound). More broadly, I am using the term fidelity to indicate the faithful reproduction of a creative idea.

15 Maserati, interview with the author.

16 The categories "listeners" and "artists/producers/engineers" are not presented as oppositional categories to illuminate difference between groups. Rather, I intend to highlight the plasticity of these categories. As I have already stated, there was a less rigid stratification of roles in many hip-hop recording studios as engineers often contributed to production work and vice versa. Furthermore, it is important to emphasize that the majority of personnel working on a recording in a studio setting are adept at shifting listening perspectives in order to make sure that the work "translates" to any number of social, acoustical, and technical settings.

17 Maserati, interview with the author.

18 It should be noted that many of the production credits in the liner notes from albums during the period in question are disorganized and apocryphal. The fast-paced manner in which songs were recorded, as well as the variety of locations used for recording, overdubbing, and mixing made the paperwork difficult to trace and validate. Each studio had a different set of support staff responsible for managing the paperwork, and the paperwork itself was often of questionable veracity. For instance, if a mix was done by "Prince" Charles Alexander, but not accepted as a final master, it is unlikely that Alexander would file that change on the official documentation used to compile liner notes. In instances where the liner notes conflict with the account I have been told, I have chosen to err on the side of believing my interlocutor over the liner notes. Furthermore, in these moments, I have been able, to the best

of my ability, to identify certain sonic traces within Maserati's mixes in particular that lead me to believe his stated involvement in the record is accurate.

19 Maserati, interview with the author.

20 Paul Verna, Marilyn A. Gillen and Peter Cronin, "Album Reviews: My Life by Mary J. Blige," *Billboard*, December 10, 1994, p. 7.

21 The term "hip-hop soul" began to catch on around the time of Mary J. Blige's recording career was beginning, particularly with her album *What's the 411?* (1992). While "Queen of Hip-hop Soul" was the original marketing term used by Uptown Records to promote Blige's invention of (and subsequently dominance within) a genre, the term caught on as a subgenre of R&B marked by a smoother and less aggressive sonic character than its counterpart, new jack swing. The delineations between hip-hop soul, neo soul, and hip-hop/R&B are tenuous at best. However, what is critical to note about these subgenres is that they provided a more palatable way for urban music to be ushered into mainstream radio markets, all the while paying tribute to the pantheon of R&B and soul artists from decades prior.

22 Maserati, interview with the author.

23 See Amanda Bayley, *Recorded Music: Performance, Culture and Technology* (Cambridge University Press, 2010); Michel Chanan, *Repeated Takes* (London: Verso, 1995); Mark Katz, *Capturing Sound: How Technology Has Changed Music* (Berkeley: University of California Press, 2004); Veit Erlmann, *Hearing Cultures* (Oxford: Berg Publishers, 2004); Jonathan Sterne, *The Audible Past* (Durham, NC: Duke University Press, 2002).

24 Maserati, interview with the author.

25 Sterne, *The Audible Past*, p. 1.

26 Rob Young (ed.), *Undercurrents: The Hidden Writing of Modern Music* (London: Continuum, 2002), pp. 28–29.

27 As in "What'd I Say" and Bach's "Goldberg Variations" respectively.

28 Don Ihde, *Listening and Voice: Phenomenologies of Sound*, 2nd edn. (State University of New York Press, 2007), pp. 185–186.

29 Angela Davis, *Blues Legacies and Black Feminism: Gertrude "Ma" Rainey, Bessie Smith and Billie Holiday* (Vintage Books, January 1999), p. 165.

30 *Ibid.*, p. 387, n. 16.

31 I am reminded, as was Eisenberg, of Ralph Ellison's narrator in *Invisible Man* who intimated, "I'd like to hear five recordings of Louis Armstrong playing and singing 'What Did I Do to Be so Black and Blue' – all at the same time . . . Perhaps I like Louis Armstrong because he's made poetry out of being invisible . . . " See Evan Eisenberg, *The Recording Angel: Music, Records and Culture from Aristotle to Zappa.* (New Haven, CT: Yale University Press, 2005), p. 25.

32 To be clear, I am highlighting the ways in which the voice is closely tied to language and subjectivity. Thus, there is an experiential baseline established that fosters a connection between hearing a voice and hearing one's own that does not place musical ability as a prerequisite. That is to say, one does not have to be a singer to make a profound connection to a recorded vocal performance in the same way one might have to be a guitarist to have a similar experience with a recorded guitar performance.

33 All lyrics from Mary J. Blige.

34 Eisenberg, *The Recording Angel*, p. 116.

35 Henry Louis Gates, Jr., *The Signifying Monkey* (New York: Oxford University Press, 1989).

36 A similar interpretation of the DeBarge melody was performed by Faith Evans in the Notorious B.I.G.'s "One More Chance (Remix)" (1994), also engineered and mixed by Maserati.

11 Hip-hop and racial identification: an (auto)ethnographic perspective

ANTHONY KWAME HARRISON

Introduction: the arrival story

My first time attending the Day One DJs' hip-hop open microphone at Haight Street's (San Francisco) Rockin' Java Café, I was fortunate to see one familiar face: underground rapper Murs, who, at the time, was most popularly associated with the Living Legends collective. Since that chance meeting over a decade ago, Murs's career has blossomed through a series of critically heralded releases and collaborations with artists including 9th Wonder, Slug (of Atmosphere), will.i.am, and Snoop Dogg. Yet even at this early stage in his career, within the interior spaces of Bay Area underground hip-hop open mics, Murs's presence was a big and noticeable deal. Had I spotted him first, I imagine I would have been hesitant to approach him: conventions of subcultural posturing dictate that one does not unnecessarily crowd local celebrities. Fortunately, he saw me and immediately came over, greeting me with a handclasp and a hug, and the question, "What are you doing here?"

I had arrived in California three weeks earlier to begin a year-long ethnographic research project within the San Francisco Bay area's multiracial underground hip-hop scene.[1] Ethnography is a specific form of qualitative research methodology based on long-term participant observation within a cultural setting. Ethnographers typically take up residence in a community and seek to understand people's everyday lives by watching what happens, listening to what is said, asking questions, and sometimes joining them in what is going on.[2]

Serendipitously, part of my own ethnographic immersion involved landing a job working two doors down from Rockin' Java at Amoeba Music – the then-largest independent record store in America,[3] and a key hub of the local hip-hop scene. The Day One open mic had been recommended to me by an Amoeba co-worker and thus, even before realizing it was one of the largest and longest-standing weekly hip-hop open-microphone events in the Bay, I anticipated it being an important research site.

I had met Murs once before, in 1998 when the Living Legends embarked on their first-ever national tour as an opening act for fellow Bay Area hip-hoppers Hieroglyphics. Following a canceled show in Albany, the first

actual performance of the tour took place in Northampton, Massachusetts –
not far from where I grew up and went to school as an undergraduate.
Through a combination of my familiarity with the venue and what I suspect
was an instance of racial (mis)recognition, my friend Dustin and I managed
to not only get a room in the same motel as the tour, but to get one right
in the middle of the Hieroglyphics room block. Since Black men with
dreadlocks rarely passed through the "small, liberal-minded, 90 percent
white college town," I imagine the clerk took one look at me and assumed I
was a late-arriving member of the crew.[4] I didn't mind the misrecognition.
That's what we were there for.

A few hours before the start of the show, the most-renowned member
of Hieroglyphics, Del the Funky Homosapien, walked into our room. With
the door open and the music turned up, Del most likely mistook ours for
a Hiero room. I immediately offered him a beer and a seat. Del ended up
spending most of the night – both before and after the show – in our room.
Subsequently, a few other Hiero members and most of the Living Legends
camped out there as well. Through my regular participation on the Living
Legends online forum (the Legends Labyrinth), I had learned that Murs
knew and was a fan of a German hip-hop artist named Juks, whom my friend
Owa had met the previous summer while visiting Berlin. In anticipation of
seeing the Legends for the first time in Northampton, I had brought along a
second-generation dub of Juks's underground cassette-tape specifically for
Murs, thus reconciling three degrees of transatlantic separation between the
two artists. He seemed genuinely thankful to receive it.

Now in San Francisco, possibly as a gesture of reciprocity, Murs was
handing me his newly pressed CD, *F'Real*.[5] Initially, I assumed he was only
showing it to me. "No. That one's for you," he said.[6] We spoke for a few
minutes: he happened to be passing through Rockin' Java on his way to drop
off copies of *F'Real* at Amoeba; I told him about my research and explained
how I planned to be in the Bay for the next year; he bemoaned my choice
of city, suggesting that Los Angeles – where he and the rest of the Legends
had recently relocated – would have been a better fieldwork site; "I know
you're having a good time though," he affirmed. Murs stayed for the entire
open mic. It was the only time I ever saw him there.

Although Murs did not get on the microphone to perform that evening,
as an established artist in the scene – arguably the most celebrated artist
I saw at the Rockin' Java – his mere presence involved a performance or,
to borrow Erving Goffman's terminology, "presentation-of-his-celebrity-
self."[7] As a Living Legend – the crew which, according to Amoeba Music's
head hip-hop buyer, "all these [Bay Area hip-hop] kids have taken a page
from" – with the foremost reputation as a fierce freestyler and battle MC,
Murs was the object of aspiring hip-hoppers' clandestine gazes from the

moment he entered the coffee shop.[8] And fortuitously for me, those people he showed familiarity with and warmth to were, if nothing else, worth taking note of.

Within popular music scenes, especially those governed by authenticity demands, the identity-work participants perform serves as an (subjective) experience of and (objective) occasion for what Simon Frith describes as "self-in-process."[9] Certainly all hip-hoppers engage in forms of "impression management" while vying for subcultural acceptance, status, and/or validation.[10] Murs, through the rare occasion of his presence in a pungent music-scene space like the Day One open mic, was involuntarily pressed into a profound performance-of-self. Such is the price of celebrity at any level. A known figure is subject to surveillance upon recognition. At the same time, for a first time attendee at the open mic – an unknown figure – the performance-of-self can be similarly consequential. First impressions matter, as the example of Murs's greeting me for only the second time attests. Thus, in that moment of mutual recognition, Murs and I entered into a heightened performance of who's who in the underground hip-hop scene – "There goes Murs! And who's that he's talking to?" His knownness and my unknownness became symbiotic – the valences between the two were pregnant with the potential for misrecognition.

There is yet another valence through which our off-stage performances that evening can and should be recognized. In fact, my own recognition of it in the weeks and months that followed became a jumping-off point for theorizing the implications of social identification within a music scene where it was widely said – and widely known to be said – that a person's race had no direct bearing on the artistic evaluation of their performative prowess (i.e. "it's all about an MC's skills"). This valence, of course, is the "vast veil" of separation and difference that W. E. B. DuBois, in contemplating the Black experience in America, wrote about over a century ago.[11] That Murs and I were two of only a handful (perhaps a half dozen) of recognizably African American people at the hip-hop open mic undeniably added to my visibility there. Whereas Murs's recognition of me as the person he had met in Northampton made me someone notable, it was through recognition of *race* – the historically contingent meanings which we inconsistently assign to a constellation of phenotypical signifiers (such as skin color, hair, and facial features) – that I became noticeable.

Over the course of the following year, as I seamlessly made the transition from an at times tentative ethnographer to a central figure in the Day One open microphone "microscene" (i.e. scene within a scene), I would realize how much being recognized as a (particular type of) racial subject, and the performance of race that accompanied such recognition, enabled and accelerated my journey.[12] I would also become profoundly aware of the extent to which a second type of racial recognition – that is, the acknowledgment of specific aesthetic and/or political traditions associated with distinct racial identities – conspired with the first type to betray the colorblind ideals of this multiracial community.

In this chapter I present a snapshot of critically grounded hip-hop ethnography that examines the implications of racial recognition and identification within a purported colorblind underground hip-hop scene. To do this, I focus on a few thickly described autoethnographic episodes which showcase some of the ways in which these racial identifications perform identity-work.[13] My analysis issues from considerations of how my own racial visibility impacted my early experiences of acceptance as a researcher and, ultimately, an MC. Ethnographic research within hip-hop music scenes offers an important on-the-ground perspective through which to explore the dynamics of power that shape a number of interpersonal encounters and social processes, not the least of which surround race. In the following pages, I develop a theory of racial identification (in underground hip-hop) that is both an outgrowth of my own positioned subjectivity and a guiding framework for what I witnessed among the hip-hoppers I met and interacted with – people who, like me, had to negotiate the terrain of identification, authenticity, and community belonging as part of their everyday movements within the scene. I first offer some preliminary comments on the practice of ethnographic research: its history, what it currently entails, and its place as an emergent mode of hip-hop scholarship.

Ethnography and hip-hop

Considering the extent to which hip-hop has been represented and discussed – in both the academy and everyday discourse – as a culture, it is surprising that the research methodology traditionally most associated with the study of culture has been utilized so sparingly within the history of hip-hop scholarship. Although ethnography has a long tradition within sociocultural anthropology, cultural sociology, and ethnomusicology, and has more recently been adopted by a broad range of disciplines, within the field of popular music studies its development has been relatively slow.[14] As a mode of research that came of age during the colonial era, classic ethnography involved traveling to distant cultures, attempting to live alongside and, to the extent feasible (or comfortable), similarly to indigenous peoples, with the goal of "grasp[ing] the native's point of view."[15] Ethnography today is recognized as a distinctly interpersonal research endeavor that is often practiced close to home.[16] Thus the ethnographer's ability to live identically to community members – and to be (mis)recognized as a member to the point where daily life proceeds as if she were not there[17] – is generally increased and specifically impacted by particulars relating to both her identity and the boundary-maintaining measures of the community she aspires to conduct research within. Ethnographic projects are furthermore influenced by countless arbitrary, idiosyncratic, and unforeseen factors including, but by no means limited to, the personality characteristics of both the researcher and the specific people she encounters, and the circumstances under which she is introduced to the research community – even who happens to show up on her first night attending an open mic.

With these revelations at the fore, contemporary ethnography developed into a highly self-conscious research methodology concerned with both the power relations surrounding ethnographic projects and the politics of ethnographic representation.[18] At the micro-social level of everyday interactions, such considerations compel ethnographers to be cognizant of what Peter McLaren calls "reception formations" – that is, historically and culturally based understandings of the research enterprise that impact on how an ethnographer is both perceived and received – as well as the constant negotiations of identities taking place throughout the course of research.[19]

Popular music scenes offer uniquely suited sites for ethnographers to productively work through many of these methodological complexities. These decidedly social arenas exist as communities of practice through which the usual designators of collective identity (i.e. race, class, gender, ethnicity, sexuality, and religion) are often secondary to matters of mutual engagement and shared repertoires.[20] This is not to suggest that race, gender, and (especially) age are not consequential to perceptions of in-scene belonging – indeed one of my principal arguments in this chapter is for the ongoing salience of racial identifications in the face of underground hip-hop's professed colorblindness – but rather that (a) joint participation in activities through which subcultural meanings are negotiated, and (b) collectively recognized ways of doing and saying things serve as two key aspects of a music scene's production and maintenance of community.[21] As a particular type of music around which scenes often form, hip-hop has a robust history of being authenticated around specific discourses of race (Black), gender (male), sexuality (hyper-heterosexual), and class (poor/working class).[22] The emergence of underground hip-hop – as a multiracial, more socially conscious alternative to commercial rap music, which has strong resonances within middle-class enclaves such as college towns – threatens to unsettle some of these ascriptive historical associations.[23] Through the virtues of its relationally and contextually situated attentions to the lived experiences of individuals, ethnography, when applied to (underground) hip-hop communities of practice, can help shed light on the dynamic and nuanced relationship between (largely exclusive) ascribed social identities and (largely inclusive) engaged communities – a tension that is crucial to the development of healthy and just twenty-first-century societies.

Arising largely out of interests in documenting the textures of hip-hop's global spread, a small canon of hip-hop ethnographies set outside the USA began emerging around the start of the twenty-first century, including studies in northeast England, Berlin, Sydney, Tokyo, and Havana.[24] More recently there has been an upsurge in USA-based ethnographies on hip-hop – represented most notably through academic books authored by second-generation hip-hop scholars like Joseph Schloss, Ali Colleen Neff, Andreana Clay, and Emery Petchauer.[25] Collectively, these works seek to legitimate hip-hop's aesthetics and practices through (re)presenting the actions, viewpoints, and voices of hip-hoppers themselves. Rather than relying on pre-established theories or emphasizing large-scale structural shifts that have little to no resonance with people's daily experiences, ethnography is more adept at presenting situational thick descriptions in an explanatory tone. Hip-hop ethnographers, while still drawing on theory and aiming to contextualize broad patterns of behavior, privilege the grounded perspectives of everyday social actors – which are notably distinct from the standpoints of invested celebrity artists or spokespersons. Indeed, the best contemporary ethnographers understand their enterprise as a project of sharing voice. And perhaps not surprisingly, several members of this new generation of hip-hop scholars – including Schloss, Neff, Petchauer, Sujatha Fernandes, Oliver Wang, and Jooyoung Lee – consider (or have at one time considered) themselves scholar-practitioners.[26] I include myself among these. Yet, the path of welcome that led me to becoming an open-mic performer who was known and recognized in this (micro)scene cuts through a forest of racial recognition and MC misrecognition, with an understory that illustrates just how much we ask and continue to make of the complex combination of visible attributes we understand as race.[27]

... back at the open mic

The following week, when I arrived at the Rockin' Java a couple of hours early to enjoy the pre-open microphone music and get caught up on fieldnote writing, three-and-a-half pages into my work I was pleasantly interrupted by one of the stand-out MCs from the week before. Lord Top Ramen (aka Top R) was a large, loud, and bodacious freestyle rhymer who dominated just about every open mic or rhyming cypher I ever saw him in (and I saw him in many). Although he had family ties back east, within the Bay Area scene Top R was known as a graffiti artist and MC from Santa Cruz who had made a name for himself – or at least a reputation as a big white guy with dope rhymes[28] (see Harrison 2009: 139–140) – through his membership of a group called the Earthlings and by working security at Maritime Hall. Prior to its closing in 2001, Maritime was the largest venue for Black music in San Francisco. As a security person there, Top R seized any and all opportunities to get in front of the crowd and freestyle or battle other MCs both on stage and backstage. Having been in the Bay for less than a month, I knew none of this. What I did know from the previous week was that Top R, a self-designated "mic hog," rhymed longer and more frequently than anyone else, had a commanding presence, and had what in Bay Area underground hip-hop vernacular one might call the "cleanest" rhymes – meaning that, even though he rhymed off the top of his head, he rarely stumbled or messed up.[29] Indeed, Top R's impromptu performances, which often included witty punchlines, very much resembled written rhymes – a fact his MC adversaries were not above calling him on.[30]

Top R first approached me asking if I was writing rhymes. His misrecognition of me as an MC was not the first or the last; in this instance, it provided a convenient opportunity to introduce myself and my research. After listening to me describe my interest in studying the multiracial character of Bay Area underground hip-hop for my doctoral thesis in cultural anthropology, Top R immediately decided to educate me on several historical and contextual aspects of my proposed study. The first regarded the history of African American migration to the Bay Area – most notably around World War II to work in the Oakland shipyards – and how it gave Black music from "the (Oak)Town" a certain "country" sound.[31] The second concerned hip-hop and cultural appropriation. Whereas many African American scholars have written about the injustices of white appropriations of Black culture, and some have debated the extent to which white hip-hop enthusiasts are simply repeating this historical cycle, being a white hip-hopper himself, Top R felt obliged to share his views on this controversial issue.[32] Rather than seeing the Bay Area's tremendous racial/ethnic diversity – which in many ways anticipates mid-twenty-first-century US population projections[33] – as limiting cultural appropriation or leading to a more genuine form of cross-cultural blending, Top R thought the Bay was nationally at "the forefront of the appropriation of Black cultural styles." Furthermore, speaking as a white MC, he stressed the importance of being conscious of his position in hip-hop and aware of how his actions conformed to, disrupted, and/or otherwise engaged this historically exploitative dynamic. A third aspect of Bay Area hip-hop which Top R schooled me on was the local history of activism – namely the Black Panthers and the anti-Vietnam War protests – and how it informed the do-it-yourself ethos of hip-hop career-building introduced by Oakland's Too $hort, continued by artists like Vallejo's Mac Dre and E-40, and, at that time, currently exploding within the hip-hop underground through exemplars like the Living Legends and San Francisco's Bored Stiff.

Finally, Top R and I discussed anthropology, most specifically its methodology. When I shared my own misgivings about the politics of ethnographic research and the vagaries of its methodological prescripts, Top R countered that anthropology, indeed, had a definitively purposeful method: "[first] you immerse yourself and [then you] gain trust." As he went on making less than flattering comments about the history and implications of the research tradition I was participating in – adding a line or two about the pretentiousness of academics in general and graduate students in particular – he made sure to intersperse explicit recognitions of my personhood via statements like "not to diss on you" or "but you're not like that."[34] Through this first conversation with Top R, I (1) learned and/or confirmed many things about Bay Area hip-hop, (2) discovered that his freestlye proficiency could, in part, be attributed to the fact that he was well read and had a sharp mind, and (3) realized that his extroversion was not limited to rhyme cyphers and open microphones. Later that evening, during one of his freestyles on stage, Top R pointed over to me and said, "my man's an anthropologist."

Theorizing race through (mis)recognitions

Both Top R's misrecognition of me as an MC and his subsequent recognition of me as a person who, perchance in a deliberate gesture to avoid offending, he distanced from the anthropological enterprise as he understood it, offer instructive instances for beginning to think through how the visibility and conception of race and the performance of racialized selves-in-process shape underground hip-hop community-building – not to mention the research encounters of hip-hop ethnographers. To begin, we might simply (but quite significantly) consider how I was fortunate enough to, through no great effort on my part other than simply *being there*, quickly establish what became a solid (and trusting) relationship with the dominant persona at the Rockin' Java open mic.[35] My experience of ethnographic immersion into this open-microphone-based hip-hop microscene was notably different from Jooyoung Lee's, who, even as a hip-hop practitioner (a turntablist and popper), recounts that months into research people still periodically reminded him of his "provisional status."[36] The most obvious explanation for my welcome reception is racial.[37] By this proposition, Top R's initial misrecognition of me was no different from the motel clerk's described in this chapter's introduction. As a perceived African American with a recognizably underground hip-hop look – including dreadlocks, baggy jeans, and an Ecko Unltd. messenger bag – what else besides rhymes could I have possibly been writing prior to a hip-hop open mic?[38]

I cannot be certain this was Top R's thought process. However, based on several similar misrecognitions as well as various opportunities and encouragements I received to freestyle and/or record music over the course of the following weeks (see below), it is evident to me that perceptions of my racial identity aligned with *norms of identification* – i.e. notions of what certain people ought to do and ought not to do – surrounding race and hip-hop.[39] Despite the colorblind ideals aspired to within the scene, a clear association between recognized/ascribed Blackness and the practice of MCing endured. Yet Top R's misrecognition could have been attributable to a second recognition in addition to race: this would be his recognition of me (from the previous week) as someone Murs knew – and if he was paying close enough attention he would have recognized that Murs knew me well enough to give me a CD.[40] Of course these two possibilities are more complementary than mutually exclusive. And there is always the possibility that he would have made such an inquiry of anyone putting pen to paper prior to an open mic.

The specter of race, as DuBois observed in his famous double-consciousness postulation, steadily pursues and perpetually preoccupies those who have its markings involuntarily cast upon them.[41] This means that the possibility of being treated in a certain way – whether that way is bad, good, or simply distinct – as a result of being recognized as belonging to a certain race is consistently present. This can range from experiences as innocuous as being selected first (or last) in a pick-up basketball game to something as consequential as being racially profiled. Where and when racial identity is unmarked – this would apply mainly to white Americans (or Europeans or Australians) in most ordinary social settings – the idea of being treated in a certain way as a result of one's race tends to only arise under extraordinary circumstances. Of course, within the broad domain of hip-hop (underground and commercial, national and global) whiteness is often marked – thus Top R becomes "a white guy with dope rhymes" (see above). Yet as part of a larger American (or British, German, Australian, etc.) society, non-whiteness is also marked. Consequently, hip-hop scenes become profitable venues for examining the complex structures and negotiations surrounding race.

The relational dynamics of racial identification that I have thus far sketched correspond with Kwame Appiah's perceptive thoughts on the role that identities play in structuring the terms of mutual conduct through which people interact. Appiah's framework, designed to shed light on "important features of the way social identities work," resonates powerfully with both my own experiences as a racially recognized ethnographer and the regimes of racial understandings and expectations I observed Bay Area underground hip-hoppers continually negotiating.[42] Whereas Appiah's model concerns social identities in general, here I am applying it specifically to race.

Appiah develops his thinking around four processes through which identities take on interrelational salience: "ascription," "identification," "treatment," and (the aforementioned) "norms of identification". Ascription refers to the invariably imperfect schemas people develop which enable them, in most instances, to classify persons as either determinately in or determinately not in an identified (in my case racial) group. This is what I have been calling "racial recognition": I am (recognized as) Black, Top R is (recognized as) white, several MCs at the Rockin' Java open mic are neither Black nor white but are still labeled racially, sometimes as a combination of recognized groups. Appiah's second process, identification, extends ascription's often visually based recognition (of race) to an acknowledged self-recognition that "figures in a certain typical way into [one's] thoughts, feelings and acts."[43] Importantly, how it figures is not prescribed: the fact that I self-recognize as Black does not mean that (in a hip-hop context) I should MC; and the fact Top R identifies as white and an MC does not mean that he should avoid or become defensive during discussions of cultural appropriation. What's vital is that my feeling Black, or his feeling white, or another hip-hopper's feeling Latino or Asian American matters in a relevant way that leads us to consciously act from our positions of subjective racial self-recognition.[44] In chorus with John L. Jackson, I believe that this distinction between restrictive scripts of racial authenticity and (inter-)subjective performances of racial sincerity is critical to understanding the complex and nuanced ways in which race persists as a basis for social solidarity and is lived both "intimately" and "affectively."[45]

For Appiah, the differential treatment of people – ranging from "supererogatory kindness" to "opprobrious unkindness" – as a result of their being recognized as belonging to a certain (racial) group becomes a third way in which social-identity labels function.[46] This process of treatment, of course, in the interactional context of underground hip-hop sociality and/or ethnographic research, can be especially consequential to how these relational performances-of-self play out. Although Appiah (rightfully) acknowledges the degree of latitude surrounding the ways in which modes of identification and treatment shape everyday encounters and life plans, he does not overlook the norms of identification – both self- and collectively imposed regimes of "appropriate" behavior – which work to rein in eccentric excesses and provide common grounding for group membership. This is where the racial recognition of being Black or white or Native American, even in a multiracial underground hip-hop context, gets tethered to an insistence that certain additional things are recognized and/or to be expected.

You better recognize

The occasion of my meeting Top R and his meeting me – our initial selves-in-process interactive moment – intimately illustrates a performative dialectic I observed playing out in the situational acts of racialization taking place throughout the Bay Area's underground hip-hop scene. Curiously, our most telling exchange might have had more to do with my identification as an (African American) anthropologist than with his as a (white) hip-hopper. I am alluding to Top R's recognition of my personhood, actualized through the comment "but you're not like that." The "that" to which he referred is an established (if at times embellished) narrative of anthropology's collusion with and complicity in matters of institutional surveillance and colonial domination, which people knowledgeable of the discipline and possessing a critical disposition are well aware of.[47] I had introduced myself as an anthropologist, but through the combination of Top R's racial recognition of me (as Black) and my performance-of-self in conversation with him – here I would spotlight my confessed misgivings about the politics of research – I became "not that kind of anthropologist." Within underground hip-hop circles, this history of anthropology is relatively obscure; yet the narratives surrounding the history and essential qualities of hip-hop, and notably those concerning white participation in hip-hop, are well rehearsed.[48] Any white hip-hopper journeying outside of exclusively white enclaves has likely been tested and challenged on certain to-be-expected grounds. Through Top R's performance-of-self, he, in so many words, sought to solicit my recognition of him as "not that kind of white hip hopper." Just as I was a part of, but not contained within, an anthropological tradition that included colonial complicities, he became a white MC who acknowledged but was not defined by the history of white participation in Black music. What's significant here is that my deviation from a practiced anthropological tradition was, in part, attributable to my recognized race, whereas Top R's deviation from an ascribed racialized tradition was in spite of his.

Where the terms of subcultural authenticity are well known if not well worn, the most sincere bids to belong involve, first, acknowledging oneself as a particular type of positioned subject in relation to a community of practice – along axes of race, gender, age, (possibly) class, and/or any other type of (usually) visually based identity ascription – and, then, performing one's identity, regardless of the performed content, in dialogue with recognized identity scripts. Through such propositions we not only become more aware of the remarkable diversity of subjective positions (i.e. the untethered counterpoints to positioned subjects) contained within ascriptive labels, but also modify existing norms of identification, and better recognize the constructed nature of social identities.

(W)rapping it up

In terms of my own journey, being recognized as someone Top R knew – and who knew Top R – would favorably mark my movements within the underground hip-hop scene from that day forward. Through our association, my racial noticeability became notable as well. As summer arrived and the open-mic crowds grew larger, I came to be both a fixture (i.e. object of other people's gazes) and a known person at the Rockin' Java open mic. Three months after meeting Top R, I would take my first steps toward freestyling publicly by joining him in a rhyme cypher one evening in Golden Gate Park.[49] In the weeks leading up to that night, several open mic regulars had inquired about my reluctance to rhyme on stage and/or encouraged me to "just go up there." When I finally decided to go, my reception was favorable and supportive – especially from those who had been expectantly waiting, but also from several MCs who, over the course of my year in the Bay, happened to pass through the open microphone. I extensively got recognized as an MC at other hip-hop venues around the city and even while walking its streets. Notably, Top R – although genuinely appreciative of my first attempt to rhyme with him in the park – seemed ambivalent toward my continued efforts. Once, following one of my better freestyles, he noted with a tone of indifference that I was "up there rapping" as he turned to look for someone else in the crowd. And years later, after the fruits of these initial rhyming experiences had led to the release of three albums (with two different groups), Murs bluntly asked me what my motivation for rapping was.

The focus of this chapter has been to examine how particular types of racial recognition foster certain kinds of self-in-process identifications in an underground hip-hop context. As the precarious and contingent nature of much of what I have described illustrates, this is nothing if not complicated terrain. A closing note on the racial and relational performances-of-selves I have sought to theorize here concerns the potential for widely recognized norms of identification to become self-fulfilling prophecies. In interactional exchanges such as those outlined above, the demands associated with expected behavior(s) are either realized or not realized through a dialectic between their (subjective) self-recognition as a basis of identification and their (objective) recognition by others as a basis for treatment. In the case of the ethnographer mistaken for an emcee, it was this treatment that foremost stimulated the transition from misrecognition to recognition.

Further reading

Fernandes, Sujatha, *Close to the Edge: In Search of the Global Hip Hop Generation* (New York: Verso, 2011).

Harrison, Anthony Kwame, *Hip Hop Underground: The Integrity and Ethics of Racial Identification* (Philadelphia: Temple University Press, 2009).

Jackson, John L., Jr., *Real Black: Adventures of Racial Sincerity* (University of Chicago Press, 2005).

Jeffries, Michael P., *Thug Life: Race, Gender, and the Meaning of Hip Hop* (University of Chicago Press, 2011).

Morgan, Marcyliena, *The Real Hiphop: Battling for Knowledge, Power, and Respect in the LA Underground* (Durham, NC: Duke University Press, 2009).

Neff, Ali Colleen, *Let the World Listen Right: The Mississippi Delta Hip-hop Story* (Jackson, MS: University Press of Mississippi, 2009).

Petchauer, Emery, *Hip-hop Culture in College Students' Lives: Elements, Embodiment, and Higher Edutainment* (New York: Routledge, 2012).

Schloss, Joseph G., *Making Beats: The Art of Sample-Based Hip-Hop* (Middletown, CT: Wesleyan University Press, 2004).

Taylor, Paul C., "Does Hip Hop Belong to Me? The Philosophy of Race and Culture," in Derrick Darby and Tommie Shelby (eds.), *Hip Hop and Philosophy: Rhyme 2 Reason* (Chicago: Open Court Publishing, 2005), pp. 79–91.

Notes

1 Anthony Kwame Harrison, *Hip Hop Underground: The Integrity and Ethics of Racial Identification* (Philadelphia: Temple University Press, 2009).

2 Martyn Hammersley and Paul Atkinson, *Ethnography: Principles in Practice*, 2nd edn. (New York: Routledge, 1995), p. 1.

3 Will Hermes, "The World's Greatest Record Store?" *Rolling Stone* 780, February 19, 1998, pp. 19–20.

4 The description of Northampton comes from Jason Rodriquez's ethnographic study of colorblind ideology among hip hoppers there: "Color-Blind Ideology and Cultural Appropriation in Hip-Hop," *Journal of Contemporary Ethnography* 35/6 (2006): 651.

5 Murs had released *F'Real* as an underground tape three years earlier.

6 Both this conversation with Murs and the conversation below with Lord Top Ramen were reconstructed from ethnographic fieldnotes written on April 26, 2000 and May 1, 2000 respectively.

7 Erving Goffman, *The Presentation of Self in Everyday Life* (Woodstock, NY: The Overlook Press, 1973 [1959]).

8 Harrison, *Hip Hop Underground*, p. 39.

9 The late Richard Peterson and Andy Bennett authored the definitive description of music scenes as "contexts in which clusters of producers, musicians, and fans collectively share their common musical tastes and collectively distinguish themselves from others." "Introducing Music Scenes," in Andy Bennett and Richard Peterson (eds.), *Music Scenes: Local, Translocal, Virtual* (Nashville, TN: Vanderbilt University Press, 2004), p. 1. Of course, an aspect of this collectivity – of sharing and distinguishing – involves the co-performance and experience of "the social in the individual and the individual in the social." Simon Frith, "Music and Identity," in Stuart Hall and Paul du Gay (eds.), *Questions of Cultural Identity* (London: Sage Publication, 1996), p. 109.

10 "Impression management" refers to the strategic process through which social actors attempt to influence others' perceptions of them by avoiding "inadvertent acts" and "unmeant gestures" which may portray them in a less than flattering light. See Goffman, *The Presentation of Self*, pp. 208–237.

11 W. E. B. DuBois, *The Souls of Black Folk* (New York: Penguin Books, 1996 [1903]), p. 4.
12 The concept of "microscene" – in reference to "a distinct component of a music scene located in a delimited space of mutual social activity, where certain clusters of scene members assemble and generate socio-cultural cohesion through collective ideologies, attitudes, preferences, practices, customs, and memories that distinguish them from the larger scene" – was developed in Geoff Harkness, "Gangs and Gangsta Rap in Chicago: A Microscenes Perspective," *Poetics* 41/2 (2013): 159.
13 "Thick description" is an interpretive approach to ethnographic analysis popularized by anthropologist Clifford Geertz. It involves densely textured depictions and explanations of social acts and activities, which strive to uncover the layers of cultural significance that underlie them. Clifford Geertz, *The Interpretation of Cultures* (New York: Basic Books, 1973), pp. 3–30. Norman K. Denzin defines autoethnography as "a turning of the ethnographic gaze inward on the self (auto), while maintaining the outward gaze of ethnography, looking at the larger context wherein self-experiences occur." Denzin, *Interpretive Ethnography: Ethnographic Practice for the 21st Century* (Thousand Oaks, CA: Sage, 1997), p. 227. Similarly, Tami Spry describes it as "a self-narrative that critiques the situatedness of self with others in social contexts" and "a vehicle of emancipation from cultural and familial identity scripts." Spry, "Performing Autoethnography: Embodied Methodological Praxis," *Qualitative Inquiry* 7/6 (2001): 710, 708. Whereas most contemporary ethnographies have autoethnographic dimensions to them, here I showcase these aspects in order to efficiently and effectively present the micro-social interactive dynamics I am theorizing.
14 Other disciplines that have embraced ethnography include education, geography, history, planning, political science, psychology, tourism and leisure studies, criminology, architecture, social work, and law. For an early commentary on the death and potential value of ethnography in popular music studies, see Sara Cohen, "Ethnography and Popular Music Studies," *Popular Music* 12/2 (1993): 123–138.
15 Bronislaw Malinowski, *Argonauts of the Western Pacific* (London: Routledge and Kegan Paul, 1966 [1922]), p. 25. Malinowski is generally regarded as the "founding father" of ethnography and many of the methodological precepts he introduced (or popularized) – including participant-observation, learning the local language, and spending a minimum of one year in the field – are still widely observed among ethnographers today. Julie S. Jones, "Origins and Ancestors: A Brief History of Ethnography," in Julie S. Jones and Sal Watt (eds.), *Ethnography in Social Science Practice* (New York: Routledge, 2010), pp. 17–18.
16 For a discussion of close-to-home ethnography, see Mary Pattillo-McCoy, *Black Picket Fences: Privilege and Peril among the Black Middle Class* (University of Chicago Press, 1999), pp. 7–10.
17 The modification of behavior in response to being studied is commonly referred to as the "Hawthorne effect" – named after the factory in which a series of 1920s and 1930s workplace studies were conducted (for a critical commentary, see Stephen R. G. Jones, "Was There a Hawthorne effect?" *American Journal of Sociology* 98/3 (1992): 451–468). Through long-term residence, participation in daily life, and additional efforts to "fit in," anthropologists strive to minimize such behavior modifications.
18 For a comprehensive treatment of these developments, see Dennison Nash and Ronald Wintrob, "The Emergence of Self-Consciousness in Ethnography," *Current Anthropology* 13/5 (1972): 527–542; James Clifford, "Introduction: Partial Truths," in James Clifford and George E. Marcus (eds.), *Writing Culture: The Poetics and Politics of Ethnography* (Berkeley, CA: University of California Press, 1986), pp. 1–26; Diane L. Wolf, "Situating Feminist Dilemmas in Fieldwork," in Diane L. Wolf (ed.), *Feminist Dilemmas in Fieldwork* (Boulder, CO: Westview Press, 1996), pp. 1–55.
19 Peter McLaren, "Field Relations and the Discourse of the Other: Collaboration in Our Own Ruin," in William Shaffir and Robert A. Stebbins (eds.), *Experiencing Fieldwork: An Insider View of Qualitative Research* (Thousand Oaks, CA: Sage Publications, 1991), pp. 153–157. For an exemplary discussion of identity negotiations in ethnographic research, see Takeyuki Tsuda, "Ethnicity and the Anthropologist: Negotiating Identities in the Field," *Anthropological Quarterly* 71/3 (1998): 107–124.
20 Etienne Wenger, *Communities of Practice: Learning, Meaning, and Identity* (Cambridge University Press, 1998).
21 Sarah Thornton argues that social class may not be as important to this sense of subcultural belonging, since subcultures tend to embrace a fantasized classlessness. Sarah Thornton, *Club Cultures: Music, Media and Subcultural Capital* (Cambridge: Polity, 1995), p. 12.
22 The definitive analysis of authenticity in hip-hop was conducted by Kembrew McLeod, "Authenticity within Hip Hop and Other

Cultures Threatened with Assimilation," *Journal of Communication* 49/4 (1999): 134–150.

23 Elsewhere, I have argued that the discourses surrounding underground hip-hop seek to disrupt dominant conceptions of hip-hop's racial and class-based identities while largely overlooking gender (see Harrison, *Hip Hop Underground*).

24 The first comprehensive global survey of hip-hop was Tony Mitchell (ed.), *Global Noise: Rap and Hip Hop Outside the USA* (Middletown, CT: Wesleyan University Press, 2001). The referenced ethnographic studies are Andy Bennett, "Rappin' on the Tyne: White Hip Hop Culture in Northeast England – an Ethnographic Study," *Sociological Review* 47/1 (1999): 1–24; Ian Condry, *Hip-Hop Japan: Rap and the Paths of Cultural Globalization* (Durham, NC: Duke University Press, 2006); Sujatha Fernandes, *Cuba Represent Cuban Arts, State Power, and the Making of New Revolutionary Cultures* (Durham, NC: Duke University Press, 2006); Ayhan Kaya, "*Sicher in Kreuzberg.*" *Constructing Diasporas: Turkish Hip-hop Youth in Berlin* (Bielefeld: Transcript, 2001); Ian Maxwell, *Phat Beats, Dope Rhymes: Hip Hop Down Under Comin' Upper* (Middletown, CT: Wesleyan University Press, 2003).

25 Andreana Clay, *The Hip-Hop Generation Fights Back: Youth, Activism, and Post-Civil Rights Politics* (New York University Press, 2012); Ali Colleen Neff, *Let the World Listen Right: The Mississippi Delta Hip-hop Story* (Jackson, MS: University Press of Mississippi, 2009); Emery Petchauer, *Hip-hop Culture in College Students' Lives: Elements, Embodiment, and Higher Edutainment* (New York: Routledge, 2012); Joseph G. Schloss, *Making Beats: The Art of Sample-Based Hip-Hop* (Middletown, CT: Wesleyan University Press, 2004); Joseph G. Schloss, *Foundation: B-Boys, B-Girls, and Hip-Hop Culture in New York* (New York: Oxford University Press, 2009). I should also mention important ethnographic works by first-generation hip-hop scholars including: Cheryl L. Keyes, *Rap Music and Street Consciousness: Music in American Life* (Chicago: University of Illinois Press, 2004); Marcyliena Morgan, *The Real Hiphop: Battling for Knowledge, Power, and Respect in the LA Underground* (Durham, NC: Duke University Press, 2009).

26 I credit this notion of scholar-practitioner to a roundtable discussion I participated in with Neff, Schloss, Wang, and Fernandes at the 2012 EMP/IASPM – US branch joint conference in New York University. For a discussion of the virtues of ethnographic outsiderness when researching hip-hop, see Ian Maxwell, "The Curse of Fandom: Insiders, Outsiders and Ethnography," in David Hesmondhalgh and Keith Negus (eds.), *Popular Music Studies* (London: Arnold, 2002), pp. 103–116.

27 This idea of what we *ask* of race comes out of Kwame Appiah's assertion that "There is nothing in the world that can do all we ask race to do for us." Appiah, *In My Father's House: Africa in the Philosophy of Culture* (New York: Oxford University Press, 1992), p. 45.

28 Harrison, *Hip Hop Underground*, pp. 139–140.

29 The Day One open mic has an informal "pass the mic" format, in which emcees are usually expected to freestyle for about a minute and it's generally understood that everyone will take a turn before an MC goes again (see Harrison, *Hip Hop Underground*, p. 75).

30 At one point that summer, Top R recorded and sold a 90-minute (TDK) cassette tape of himself freestyling over various hip-hop instrumentals for five dollars a unit. See Anthony Kwame Harrison, "'Cheaper Than a CD, Plus We Really Mean It': Bay Area Underground Hip Hop Tapes as Subcultural Artefacts," *Popular Music* 25/2 (2006): 293. According to a local hip-hop retailer and close friend of Top R's, the underground freestyle tape took only a couple of hours to record. That same retailer approached me a few weeks later asking if he could borrow my copy in order to dub it. He had apparently sold out of Top R's freestyle tape and was looking to make more copies.

31 Oakland is affectionately called "the (Oak)Town," which is juxtaposed to "the (San Francisco) City."

32 For discussions of white appropriation of Black culture, see Margo Jefferson, "Ripping off Black Music: From Thomas 'Daddy' Rice to Jimi Hendrix," *Harpers*, January (1973): 40–45; Perry A. Hall, "African-American Music: Dynamics of Appropriation and Innovation," in Bruce Ziff and Pratima V. Rao (eds.), *Borrowed Power: Essays on Cultural Appropriation* (New Brunswick, NJ: Rutgers University Press, 1997), pp. 31–51; Greg Tate, "Introduction: Nigs R Us, or How Blackfolk Became Fetish Objects," in Greg Tate (ed.) *Everything but the Burden: What White People are Taking from Black Culture* (New York: Broadway Books, 2003), pp. 1–14. For commentaries on white hip-hoppers' position in this dynamic, see Nelson George, *Hip Hop America* (New York: Viking Press, 1998); Paul C. Taylor, "Does Hip Hop Belong to Me? The Philosophy of Race and Culture," in Derrick Darby and Tommie Shelby (eds.), *Hip Hop and Philosophy: Rhyme 2 Reason* (Chicago: Open Court Publishing, 2005), pp. 79–91.

33 According to the then-most-recent (2000) census, the Bay Area population was 50 percent white, 7 percent Black, 19 percent Hispanic, and 19 percent Asian/Pacific-Islander, with just over 3 percent of people identifying as "two or more races." Of course, these numbers vary with regards to specific Bay Area cities and districts (see Harrison, *Hip Hop Underground*, pp. 18–21).

34 For critical commentaries on anthropology's sordid history, see Bernard Magubane and James C. Faris, "On the Political Relevance of Anthropology," *Dialectical Anthropology* 9/1–4 (1985): 91–104; Faye V. Harrison, *Decolonizing Anthropology: Moving Further Towards an Anthropology for Liberation*, third revision (Washington, DC: American Anthropological Association, 1997 [1991]).

35 For a discussion of the importance of being there in anthropology, see Clifford Geertz, *Works and Lives: The Anthropologist as Author* (Stanford University Press, 1988), pp. 1–24.

36 Lee offers the most comparable accounting of ethnographic immersion into a hip-hop open microphone (micro)scene. See Jooyoung Lee, "Open Mic: Professionalizing the Rap Career," *Ethnography* 10/4 (2009): 479–483. Although Morgan immersed herself in the same (Project Blowed) open mic scene as Lee, she offers little to no description of her direct experiences aside from saying that she was "constantly tested and challenged" (*The Real Hiphop*, p. 15). While my discussion in this chapter focuses on race, I think it is worth considering the extent to which gender impacted Morgan's (less-disclosed) experiences as an African American woman.

37 Lee was a Korean American conducting research within a predominantly African American Los Angeles open-microphone scene ("Open Mic," pp. 479–481).

38 Ecko Unltd. is a brand of urban apparel often associated with hip-hop.

39 My understanding of norms of identification is developed from Kwame A. Appiah, "Does Truth Matter to Identity?," in Jorge J. E. Garcia (ed.), *Race or Ethnicity? On Black and Latino Identity* (Ithaca, NY: Cornell University Press, 2007), pp. 29–30.

40 Top R and Murs were certainly friends. In fact, later that year when Murs released his *Murs Rules the World* CD, one of the songs ("Way Tight") included a "What's up to . . . Top R."

41 DuBois, *The Souls of Black Folk*.

42 Appiah, "Does Truth Matter to Identity?," p. 21.

43 *Ibid.*, p. 27.

44 Of course, where Black and white have historically been the most tightly bound racial classifications in American society, people identifying broadly as Latino or Asian/Pacific-Islander are more inclined to identify as members of ethno-racial, or simply ethnic, groups such as Puerto Rican, Filipino, or Mexican.

45 John L. Jackson, Jr., *Real Black: Adventures of Racial Sincerity* (University of Chicago Press, 2005), p. 13; for a thoughtful discussion of racial sincerity in hip-hop, see *ibid.*, pp. 173–196.

46 Appiah, "Does Truth Matter to Identity?," p. 28.

47 See Harrison (ed.), *Decolonizing Anthropology*.

48 When William "Upski" Wimsatt published his exposé of white rappers in the May 1993 issue of *The Source*, it immediately became "the most responded to article in the history of hip hop journalism." William U. Wimsatt, *Bomb the Suburbs*, 2nd edn. (Chicago: The Subway and Elevated Press Company, 1994), p. 22. Ten years later, *The Source* would publish a scathing critique of Eminem authored by Public Enemy Media Assassin Harry Allen ("The Unbearable Whiteness of Emceeing: What the Eminence of Eminem Says About Race," *The Source*, February [2003]: 91–92). I would add, quite simply, that the mere mention of Vanilla Ice's name continues to be a punchline in most contexts where I've seen the white rapper brought up.

49 This episode is recounted in the opening pages of Harrison, *Hip Hop Underground*, pp. 1–4.

12 Thirty years of Rapsploitation: hip-hop culture in American cinema

GEOFF HARKNESS

Rap music's rise to prominence, which dovetailed the trajectories of television outlets such as MTV and BET, made rap videos a natural resource for scholarly analysis. There is an extended history of studies that examine rap videos as primary texts, particularly in their limited and often stereotypical portrayals of women.[1] The relationship between hip-hop culture and cinema has generated less attention. Yet the sweeping popularity of rap music has spilled over into nearly every genre of film, including comedy, drama, action, gangster, biopic, documentary, mockumentary, horror, musical, dance, and even pornography. Unlike music videos, however, cinematic representations of hip-hop culture differ from the expressions that emanate from its practitioners. Hip-hop-themed or Rapsploitation movies are calculated to appeal to these practitioners, who constitute their target audience, but like most films are crafted to reach the largest possible audience.

As a cinematic subgenre Rapsploitation consists of a small canon of a few dozen movies, only a handful of which have earned much at the box office. More common is the use of hip-hop culture in films: a goofy white wannabe thrown in for comedic effect, a celebrity rapper cast in a non-hip-hop-related role, or a rap music soundtrack calculated to provide an aura of so-called authentic Black street culture. Producing a movie is an expensive endeavor whose costs typically dwarf those related to creating songs and music videos. The highest grossing Rapsploitation film of all time, the 2002 Eminem vehicle *8 Mile*, cost $41 million to produce and generated nearly $243 million in box office sales before earning even more revenues in DVD and streaming dollars.[2] Conversely, *Marci X*, a 2003 Rapsploitation comedy starring Lisa Kudrow and Damon Wayans, had a $20 million budget but earned a mere $1.675 million at the box office, a catastrophic financial failure. With this type of money at stake, little is left to chance. Films – Rapsploitation and otherwise – necessitate adhering to genre conventions that include stock storylines and characters and plenty of action, violence, and sex.[3]

Mic, lights, camera, action

Hip-hop is an inherently visual culture; the vivid graffiti colors, the awe-inspiring breakdance moves, and the theatrical drama of rap battles readily lend themselves to cinematic depictions. It comes as little surprise, then, that film-makers leapt at the opportunity to capture hip-hop culture on celluloid, almost from its inception. The earliest forays into Rapsploitation were low-budget affairs, reflecting hip-hop culture's then-status as an underground, noncommercial phenomenon. The 1983 documentary *Style Wars* chronicled the primordial scene in New York, focusing largely on graffiti. *Wild Style*, a feature film released the same year, was an indie attempt to fictionalize this scene, recounting the tale of a young graffiti artist struggling to gain respect amid the rap, DJ, and breakdance pioneers who also contributed to the burgeoning culture. *Beat Street* and *Breakin'*, issued in 1984, and 1985's *Krush Groove*, offered more of the same, but with bigger budgets that reflected rap's growing commercial presence. These films, shot in vivid color and cast with multicultural young men and women joyfully participating in hip-hop culture, are almost startling in contrast to today's mostly dour, violent, and hypermasculine depictions.

Spike Lee's influence on Rapsploitation cannot be overstated. Though Lee has never directed a feature film about rap music, movies such as 1989's critical smash *Do the Right Thing* were steeped in hip-hop culture, and Lee's prominence as a writer-director helped launch a Black cinema renaissance that continues to resonate today. Lee's considerable imprint on film-making inspired a number of critically acclaimed and commercially viable successors, including John Singleton, Reginald Hudlin, Mario Van Peebles, and the Hughes Brothers, all of whom have directed films that heavily reference hip-hop culture.

In the mid to late 1980s, rap music rose in prominence as independent rap record labels partnered with major labels to increase distribution and visibility. The rise in popularity of hip-hop culture led to co-option by the major media conglomerates, whose marketing savvy and business acumen put the spotlight increasingly on rap music, to the detriment of the culture's other elements.[4] Black male rappers effectively became the popular face of hip-hop culture and a number of rap superstars were cast in movies during this time. Film scholar Melvin Donalson suggested that "the screen presence of many rappers in music videos encouraged a casting of those rappers in fictional roles; at the very least, the familiarity of hip-hop fans with those rappers guaranteed a substantial viewing audience."[5]

Featherweight flicks such as 1990s' *House Party* and 1991's *Cool as Ice* depicted hip-hop as a natural extension of youth culture, a benign social force not unlike the sock-hops of the 1950s. As gangsta rap rose in prominence during the late 1980s and early 1990s, however, a new genre of film emerged, hood cinema. The plotlines of *Colors, New Jack City, Boyz N the Hood*, and *Menace II Society* had little to do with hip-hop culture, but were heavily influenced by it nonetheless. These violent films, which offered a postmodern spin on the Blaxploitation movies of the 1970s, were set in gritty urban environs, featured celebrity rappers in pivotal roles, and were set to rap-music soundtracks. In response, another set of movies from this era (*CB4, Fear of a Black Hat, Don't be a Menace to South Central While Drinking Your Juice in the Hood*) satirized gangsta rap and the hood cinema trend.

Early Rapsploitation cinema regularly featured women as key participants. Movies such as *Breakin'* and *Krush Groove* included scenes where female artists held their own alongside their male counterparts. This trend, however, began to reverse in the Rapsploitation films of the early 1990s. Female MCs such as Salt-N-Pepa, Queen Latifah, and Monie Love were integral to the rap music produced during this era, but women were largely sidelined on screen, reduced to auxiliary roles that emphasized sexuality over musical skills. Most often women were cast as wives, girlfriends, one-night stands, and audience members. The few females portrayed as participants of hip-hop culture were generally cast in minor roles (dancers, back-up singers), a cinematic tradition that remains largely intact.

The growing recognition that white male teenagers were enchanted by hip-hop culture led to a number of films that grappled with this phenomenon, sometimes seriously and at other times for comedic effect. *White Boyz* and *Black and White* (both released in 1999), *8 Mile* (2002), and *Malibu's Most Wanted* (2003) toyed with white involvement in rap music and (to a lesser degree) hip-hop culture. These films often depicted the allegedly transformative power of rap music when crossing the Black–white color line. In 1998's *Bulworth* a cynical white democratic senator from California regains his Civil Rights-era values after taking up rapping as a campaign tool. By the end of the movie its titular character effectively becomes a Black "street" caricature, dropping his cookie-cutter suit-and-tie combos in favor of knit caps, sportswear, and sunglasses. "You know you my nigga," the Black female protagonist tells Bulworth near the film's end.

By the turn of the century, rap music had effectively become the soundtrack of American youth culture. Many hip-hop scholars point to the year 2000 as important "because that year marked a turning point in the industry's increasing commercialization and greater detachment from its neighborhood sources."[6] Concurrent with rising commercialization was a shift toward what Roopali Makherjee dubbed the "ghetto fabulous aesthetic,"[7] which emphasized hypermaterialism and conspicuous consumption. While early celluloid depictions of hip-hop culture were rooted in a working-class aesthetic, and hood cinema depicted lower-class life in urban ghettos, the new millennial trend juxtaposed near parodic displays of wealth with so-called "street" behaviors and attitudes that kept a foot firmly planted in the hood. Films such as 1999's *Murda Musik* and 2003's *Death of a Dynasty* illustrated this trend.

The dramatic decline in music sales in the post-Napster era, combined with the increasing availability of inexpensive movie-making technology, helped spawn an independent Rapsploitation cinema. Master P in particular cashed in on the opportunity to produce and distribute a series of microbudget indie films, several of which earned small fortunes for the New Orleans mogul. 1998's *I Got the Hook Up* was a modest box-office hit that earned $10 million against a budget of $3.5 million, and P was the tenth highest-paid American entertainer that year, according to *Forbes Magazine*.

The movie industry's increasing focus on big-ticket franchise films has led to a decline in low-budget movies that do not earn hundreds of millions of dollars.[8] While rap music remains popular, the pairing of hip-hop culture and the major movie studios has declined sharply in recent years. Of the ten highest-grossing Rapsploitation films of all time, half were made between 2002 and 2005, and only one (2009's *Notorious*) was released after this period. The exception to this trend is in the dance genre; updates of early Rapsploitation films such as *Breakin'*, *You Got Served* (2004), *Step Up* (2006), *How She Move* (2007), and *Video Girl* (2011) are notable in that they almost always feature a middle-class female lead whose traditional, conservative dance moves are transformed upon meeting a working-class ethnic minority male. While these movies are not about hip-hop culture, they borrow heavily from its aesthetics and ideology.

S. Craig Watkins noted that, "[i]ndependent distributors are more likely to seek out 'fresh' material that can be differentiated from the imitative and formulaic cycles that tend to dominate film production in Hollywood."[9] Today's Rapsploitation films are often microbudget indies that cater to niche audiences. In that sense, the medium has come full circle and is back in the hands of independent film-makers with a direct – and often firsthand – appreciation of the culture. Movies such as *Akira's Hip Hop Shop* (2007) demonstrate a genuine affection for old-school hip-hop, but most of today's Rapsploitation fare depicts a culture enmeshed in gangsta-rap tropes. Drugs, street gangs, prisons, and deadly gun battles are the *mise-en-scène* of recent low-budget films such *A Day in the Life* and *Know Thy Enemy*, both released in 2009. The few larger budget Rapsploitation films produced in recent years – *Get Rich or Die Tryin'* (2005), *Hustle and Flow* (2005), *Notorious* (2009) – faithfully repeat the same clichés. Hip-hop culture as currently depicted on screen is a social world populated by shady promoters, greedy managers, crooked cops, disapproving parents, outraged politicians, hypersexual women, and violent male criminals.

A typology of characters in rapsploitation cinema

Movie characters in any genre are rarely multidimensional or complex. Rather, in service of a film's plot, people in films are generally depicted as instantly recognizable archetypes: superheroes, bad boys, femmes fatales, business tycoons, mad scientists, sassy best friends, and manic pixie dream girls. This one-dimensional rendering makes movie characters fairly easy to categorize, but these archetypes also reveal something larger about the social, cultural, and political issues of the era in which the films were produced. For example, early Hollywood portrayals of African Americans as subservient butlers and maids enable critical viewers to better understand racial attitudes of that time. More recently, the stereotyping of Arabs as terrorists in contemporary Hollywood cinema exposes the fears and anxieties of post 9/11 America.[10]

Scrutiny of Rapsploitation cinema reveals a number of stock characters who illustrate these larger issues. In creating a typology of these characters, I analyzed fifty-three hip-hop themed films, paying particular attention to how characters directly involved in hip-hop culture were portrayed. The central attributes of these stock characters were signified through language, speech, dialect, clothing, body language, behavior, attitudes, ideology, cultural practices, and the production of cultural objects such as songs and live performances. These stock characters represent Weberian "ideal types," rather than hard, fixed categories with no room for overlap.[11] While most of the characters were one dimensional, they sometimes embodied more than one category.

Hip-hop's multi-faceted crossover onto the big screen necessitated the creation of certain boundaries in creating this typology. Requisite was that the film included one or more lead characters whose involvement in hip-hop culture was foregrounded. Thus, films with a hip-hop "sensibility" but that were not about hip-hop culture (e.g. *New Jack City*, *Boyz N the Hood*, *Baller Blockin*) were not included. Also excluded were documentaries and the burgeoning genre of hip-hop themed pornography.[12]

My interest was to understand the various means by which hip-hoppers were portrayed on screen, the central characteristics of these archetypes, how these archetypes have changed over time, and the larger implications of these findings. I begin with a typology of archetypal characters and the central characteristics associated with each. I conclude by exploring the larger implications of these findings.

Bad girls are sexually insatiable females who emphasize their physical attributes and downplay other aspects of identity. Exemplars include Lil' Kim in *Notorious* and Yanesha Kon in *Play'd: A Hip Hop Story*. Bad girls dress in provocative clothing, curse like sailors, and often appear nude on screen. Shug, a bad girl who sings over rap tracks in *Hustle and Flow*, is a pregnant prostitute. Many bad girls are punished for their wayward behavior. For example, in *Notorious*, Lil' Kim is portrayed as a hysterical stalker who is physically and verbally assaulted by Biggie Smalls, who quickly dumps her and marries Faith Evans.

Commercial sellouts utilize hip-hop as a commodity rather than an artistic expression, even if that means compromising personal ideals. Exemplars include Wacky Dee in *CB4*, Ren and Ten in *Brown Sugar*, and Jaxx in *Play'd: A Hip Hop Story*. Commercial sellouts are aligned with the mainstream rather than the underground, and follow mass trends rather than staying true to themselves. Kembrew McLeod defined selling out as "the distancing of an artist's music and persona from an independently owned network of distribution (the underground) and repositioning oneself within a music business culture dominated by the big five multinational corporations that control the U.S. music industry."[13]

In Rapsploitation films, commercial sellouts are typically played for laughs, but Jaxx, the protagonist of *Play'd: A Hip Hop Story*, illustrates the complications that can arise from selling out. Jaxx, who is one half of a successful rap duo, signs on with a commercial gangsta rap label, modeled on Death Row Records. Jaxx has few connections to the streets, but adopts a gangsta persona and lifestyle in a bid to launch a successful solo career. He sells three million copies of his solo debut, but things quickly turn violent. At the end of the movie, Jaxx forfeits all publishing and royalties for his next album in an attempt to extract himself from the gangsta-rap record label. But it's too late; Jaxx is murdered at the conclusion of the film.

Divas serve as clean-cut female counterparts to bad girls. Middle class, modest in dress and appearance, willowy, and often light skinned, divas have sweet dispositions that are appealing to men. Exemplars include Roxie in *Let It Shine*, Sidney in *Brown Sugar*, and Faith Evans in *Notorious*. According to Stephens and Few, divas "appear independent yet select partners that primarily bolster social status and provide companionship. [Their] sexuality is framed from a traditional view of power in relationships, such that males are viewed as central to defining who [they are]."[14] As the female protagonists of Rapsploitation films, divas are always rewarded for "appropriate" behavior; they typically secure the most desirable male in the movie, sometimes against heavy odds. In *Notorious* and *Brown Sugar*, the male leads break up with significant others and even end marriages in order to consort with a seemingly irresistible diva.

Hip-hop heroes are protagonist purists whose involvement in hip-hop serves as its own reward – they emphasize art for art's sake, rather than as a money-making tactic. Hip-hop heroes are aligned with the underground and the old school, and stay true to their core values and beliefs. Exemplars include Zoro in *Wild Style*, Cyrus in *Let It Shine*, and Dre in *Brown Sugar*. Hip-hop heroes do not follow mass trends or commercial, mainstream interests. They are versed in the history of hip-hop, and display allegiance to all aspects of the culture, rather than just rap music. "The old school refers to a more close-knit community of break dancers, DJs, MCs, and graffiti artists who helped nurture and develop hip-hop as a culture, and who were not necessarily concerned with making money."[15] Hip-hop heroes are generally working class. Cyrus, the lead character in *Let It Shine*, works as a bus boy in a nightclub. Cav, a rapper portrayed by Mos Def in *Brown Sugar*, drives a cab. Akira – a Japanese rapper, DJ and producer and the titular character of *Akira's Hip Hop Shop* – has encyclopedic knowledge of the old-school hip-hop records he sells for a "fair price" from the independent record store he owns. In *Brown Sugar*, Dre is an upwardly mobile executive at a commercial rap record label. In one scene, he reminisces about the old school rap music of his youth: "Back in the day. Do you remember that feeling, just how hip-hop used to make you feel? Especially back then. It was so real, it was like air." Dre quits his high paying job and starts his own independent record company, one focused on authentic, old school rap music, rather than cynical commercial fare. "I was tired of making bullshit and calling it hip-hop," he avows.

Playas are hypermasculine male characters whose primary trait is their ability to attract members of the opposite sex. Exemplars include Dr. S in *Marci X*, Stabmaster Arson in *CB4*, and Kris in *Let It Shine*. Playas are hard rather than soft, emphasizing allegedly masculine traits such as aggression and competition. Writing about hip-hop dance as depicted in film, Sara LaBoskey noted that its "synonymy with competition has kept it a primarily male-dominated realm; it is the male ego on trial. Each challenge is an opportunity to gain dominance and respect or be defeated."[16] So it is with the playa, who claims status via sexual conquest. Playas are depicted as possessing a natural ability to attract women, rather than having a skill developed over time. In Rapsploitation films, they are regularly featured in scenes surrounded by not one, but a large number of attractive, willing females. In *House Party*, Play arrives in a car so full of women, there is no room for the DJ or his equipment. In *Hustle and Flow*, the lead character is literally a pimp. "The term pimp is often synonymous with 'player,' a man who excels at attracting women or glamorized hustlers who conspicuously display their riches . . . The celebration of both pimp imagery and real pimps is pervasive in rap culture."[17] Homophobia is another trait of the playa.

"Within hip-hop, being a real man doesn't merely entail having the proper sex organ; it means acting in a masculine manner . . . To claim one is a real man, one is defining himself not just in terms of gender, but also sexuality, that is, not being a 'pussy' or a 'faggot.'"[18]

Political panthers employ hip-hop as a tool of political expression and social activism. In doing so they take "dead aim at institutions of power within the United States in an attempt to address the blatant and growing racial inequities in American society."[19] Exemplars include Dead Mike in *CB4*, Zora in *House Party 2*, and Radio Raheem in *Do the Right Thing*. In *Bulworth*, the titular character takes to rapping as a political campaign tool, using the medium as a platform for telling politically incorrect truths. In *Do the Right Thing*, Radio Raheem carries a large, portable stereo that he uses to blast political rap music everywhere he goes. According to historian Robin Kelley, hip-hoppers deploy loud rap music strategically as "weapons in a battle over the right to occupy public space. Frequently employing high-decibel car stereos and boom-boxes, black youth not only 'pump up the volume' for their own listening pleasure, but also as part of an indirect, ad hoc war of position."[20] While political panthers garner respect from their local communities, they are generally portrayed as martyrs: both Radio Raheem and Bulworth have been murdered by the time the final credits roll.

Rapitalists embody the "spirit of rapitalism" in that they are capitalist entrepreneurs who simultaneously maintain an aura of so-called street credibility.[21] Exemplars include Sean "Puffy" Combs in *Notorious* and A-Maze in *Just Another Day*. Rapitalists view rap music through the lens of business and frame their involvement as work, rather than leisure. They are commercial and mainstream, yet aligned with the streets, rather than the suburbs. Unlike the thug lifer archetype, rapitalists are not criminals, but businessmen. "Stop thinking about all this little shit all the time," A-Maze admonishes a colleague in *Just Another Day*. "We out here trying to do business, man. Let's take care of business. Don't nothing else really even fuckin' matter. What you gonna do with a double extra crispy number three with sesame seeds and shit you ain't got no money to busy it with? Stay focused."

Skilled sincerists are outsiders whose knowledge of the art, aesthetic, and history of hip-hop are invoked via skills and sincerity. Exemplars include Shelby in *Hustle and Flow*, Johnny Van Owen in *Cool as Ice*, and B Rabbit in *8 Mile*. Skilled sincerists stay true to themselves and eschew mass trends. Their skin color, social class, and/or gender renders them outsiders, a status they overcome via elaborate displays of hip-hop skills. "Once they hear you, it won't matter what color you are," Future, a black hip-hopper says to Rabbit, a white rapper portrayed by Eminem in *8 Mile*. Indeed, in

8 Mile's most famous scene, Rabbit triumphs at a rap battle before a mostly Black audience by making explicit his whiteness and circumventing the criticisms aimed at white rappers. Rabbit also flips the script by augmenting his working-class job and trailer-park dwelling. In doing so, Rabbit uses situational authenticity, which

> occurs when a person makes a claim to "realness" that emphasizes certain categories within the normative cluster of conditions that govern authenticity, while downplaying others . . . Outsiders emphasize interpretive categories and de-emphasize those that are fixed . . . and reorder the normative cluster of conditions to suit their own habitus.[22]

Thug lifers combine unpredictability with a willingness to commit violence and/or other criminal acts. Exemplars include Marcus in *Get Rich or Die Tryin'*, Tupac Shakur in *Notorious*, and Young Eastie in *Just Another Day*. The thug lifer embodies hypermasculinity, profanity, and is aligned with the streets rather than the suburbs. Like rapitalists, thug lifers aspire to fortune and fame, but unlike rapitalists they are willing to fund their music careers through criminal acts such as robbery and drug dealing. In *Just Another Day*, aspiring rapper Young Eastie sells drugs from a fast-food drive thru' window. In *Get Rich or Die Tryin'*, Marcus deals crack to fund his rap-music ambitions. Thug lifers are a staple of dramatic action Rapsploitation films, but they are also found in comedies.

Wannabes are phonies whose participation in hip-hop culture is insincere or lacks credibility. Exemplars include B-Rad in *Malibu's Most Wanted*, Papa Doc in *8 Mile*, Albert/MC Gusto in *CB4*, and Vanilla Sherbert in *Fear of a Black Hat*. White wannabes are satirized for over-identification with stereotypical elements of so-called Black street culture. They speak in African American vernacular English (AAVE) and Black street slang, and wear clothing that signifies an unearned alliance with so-called Black ghetto culture. In *Malibu's Most Wanted* and *Fear of a Black Hat* white wannabes say the n-word and encounter violence from blacks. Black wannabes are portrayed as middle-class suburbanites who attempt to pass themselves off as street denizens; fake because they do not stay true to themselves. In the final battle scene in *8 Mile*, Rabbit exposes his Black gangsta-rap opponent as a private-school graduate named Clarence who "lives at home with both parents." Be they Black or white, wannabes are criticized and otherwise punished for not being true to themselves, for pretending to be something they are not. Wannabes are the antithesis of hip-hop's mandate to "keep it real."

The aftermath

As a cinematic body, Rapsploitation reflects, reaffirms, and comments on issues of race, gender, and social class in some of the same ways found in hip-hop culture. Early Rapsploitation cinema illustrated the contributions of Latinos to hip-hop culture, but mid-period movies depicted hip-hop primarily as a Black culture threatened with white assimilation. Films such as 1999's *Black and White* feature clueless Caucasians whose interest in hip-hop culture is academic and colonialist or those who over-identify to the point of parody. A few Rapsploitation efforts made clumsy attempts to demonstrate white transformation via hip-hop culture: the titular character of *Bulworth* finds himself by becoming a Black ghetto stereotype but he never pulls off the look or the rhymes with anything resembling credibility. In *Marci X*, after taking up with a playa named Dr. S, the female lead (played by *Friends* alum Lisa Kudrow) begins sporting African kaftans and gele head wraps to unintended comedic effect. Slightly more convincing is Flip, the lead character in *Whiteboyz*, a rapping wannabe who learns to stop acting like a Black hood stereotype and start being himself. But it was *8 Mile* that offered a successful strategy for white involvement in hip-hop: sincerity combined with skills could lead to acceptance from non-whites. *Hustle and Flow* (2005) features Shelby, a skilled sincerist whose skin color is barely commented on.

Hip-hop heroes fare the best of all characters in the Rapsploitation subgenre, portrayed as authentic in that they are dedicated to ideals and art instead of cash. Most heroes are Black, but a small number of Latinos and Asians are also found in this category. The few Black political panthers are portrayed as enlightened, but some are punished for this behavior. Those who are not murdered are portrayed as overbearing conspiracy theorists. The majority of Rapsploitation's Black males are depicted in a negative light, re-creating many of the same stereotypes still found in Hollywood films. Black men are painted as criminals, thugs, gang members, sellouts, wannabes, calculating capitalists, and oversexed lotharios. And these are the protagonists, most of whom are surrounded by an even worse cast of low-lifes. This is especially true for recent Rapsploitation entries, but those who believe that earlier films were wholly positive should have another look at 1983's *Wild Style*, where a faction of male rappers talks a group of women into a drug-fueled orgy.

Reflecting hip-hop culture's hypermasculinity, the majority of women in Rapsploitation cinema are either insulted or ignored. Many of the movies feature women, some prominently, but most females are cast as love inter-est, prostitutes, mothers, sidekicks, one-night stands, and other periph-eral characters. Very few women in today's Rapsploitation fare actually participate in the culture itself. This is a marked shift from earlier portray-als of females, whose involvement was more direct. *Beat Street*, *Breakin'*, and *Krush Groove* featured empowered women in starring roles. 1991's *House Party 2* included Zora, a female activist who raps a socially conscious song called "Knowledge is Power" at a rally for a campus ethnic studies program.

Sidney, the female lead in 2007's *Brown Sugar*, is one of the rare exceptions found in recent years. Although Sidney is a hip-hop journalist, rather than a cultural practitioner, her romanticization of old school rap music and commitment to the culture is foregrounded. It is a shared love old school rap music that is at the heart of the attraction between Sidney and Dre, the male lead. With the exception of these few roles, however, women are underrepresented as participants of hip-hop culture, and Rapsploitation films both reflect and reproduce this phenomenon.

If Rapsploitation has not done much to improve upon Hollywood's demonization of Black males and sexualization of women of all colors, it has made perhaps a marginal contribution toward challenging racialized notions of social class. Early Rapsploitation was rooted in a working-class aesthetic, which eventually gave way to the ghetto fabulous aesthetic and capitalism by any means necessary. But there have always been Rapsploitation films that play with ideas of social class. *House Party* (1990) has been esteemed as a film that depicted Black middle-class adolescence without questioning the "street" authenticity of its clean-cut central characters. The double meaning of 1992's *Class Act* (also starring the *House Party* leads, rap duo Kid and Play) is no accident. A prince-and-pauper rehash, the film features nerdy Duncan Pinderhughes, a straight-A student with perfect SAT scores, who becomes more "Black" after being taught how to rap and dance by his "hood" counterpart, Blade. But Blade finds a softer side of himself, too, after exposure to the Pinderhughes way of life. While the tale is simplistic, it lightly challenges the notion that authentic blackness is synonymous with so-called street life. The plot of 1993's *CB4* centers around three suburban, middle-class Black teens who assume criminal personas in a quest for rap fame. 2002's *Brown Sugar* depicts middle-class Black adults as serious, hard working, and looking for fulfillment through both marriage and employment. More recently, 2012's Disney-helmed *Let It Shine* is set in a world that depicts Black middle-class tween life as largely free of drama. Critics may charge – as they have with some Tyler Perry movies or Bill Cosby roles – that the middle-class Blacks in these films are simply "acting white," but the hip-hop culture at the core of these films make those accusations easier to deflect. Rapsploitation, then, may represent one of the few cinematic spaces where the hip-hop culture belongs as much to the Black middle class as it does to Blacks on the lower rungs of the socio-economic strata.

So long as rap music remains commercially viable, Rapsploitation films will continue to be produced. It is doubtful that they will ever be a force for social change, largely due to the nature of their existence. Exploitation films of any stripe are designed to cash in on existing trends, rather than to generate new ideas or ways of thinking. Reflective of creative industries that craft commercial products calculated for mass, rather than niche, audiences, original cinematic depictions of hip-hop culture are unlikely to receive wide distribution. With the increasing democratization of cinematic production and distribution, such films will continue to be produced and consumed at the underground level, the location where the most creative and interesting hip-hop culture has always existed. In that regard, Rapsploitation film is reflective of hip-hop culture, both in content and in character.

Notes

1 Two decades of scholarship have examined the negative portrayals of women in hip-hop music videos. For examples, see Rana Emerson, "'Where My Girls at': Negotiating Black Womanhood in Music Videos," *Gender & Society* 16 (2002): 115–135; Margaret Hunter, "Shake it, Baby, Shake it: Consumption and the New Gender Relation Hip-hop," *Sociological Perspectives* 54 (2001): 15–36; Cheryl L. Keyes, "Empowering Self, Making Choices, Creating Spaces: Black Female Identity via Rap Music Performance," *The Journal of American Folklore* 113 (2000): 255–269; Ladel Lewis, "White Thugs & Black Bodies: A Comparison of the Portrayal of African-American women in Hip-hop Videos," *The Hilltop Review* 4 (2011): 1–17; Robin Roberts, "'Ladies First': Queen Latifah's Afrocentric Feminist Music Video," *African American Review* 28 (1994): 245–257; Dionne Stephens, and Layi Phillips, "Freaks, Gold Diggers, Divas, and Dykes: The Sociohistorical Development of Adolescent African American Women's Sexual Scripts," *Sexuality & Culture* 7 (2003): 3–49; and L. Monique Ward, Edwina Hansbrough, and Eboni Walker, "Contributions of Music Video Exposure to Black Adolescents' Gender and Sexual Schemas," *Journal of Adolescent Research* 20 (2005): 143–166.

2 These and subsequent financial data came from BoxOfficeMojo.com. While Eminem's skills are widely acknowledged, many also believe that the rapper's mainstream success is attributable to his whiteness and rap music's large white audience. For example, see Edward G. Armstrong, "Eminem's Construction of Authenticity," *Popular Music and Society* 27/3 (2004): 335–355.

3 A contemporary sociological analysis of Hollywood conventions is found in David Grazian, *Mix It Up: Popular Culture, Mass Media, and Society* (New York: W. W. Norton, 2010).

4 See Greg Dimitriadis, "Hip-hop to Rap: Some Implications of an Historically Situated Approach to Performance," *Text and Performance Quarterly* 19 (1999): 355–369; and Keith Negus, "The Music Business and Rap: Between the Street and the Executive Suite," *Cultural Studies* 13 (1999): 488–508.

5 Melvin Donalson, *Hip Hop in American Cinema* (New York: Peter Lang Publishing, 2007), p. 36.

6 Ronald Weitzer and Charis Kubrin, "Misogyny in Rap Music: A Content Analysis of Prevalence and Meanings," *Men and Masculinities* 12 (2009): 10.

7 Roopali Makherjee, "The Ghetto Fabulous Aesthetic in Contemporary Black Culture," *Cultural Studies* 20/6 (2006): 599–629.

8 See Grazian, *Mix It Up*, Chapter 6.

9 S. Craig Watkins, *Representing: Hip Hop Culture and the Production of Black Cinema* (University of Chicago Press, 1998), p. 101.

10 A thorough analysis of Arab stereotypes in post-9/11 films is found in Jack Shaheen, *Guilty: Hollywood's Verdict on Arabs after 9/11* (Northampton, MA: Olive Branch Press, 2008).

11 See Philip Gossett, "Carl Dahlhaus and the 'Ideal Type,'" *19th-Century Music* 13 (1989): 49–56.

12 For a scholarly analysis of the latter see Mireille Miller-Young, "Hip Hop Honeys and da Hustlaz: Black Sexualities in the New Hip Hop Pornography," *Meridians: Feminism, Race, Transnationalism* 8 (2008): 261–292.

13 Kembrew McLeod, "Authenticity within Hip Hop and Other Cultures Threatened with Assimilation," *Journal of Communication* 49/4 (1999): 141.

14 Dionne Stephens and April Few, "Hip-hop Honey or Video Ho: African American Preadolescents' Understanding of Female Sexual Scripts in Hip-hop culture," *Sexuality & Culture* 11 (2007): 51.

15 McLeod, "Authenticity within Hip Hop," pp. 143–144.

16 Sara LaBoskey, "Getting off: Portrayals of Masculinity in Hip-hop Dance in Film," *Dance Research Journal* 33 (2001): 113–114.

17 Weitzer and Kubrin, "Misogyny in Rap Music," p. 20.
18 McLeod, "Authenticity within Hip Hop," p. 142.
19 Erik Nielson, "'Here Come the Cops': Policing the Resistance in Rap Music," *International Journal of Cultural Studies* 15 (2012): 349.
20 Robin D. G. Kelley, *Race Rebels: Culture, Politics, and the Black Working Class* (New York: The Free Press, 1994), p. 206.
21 See Geoff Harkness, "The Spirit of Rapitalism: Artistic Labor Practices in Chicago's Hip Hop Underground," *Journal of Workplace Rights* 16 (2012): 251–270.
22 Geoff Harkness, "True School: Situational Authenticity in Chicago's Hip Hop Underground," *Cultural Sociology* 6 (2012): 288.

13 Barbz and kings: explorations of gender and sexuality in hip-hop

REGINA N. BRADLEY

In March 2013, a verse by Rick Ross for rapper Rocko's mixtape track "U.O.E.N.O."[1] leaked on the internet. In it, Ross talked about his plans to sexually engage a woman without her consent. Ross raps, "put molly all in her champagne, she ain't even know it/I took her home and enjoyed that, she ain't even know it." In another incident around the same time, rapper Lil' Wayne boasts of "beating the pussy up like Emmett Till." A year before these incidents, Oakland pioneer rapper Too $hort released a Valentine's Day video instructing boys how to approach girls: "Take your finger and put a little spit on it and you stick your finger in her underwear and you rub it on there and watch what happens." Although all three rappers would later apologize for their words – Ross apologized three times for his lyrics – the controversy surrounding Ross, Lil' Wayne, and Too $hort demands a (re)visitation of the gendered and racialized identity politics at play in contemporary popular culture.[2]

Overarching tropes of misogyny, rape culture, and violence against women present hip-hop as a hypermasculine and gendered space of (Black) American cultural expression that is profitable. The privilege of what is marketable comes with hypervisibility and increased normalcy and vice versa. Conceiving gender in commercial hip-hop as a commodity gives lee-way for the frequent clashes of gender that occupy a hip-hop space. For example, the most brazenly commodified representation of gender in hip-hop is women's sexuality. Returning to Rick Ross's date rape lyrics, Ross's delivery situates women's bodies as disposable sources of sexual pleasure and income; he uses champagne – one commodity – to buy the woman's attention – another commodity – and ultimately engages her in sex without her consent. The simultaneous detachment of women's agency and empha-sis of women's sexuality imposed upon women's bodies exhibited in lyrics like Ross's inadvertently point to the complexities of gender performance that frame hip-hop's commercial and cultural identity.

Ross's realization that his lyrics are problematic did not come to full fruition until after his pockets were hit. Outcries on social media out-lets Twitter, Youtube, and Facebook and demonstrations by women's group UltraViolet in front of Ross's endorsement partner Reebok resulted in their dropping Ross as a spokesperson. Ross's loss of endorsements further emphasizes the intervention of capitalism as a lens of hip-hop gender politics. The gender performances that are most commodified transition into those performances considered normative, culturally relevant, and representative of hip-hop aesthetics. The challenge, however, is considering how capitalism impacts gender as it intersects with other underlying factors of hip-hop like race, social-political agency, and class.

Hip-hop's gender politics extend outside of their performative qualities into the realms of lived experience and expectation, and are often short-sighted about the complexities of Blackness and humanity that hip-hop could (and should) represent. Hip-hop gender politics are often considered oppositional and frequently in a power struggle that intersects with race and class. Tricia Rose argues in *The Hip Hop Wars* that the stereotypical expectations and representations of race and gender in hip-hop satiate a larger paranoia about Black gender roles that exists at the crux of hip-hop as a lens of Black (gender) performance and reality. She writes,

> the history of association of blacks with ignorance, sexual deviance, violence, and criminality has not only contributed to the believability of hip-hop artists' fictitious autobiographical tales among fans from various racial groups but has also helped explain the excessive anxiety about the popularity and allure of these artists.[3]

Hip-hop masculinity is aggressive, dominant, and flattened while hip-hop femininity is submissive, (hyper)sexual, and silenced. This is especially prevalent in the visual aspect of hip-hop, with women being very much seen as video vixens. The sonic and visual markers of hip-hop's gender roles and the feelings and anxieties associated with those roles seep out into a larger national American narrative of race. For example, the recent deaths of Oscar Grant, Chavis Carter, Jordan Davis, and Trayvon Martin reflect not only the anxieties surrounding the believed inherent pathology of young Black men but also hip-hop as a breeding ground for their pathology. As I have previously written in "Fear of the Sonic [Un]Known":

> The deaths of Trayvon Martin [and] Jordan Davis . . . have tested the limits of a visualizing logic vis-à-vis black manhood in the American (popular) narrative . . . Of course, the publicity of their bodies is doubly bound to an easily digestible rhetoric of black pathology and the expectations of violence surrounding black men's existence. In a word, black men's existence does not breathe, it is restricted to a one-dimensional portrayal. That is to say, black men are often rendered incapable of exhibiting emotions or experiences outside of anger or even in death.[4]

These polarized negotiations of hip-hop gender roles extend outside of hip-hop aesthetics into other (popular) cultural discourses that use hip-hop to register racial and gender identity politics for Blacks in America.

Consider, for example, the 2008 presidential campaign of Barack Obama (see also Chapters 14 and 25). As America's first Black presidential candidate (and now president), Obama negotiated not only the literal arena of American politics but its attached racial identity politics. To do so, Obama utilized hip-hop aesthetics to establish his cultural and political identity as cool, accessible, and authentically (Black) American. He homed in on his absent father, namedropped hip-hop heavy hitters like Jay-Z and Lil' Wayne, and, when asked about Hillary Clinton's harsh critique of him during democratic primary elections, dusted his shoulders off like Jay-Z's eponymous song from *The Black Album*. Obama meticulously constructed a narrative of his blackness and manhood that could be accessible not only to middle-class Blacks but to working-class Blacks who are deemed the core of hip-hop and authentic Black identity. Obama utilized hip-hop and its cool as a political tool to reach out to a younger demographic of voters who had low voter turnout in previous presidential elections. Situating his masculinity within a hip-hop framework provided Obama with an avenue to maneuver this demographic and culturally signify him as Black.[5] Still, Obama recognized that he needed to attract members of the Black American community without isolating white voters. Obama utilized hip-hop and its associated culture signifiers – and stereotypes – to the extent that did not distort "his white side," the side considered socially, culturally, and politically respectable. Obama sustained a critical distance from hip-hop that could be read as denigration instead of appreciation. Michael P. Jeffries writes in *Thug Life* how Obama's investment in hip-hop doubly serves him as a cultural inducer of his Blackness and as a vehicle to divest away from it: "the president consistently displayed enough knowledge of hip-hop events and personalities to build connections with young voters, all the while maintaining a politically astute detachment from the hip-hop generation."[6]

Obama's criticism of rapper Ludacris's diss rap of Hillary Clinton – a fundamental staple of hip-hop masculinity and braggadocio – in support of Obama's election is one instance of Obama's arm's length embrace of hip-hop. Yet Obama's investment in hip-hop gender politics parallels those of rappers like Ludacris and extends beyond shallow points of (hyper)visibility to more intricate intersections of performativity and expectations of those performances imposed upon Black male bodies in hip-hop. Jeffries astutely points out how:

> The key to this coolness is not just that Obama and thug narrators showcase their personal unflappability; it is that these figures are forthright about their experiences that produce a cool response, which invalidates understandings of hip-hop coolness as a shallow and self-defeating façade . . . the "cool" element of these performances is not simply the outward projection of detachment; it is the entire *process* that each performer goes through.[7]

Obama, like other Black men, navigates numerous gender sensibilities that intersect with the politics of respectability that frame both the public and private spaces that Black men occupy. Mark Anthony Neal's essay "A (Nearly) Flawless Masculinity?" addresses Obama's maneuvering of personal politics and national expectations placed upon his Black masculinity. Neal points out that Obama's critical distance from any negative connotations associated with Black masculinity serves as "an index of the tolerance within said polite society" and that "black men do not live in polite society – however effectively they earn their keep within those spaces."[8] Obama's performance of Black masculinity exists at the fringes of (white) respectable society and the interstitial space of hip-hop and Black respectability. Black respectability mirrors white respectability in the sense it is a medium for recognition of Blacks' humanity. It is also a sliding site of commodity and performance, which hip-hop signifies in larger spaces of public opinion and popular culture.

In its current state, the discourse surrounding hip-hop's gender politics does not reflect the complex interstitial spaces in which many bodies of hip-hop – consumers included – reside. For example, how can one view the queerness of Frank Ocean or the consistently fluctuating performances of gender donned by rapper Nicki Minaj through these polarities? There is a need for renegotiating how we conceive hip-hop gender politics to manifest. This chapter offers some alternative insight into how we can (re)negotiate hip-hop gender and identity politics in ways that bend to the complexities in which hip-hop performers and their audience(s) function.

Again, there is a tangible connection between hip-hop's capitalist impulses and its gender politics. Consider its initial forays into American popular culture. Before its crossover into the national imagination – arguably pinpointed to 1986's smash hit collaboration "Walk This Way" by Aerosmith and Run-D.M.C. – hip-hop remained an openly experimental and creative space that allowed for a broader interpretation of masculine and feminine expression. Men and even women in hip-hop followed various lines of gendered performance including the "conscious" MC, the b-boy/b-girl, the griot/storyteller, the gangsta, and even the party MC. In her article "Empower Self, Making Choices, Creating Spaces," Cheryl Keyes argues that there are four major categories of women in hip-hop: the "queen mother," "fly girl," "sista with attitude," and "lesbian."[9] These four hip-hop archetypes for (Black) women help identify the breadth of experiences that women contributed to an evolving hip-hop narrative. Even during its early cycles of commodification, the wider range of gender performances seen and heard in rap did not need or desire to reflect hip-hop's potential as an American commodity. Yet its cultural and commercial crossover *does* impact not only hip-hop's narratives but the performers who deliver those narratives. Commercialism flattens hip-hop's gender roles to those that are most easily digestible and profitable, those roles that are readily identified as "Black" and stereotypical. Gender's intersection with hip-hop as a capitalist space suggests the flightiness of commercial rap as a space for negotiating the complex intersections of race, gender, and class.

Hip-hop masculinities

In *New Black Man* Mark Anthony Neal discusses the need for a reconceptualization of language surrounding Black masculinity in post-Civil Rights America. Neal writes:

> The post-civil rights era has witnessed a relative explosion of what I call black-meta identities, a diversity of black identities that under the logic of segregated America, remained under wraps, mentioned in hushed tones like the crackhead uncle nobody wants to talk about . . . while some many aspects of black identity have flourished in the post-Civil rights era, allowing for rich and diverse visions of blackness, black masculinity has remained one aspect of black identity still in need of radical reconstruction.[10]

As a cultural by-product of the Civil Rights movement, hip-hop culture can be used as a framework for initiating the renegotiation of Black male discourses Neal calls for. In order to negotiate Black masculinity through hip-hop discourse, one must be able to identify the archetypes or characterizations of masculinity that are grounded in hip-hop. To do this, I suggest borrowing from Cheryl Keyes's categorization of women's roles in hip-hop culture. While Keyes focuses on women in hip-hop, constructing hip-hop male archetypes provides a useful blueprint for articulating frequently shifting hip-hop masculinities. It is important to note that, as Keyes observes with female rap archetypes, these categories can blur boundaries, overlap, and intersect to signify the complexity of their performer. I suggest the following primary categories to reflect this moment of gender in (commercial) hip-hop: philosopher king, playa/pimp, dope boy/trap star, and hustler.

Philosopher king

The hip-hop philosopher king – a contextualization borrowed from Julius Bailey – is a leg of hip-hop masculinity that blends emotional vulnerability and intellect. While Bailey focuses on Jay-Z, his definition of a hip-hop philosopher king is applicable to other performers of this type of masculinity within hip-hop: "his music, like hip-hop more broadly, serves as a force, particularly for minorities, of creating a new identity – but also a new rhetoric to augment the identity, a new lingo, new symbols of identity that have become part of a metamorphosis of black and brown youth."[11]

Philosopher kings in hip-hop are those performers who expand on the complexities of the world around them, their position in the world around them, and what that may or may not represent. Philosopher kings are able to easily negotiate between the (Black) essentialisms of hip-hop and a larger, non-hip-hop audience. Their gender and racial politics are signified in hip-hop but do not rely solely on the culture to manifest in other expressive spaces. They are viewed as touchstones of hip-hop culture's analytical possibilities as well as portals to experiences lodged in hip-hop that may not translate to a white audience. Examples of philosopher kings include KRS-One, Tupac Shakur, Lupe Fiasco, Andre 3000, Kid Cudi, Kendrick Lamar, and Kanye West.

Playa/pimp
The playa/pimp archetype in hip-hop is signified by the hypermasculinity and hypersexuality of commercial hip-hop culture. Their braggadocio is embedded in their sexual skills and prowess. They are an updated representation of the buck archetype from slavery and the Blaxploitation era pimp of the 1970s. Playas and pimps in hip-hop are highly visible, heterosexual, misogynistic, and the crux of hip-hop's Black cool pose. They signify the idea of pleasure in hip-hop as male dominated and at the expense of women. Examples of the playa/pimp archetype include Kurtis Blow, LL Cool J, Too $hort, (Uncle) Luke, and Big Boi.

Dope boy/trap star
Dope boys and trap stars in hip-hop are those performers whose dominant lens for their identity is drug culture. Their origins are arguably situated in the heroin epidemic of the 1970s and crack cocaine epidemic of the 1980s. It is important to note that the idea of "the trap" is separated from the dope boy persona because of its significance as a regional signifier of drug culture outside of (northeastern) urbanized spaces. The trap is a space in the American South where drug dealers conduct drug transactions but it is also a space that signifies the despair and socio-economic anxieties of southern Black men. Dope boys' and trap stars' narratives are nihilistic, violent, and quick-witted disclosures about their knowledge of the drug game. They are cynical capitalists. Examples of the dope boy/trap star archetype include Easy-E, Young Jeezy, T.I., The Game, and Rick Ross.

Hustler
Hip-hop's hustler archetype is quick witted and ambitious. Hustlers are a hybrid of other personas of (Black) masculinities found in hip-hop. Their narratives are the pull one's self up by the bootstraps stories that contextualize hip-hop as an entrepreneurial space. It is important to note that their

187 Gender and sexuality in hip-hop

narratives also have the possibility of being (over) exaggerated to high-light their struggle and path to success. Unlike popular conceptions of the thug or even the dope boy/trap star who remain tethered to the corner or the trap, the hustler utilizes street smarts and skills to translate them into other arenas and industries outside of the hood. Hustlers can maneuver the juxtapositions of the street and a corporate meeting or classroom. Their multidimensionality allows them to keep one foot in the hood even after their transition from those impoverished spaces. It allows them to remain attached to the working-class ideals that authenticate their hustler status. Hustlers are often the foundation for what we recognize as mogul figures in hip-hop. Examples of hustlers in hip-hop include Puff Daddy, Bird Man, Jay-Z, Notorious B.I.G., and Master P.

Hip-hop femininities and sexual politics

Discourses surrounding women in hip-hop are in desperate need of renova-tion. Joan Morgan's groundbreaking monograph *When Chickenheads Come Home to Roost* initiates this cultural work. Morgan borrows from her own background and career as a journalist to collapse the binaries of victimiza-tion or hypersexuality that women occupy in hip-hop. Morgan's assertion to "fuck with the grays" in terms of gender performance and pronunciation moves away from considerations of Black women as flat figures of misogy-nistic abuse toward recognition and analysis of (Black) women's complicity in hip-hop culture. Morgan argues that there is a need to divest from out-dated structures of analysis like earlier cycles of Black feminist thought that came into fruition previous to hip-hop or ignored its relevance toward more rounded and dynamic frameworks that engage women's multidimension-ality. Morgan writes: "[t]he keys that unlock the riches of contemporary black female identity . . . [lie in] the juncture where 'truth' is no longer black and white but subtle, intriguing shades of gray."[12] Morgan's demand for a feminine space that allowed for various representations of Black women's identities in the form of hip-hop feminism springboards later explorations of women in hip-hop like Tracy Sharpley-Whiting's *Pimps Up Hoes Down*, Gwendolyn Pough's hip-hop feminist anthology *Check It While I Wreck It*, and the social media-driven Crunk Feminist Collective. As previously stated, Keyes's categorization of women in hip-hop provides useful analysis of the means to dislocate hip-hop women's narratives away from simplistic renderings of hip-hop and women.

In addition to the "queen mother," "fly girl," "sista with attitude," and "lesbian," I'd like to extend Keyes's archetypes to include Imani Perry's com-plication of "sista[s] with attitude" as "badwomen" and Sharpley-Whiting's discussion of the groupie as an archetype that complicates the binary of Black women's sexuality and power. In her book *Prophets of the Hood* Imani Perry complicates hip-hop to mean "a dialogic space in which artists' voices articulate about existence on a number of registers. The space of hip-hop is public and yet interior."[13] Perry's exploration of these registers of hip-hop identity and agency primarily takes place in hip-hop gender politics. Perry's categorization of powerful women in hip-hop as badwomen is a useful tool of analysis in renegotiating intersections of sex and power in public and private hip-hop spaces. Like Morgan before her, Perry acknowledges women's complicity with sexism in hip-hop but its potential as a site of Black women's resistance:

> in this space, one finds both clearly articulated feminisms as well as complicity with sexist paradigms. On the one hand, within women's roles as badasses, the ideal of an appropriate male partner is often one who trumps the badness of the woman herself. However, one does find voices in which badassness most fundamentally becomes a strategy for expressing feminism.[14]

Perry asserts that "badass" Black women are afforded space for a more complicated narrative because they carve it out for themselves. Badwomen's narratives are

> a space for rage and frustration in the [contemporary] black female [hip-hop] experience, realities often imagined as male in the black community. Many black women – racially oppressed, sexually abused, robbed of gender roles, and overburdened by community responsibility – rarely acknowledge rage.[15]

Perry initially builds upon Keyes's "sista with attitude" as well as the angry black woman archetype to complicate the notion that rage is a privilege reserved for Black men (rappers):

> in addition to the occupations of a male space, which grants a certain level of legitimacy to the female MC in the masculinist world of hip-hop, black women rappers have also used traditionally black female expressions of "badness" in the form of assertiveness, attitude, and independence in their lyrics.[16]

To consider anger as a validated dimension of women in hip-hop pushes the idea that Black women are solely victims into a more complex space where Black women who are mistreated in hip-hop can also voice their frustrations and move past the all-consuming role of victim. Examples of badwomen in hip-hop include Lady of Rage, Nicki Minaj, and Azalea Banks.

In addition to acknowledging anger as a valid dimension of hip-hop femininity, Tracy Sharpley-Whiting reconsiders the role of hypersexuality as a flattened space of victimization and marginalization for women in hip-hop. While Sharpley-Whiting acknowledges that there *is* misogyny in commercial rap, she complicates the interchangeability of hip-hop sexuality and misogyny. I propose that Sharpley-Whiting utilizes the groupie as an updated archetype for the jezebel and sapphire figures of previous Black cultural expressions to navigate hip-hop sexual politics. The groupie is not strictly whorish. She is doubly bound as an enabler and self-aware capitalist of her body. Sharpley-Whiting argues she is the crux of hip-hop masculinity, pivotal in situating men in the rap industry as successful. Sharpley-Whiting writes:

> The presence of groupies is integral to safeguarding a seemingly fragile masculinity that is heavily contingent upon female acquiescence and accessibility . . . the bedroom, once a private space, has become a public one via music videos, porn flicks, and music tracks. In this space, the mythic dominance of black men and their perfected craft of "dicksmithing" appear uncontested by all, irrespective of race, class, and gender. In general, groupies authenticate a hip hop star's successful cultivation of his craft, his flow, his game, which is thoroughly part and parcel of his selfhood. Groupies may be handy, interchangeable, throwaway women, but they are also ego-intoxicating and self-affirming for hip hop stars.[17]

In addition to the risk of their belittlement and disposability, Sharpley-Whiting points out how hip-hop's groupies utilize their bodies and hypersexuality as capital. This blurred binary suggests the potential of hypersexualized women to negotiate their worth through both their own interpretations of sexual prowess and the expectations of the Black male rappers that pursue them. It is important to note that Tricia Rose's discussion of hip-hop and Black women's eroticism buoys Sharpley-Whiting's reclamation of the hip-hop groupie as empowering. Rose writes:

> Yet even when such performers [i.e. Lil' Kim or Foxy Brown] seem to be expressing women's sexual power, they use sexually exploitative images and stories and sexually dominating personas similar to those expressed by many male rappers. They are hustlers instead of victims, but the male-empowering terms of hustling, victimizing, and sexual domination as a legitimate power remain intact.[18]

The challenge of renegotiating hypersexuality in hip-hop is its staunch attachment to the hypermasculine policies – and policing – that dictate women's experiences in hip-hop spaces. Still, to complicate sexual politics within hip-hop's current state allows for some reconsideration of the significance of sexuality as an intervention of gender and identity in hip-hop culture. New ground is breaking to reconsider the role of sexuality in interpreting women's roles in hip-hop. The notion of pleasure as a tool of sexual empowerment is intriguing this recent wave of hip-hop feminists and Black gender scholars who consume and critique hip-hop. In addition to Joan Morgan, young scholars including Treva Lindsey, Brittney Cooper, Kaila Story, and Heidi Lewis are currently at work building scholarship that centralizes pleasure politics as the foundation of women's empowerment in popular spaces.

Sounding hip-hop gender politics

In addition to using notions of pleasure to destabilize women's sexual politics and reconfiguring categories of gender performances in hip-hop, sound studies provides an intriguing alternative for understanding the gender performances that may not register through language currently in place to talk about gender and hip-hop. For the purposes of this chapter, sound studies is the use of musical and nonmusical markers in hip-hop to construct an alternative discourse. Sounding gender means acknowledging sonic cues heard frequently in rap – i.e. wails, grunts, moans, laughter, gun shots, abrupt moments of silence – and identifying what their inclusion in a track or other soundbite represents. This is especially helpful in complicating Black masculine narratives heard in rap. For example, Master P's moan, Young Jeezy's chuckle, and Rick Ross's grunt sonically cue the audience to their presence on the track before they say a (literal) word. These non-musical cues suggest not only the expected hip-hop braggadocio seen (and heard) in male rappers but leave room for non-normal readings of Black masculinity like pain. Where words fall short, these sounds provide space to sonically represent emotions that do not and cannot be translated through literal text. Further, sounding gender provides a tangible intersection of capitalism and hip-hop's gender roles that may be overlooked otherwise. In this case, sounding gender also establishes a sonic brand that earmarks the performer and one's profitability.

In addition to a performer's sonic branding, the production of the track itself is also useful in analyzing gender using sound. While rappers provide a point of reference for sounding gender politics in hip-hop, hip-hop's track producers can also provide an insight into gender politics that may not be spoken.

In addition to acknowledging hip-hop culture as a complicated space for (contemporary) hip-hop gender politics, there is equal need for frameworks that recognize and engage these complexities within the music and in research. By using alternative media of critical observation like sound studies and pleasure politics, the study of expressions of gender in hip-hop are allowed space to breathe and organically evolve.

Further reading

Chaney, Charise, *Brothers Gonna Work it Out: Sexual Politics in the Golden Age of Rap Nationalism* (New York University Press, 2005).

Gaunt, Kyra, *The Games Black Girls Play: Learning the Ropes from Double-Dutch to Hip-Hop* (New York University Press, 2006).

Jeffries, Michael, *Thug Life: Race, Gender, and the Meaning of Hip Hop* (University of Chicago Press, 2011).

Love, Bettina, *Hip Hop's Lil Sistas Speak: Negotiating Hip Hop Identities and Politics in the New South* (New York: Peter Lang, 2012).

Pough, Gwendolyn, *Homegirls Make Some Noise! Hip Hop Feminist Anthology* (Mira Loma, CA: Parker Publishing, 2007).

Notes

1 Possibly a phonetic acronym for the American southern pronunciation of You Don't Even Know It.

2 Ross issued public apologies via the social media network Twitter.

3 Tricia Rose, *The Hip Hop Wars: What We Talk about When We Talk about Hip Hop* (New York: Basic Civitas, 2008), p. 39.

4 Regina Bradley, "Fear of the Sonic [Un]Known," *Feminist Wire*, March 13, 2013. Available at http://thefeministwire.com/2013/03/11082/ (accessed June 1, 2014).

5 It should be noted that the hip-hop sensibility Obama demonstrates still satiates the overarching push for multicultural inclusion in his "Yes We Can" campaign slogan. His use of hip-hop demonstrates not only an awareness of Black culture and identity in the USA but hip-hop as a youth culture, attracting a younger voter demographic often overlooked in presidential campaigns.

6 Michael Jeffries, *Thug Life: Race, Gender, and the Meaning of Hip-Hop* (University of Chicago Press, 2011), p. 202.

7 *Ibid.*, p. 204.

8 Mark Anthony Neal, "A Nearly Flawless Masculinity? Barack Obama," *New Black Man*, November 17, 2009. Available at http://newblackman.blogspot.co.uk/2009/11/nearly-flawless-masculinity-barack.html (accessed June 1, 2014).

9 Cheryl L. Keyes, "Empowering Self, Making Choices, Creating Spaces: Black Female Identity via Rap Music Performance," *American Folklore Society* 113 (2000): 255–269.

10 Mark Anthony Neal, *New Black Man* (London: Routledge, 2005), p. 28.

11 Julius Bailey (ed.), *Jay-Z: Essays on Hip Hop's Philosopher King* (Jefferson, NC: McFarland Press, 2011), p. 4.

12 Joan Morgan, *When Chickenheads Come Home to Roost: A Hip Hop Feminist Breaks it Down* (New York: Simon and Schuster, 1999), p. 62.

13 Imani Perry, *Prophets of the Hood: Politics and Poetics in Hip Hop* (Durham, NC: Duke University Press, 2004), p. 43.

14 *Ibid.*, p. 168.

15 *Ibid.*, p. 159.

16 *Ibid.*, p. 167.

17 Tracey Sharpley-Whiting, *Pimps Up, Hoes Down: Hip Hop's Hold on Young Black Women* (New York University Press, 2008), p. 88.

18 Rose, *The Hip Hop Wars*, p. 124.

14 Hip-hop and politics

CHRISTOPHER DEIS

The claim that hip-hop music and culture is somehow "political" is a common one. MCs and other hip-hop artists frequently comment on how their music is a type of social commentary and a description of the challenges facing poor Black and Brown communities in the USA. This observation is mirrored by other artists in hip-hop's global diaspora as well – where hip-hop has been used as a means of social protest and to (ostensibly) give voice to marginalized or otherwise disempowered communities.

Hip-hop culture was "born" during the 1970s in the South Bronx, New York in a moment of rampant poverty, crime, and gang activity. Consequently, hip-hop's origins – and how they are (often) mythologized – are imbued with a sense of struggle and resistance on the part of poor and working-class urban youth to limited life chances and other challenges.

As such, academics and cultural critics often proceed from an assumption in their scholarly work that hip-hop music and culture is "oppositional" and/or "political."[1] Moreover, hip-hop's assumed "political" nature is one of the common threads tying together the discipline loosely known as "hip-hop studies."

As with other types of popular music, fans and listeners interpret, process, and live through hip-hop. Yes, hip-hop is a type of cultural product that is sold and circulated by the culture industry and purchased by the public. But – to paraphrase Fiske and Frith – hip-hop, because it is a type of popular culture, still personally "matters" to its listeners and fans.[2] And as popular culture, hip-hop is also a space for identity formation, where claims about the relative value and artistic merit of a given song or hip-hop cultural practice are also a type of value judgment. Popular culture is not politically neutral: it is an ideological space. Hip-hop music and culture are ideal-typical examples of that reality in practice.

Moreover, for many consumers of hip-hop music, especially white suburban youth in the USA, the appeal of hip-hop as a type of popular Black music, one whose most commercial and successful varieties reflect and reproduce a very complex (and problematic) mix of "Black" authenticity, social taboos, as well as narratives of Black banditry, criminality, and consumer excess, is exactly why it is perceived as being resistant and deviant to white bourgeois norms of "respectability" and "normality."[3]

In all, there is a sense that hip-hop music and culture has something to say about society. The logic at work here is direct and simple: because hip-hop is a type of social commentary, it is therefore inherently "political." My purposes in this chapter are to challenge such a superficial and problematic assumption.

My goals and approach are threefold. First, I provide an overview of the various ways that hip-hop music can be interpreted as a political discourse space. Second, I also try to provide examples of hip-hop culture's varied politics in practice. Third, I conclude this chapter by highlighting how hip-hop music and culture also overlap with the more formal and traditional politics of the public sphere. These elements are the foundation for a framework that I describe as "a critical theory of hip-hop and politics."

By taking a critical approach to hip-hop's relationship to the politics of popular culture, our understandings of hip-hop music and culture are broadened and enriched. In what follows, I suggest that hip-hop as a music and cultural practice, and across its various subgenres and styles (e.g. "commercial" vs. "underground" or "alternative") can, depending on the context and specific example, be understood as being political in a number of ways:

- Hip-hop is a discursive space where sociopolitical issues are discussed.
- Hip-hop is a site where the very nature and understanding of what constitutes politics and political behavior are broadened and challenged.
- Hip-hop music and culture influence and reflect the political attitudes and beliefs of its listeners and fans.
- Hip-hop is politicized by outside actors and agents; there have also been efforts in the USA, France, the UK, and in other countries such as Cuba, Brazil, and across the Middle East to use hip-hop as a way of raising public awareness about specific political issues, for political organizing, and "social movement" activity.

Instead of assuming that hip-hop music and culture is in fact inherently "political", I reframe that claim in terms of a question: How do we define politics? And if hip-hop is in fact political, how do we locate it within a broader context for thinking about the relationship between politics and popular culture?

A disciplinary specific understanding of what constitutes politics as informed by political science would suggest that it involves the question of access to resources in the polity, and how the concept of power shapes their distribution. In the classic formulation offered by the preeminent political scientist Harold Lasswell, politics is about "who gets what, when, and how."[4] In a similar fashion, David Easton defined politics as the "process that determines the authoritative allocation of values."[5]

A complementary definition/understanding of "the political" is that "real" politics (or what can also be described as "high politics") involves openly contestational behavior such as voting, elections, public opinion polling, lobbying, organizing, and interest group behavior. Politics is the terrain of social and political institutions which help to organize and govern the polity. By implication, these understandings narrowly define and bind "political" issues to include such topics as war, the economy, and the behavior of the mass public(s).

Popular culture has a tenuous relationship to traditional understandings of politics. Consequently, from the latter's perspective, "popular culture" is understood to be ephemeral and disposable. Alternatively, popular culture is a tool that can be manipulated and used by elites to create a passive public. The most generous interpretation of the politics of popular culture views it as a mirror for reflecting broader social issues.[6] From this framework, music and popular culture may be symbolically political or a type of informal barometer of the public mood where, "if music is popular within a particular cultural economy of desirability then it will develop political and economic values symptomatic of that popularity."[7]

For the most narrowly defined versions of "formal" or "traditional" politics, music and popular culture are not "political" in a substantive and important way:

> In the 3½ centuries since settlers landed in America, music has always served
> as a barometer of political sentiments, whether or not those listening
> reflected on what it told of their era. Politically oriented musicians have tried
> to collapse the distance separating singing and organizing, but music has
> often seemed ephemeral when compared to bullets or votes. Music's effect
> on the political process is subtle and virtually impossible to measure, even in
> retrospect.[8]

Thus, popular culture contains little to no emancipatory or resistant potential because popular culture is a product of the culture industry which distracts "the people" from the real dynamics of power and social inequality in a given society.[9] Thus, in order to "see" hip-hop as having "political" potential or content (which is not necessarily "progressive" or "liberating" – this is an important qualifier), we have to push back against these narrow definitions and understandings.

Working through the political possibilities of hip-hop music and culture (and popular culture, more generally) is challenging precisely because of how the cultural and political practices of the day to day resist simple binary models and categorizations. A "critical theory of hip-hop and politics" which I offered earlier tries to negotiate this puzzle by locating hip-hop within a given political and social context, rigorously defining what exactly is "political" about hip-hop as a musical and cultural practice, and acknowledging how hip-hop can be both a tool for liberation and resistance – while also possessing the capacity to serve elite interests and hegemonic power – and is a partial answer to this dilemma.

As I apply it in this chapter, a critical theory of hip-hop and politics identifies the intersection of politics and popular culture as not one set of behaviors or practices, but rather as existing along a continuum. Ultimately, "reading" the politics of popular culture is an interpretive process, one that leverages a variety of frameworks and critical lenses to that end.[10]

The critical framework loosely known as "populism" exists in juxtaposition to more restrictive and cynical understandings of the liberating or resistant potential of popular culture. Widely associated with the work of John Fiske, a populist perspective on popular culture provides an alternative means for analyzing popular culture and its relationship to politics. Populism imbues popular culture with political meaning by virtue of how diverse publics interpret and apply popular culture on their own terms. From this perspective, popular music, movies, and other cultural texts that may be rejected out of hand as being apolitical can be given political relevance by virtue of how they are interpreted and given meaning by diverse public(s) and audiences.

Populism also suggests that "high politics" is not the exclusive terrain of political behavior. Politics can be expanded beyond political institutions and such formal political behavior as voting, campaigns, and elections. Consequently, a space is created for conceptualizing popular culture, and by implication, hip-hop music and culture, as having political content and meaning.

In his book *Race Rebels*, Robin Kelley highlights how the terrain for understanding what constitutes "politics" and "the political" should be broadened when studying communities that have been disadvantaged by unequal arrangements of power:

> Writing "history from below" that emphasizes the infrapolitics of the Black working class requires that we substantially redefine politics. Too often politics is defined by how people participate rather than why; by traditional definition the question of what is political hinges on whether or not groups are involved in elections, political parties, or grass-roots social movements. Yet the how seems far less important than the why, since many of the so-called real political institutions have not always proved effective for, or even accessible to, oppressed people . . . In other words, I am rejecting the tendency to dichotomize people's lives, to assume that clear-cut "political" motivations exist separately from issues of economic well-being, safety, pleasure, cultural expression, sexuality, freedom of mobility, and other facets of daily life.[11]

Timothy Brennan, writing in *Spectacular Devotion*, makes a complementary observation to Kelley's, one that is well worth considering for how it challenges the boundaries placed around political behavior, desire, commerce, and "authenticity" with regard to hip-hop music:

> If the paradoxical strategy of choice for a political genre is to bring it into the category of art, the paradoxical strategy for the dispossessed is to bring it into the category of business.[12]

These arguments for an expansion of where we look to for politics, resistance, and oppositional behavior, suggest that the realm of "the popular" and of "the cultural" are viable locations for investigating how marginalized communities give voice to their concerns and (re)imagine their political possibilities. By extension, when politics is imagined as consisting of more than the high politics of formal institutions and participation, we are able to frame the politics of popular culture as possessing a potential to be a robust and meaningful site of both political contention and political expression.[13]

A populist view of the politics of popular music is also operative in the various ways that diverse audiences – audiences who experience power relationships differently by virtue of their position relative to the public sphere (and belonging to diverse counter-publics) – decode, interpret, and construct meaning around popular culture. For example, young people have appropriated certain clothing styles as a statement of rebellion or allegiance to a counter-culture. Musical forms such as punk and early hip-hop were efforts to establish a space for pleasure and release in a system of political economy that marginalized poor and working-class youth. What has been described as an "oppositional approach" to interpreting and forming meaning in response to various types of popular culture, may also involve how "marginalized" publics often reframe and reinterpret a text or practice so that it has meaning for their personal experiences.[14]

Narrowing our focus down from the larger questions surrounding the boundaries of the politics in popular culture, hip-hop music can also be considered political because it is part of a Black musical tradition that reflects on Black freedom struggles and life in a racially ordered society.[15] Writing in *Hip-hop's Inheritance*, Reiland Rabaka links together these themes with Ralph Ellison's essential *Shadow and Act* (1964):

> Returning to the notion that for black America music is much more than music . . . it is important here to bear in mind Ralph Ellison's contention in Shadow and Act (1964), where he eloquently argued that African American popular music constitutes an indispensable element and cultural indicator of African Americans' life worlds and life-struggles. African American popular music, then, is much more than the soundtrack to black popular culture. It is more akin to a musical map and cultural compass that provides us with a window into black folks' world, and also a window into the ways in which African Americans' aforementioned "second sight" shapes and shades their worldview.[16]

Rather than be viewed as something separate from the Black musical tradition (or peripheral to it), as critics such as Stanley Crouch, Wynton Marsalis, and Andre Craddock-Willis have argued,[17] hip-hop music is the latest development of and iteration in what music scholar Guthrie Ramsey describes as Afro-modernism in Black music:

> If we consider, for example, the way in which jazz in the 1940s represented the quintessential Afro-modernist expression of Black urbanity, we can better understand how the musical styles most closely associated with hip-hop represent "the urban contemporary" for the present generation. If the blues muse of the World War 2 years existed as a basic ingredient in various styles, then we need to try to identity, codify, and theorize the elements that make up the decidedly hybrid hip-hop sensibility and "worldview." One might learn, for example, that the idea of Afro-modernism might be extended in the late twentieth century.[18]

The assertion that hip-hop music is politicized by virtue of its relationship to Black music is also a nuanced one. We must be careful not to overstate "the rhythm and resistance" contained within or to essentialize Black music as resistant and political because it is identified with the African diaspora. Essentializing Black music is problematic because it naturalizes and masks the complexity, intelligence, and genius of Black music as both a reflection of universal human experiences and the particular and unique historic and contemporary experiences of the Black diaspora. Asserting that all Black music is equally political or resistant, or that the "small acts of resistance" in the language, symbols, and themes of Black music are constructed in the same way, homogenizes away the diversity of Black music generally, and hip-hop specifically.[19]

"For African Americans, partly because of their marginal status and often violent exclusion from the realms of formal politics, popular culture was an integral and important aspect of the making of politics throughout the pre-civil rights era and the civil rights era itself."[20] Hip-hop continues this trajectory.

Hip-hop music can also be considered a space for political discourse by virtue of its explicit references to politics, as well as songs that purport to function as political commentaries because of how a given artist may make claims on "social realism" through their lyrics. In this way, hip-hop music has served as a space for discussing a variety of political topics and controversies ranging from the war in Iraq (Outkast "War"; the 4th 25 "Live from Iraq"; Mr. Lif "Home of the Brave"; Talib Kweli "The Proud"), terrorism (Immortal Technique "Bin Laden"; Eminem "Mosh"), police profiling (N.W.A. "Fuck the Police"; Chamillionaire "Ridin Dirty"; dead prez "I Have a Dream Too"), racism (Yaslin Bey "Niggas is the Poorest"), the prison industrial complex (Killer Mike "Reagan"), urban gun violence (the Roots' concept album "Undun"; Lupe Fiasco "Kids with Guns"; Jay-Z and Kanye West "Murder to Excellence"; Nas "I Gave You Power"; Rhymefest "Pull Me Back"), and gender politics (see the oeuvre of MCs such as Jean Grae, Psalm One, and MIA).

The degree and way in which a given hip-hop artist chooses to explicitly engage "political" matters is one of the divides between hip-hop subgenres – what have conveniently (and however imprecisely) been described as "commercial," "underground," "conscious," or "political" hip-hop.

These divisions are not fixed. They are fluid and often overlap. For example, "political" hip-hop artists such as Talib Kweli, Mos Def, Immortal Technique, and others engage and discuss explicitly political subject matter in their song lyrics while also wanting the freedom to be identified as MCs with a broad repertoire of subject matters, and even in some instances rejecting the title of being "political" rappers as a curse and a stigma.[21]

"Alternative" hip-hop artists such as Lupe Fiasco, Jay Electronica, and Kid Cudi embody an aesthetic sensibility that is centered upon a reconfigured Black male authenticity that exists in direct contrast to that of more "commercial" artists such as Jay-Z, 50 Cent, Young Jeezy, Lil' Wayne, T.I., Rick Ross, and others. In the broad middle ground, there are artists such as the Roots, Nas, Kendrick Lamar, Common, Phonte, Little Brother, Out-Kast, Kanye West, and others who are located between these two poles. These pairings are a negotiation of the binaries of performance and identity which in turn serve as archetypal models in a broader hip-hop imaginary with its struggles over labor, identity, and authenticity. Joe Jackson's *Real Black: Adventures in Racial Sincerity* offers a helpful illumination of this tension:

> The vibrant field of hip-hop emceeing, most specifically harbors several notable binaries of labor: between the male emcee and the female rapper, between the black rapper and the white rapper, between the "gangsta" and the neo-black nationalist, between the "bling-bling" lyricist and the conscious rapper. These same divisions mirror hip-hop's larger cultural project: constructing and deconstructing the social, cultural, and political boundaries placed around black bodies, boundaries that prop up the very category of blackness itself, but in situation-specific ways. Such divisions help to define the parameters of contemporary black aesthetics . . . [22]

While there have been ebbs and flows in the popularity of political hip-hop (or what were once called "message raps"), beginning in the late 1970s with the landmark song "The Message" by Grandmaster Flash and the Furious Five, to the Black Nationalist era in the late 1980s of which the celebrated group Public Enemy was central, to more "conscious" artists and groups of the present, such as Talib Kweli, Mos Def (Yusef Bey), Common, dead prez, Jean Grae, MIA, Immortal Technique, Jasiri X, and Brother Ali, politically expressive artists have long been a fixture in hip-hop music. These debates about hip-hop's political content are also claims about who qualifies as an "authentic" or legitimate "hip-hop artist." In a less explicit fashion, debates regarding hip-hop's aesthetic conventions and authenticity can also be understood as political conversations regarding the ways in which Black expressive culture should represent and/or affirm the Black community, as well as further the politics of Black respectability.

Building upon my earlier suggestion that hip-hop music can be understood to be a type of social soundtrack or informal barometer for a society or community's mood and sentiments, we can also see how changes in hip-hop genre conventions can also be interpreted as reflections of larger political and social dynamics in society.

For example, as scholars such as Rose, Forman, George, Spence, and Chang have exhaustively documented, hip-hop music and culture's origins in the South Bronx in the 1970s is inseparably linked to narratives regarding de-industrialization, neo-liberalism, and failed urban renewal policies.[23]

Moving forward, the rise of Black Nationalist hip-hop music in the late 1980s and early 1990s in the USA reflected a resurgent Black politics that was linked to Jesse Jackson's two presidential campaigns, a reaction to the rightward move in American political culture, and to the successful mayoral campaigns of David Dinkins in New York City – whose election was playfully wished for in the classic hip-hop song "Can I Kick It?" by Phife Dogg of the hip-hop group A Tribe Called Quest.

This genre shift was also a result of a simultaneous disappointment and cynicism by some in the Black counter-public (and among "the post-Civil Rights generation" in particular) toward the perceived inability of the Civil Rights establishment, with its policies of mass mobilizing and traditional political engagement, to respond to the particular material and economic needs of the Black community in general, as well as the urban poor in particular.[24]

Black Nationalist hip-hop (X-Clan; Poor Righteous Teachers; Public Enemy) would decline in popularity by the early 1990s, and Los Angeles centered hip-hop would rise to take its place as hip-hop's standard-bearer (for example, groups and individual MCs such as N.W.A., Dr. Dre, Snoop Dogg, Ice Cube, Too $hort, Ice-T, and others). Creatively, this move away from Black Nationalist hip-hop as the dominant genre and toward "gangsta rap," with its tales of unrepentant violence and social banditry, would be a prescient foretelling of a move westward (and eventually southward) from New York City as the exclusive creative and cultural center of hip-hop music. Politically, gangsta rap's depictions of West Coast gang culture, a general dissatisfaction with traditional Black civil society institutions and the politics of respectability, as well as an unapologetic rage against police authority and their abuses of power, would be taken as forecasting the inevitability of the 1992 Los Angeles uprising.[25]

In what historian William Jelani Cobb describes in his book *To the Break of Dawn* as an act of "ghetto clairvoyance," Ice Cube's albums *AmeriKKKa's Most Wanted* and *Death Certificate* (as well as the later *The Predator*) were prescient and powerfully descriptive of the rage about police brutality, violence, and poverty that would explode in the Los Angeles rebellion, with songs such as "Black Korea" and its lyrics: "so pay respect to the black fist/or we'll burn your store, right down to a crisp."[26]

Spurred on by the commercial success of gangsta rap, hip-hop music would subsequently grow in popularity throughout the 1990s and become a dominant, American youth culture. This rise in popularity and "crossing over" from a Black and Brown to a youth subculture would also result in what I would suggest was a problematic standardization of "hip-hop" as a musical genre with a defined "sound," a process that was aided by media consolidation.[27] "The Hip-hop Nation," as *Time* magazine announced on the cover of its February 1999 issue, had finally arrived. Hip-hop had officially "crossed over" during the Clinton administration, when during the last decade of the twentieth century "racial colorblindness" had matured, and "whiteness" was becoming "colored." This dynamic continues in the age of Obama.

Hip-hop music and culture has been politicized both from inside and outside the Black community. For the latter, as a Black music, hip-hop shares a transhistorical experience of politicization by moral panics.[28] Historically, hip-hop is part of a tradition in which for (some) white elites, hip-hop as a type of "Black music" represents deeply rooted, psycho-social fears of Black criminality and Black male sexuality.

Likewise, for a section of the Black public, and among Black elites, hip-hop music has been cast as a problem[29] – a symptom of a deep malaise, and indicative of "cultural nihilism" among Black youth and the Black underclass:

> During the 1980s and 1990s, no cultural trend more tellingly influenced public opinion on African American villainy than the valorization of rap music and its creators by mainstream youth . . . the spread of hip-hop culture was like a home invasion carried out on a grand scale. At the outset of the twenty-first century, rappers and their critics were locked in an epic struggle for the soul of the hip-hop generation. As in most morality plays, this conflict over cultural expression and racial representation pitted unblemished righteousness against unmitigated evil. Allegedly estranged from both God and good manners, offending musicians provided a

convenient lightning rod for criticism of underclass mores and helped shape
new millennial views on Black America's spiritual health.[30]

In a reversal of the negative politics of stigma and moral panics where
hip-hop culture was viewed as a "problem" to be solved, hip-hop has been a
means for local and national community groups to organize young people
(and others) in response to the specific challenges faced by Black and Brown
youth, as well as the poor, in the USA and elsewhere.

In its most ambitious iteration, from the years 2000 to 2008, community
activists and political entrepreneurs allied with hip-hop artists and hip-hop
moguls in an effort to create what they described as a "hip-hop social movement" by mobilizing "the hip-hop generation" to create political change in
the United States.

While it failed for a variety of reasons, the goal of this vision was a broad
platform which attempted to leverage hip-hop's popularity as a dominant
youth culture in order to address such issues as the criminalization of Black
and Brown youth, urban poverty, and failing schools.[31]

Ironically, while a hip-hop social movement was unable to reframe the
relationship between popular music and formal politics in 2004, it was
present in Barack Obama's 2008 presidential campaign (and through to the
first term of his administration). In this regard, hip-hop fulfilled traditional
understandings of the various roles that popular music can play in electoral
politics.[32]

For example, celebrity hip-hop artists such as Jay-Z, Common, and
others worked on fund-raising campaigns to mobilize voters, and wrote
songs in support of then candidate Senator Barack Obama. The Obama
campaign benefited greatly from bringing new voters into the political
process, and in particular, young people and racial minorities who had not
participated in earlier elections. Hip-hop artists and activists were critical
of these efforts. Barack Obama's campaign also used hip-hop artists as
spokespeople who could symbolize and personify his "hope and change"
narrative. In this way, hip-hop's narrative of cultural resistance, change, and
opposition to the status quo and "mainstream culture" was channeled in
support of "traditional" electoral politics.

One of the most prominent moments where politics overlapped with
popular culture during Obama's tenure is the song "My President" (2008)
by the rappers Jay-Z and Young Jeezy, which has the following lyrics:

> My president is black
> But his house is all white
> Rosa Parks sat so Martin Luther could walk
> Martin Luther walked so Barack Obama could run

Barack Obama ran so all the children could fly
So I'm a spread my wings and
U can meet me in the sky
I already got my own clothes
Already got my own shoes
I was hot before Barack imagine what I'm gonna do . . .

However, the choice to deploy hip-hop in the service of formal politics did not come without a cost. Hip-hop is a type of Black music. By implication, hip-hop is now a *means* that reactionary white conservatives can use toward *the ends* of "blackening" President Barack Obama through coded racial appeals (and symbolic racism).

On numerous occasions, right-wing critics of President Barack Obama have evoked hip-hop in order to encourage white racial anxiety. When President Obama hosted MC and hip-hop mogul Jay-Z, and his celebrity wife, actress, and singer Beyoncé at the White House, the meeting was described as a "hip-hop bbq," and part of a pattern wherein Barack Obama hosts "hoodlums" in the "hizzouse" (a strained use of slang intended to highlight the culturally "Black" nature of the White House since his election as viewed by racially resentful white conservatives). The American right-wing media also lambasted the Obama administration for inviting Common, a Chicago-based "progressive" hip-hop artist, to perform at the White House as "proof" that the president is a "radical" who embraces violence against police, and as further "proof" that he cannot escape his "gangster" "Chicago roots."

The song "My President is Black" by Jay-Z and Young Jeezy was also the focal point of coverage by Fox News, Bill O'Reilly, Rush Limbaugh, and other right-wing opinion leaders who argued that the song was explicitly anti-white, "disrespectful" to the office of the president, and a signal that candidate-elect President Barack Obama would pursue a "pro-Black" agenda of "reparations" and "hate" against "White America" once in office.[33]

Conclusion: toward a critical theory of hip-hop and politics

People live through and by popular culture. It circulates among the public and is one of the primary ways through which individuals are socialized into a community's norms and values. Individuals are also invested in popular culture: it is a site for pleasure, play, and emotional release. In keeping with the populist framework as offered in this chapter, hip-hop is a deep and central part of these processes because of its popularity as a global youth culture.

As a cultural practice, hip-hop is more than just music or rapping. From the point of view of artists such as KRS-One, organizations such as the

Universal Zulu Nation, and those others who practice and live hip-hop as a holistic and integrated culture, hip-hop is a lifestyle and an integral part of their "cognitive map."

Complementing this observation, empirical research has increasingly demonstrated that how a given individual relates to and consumes hip-hop culture is correlated with, and in some cases may even shape, their attitudes and values about race, class, gender, sexuality, and other issues related to citizenship, belonging, identity, and politics more broadly.[34]

Active involvement in the various aspects of hip-hop culture is central to identity formation and a sense of group belonging for its participants. Here, hip-hop culture is a type of social capital that can help its participants' self-esteem, enabling them to gain various life skills, organize to create change in their communities, and participate in the associational and organizational life of the public sphere.[35] In total, there is mounting evidence that if "the personal is indeed political" then perhaps hip-hop culture is a means to that end.

I have outlined several ways of thinking through and about hip-hop culture's relationship to politics in this chapter. While it is a working assumption by many fans and scholars that hip-hop music and culture are somehow "political," "oppositional," or "resistant," I suggest that the more productive and useful framework is one that begins with complications and context. Instead of assuming that hip-hop as a type of Black popular music is inherently and naturally "political" – a claim I am sympathetic to – I have suggested that we should begin with the questions "how?" and "in what ways?"

Ultimately, I have attempted to demonstrate how the politics of hip-hop music and culture are multi-faceted, exist on a continuum, and are heavily dependent on both context and theoretical priors.[36] Perhaps most importantly, how a person chooses to define and conceptualize what constitutes "politics" has a direct impact on their conclusions about the political nature of hip-hop music and culture.

Notes

1 The claim that hip-hop is "political" is a common one across the broad field known as "hip-hop studies." Some prominent examples include Todd Boyd, *The New H.N.I.C.: The Death of Civil Rights and the Reign of Hip Hop* (New York University Press, 2002) and Bakari Kitwana, *The Hip-Hop Generation: Young Blacks and the Crisis in African American Culture* (New York: Basic Civitas, 2002). The edited volume by Murray Forman and Mark Anthony Neal (eds.), *That's the Joint! The Hip-Hop Studies Reader* (New York: Routledge, 2004) also contains essays where the "political" nature of hip-hop music and culture is assumed as a prior, as opposed to a claim which is to be demonstrated and explored. There are also texts which examine the lyrics of hip-hop songs as (1) a political discourse space and (2) a means of engaging broader claims about the social order and the public sphere. See Michael P. Jeffries, *Thug Life: Race, Gender, and the Meaning of Hip-Hop* (University of Chicago Press, 2011); Jeffrey Ogbonna Green Ogbar, *Hip-Hop Revolution: The Culture and Politics of Rap*

(Lawerence, KS: University Press of Kansas, 2007); and Lester K. Spence, *Stare in the Darkness: The Limits of Hip-Hop and Black Politics* (Minneapolis: University of Minnesota Press, 2011) as examples of this approach.
2 John Fiske, *Understanding Popular Culture* (London: Unwin Press, 1989) and Simon Frith, *Performing Rites: On the Value of Popular Music* (Oxford University Press, 1996).
3 Bakari Kitwana, *Why White Kids Love Hip-hop* (New York: Basic Civitas, 2005).
4 Harold Lasswell, *Politics: Who Gets What, When, and How* (New York: McGraw-Hill, 1936).
5 David Easton, *A Framework for Political Analysis* (Englewood Cliffs, NJ: Prentice-Hall, 1965), p. 96.
6 Susan McClary, "Same as It Ever Was: Youth Culture and Music," in Tricia Rose and Andrew Ross (eds.), *Microphone Fiends* (London: Routledge, 1994), pp. 29–40.
7 John Shepherd, "Popular Music Studies: Challenges to Musicology," *Stanford Humanities Review* 3/2 (1993): 17–36.
8 David Dunaway, "Music as Political Communication in the United States," in James Lull (ed.), *Popular Music and Communication* (New York: Sage Publications, 1987), pp. 36–52.
9 See the summary in Dominic Strinati, *An Introduction to Theories of Popular Culture* (New York: Routledge, 1995); see also John Street, *Politics and Popular Culture* (Philadelphia: Temple University Press, 1997), Chapter 8.
10 There are a variety of approaches and frameworks for interpreting the social and political meaning of popular culture. One of the most useful and comprehensive books that details these approaches from a cultural studies perspective is David Oswell, *Culture and Society: An Introduction to Cultural Studies* (London: Sage Publications, 2004).
11 Robin D. G. Kelley, *Race Rebels: Culture, Politics, and the Black Working Class* (New York: The Free Press, 1994).
12 Timothy Brennan, *Spectacular Devotion: Afro-Latin Music and Imperial Jazz* (New York: Verso, 2008), p. 144.
13 John Street, *Politics and Popular Culture* (Philadelphia: Temple University Press, 1997), p. 22; see also James Scott, *Domination and the Arts of Resistance* (New Haven: Yale University Press, 1990), pp. 19, 157, 183.
14 For an exploration of the interpretive approach known as "oppositional reading," see bell hooks, *Black Looks: Race and Representation* (Boston: South End Press, 1992), pp. 115–131.
15 Samuel A. Floyd Jr., *The Power of Black Music* (Oxford University Press, 1995); Amiri Baraka,

Blues People: Negro Music in White America (New York: William Morrow, 1963); Ray Pratt, *Rhythm and Resistance: The Political Uses of American Popular Music* (New York: Praeger Publishers, 1990), especially Chapters 3 and 4.
16 Reiland Rabaka, *Hip Hop's Inheritance* (Maryland: Lexington Books, 2011), p. 9.
17 See the following: Michael Eric Dyson, *Race Rules* (New York: Vintage Books, 1997), pp. 125–127; Robin D. G. Kelley, *Yo' Mama's Dysfunctional! Fighting the Culture Wars in Urban America* (Boston: Beacon Press, 1997), p. 36; and John McWhorter, *All About the Beat: Why Hip-Hop Can't Save Black America* (New York: Gotham Books, 2008).
18 Guthrie P. Ramsey, *Race Music* (Berkeley, CA: University of California Press, 2003), p. 187.
19 Ramsey elaborates in *Race Music* that: "African American culture cannot be characterized solely in terms of a liberation struggle." The diverse and sprawling processes we think of as "African American culture" did not develop simply as a response to hegemony, racism, and social oppression. Recent academic studies and populist discourses reveal a feisty intra-Black dialogue about the representation of Blackness in the public and scholarly arenas: "Who," some of the debates seem to ask, "will be the representative, authentic Negro?" Which of these voices will be privileged?" (p. 24). This concern in some ways mirrors Paul Gilroy's *Modernity and Double Consciousness* observations in *The Black Atlantic* (Cambridge, MA: Harvard University Press, 1993) that we as scholars should be mindful of the potentially damaging and limiting power of the idea of racial or cultural authenticity in relation to the expressive and other cultures produced by the Black diaspora (pp. 72–110).
20 Richard Iton, *In Search of the Black Fantastic: Politics and Popular Culture in the Post-Civil Rights Era* (Oxford University Press, 2008), p. 6.
21 Rabaka, *Hip Hop's Inheritance*, pp. 204–207.
22 John L. Jackson, *Real Black: Adventures of Racial Sincerity* (University of Chicago Press, 2005), p. 182.
23 See the following: Jeff Chang, *Can't Stop Won't Stop: A History of the Hip-Hop Generation* (New York: St. Martin's Press, 2005); Murray Forman, *The 'Hood Comes First: Race, Space, and Place in Rap and Hip-Hop* (Middletown, CT: Wesleyan University Press, 2002); Nelson George, *Hip Hop America* (New York: Viking Press, 1998); Tricia Rose, *Black Noise: Rap Music and Black Culture in Contemporary America* (Middletown, CT: Wesleyan University Press, 1994); Spence, *Stare in the Darkness.*

24 Chang, *Can't Stop Won't Stop*. See also Cedric Johnson, *Revolutionaries to Race Leaders: Black Power and the Making of African-American Politics* (Minneapolis, MN: University of Minnesota Press, 2007).

25 Brian Cross, *It's Not About a Salary: Rap, Race and Resistance in Los Angeles* (New York: Verso, 1994); Chang, *Can't Stop Won't Stop*; Eithne Quinn, *Nuthin' but a "G" Thang: The Culture and Commerce of Gangsta Rap* (*Popular Cultures, Everyday Lives*) (New York: Columbia University Press, 2005).

26 William Jelani Cobb, *To the Break of Dawn: A Freestyle on the Hip Hop Aesthetic* (New York University Press Academic, 2007), p. 58.

27 Forman, *The 'Hood Comes First*, see especially Chapters 4, 5, and 7.

28 James Morone, *Hellfire Nation* (New Haven, CT: Yale University Press, 2003).

29 McWhorter, *All About the Beat*.

30 William Van DeBurg, *Hoodlum: African-American Blacks, Villains and Social Bandits in American Life* (University of Chicago Press, 2004), p. 196.

31 See the following: Yvonne Bynoe, *Stand and Deliver: Political Activism, Leadership, and Hip-hop Culture* (New York: Soft Skull Press, 2004); Boyd, *The New H.N.I.C.*; Kitwana, *The Hip-Hop Generation*; and Spence, *Stare in the Darkness*.

32 See the following sources: R. Serge Denisoff, *Sing a Song of Social Significance* (Bowling Green University Popular Press, 1972); Dunaway,

"Music as Political Communication in the United States," 36–52; Richard Eyerman and Andrew Jamison, *Music and Social Movements* (Cambridge University Press, 1988).

33 "Fox News Site Calls Obama's Picnic a 'Hip-Hop BBQ'" from the *New York Times* website, http://tinyurl.com/mfu8g2f; "Michelle Obama Invited Rapper to White House Who Called for Burning of George W. Bush" from the *National Review Online*, http://tinyurl.com/4yng8kz; "Fox News Attacks Rapper Common over White House Invite" from *Rolling Stone*, http://tinyurl.com/44brpa9; "Fox Attacks 'Black President' while Defending 'Magical Negro'" from the *Huffington Post*, http://tinyurl.com/dltydb (all accessed June 1, 2014).

34 Cathy Cohen, *Democracy Remixed: Black Youth and the Future of American Politics* (New York: Oxford University Press, 2010); Michael Dawson, *Black Visions: The Roots of Contemporary African-American Political Ideologies* (University of Chicago, 2001), pp. 44–84; Jeffries, *Thug Life*; and Spence, *Stare in the Darkness*.

35 Sujatha Fernandes, *Cuba Represent! Cuban Arts, State Power, and the Making of New Revolutionary Cultures* (Durham, NC: Duke University Press, 2006); and Joseph Schloss, *Foundation: B-Boys, B-Girls, and Hip-Hop Culture in New York* (New York: Oxford University Press, 2009).

36 Michael Hanchard, *Party Politics: Horizons in Black Political Thought* (New York: Oxford University Press, 2006), pp. 25–67.

15 Intertextuality, sampling, and copyright

JUSTIN A. WILLIAMS

Intertextuality, most broadly defined as the relationship between one text and others, is pervasive in multiple forms of popular music, and of all music in general, but is arguably most overtly presented in hip-hop music and culture.[1] This chapter will outline a number of analytical approaches to the varied forms of intertextuality in recordings of hip-hop music. Related to this are questions of ownership, copyright, and the ethics of using such material perceived by some to be foundational to the construction of new hip-hop recordings. Though the legal context has changed over time, and differs between countries, I will point to some influential cases in US copyright law which have helped shape the sonic landscape of mainstream hip-hop. As I have written elsewhere,[2] hip-hop openly celebrates its connections with the past, creating a vast intertextual network from myriad elements within and outside of hip-hop culture.

Musical borrowing, digital sampling, and signifyin(g)

From its very outset, hip-hop music was founded on the manipulation of pre-existing material. DJs originally borrowed instrumental excerpts from records (known as "breaks" or "breakbeats," see Chapters 2 and 4) to craft their sets, either looping passages with two copies of the same record or stringing passages together from different records. As digital sampling technology improved and became more affordable in the mid to late 1980s, many of the hip-hop DJ practices were adopted by the hip-hop producer, utilizing the new technologies in the process. Brewster and Broughton argue convincingly that sampling was just a faster, more complex and permanent way of re-creating what the DJs had been doing all along.[3]

With the technology of the digital age, using pre-existing material has become much easier with technology enabling composers to take all elements of a recorded performance. But even though the practice of digital sampling falls into a tradition of twentieth-century collage and an even longer history of African American and European artistic practices, the act of taking material from a recording for the financial gain of another became a legal and ethical issue. A number of high profile copyright lawsuits in the late 1980s and early 1990s set the precedent for regulating such "collage style" sampling made famous by the Bomb Squad (Public Enemy, Ice Cube) and the Dust Brothers (Beastie Boys).

Russell Potter, in addition to describing sampling as political and as postmodern, discusses the practice as a form of Signifyin(g), a concept theorized by Henry Louis Gates Jr. in African American literary studies, and adapted to Black musics by Samuel A. Floyd Jr. To quote Potter:

> Simply put, Signifyin(g) is repetition *with a difference*; the same and yet not the same. When, in a jazz riff, a horn player substitutes one arpeggio for a harmony note, or "cuts up" a well-known solo by altering its tempo, phrasing, or accents, s/he is Signifyin(g) on all previous versions. When a blues singer, like Blind Willie McTell, "borrows" a cut known as the "Wabash Rag" and re-cuts it as the "Georgia Rag," he is Signifyin(g) on a rival's recording.[4]

Like ragtime, swing, hard bop, bebop, cool, reggae, dub, and hip-hop, these musical forms were Signifyin(g) what came before them. Furthermore, musical texts Signify upon one another, troping and revising particular musical ideas. These musical "conversations" can therefore occur between the present and the past, or synchronically within a particular genre.

Signifyin(g), as Gates writes, is derived from myths of the African god Esu-Elegbara, later manifested as the trickster figure of the Signifying Monkey in African American oral tradition.[5] Gates writes, "For the Signifying Monkey exists as the great trope of Afro-American discourse, and the trope of tropes, his language of Signifyin(g), is his verbal sign in the Afro-American tradition."[6] To Signify is to foreground the signifier, to give it importance for its own sake. The language of the monkey is playful yet intelligent, and can be found in the West African poet/musician griots, in hipster talk and radio DJs of the 1950s, comedians such as Redd Foxx, 1970s Blaxploitation characters such as Dolemite, and in countless rap lyrics. It should be stated that in addition to Signifying as masterful revision and repetition of tropes, it also includes double-voiced or multi-voiced utterances which complicate any simple semiotic interpretation.

The sampling of classic breakbeats, to use but one example, is certainly a foundational instance of musical Signifyin(g) in hip-hop, musically troping on and responding to what has come before.[7] Linked with the concept of Signifyin(g) is Bakhtin's concept of dialogism, as well as that of the multi-vocality of texts, two aspects also related to hip-hop's intertextuality.[8] "Answer songs" (which of course predate hip-hop) such as "Roxanne's Revenge" by Roxanne Shante (in answer to UTFO's "Roxanne, Roxanne") would also fit in terms of intertextual relationships. Signifyin(g), dialogism, and intertextuality all form important academic frameworks in which to understand hip-hop's borrowing practices.

Hip-hop's intertextuality arguably fits within a long tradition in the Western music canon as well. Major forms of polyphony up to 1300 – organum, discant, and motet – were all based on existing melodies, usually chant. Masses in the sixteenth century could be divided in terms of cantus firmus mass (or tenor mass), cantus firmus/imitation mass, paraphrase mass, or parody mass. These earlier cultures show that a notion of musical creativity in terms of pure originality was anachronistic for that time period. Compositional practice involved reworking pre-existing material in an unconcealed manner, particularly akin to sample-based hip-hop, in contrast to nineteenth-century Romantic ideologies where composers often denied their precursors in an attempt to appear purely original. This is not to mention the works of twentieth-century composers like Charles Ives and Luciano Berio who also included a high level of pre-existing material in their works. J. Peter Burkholder, in addition to providing a thousand-year history of musical borrowing, has also engaged in a typology of borrowing which most directly relates to his extensive research on Charles Ives, but could be expanded and adapted to a number of forms of repertoire.[9]

In terms of sampling more specifically, it is worth considering what sets digital sampling apart from other forms of borrowing. Chris Cutler notes that samples are essentially "vertical slices" of sound which are then converted into binary information which is then stored as information for the eventual reconstruction of the sound.[10] In one of the most engaging studies of digital sampling to date, Katz also explains that the sampling rate is 44,100 Hz, which means that each second of sound is cut into 44,100 slices, and states, "Although sampling, particularly when done well, is far from a simple matter, the possibilities it offers are nearly limitless."[11] And as Tricia Rose wrote in *Black Noise,* hip-hop culture is at the intersection of African and African American artistic cultures and traditions and newer technologies like digital sampling which allow practitioners to extend older traditions in new and varied ways.[12]

Sampling is only one of the ways that hip-hop can borrow and reference pre-existing material: sampling as a technique is, in addition to reperforming past music (by way of a DJ or live band), referencing other lyrics, matching the style of another rapper's flow, and quoting sounds and dialogue in the music, and other intertextual techniques. In terms of the digital, non-digital divide (which does often overlap), one can make the useful distinction between "autosonic quotation" and "allosonic quotation" from Serge Lacasse. "Autosonic quotation" is quotation of a recording by digitally sampling it, as opposed to "allosonic quotation," which quotes the previous material by way of re-recording or performing the quotation in live performance.[13] To take jazz as an example, the distinction would be between digitally sampling a Charlie Parker solo phrase (or "lick") for Gang Starr's "Jazz Thing" (1990) (autosonic) versus a recording of a jazz musician in live performance quoting a similar phrase (allosonic). Additionally, it is worth analyzing the length of sample used: is it a long (e.g. four-measure) loop, or a smaller riff? Or a mix of both (such as Kanye West's "Champion" and his production on Talib Kweli's "In the Mood")? Looking at sequencing as well as sampling can help create an analogue to Middleton's distinction between "discursive" (longer-phrase) and "musematic" (riff-based) repetition which would be an additional distinction in the analysis of autosonic quotation in the "basic beat"[14] of a given rap song.

Another important distinction that can be made with borrowing in hip-hop is the difference between "textually signaled" and "textually unsignaled" forms of intertextuality. While hip-hop music is often highly intertextual, this is not meant to imply that all hip-hop musical texts draw attention to their borrowing equally. Film scholar Richard Dyer, writing on pastiche, notes that as an imitative artistic form, it is "textually signaled" as such; in other words, the text itself draws attention to the fact that it contains imitative material.[15] In the case of pastiche and film adaptation, and in forms like parody and homage, recognizing that these works are referring to something that precedes them is crucial to their identity. Hip-hop songs can textually signal their borrowing overtly or not do so, and both approaches can be manifested in a number of ways.

Take, for example, two recorded examples of hip-hop from roughly the same era and geographical location (1992–1993, Los Angeles): the Pharcyde's "Passin' me By" (from *Bizarre Ride to the Pharcyde*) and Snoop Doggy Dogg's "Who am I (What's my Name?)" (from *Doggystyle*). Both use source material from elsewhere (see Table 15.1), but the vinyl pop and hiss audible in the Pharcyde example draws attention to the fact that the material comes from an earlier source. It is also a trope we might call "vinyl aesthetics": a signifier of hip-hop authenticity associated with the sounds of vinyl (popping, hiss, and scratching to name a few). To invoke the terminology from Lacasse which is useful in the study of recorded music, the Pharcyde example is autosonic, in that it comes from a digital sample, and the Dr. Dre example is allosonic, in that its borrowed material has been re-recorded.

Furthermore, the hiss of vinyl heard faintly in the introduction of "Passin' me By" textually signals that some of the song has its roots elsewhere, that elements have been borrowed, and most likely sampled. In contrast, "Who am I?" contains many elements derived from earlier songs but was re-recorded in a studio (apart from its two-measure introduction), and does not contain any vinyl popping or hiss characteristic of sample-based hip-hop songs. In other words, "Who am I?"'s intertexuality is not

Table 15.1 *Samples and borrowed material from the Pharcyde's "Passin' me By" and Snoop Doggy Dogg's "Who am I (What's my Name?)."*

"Passin' Me By" (1992) autosonic quotations, textually signaled

Musical phrase	Derived from
Opening phrase	The Jimi Hendrix Experience, "Are You Experienced?" (1967)
Bass figure	Weather Report, "125th Street Congress" (1973)
Drums	Skull Snaps, "It's a New Day" (1973)
Keyboard	Quincy Jones, "Summer in the City" (1973)
Saxophone	Eddie Russ, "Hill Where the Lord Hides" (1974)

"Who am I (What's my Name?)" (1993) allosonic quotations, not textually signaled

Musical phrase	Derived from
Moog bass line	Tom Browne, "Funkin' for Jamaica" (1981)
Vocal Line 1	George Clinton, "Atomic Dog" (1982)
Vocal Line 2	Parliament, "Tear the Roof off the Sucker (Give up the Funk)" (1976)
"Talk box"	Zapp-style (1978–80s funk band)
Low vocal effects and vocal line 3	"Atomic Dog" (1982)

textually signaled. Its sources of material are not obvious in themselves, and to a young listener unknowledgeable of 1970s soul and funk, it can sound strikingly "original."[16]

Other instances of "textually signaled" borrowing in hip-hop could also include references and citations to earlier lyrics (50 Cent's "Snoop said this in '94: 'We Don't Love them Hoes'" in "Patiently Waiting") or using short snippets of dialogue that originate elsewhere. In the beat, this would include vinyl hiss and popping, scratching, looped beats, "chopped up" beats, as producers and rappers may use a sample as an opening phrase, and proceed to chop the phrase for its basic beat,[17] using breakbeats that fall firmly within the breakbeat canon, heavy collages of sound (The Bomb Squad, DJ Shadow), and sped up samples (such as Kanye West's "Through the Wire" (2003)). In addition, the sampling could be textually signaled if the borrowed fragment "doesn't quite fit" with the rest of the material; for example, being slightly out of tune with other elements or if the duration of the sample does not fit any "regular" pattern (i.e. four- or eight-measure pattern).

These distinctions are important to make, in light of the fact that on an abstract level, "everything is borrowed," a phrase that I myself borrow from an album title of the UK hip-hop group the Streets. But what is compelling for the study of intertextuality is how exactly particular communities incorporate borrowing, celebrate it, conceal it, and discuss it.

Sampling and copyright

Copyright emerged as a result of the invention of the printing press, and most point to the Statute of Anne in 1710 in England as the first legislation which protected authors for a certain amount of time from unauthorized use or sale of their work. Since then, countries have developed and modified legislation regarding authorship and ownership of intellectual property. One of the issues with the study of copyright cases is that many are settled out of court, but even when we do not have such data, such high-profile cases have had ramification for artists and the music industry. As McLeod and Dicola write, "Licensing negotiations always take place in the shadow of copyright law's provisions – and the ways that courts have interpreted those provisions in particular cases."[18]

In order to sample a sound, rights need to be cleared and a license needs to be given for use, both for the recording rights and for publishing. It is important, here, to draw the distinction between publishing fees and master recording (or mechanical) fees. When Dr. Dre re-records songs, he only has to pay the publishing fees and not the mechanical fees in addition to the publishing, as would be the case if he digitally sampled the sounds. Kembrew McLeod writes, "The publishing fee, which is paid to the company or individual owning a particular song, often consists of a flexible and somewhat arbitrary formula that calculates a statutory royalty rate set by Congress."[19] Those who do not pay a fee can be subject to lawsuits from those who own the rights. Sampling artists can argue fair use, or that they used an excerpt so small that it was unrecognizable or not integral to the original songs, but this is not necessarily a failsafe argument. The court cases that deal with sampling are battlefields that set important precedents and trends in creative practices. As McLeod and DiCola write:

> In particular, lawsuits play a role in determining the way and the degree to which musicians can use prior works by other musicians. When a copyright owner brings a successful claim for infringement, the range of existing music to which musicians have unfettered access can shrink. On the other hand, when a musician who has sampled without permission mounts a successful defence to copyright infringement, access might be understood to expand.[20]

One of the first cases to receive media attention was when the Turtles sued De La Soul in 1989, which was settled out of court, but was for unauthorized use of "You Showed Me" for "Transmitting Live from Mars." The lawsuit made record companies hesitant to support such heavily sample-based albums as *3 Feet High and Rising*. Two years later, *Grand Upright Music, Ltd.* v. *Warner Bros. Records, Inc.* set an important precedent. Biz Markie had used material from Gilbert O'Sullivan's "Alone Again

(Naturally)" for his song "Alone Again." Biz Markie lost the case. The judge considered any unauthorized sampling an act of theft, and all samples had to be cleared by the copyright owner (and the title of Markie's next album would be *All Samples Cleared*). Other cases, such as *Campbell* v. *Acuff-Rose Music* (1994) deemed 2 Live Crew's use of "Oh, Pretty Woman" by Roy Orbison a parody and held that the sales of the parody would not hurt the sales of the Roy Orbison recording. Uses of parody and critique in the USA can fall under "fair use" as long as the case is made that it is transformative and does not hurt the sale of the original product.[21]

Bridgeport Music, Inc., founded in 1969, is a company of one man who buys the rights to various music catalogues (most famously that of George Clinton) and sues those who use the material without license (Bridgeport had five hundred lawsuits in 2001 alone). An extremely important case involving the company was *Bridgeport Music Inc.* v. *Dimension Films* (2005), which claimed that N.W.A.'s "100 miles and Running" used a three-note chord from Funkadelic's "Get off Your Ass and Jam," albeit with the pitch lowered and looped five times. In previous cases this may have been considered transformative and so minimal (*de minimis*) as to be not considered infringement. However, Bridgeport Music did win the case, and it set a precedent that any sampled sound needs to be subject to clearance.[22] Bridgeport also successfully sued Bad Boy Records in 2006 for use of an Ohio Players' track on Notorious B.I.G.'s *Ready to Die*. This halted album sales until after the settlement (reported to be $4 million).[23] Sometimes it is too expensive to clear a sample, such as when Public Enemy wanted to use "Tomorrow Never Knows" by the Beatles in 2002 but the song had to be taken off the album. And in 2004, EMI sent a cease and desist letter to DJ Danger Mouse for the *Grey Album* (which mixes Jay-Z's *Black Album* with the Beatles' *White Album*).[24] The legal battles will continue in the foreseeable future, though both sides of the debate are getting their arguments across in various arenas (websites, articles, and other media). It is safe to say that copyright legislation over sampling has had a measurable effect on the sounds of hip-hop, and that some of the intertextual spirit of the genre is now tempered by the legal requirements of clearing samples.

Case study: Xzibit/Wendy Carlos/J. S. Bach

To provide a more substantial example in the close reading of a recorded hip-hop text, I will now turn to a specific instance of sampling from the classical music canon. I focus on the elements of the "beat" or basic beat, rather than lyrical content, in depth and choose to use them as an example of how the concepts outlined earlier in this chapter apply to a piece of recorded hip-hop. I could have chosen pieces that sample other repertoire or other genres, but there may be some wider implications in the use of pieces which have had relatively long lives (and afterlives) in the public sphere.

"Symphony in X Major" (2002) is a single from the rapper Xzibit on his fourth album *Man* v. *Machine*. The song is produced by Bay Area-based Rick Rock (active since 1996) and features a verse by accomplished producer Dr. Dre (Andre Young). Hip-hop music production since the mid 1990s is too varied to define comprehensively, but it often includes a mix of technology such as samplers, sequencers, synthesizers, drum machines, and more traditionally "live" instruments. Xzibit, Alvin Nathaniel Joiner (b. 1974), has been a professional rapper since the mid 1990s, often collaborating with other West Coast rap stars, including a featured role as guest on Dr. Dre's *Chronic 2001* (1999). The presence of Dr. Dre on "Symphony in X Major" is not uncommon for rap at this time, as there were often numerous guest artists and multiple producers on a single album.

Unlike the Dr. Dre early-1990s production mentioned earlier (e.g. "Who am I?"), "Symphony in X Major" relies more heavily on overt autosonic quotation, and textually signals the source of the sample. The samples are the most prominent aspect of the basic beat, although there is the presence of simple and unobtrusive programmed rhythmic percussion with emphasis on beats one (kick drum) and three (clap/snare). The percussive additions are minimal, but transform the sample into a track characteristic of the hip-hop genre. The song consists of two samples both taken from the same source: Wendy Carlos's *Switched on Bach* (1968) version of Bach's Brandenburg Concerto No. 3 (first movement). The excerpt is from the middle section of the movement, when the theme transitions into the relative minor key. It may be significant that the song uses the shift to the minor key of the movement, which becomes useful in reinforcing the menacing tone of the hip-hop track. I will call the two pieces of sampled material sample A (mm. 70–71 of Brandenburg Concerto) and sample B (mm. 68–69 of Brandenburg Concerto)[25] – see Examples 15.1 and 15.2.

"Symphony in X Major" follows a contrasting verse–chorus structure in that the harmonic material of the chorus differs from that of the verse (Table 15.2). The chorus consists of the two-measure sample A repeated once to create a four-measure phrase in total. The chorus includes both male and female voices singing pseudo-operatically over the primary "violin" melody of the sample. The verse consists of the two-measure sample B repeated eight times. The verse with rapped material followed by the chorus with sung material reflects a transition in hip-hop song form from free rhyming verse over a repeated riff ("Rapper's Delight" [1979]) to rap songs with sung choruses (in part, ushered in by Dr. Dre's G-Funk era (1992–1996), e.g. "Let me Ride" (1992) and "Nuthin but a 'G' Thang"(1992)).

Example 15.1 Sample A (mm. 70–71) Brandenburg Concerto No. 3, 1st movement.

The contrasting verse–chorus form is common for hip-hop at the time, as is the musematic (or riff-based) repetition in the verse (sample B) with longer (discursive) phrases on the chorus (sample A). To use Dyer's distinction, there are two primary elements which suggest that the recorded text signals the autosonic quotations rather than unsignaling them. The first eight measures of the song consist of two iterations of sample A, and we can hear the rupture between measure two and three as the sample begins to loop again. There is no attempt to cover this up with flow in the first instance. Furthermore, verse four is an instrumental which is the same loop of sample B found in the previous verses and transition section (repeated

Example 15.2 Sample B (mm. 68–69) Brandenburg Concerto No. 3, 1st movement.

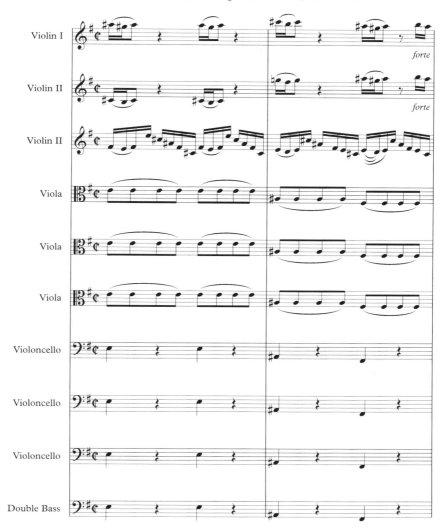

in the instrumental verse four times). The exposure of the sample, as seen in the form of the track, demonstrates that it celebrates its sample origins. In a general sense, we can analyze this particular hip-hop track as characteristic of its era: sample-based (sampling the same track rather than multiple tracks), with a level of synthesized reinforcement (in this instance, drum sounds), with a contrasting verse–chorus form, autosonic quotations in verse and chorus, allosonic quotations of the Bach melody in the form of the sung chorus, and overall, the basic beat textually signaling where its primary source comes from. By virtue of the musical material sampled, the verse includes musematic repetition as compared to the chorus material of

Table 15.2 *"Symphony in X Major" form (section/function, number of bars and sample used)*

Intro	Verse 1 (Xzibit)	Chorus	Verse 2 (Dre)	Chorus	Trans.	Verse 3 (Xzibit)	Chorus	Verse 4	Fade
2+2	2×8	2+2	2×8	2+2	2×2	2×8	2+2	2+2	2+2
A	B	A	B	A	B	B	A	B	B

sample A, which suggests more discursive repetition. While there is a high degree of flow located in the rap track, the fact that both sample A and sample B have instrumental sections without flow or singing demonstrate that these samples are placed prominently in order to be heard.

It is at this point that we might be inclined to draw multi-layered meaning from the use of this sample. Do we wish to draw meaning from its generic associations, a genre synecdoche of "classical music" (broadly defined), or perhaps even misread as opera, given the "operatic" voices on the chorus and transition section? Do we go further and give meaning to the prominence of its composer (J. S. Bach), his afterlife and reception as an important cultural figure and the multiple shades of his personal portrayal over the centuries (the divine genius, the hard-working craftsman, the subject of the refined tastes of a serial killer, or the Romantic nineteenth-century choral "reboots"/revivals of Bach's music)? There are a number of instances where this would be appropriate, in particular, when films utilize his music and character in quite overt ways.[26] But in this particular instance, one might hesitate before placing too much emphasis on the direct Bach link, in the same way that Robert Fink attaches less meaning to Pachelbel in the afterlife of Pachelbel's "Canon in D."[27] Features of classical music become a trope in this particular instance, to cite Leydon's use of Ratner to discuss sampling. In other words, classical music becomes a stylistic topic in the potential polystylism that hip-hop tracks often express.[28]

But we also need to acknowledge the "second degree" nature of the borrowing, in that the producer is not simply sampling J. S. Bach's Brandenburg Concerto No. 3 generally, but is sampling from a specific famous recorded performance of the piece, that of Wendy/Walter Carlos *Switched on Bach*.[29] In considering the synthesizer timbres, the Moog synthesizer of Carlos is fused with the contemporary (*c.* 2002) trend of heavily synthesized hip-hop beats (Eminem's production on 50 Cent's "Patiently Waiting" from 2003, for example). In this way, the sample may be more aligned to Schloss's line of argument for sampling artists' motivations, that producers sample because the material is beautiful, rather than sampling more specific political and resistant material (as Russell Potter argues, for example). Thus, it is the convergence between vinyl "crate digging" which in this case found a late-1960s album which resembles certain 00s synthesized timbres (Carlos arguably a precursor to a hip-hop based approach to reworking previous materials). Carlos, like many hip-hop producers, was Signifyin(g) on earlier material in a tradition of revision (although tellingly, the score is preserved for *Switched on Bach*, albeit "re-orchestrated") – but the use of previous material in the context is an issue of degree rather than quality. Past becomes present which then adds to the trend of producing synthesized hip-hop beats, and perhaps becomes a stylistic topic in itself: representative of mid-00s synthesizer-heavy hip-hop of Interscope/Aftermath, Shady Records, and G-Unit record labels. Wendy Carlos then becomes part of a tradition and genre culture, perhaps more so than J. S. Bach becomes a part of hip-hop culture in this instance. Such is the flexibility of musical signifiers, as they are so heavily dependent on their social contexts.

As Schloss states in *Making Beats*, too much emphasis has been placed on political readings of sampling, which may be linked to a disproportionate amount of emphasis placed on the quasi-academic location of specific sample sources. This is a feature of "hip-hop heads" or enthusiasts in production and fan communities. But I think we also need to allow for these wider significations. For example, sometimes generic signifiers (those of "jazz," or "classical," or synthesized versions of classical) become more important than the actual identity of the sample. If it "sounds jazzy," rather than originating from an authentic jazz source, then this should be investigated rather than dismissed as an example of how musical structures travel in various cultural realms.[30] This has been occurring for more than a century with the idiom of Hollywood film music and its Romantic precursors. For example, does the autosonic use of the "Rex Tremendae" in Mozart's *Requiem* for Missy Elliott's "Who You Gonna Call?" suggest Mozart or the wider "gothic choral aesthetic" found in film music (inspired by Orff's *Carmina Burana* and the requiems of Mozart and Verdi)?[31] This is dependent on the specific interpretive community, but it does reinforce Leydon's notion that we are moving toward a focus on sampling "stylistic topics" rather than detailed information from specific examples. In the case of Xzibit, sampling something that, albeit synthesized, still sounds "classical" has a range of meanings which means that while we might be in a "post-canonic era" for classical music, as Fink argues,[32] we are nowhere near a post-genre era for either interpretive communities of music or historical musicology as a discipline.

In studies of borrowing, there is always the question of whether to favor compositional process or cultural reception, or, to invoke Nattiez, to place emphasis on the poietic dimension or the esthesic.[33] In other words, if we do not hear Bach in "Symphony in X Major" is it still a worthy topic for the study of quotation and musical borrowing? Or on the compositional/poietic side, if the producer did not intend to allude to Bach or Carlos, does it still tell us anything? And if the reception is important, whose reception is it? Is it simply the private reflections of an idiosyncratic white middle-class academic risking the danger of implicitly making spurious claims that these references can generally be heard by "all"?

The answer lies within the imagined community of hip-hop. Most crucially, as I have written elsewhere, this imagined community is also an "interpretive community," to make reference to Stanley Fish and reader-response theory.[34] In any given reference in a rap song, some listeners will understand the reference, and some will not, to varying degrees. This is not to suggest there are one or more fixed meanings, nor a dialectic between "past" and "present," or necessarily between a hip-hop song and its "source" sample, but multiple imagined "sources," based on the previous knowledge of specific songs, artists, or genres. It is the reading and misreading of these sources as reflected by constantly shifting and negotiating interpretations within hip-hop's imagined communities that form its foundations. These hip-hop interpretive communities bring their experiences to the understanding of hip-hop texts, shaping and inflecting that text through the interaction involved in the listening and interpreting experience.

Despite variations inevitable with a group's interpretation of any given utterance, I would argue that there exists an audience expectation that hip-hop is a vast intertextual network that helps to form and inform the generic contract between audiences and hip-hop groups and artists. And in many cases, hip-hop practitioners overtly celebrate their peers, ancestors, and musical pasts, though reasons why this is so may diverge, and how references and sources are textually signaled (or not) varies on an imaginary spectrum that roughly corresponds to a timeline of traditions and technical innovations. Whereas certain rock or "new music"/contemporary classical ideologies that borrow from Romantic notions of musical genius attempt to demonstrate an illusionary originality, hip-hop takes pride in appropriating and celebrating other sounds and ideas. It is reflective of a long lineage of African American and pre-Romantic Western music-making which has embraced the collective in multifarious ways.

Further reading

McLeod, Kembrew, *Owning Culture: Authorship, Ownership, and Intellectual Property Law* (New York: Peter Lang, 2001).

McLeod, Kembrew and Peter DiCola, *Creative License: The Law and Culture of Digital Sampling* (Durham, NC: Duke University Press, 2011).

Schloss, Joseph, *Making Beats: The Art of Sample-Based Hip-Hop* (Middletown, CT: Wesleyan University Press, 2004).

Williams, Justin, *Rhymin' and Stealin': Musical Borrowing in Hip-Hop* (Ann Arbor: University of Michigan Press, 2013).

Discography

Carlos, Wendy/Walter, *Switched on Bach* (CBS/Columbia Masterworks, S 63501, 1968).

The Pharcyde, *Bizarre Ride II the Pharcyde* (Delicious Vinyl, 828 749–2, 1992).

Snoop Doggy Dogg, *Doggystyle* (Interscope/Death Row Records, 6544–92272–2, 1993).

Xzibit, *Man Vs. Machine* (Columbia, CK 85925, 2002).

Notes

1 More specifically, citing Genette, intertextuality is the "relationship of copresence between two texts or among several texts." Gérard Genette, cited in Serge Lacasse, "Intertextuality and Hypertextuality in Recorded Popular Music," in Michael Talbot (ed.), *The Musical Work: Reality or Invention?* (University of Liverpool Press, 2000), p. 36.

2 See Justin A. Williams, *Rhymin' and Stealin': Musical Borrowing in Hip-Hop* (Ann Arbor: University of Michigan Press, 2013).

3 Bill Brewster and Frank Broughton, *Last Night a DJ Saved my Life: The History of the Disc Jockey* (London: Headline Publishing, 2007), p. 267.

4 Russell Potter, *Spectacular Vernaculars: Hip-Hop and the Politics of Postmodernism* (State University of New York Press, 1995), p. 27.

5 Henry Louis Gates, Jr., *The Signifying Monkey: A Theory of African-American Literary Criticism* (New York and Oxford: Oxford University Press, 1989), pp. 55–56. See also Potter, *Spectacular Vernaculars*, p. 83.

6 Gates, *Signifying Monkey*, p. 21. For Signifyin(g) in jazz contexts, see David Metzer, *Quotation and Cultural Meaning in Twentieth-century Music* (Cambridge University Press, 2003), Chapter 2, "Black and White: Quotations in Duke Ellington's 'Black and Tan Fantasy,'" pp. 47–68; Ingrid Monson, "Doubleness and Jazz Improvisation: Irony, Parody, and Ethnomusicology," *Critical Inquiry* 20/2 (1994): 283–313; Gary Tomlinson, "Cultural Dialogics and Jazz: A White Historian Signifies," *Black Music Research Journal* 22 (2002): 71–102. David Brackett uses the concept in his analysis of James Brown's "Superbad"; see David Brackett, *Interpreting Popular Music* (Berkeley, CA: University of California Press, 2000).

7 For more on dialogism, Signifyin(g), and intertextuality, see Graham Allen, *Intertextuality* (New York: Routledge, 2000); and Mikhail Bakhtin, *Discourse in the Novel*, in Michael Holquist (ed.), *The Dialogic Imagination: Four Essays* (Austin, TX: University of Texas, 1982), pp. 259–422.

8 Elizabeth A. Wheeler, "'Most of my Heroes don't Appear on no Stamps': The Dialogics of Rap Music," *Black Music Research Journal* 11/2 (1991): 193–216.

9 J. Peter Burkholder, "Borrowing," in Laura Macy (ed.), *Grove Music Online* (Oxford University Press). Available at www.oxfordmusiconline.com/ (accessed June 1, 2014); see also J. Peter Burkholder, "The Uses of Existing Music: Musical Borrowing as a Field," *Notes* 50/3 (1994): 851–870.

10 Chris Cutler, "Plunderphonia," in Christoph Cox and Daniel Warner (eds.), *Audio Culture* (London: Continuum, 2004), p. 149.

11 Mark Katz, *Capturing Sound: How Technology Has Changed Music* (Berkeley, CA: University of California Press, 2004), p. 139.

12 Tricia Rose, *Black Noise: Rap Music and Black Culture in Contemporary America* (Middletown, CT: Wesleyan University Press, 2004), p. 64.

13 Lacasse, "Intertextuality," pp. 35–58.

14 Richard Middleton, *Studying Popular Music* (Open University Press, 1990), 269–284. For more on the "basic beat," see Williams, *Rhymin' and Stealin'*, p. 2.

15 Williams, *Rhymin' and Stealin'*, pp. 7–10.

16 For more on Dr. Dre's compositional process in his early 1990s productions, see Williams, *Rhymin' and Stealin'*, pp. 82–88.

17 Examples would include Kanye West's production on his own "Champion" (2007) and on Talib Kweli's "In the Mood" (2007).

18 Kembrew McLeod and Peter DiCola, *Creative License: The Law and Culture of Digital Sampling* (Durham, NC: Duke University Press, 2011), p. 128.

19 Kembrew McLeod, *Owning Culture: Authorship, Ownership, and Intellectual Property Law* (New York: Peter Lang, 2001), p. 91. See also Schloss, *Making Beats*, p. 175.

20 McLeod and DiCola, *Creative License*, pp. 128–129.

220 *Justin A. Williams*

21 For more on "fair use" in the US legal context, see the Stanford Law School Fair Use Project. Available at http://cyberlaw.stanford. edu/focus-areas/copyright-and-fair-use (accessed May 19, 2014).
22 McLeod and DiCola, *Creative License*, pp. 144–147.
23 K. Matthew Dames, "Uncleared Sample Halts Sale of Seminal Album," *Copycense*, March 20, 2006. Available at http://copycense.com/2006/03/20/uncleared_sampl/ (accessed May 19, 2014).
24 McLeod and DiCola, *Creative License*, pp. 176–182.
25 Although sample A occurs chronologically after sample B in the Brandenburg, sample A is the first sample we hear in "Symphony in X Major," in the introduction to the song.
26 For example, see Carlo Cenciarelli, "Bach and Cigarettes: Imagining the Everyday in Jim Jarmusch's Int. Trailer. Night," *Twentieth-century Music* 7/2 (2010): pp. 219–243; and Carlo Cenciarelli, "Dr. Lecter's Taste for 'Goldberg', or: The Horror of Bach in the Hannibal Franchise," *Journal of the Royal Musical Association* 137/1 (2012): 107–134.
27 Robert Fink, "Prisoners of Pachelbel: An Essay in Post-canonic Musicology," *Hamburg Jahrbuch* (2010). Available at http://ucla. academia.edu/RobertFink/Papers/583880/Prisoners_of_Pachelbel (accessed September 23, 2012).
28 Leydon argues that the era of sampling has now shifted from explicit sampling toward multiple stylistic allusions, and that sampled

sounds have become yet another topic in this range of topoi. Rebecca Leydon, "Recombinant Style Topics: The Past and Future of Sampling," in Mark Spicer and John Covach (eds.), *Sounding out Pop: Analytical Essays in Popular Music* (Ann Arbor: University of Michigan Press, 2010), pp. 193–213. I would argue, however, that stylistic allusion has been an important feature since the beginning of hip-hop (styles including funk, disco and rock music to name a few), and that we can have a degree of explicit quotation concurrently with its function as stylistic topic.
29 Cenciarelli coins the term "second degree" borrowings within the Bach context; see Carlo Cenciarelli, "'What Never Was Has Ended': Bach, Bergman and the Beatles in Christopher Munch's The Hours and Times," *Music & Letters* 94/1 (2013): 119–137.
30 Justin Williams, *Rhymin' and Stealin'*, pp. 47–72.
31 Melanie Lowe, "Claiming Amadeus: Classical Feedback in American Media," *American Music* 20/1 (2002): 102–119.
32 Robert Fink, "Elvis Everywhere: Musicology and Popular Music Studies at the Twilight of the Canon," *American Music* 16/2 (1998): 135–179.
33 Jean-Jacques Nattiez, *Music and Discourse: Toward a Semiology of Music*, trans. Carolyn Abbate (Princeton University Press, 1990), pp. 11–15.
34 Stanley Fish, *Is There a text in this class? The Authority of Interpretive Communities* (Cambridge, MA: Harvard University Press, 1980), p. 14.

PART III

Case studies

16 Nerdcore hip-hop

AMANDA SEWELL

Nerd-ho! Warm the mic up.
Yo, we 'bout to strike up
This band of nebbishes
Who cultivate nebulous fetishes

The FPS, RPG, or MMPOG[1]
Any obsession to blather over by blog or BBS.[2]
Step and possess,
Hone thy geekishness.

MC Frontalot, "Nerdcore Hip-Hop"

Welcome to the world of nerdcore hip-hop. The rhymes address topics ranging from *Star Wars* (mc chris's "Fett's 'Vette") to music file sharing (MC Lars's "Download this Song") to science (MC Hawking's "Entropy") to online role-playing games (Beefy's "Join My Guild") to the woes of higher education (Monzy's "So Much Drama in the Ph.D.").

Nerdcore hip-hop happens when technologically savvy, verbally precocious, and socially marginalized people begin to make hip-hop using their skill sets and experiences. Unlike the Black and Latino youths who created the earliest hip-hop under similar circumstances in the late 1970s, nerdcore rappers are almost all white, middle-class, and come from the suburbs. Although critic Dan LeRoy suggests that the Beastie Boys' 1989 "The Sounds of Science" opened the doors for nerdy white rappers to gain acceptance in the hip-hop scene, most nerdcore rappers acknowledge the Beastie Boys as an influence only in the broadest sense of being white and successful hip-hop artists.[3] According to MC Lars, "The Beastie Boys definitely made it less awkward for white people who wanted to express themselves through rap."[4] MC Frontalot (Figure 16.1), who coined the term "nerdcore hip-hop" in a song of the same name, describes a collision of interests in the genesis of the genre: "I liked [nerdcore] as a theme because it gave me an excellent excuse to rap about things I already wanted to rap about, like data encryption and text adventures and comic shops and the defeat of coolness in general."[5] Most nerdcore hip-hop artists describe a similar process: they wanted to rap, they wanted to rap about familiar topics, and the topics familiar to them were nerdy.

Figure 16.1 MC Frontalot. Credit: Phil Palios / Philthy Photography (with permission from Damien Hess).

Most nerdcore rappers are college-educated, and many hold at least one graduate degree: MC Lars studied English literature at Stanford and Oxford, Monzy has a Ph.D. in computer science from Stanford, and MC Frontalot double-majored in English and electronic music at Wesleyan University. As MC Hawking wryly notes, nerdcore artists are "young, gifted, and tenured."[6]

Nerdcore hip-hop is a relatively marginal genre, both in its subject matter and in its audience. Perhaps the three best-known artists are mc chris, MC Frontalot, and MC Lars. mc chris provided the voices for the characters MC Pee Pants and Sir Loin on *Aqua Teen Hunger Force*. MC

Frontalot appeared as a guest judge on the TBS reality show *King of the Nerds* and recorded the song "Toilet Paper Factory" for the direct-to-DVD *Elmo's Potty Time*. MC Lars co-hosted the 2012 Scholastic Art and Writing Awards Ceremony at Carnegie Hall, where he performed "Flow Like Poe," a rapped analysis of poetic meter in the works of Edgar Allen Poe. MC Frontalot and his crew were the subjects of *Nerdcore Rising*, a 2008 documentary which also included interviews with mc chris and MC Lars.[7]

Although nerdcore rappers are superficially connected by a set of interests in games, computer science, and science fiction or fantasy, according to MC Frontalot, they are truly united by their own sense of isolation and marginalization:

> Nerds end up in a lot of sub-categories, often based on what kinds of escapist media they consume (fantasy, sci-fi, games, comics, anime) or what professional talents they've developed (astrophysics, software engineering, genetics). But the question that always seemed more important to me was, what drove them into these obsessions or specializations in the first place? And I think that in every nerd there is a genesis story, an early period of perceived inadequacy, failures of athleticism and charisma, social exclusion, and then isolation.[8]

Most nerdcore rappers felt socially marginalized, particularly during their teenage years. As mc chris explains succinctly, "I was made fun of a lot because I was different."[9]

Nerdcore rappers' rhymes address either their interests or some aspect of social and romantic relationships, generally centering on awkwardness or ineptitude. For example, MC Lars's "Internet Relationships (Are Not Real Relationships)" cautions listeners that seemingly interested online parties are probably lying about their age, location, appearance, gender, or interests. In "Wallflowers," MC Frontalot invites his listeners to do a dance called the Margaret Thatcher; he assures them not to feel self-conscious because "you only ever do it when there's nobody watching you." These rappers focus on their own knowledge and experiences instead of imitating rap tropes or creating fictional stories. As mc chris explains, "If you try to act like you're a tough rapper when you're really just a skinny white guy who knows how to play video games, then no one's really going to buy it."[10]

Unlike bravado-laden mainstream hip-hop, many nerdcore rappers address their romantic and sexual ineptitude rather than prowess. As MC Lars confesses, "I was always very awkward, and it was hard to relate to girls."[11] For example, mc chris's "On*" is a plea to the navigation program OnStar to help him find the elusive clitoris. Further, nerdcore artists often address specific groups or types of females, including mc chris's "Nrrrd

Grrrl," Beefy's "Game Store Girl," MC Lars's "Hipster Girl," and MC Frontalot's "Goth Girls." In these and other tracks, nerdcore rappers lament their inability to talk to girls or else criticize certain girls for failing to take notice of them. When nerdcore rappers do spin tales of dating success, the girls involved are usually nerds, too. For example, in "Dork Date," Beefy invites a girl to the comic book store, Comic-Con, an mc chris show, and eventually, back to his place.

Although most love and sex tales in nerdcore hip-hop portray heterosexual relationships, nerdcore hip-hop shies away from heteronormative notions of masculinity. In fact, although most nerdcore rappers are straight-identified, many have conveyed an alliance with GLBT communities. Many nerdcore rappers identify with the GLBT community because they too were marginalized by their peers' ideas of heteronormative behavior. According to MC Frontalot, "That's part of nerd life. You don't fit into the traditional expectations of masculinity, especially as a teenager. If you're not actively struggling to maintain those goals of masculinity, then you get chastised by the word 'fag.'"[12] MC Frontalot's "I Heart Fags" is simultaneously an ode to his hometown of San Francisco and the numerous GLBT people (and "non-gender-identified Spivaks seeking nerd love") who inhabit it. MC Lars calls on figures such as Alfred Kinsey, Henry David Thoreau, Leonardo da Vinci, and the Village People to convince his listeners that "everyone's a little bit gay" in a song of the same title. Even though they are largely straight-identified, most nerdcore rappers endured the same kinds of bullying as their gay peers because their behaviors and interests did not fit neatly into a gender paradigm.

Nerdcore rappers also avoid other rap tropes such as drugs, violence, and guns. While some nerdcore tracks may seem like exceptions, they are still a far cry from the world portrayed in gangsta rap. Perhaps the most representative example of drug abuse in nerdcore hip-hop is mc chris's "The Tussin," an ode to "robo-tripping," or the abuse of dextromethorphan, an ingredient in cough medicine. However, "The Tussin's" lyrics chronicle the vomiting and headaches following the abuse, rather than glorifying the drug use itself.

Additionally, the lyrics of MC Hawking's "All My Shootings Be Drive-Bys" seem at first to celebrate drug use and drive-by shootings:

> I'm rolling through the hood on a Saturday night
> Got a 40 in my left hand, my dick in my right,
> Some chronic in my lap, a pager in my cap,
> And a 9 millimeter in the small of my back.

One might argue that these lyrics are in the same vein as gritty tales related by N.W.A. or the Wu-Tang Clan, but MC Hawking's rhymes are rendered in

WillowTalk, the same computer program that physicist Stephen Hawking uses to communicate.[13] Out of context, MC Hawking's lyrics address stereo-typical rap topics, but the aural delivery in Stephen Hawking's voice turns them into a farce: the vision of the wheelchair-bound theoretical physicist participating in the events described appears ludicrous.

Nerdcore is one of the earliest forms of "laptop hip-hop" or "laptop rap," in which all the materials needed for production and recording are contained in a laptop. MC Lars proclaims himself the originator of "post-punk laptop rap" because he was one of the first hip-hop artists to sample post-punk recordings in his production. Most live nerdcore hip-hop shows feature a lyricist rapping over beats that pour from his laptop into the venue's sound system. A few nerdcore rappers such as MC Frontalot and MC Lars have instrumental backing for their live shows, but the majority of rappers perform exclusively with their laptops. Although most nerdcore rappers also produce their own beats, some do collaborate with producers. Producer Baddd Spellah works extensively with MC Frontalot, rapper MC Router frequently collaborates with producer T-Byte, and the duo Dual Core consists of rapper Int Eighty and producer C64.

Most nerdcore hip-hop is disseminated free online, either through artists' websites or through file-sharing programs such as BitTorrent. No nerdcore artist is signed to a major label, although MC Lars founded his own independent record label, Horris Records. Most nerdcore rappers have accepted that they will not earn much money from selling their music because most of their listeners are technologically savvy enough to acquire it without paying. According to mc chris, "It's never fun to lose money, but you can't stop them. It's a humongous zombie army. Have you tried?"[14]

Some critics consider nerdcore a form of parody, an assessment not supported by most nerdcore rappers. Insinuations of nerdcore's parody are probably perpetuated by those who associate white, geeky rap acts with satirical parodies by Weird Al Yankovic. For example, in 2006, Weird Al recorded "White and Nerdy," a parody of Chamillionaire and Krayzie Bone's "Ridin'," released earlier that same year. The listener's familiarity with the original, when confronted with the clever revision of the lyrics, creates the humor and effectiveness of the parody. In both the lyrics and the music video of "White and Nerdy," Weird Al juxtaposes the depictions of racial profiling, police brutality, and transporting contraband in "Ridin'" against images of a white nerd who enjoys *Dungeons and Dragons*, calculus, and coding. The success of "White and Nerdy" relies on the listener's familiarity with "Ridin'," as well as the way Weird Al creates new lyrics completely opposite in meaning compared to the original. While the white rapper and the subjects of "White and Nerdy" superficially connect the track with nerdcore hip-hop, the fact that the song is a parody exempts it from nerdcore status. Nerdcore artists insist, as MC Frontalot has, that "nerdcore is not a parody of or a critique of hip-hop."[15]

Although nerdcore hip-hop is not parody in the sense that it mocks or ridicules hip-hop, the literary conception of parody as described by Linda Hutcheon is a useful lens for viewing nerdcore hip-hop. As she writes, "As a genre, musical parody is an acknowledged reworking of pre-existent material, but with no ridiculing intent."[16] While the term "parody" is often associated with satire, thus bringing to mind such parodies as those of Weird Al, the parody of nerdcore hip-hop is respectful rather than mocking: as Hutcheon points out, parody can imply either contrast or similarity.[17] Parody means doubleness, or one text standing clearly in relation to another. By this definition of parody, then, nerdcore hip-hop artists maintain respect for hip-hop by reworking it to suit their own messages.

This type of parody is evident in Monzy's track "So Fucking Pimp." When Monzy posted the song on his blog, he commented,

> Naturally, geeks are not pimp for the reasons traditionally cited in rap songs (wealth, women, jewelry, cars, strength, etc.), but certainly everyone has their own special skills to be proud of, and nerdcore is all about embracing the things that make you unique, even if they are not widely appreciated.

Monzy touts these attributes – such as a graduate degree from MIT, video-game mastery, and the ability to solve a Rubik's cube quickly – in "So Pimp" but frames them in language borrowed from mainstream hip-hop:

> I'm so pimp it should be a crime
> My site's been Slashdotted four separate times[18]
> I can factor numbers into their constituent primes
> Oh, and did I mention that I spit the dopest rhymes?

As Monzy's lyrics reveal, many nerdcore artists borrow the musical and verbal language of hip-hop to express their own sources of pride and achievement.

Nerdcore artists frequently express gratitude toward their hip-hop influences and insist that they take their parent genre seriously. As MC Frontalot has said, "I was worried that I would run into people who think I'm making fun of hip-hop, and no one has had that response. I don't find hip-hop absurd in any way."[19] Monzy explains, "I've always looked at nerdcore as an homage. I've always thought, 'Wow, I wish I was as cool as these rappers I've listened to.'"[20] Their musical contributions reflect their own experiences rather than imitating or attempting to identify with a culture of which they are not a part. Nerdcore rappers represent their own experience and culture within the musical confines of a genre they respect.

Nor do nerdcore rappers ignore or discount the roots of hip-hop and the inherent debt to African American musicians. As MC Lars explains, "The only way you truly appreciate the nerdcore movement is seeing it in relationship to its greater history. [I'm] an adamant proponent of knowledge of old-school [hip-hop] and respecting the culture's roots."[21] For example, MC Frontalot's "Good Old Clyde" is an homage to Clyde Stubblefield's famous drum break in James Brown's "Funky Drummer." In "Good Old Clyde," MC Frontalot acknowledges not only hip-hop's origins but also the funk music sampled to create hip-hop grooves. Nerdcore artists recognize and honor those who paved the road of hip-hop.

This admiration for hip-hop and a desire to produce a nerd version echoes the attitude Amiri Baraka perceived in early white jazz artists such as Bix Beiderbecke and the New Orleans Rhythm Kings. Baraka wrote, "They had caught the accent, understood the more generalized emotional statements, and, genuinely moved, set out to involve themselves in this music as completely as possible."[22] Many nerdcore artists reflect their love for hip-hop without necessarily copying what they have heard. As MC Frontalot has said, "We love rap music. We wish we could be like real rappers, but we're stuck with who we are. And we do what we do for that reason."[23] Nerdcore artists, like the white jazz musicians Baraka mentions, "wanted to play the music because they thought it emotionally and intellectually fulfilling."[24]

Nerdcore hip-hop's respect for hip-hop is frequently returned by other hip-hop artists. In fact, legendary hip-hop producer Prince Paul has said that nerdcore is "keeping it real" more than many other genres of hip-hop:

> I don't think [nerdcore] has anything to do with appropriation of black culture. I think it's going back to originally what I think hip-hop was all about, and that's to be yourself and talk about what you're into, not what the masses are into. For those guys to do what they do takes a lot of guts . . . Whoever is doing it is actually being honest and keeping real to themselves. You can't beat it. To me, that's true hip-hop.[25]

Other hip-hop artists have affirmed nerdcore's presence and viability through collaboration. MC Lars has opened for Nas and Snoop Dogg, and KRS-One delivered a guest verse on the track "What is Hip-Hop?" Kool Keith produced Beefy's track "The God of Rap Dr. Dooom2." MC Frontalot has included rappers such as Jean Grae and Kid Koala on his albums, an act he says "makes me feel like I could build a little credibility within parts of the hip-hop world that do not overlap entirely with the nerd bubble."[26]

To MC Frontalot, nerdcore "seeks only to be itself, to create a vivid and forthright presentation of topics and identities that might normally be shrouded in shame or embarrassment."[27] Nerdcore artists produce their own interpretations and visions of what hip-hop means to them, rather than emulating a culture of which they are not a part. Nerdcore hip-hop gives voices to musicians and speaks to listeners who feel marginalized both in life and in their music choices. When asked who his audience is, MC Lars replied, "Kids who feel pop culture talks down to them. It's the mavens and the misfits, and kids who discover things independently and the ones who are very passionate and of course, a little awkward and creative and smart."[28] One of the most touching scenes in *Nerdcore Rising* shows fan after fan hugging MC Frontalot after a show, some on the verge of tears. Footage of Frontalot is interspersed as he relates the isolation of his teenage years:

> I didn't have that much luck connecting with people in real life. These assholes over here make fun of me, these other people think I'm weird and want to have distance, and maybe a couple people like me and get me, but we're all rejects. If I could be disembodied and just have intellectual connection with other people through typing power, wouldn't that be utopia?[29]

For both the musicians and the listeners, nerdcore hip-hop is a chance to belong to a musical community. It offers them a musical connection to others who have the same interests and experiences with being on the fringes of society. To MC Lars, creating this community for his listeners is one of his greatest accomplishments: "To be able to give these kids a culture they can call their own, to embrace, that's beautiful. That's the only thing I really care about."[30]

Notes

1 FPS: first-person shooter; RPG: role-playing game; MMPOG: massive multiplayer online game.

2 BBS: bulletin-board system.

3 Dan LeRoy, *Paul's Boutique* (New York: Continuum, 2009), p. 86.

4 MC Lars, email message to the author, March 21, 2013.

5 MC Frontalot, email message to the author, March 18, 2013.

6 Quoted in Cary Darling, "Beats and Geeks: White Rappers Merge the Worlds of Hip-Hop and Computers in an Underground Scene Called 'Nerdcore,'" *Fort Worth Star-Telegram* (TX), February 16, 2007.

7 Another 2008 documentary, *Nerdcore for Life*, also featured a number of nerdcore hip-hop artists.

8 Email message to the author, March 18, 2013.

9 mc chris, interview with the author, November 14, 2008.

10 mc chris, interview with the author, November 14, 2008.

11 MC Lars, interview with the author, March 11, 2013.

12 *Nerdcore Rising*, dir. Negin Farsad (2008), 1:01:40.

13 MC Hawking is one of the very few non-white nerdcore rappers, but by delivering his rhymes in Stephen Hawking's voice rather than his own, he avoids aural association with his own blackness and instead maintains an aural association with Hawking's whiteness and nerdiness.

14 *Nerdcore Rising*, 13:27.

15 MC Frontalot, email message to the author, March 18, 2013. In nearly every interview he has given, MC Frontalot asserts that nerdcore is not a parody of hip-hop. See, for example, Brian Braiker, "Geeksta Rap Rising," *Newsweek*, February 5, 2007.

16 Linda Hutcheon, *A Theory of Parody: The Teachings of Twentieth-Century Art Forms* (New York: Methuen, 1985), p. 67.

17 *Ibid.*, p. 32.
18 Slashdot: a news website devoted to technology whose slogan is "News for Nerds: Stuff that Matters."
19 Quoted in Darling, "Beats and Geeks."
20 Quoted in Jeff Miranda, "Refrain of the Nerds: In this Hip-hop Universe, Science – not Violence – is What They Rap about," *Boston Globe*, November 4, 2007.
21 MC Lars, interview with the author, March 11, 2013.
22 Amiri Baraka [LeRoi Jones], *Blues People: Negro Music in White America* (New York: William Morrow, 1963), reprinted with introduction by the author (New York: Harper Collins, 1999), p. 149.

23 Quoted in Jim Colgan, "Profile: Nerd Hip-Hop, Flowing Like Han Solo," *Day to Day* (National Public Radio), November 7, 2005.
24 Baraka, *Blues People*, p. 150.
25 *Nerdcore Rising*, 57:00.
26 MC Frontalot, email message to the author, March 18, 2013.
27 MC Frontalot, email message to the author, March 18, 2013.
28 MC Lars, interview with the author, March 11, 2013.
29 *Nerdcore Rising*, 1:03:42.
30 MC Lars, interview with the author, March 11, 2013.

17 Framing gender, race, and hip-hop in *Boyz N the Hood, Do the Right Thing,* and *Slam*

ADAM HAUPT

Gangsta rap's global appeal in the early 1990s was partly facilitated by its use in 'hood films, such as *Boyz N the Hood* (1992; hereafter referred to as *Boyz*). This is largely because such films employed gangsta rap on their soundtracks and because gangsta rappers, like Ice Cube, were cast,[1] thereby authenticating the film narratives and globalizing narrow representations of Black masculinity. The relationship between Hollywood film-makers and certain rappers was mutually beneficial because these artists' film and television careers were kick-started. This film genre, and its associated music, found both US and global audiences. This allows us to consider stereotypical representations of Black masculinity in US cinema and gangsta rap.[2] However, these narrow depictions have not gone uncontested, as the Wayans brother's parody, *Don't Be a Menace to South Central While Drinking Your Juice in the Hood*, as well as Sacha Baron Cohen's spoof of gangsta rap via his persona, Ali G, reveal. Spike Lee provides more serious critical engagements with the 'hood genre in *Clockers*, but *Do the Right Thing* (1989) – which precedes the ascendance of the 'hood genre – points to more lateral ways in which hip-hop could be used to represent marginal Black subjects' struggles. His work challenges racially problematic cinematic depictions by resisting mainstream, commercial film conventions. Likewise, Marc Levin's *Slam* (1998) casts hip-hop slam poet Saul Williams in the lead role and features his performances as a means, not to create stereotypical representations of Black men, but to explore the concept of redemption through taking personal responsibility for one's actions. This casting choice is apt because Williams is critical of gangsta rap, which, he says, "has strayed too far from the source."[3] Ultimately, the different ways in which hip-hop is employed in the films under consideration here will reveal competing representations of Black masculinity in popular culture.

Singleton's *Boyz* sparked the wave of 'hood films by providing key insights into the lives of young Black males in South Central, Los Angeles. *Boyz* tells the story of Tre (Cuba Gooding Jr.) and his friendship with neighborhood friends Doughboy (Ice Cube) and Ricky (Morris Chestnut). Singleton focuses on the difficulties young African American men face in poor, gang-ridden neighborhoods. Films like *Boyz:*

[232]

create an effect of realism by creating an overlap between the rite of passage into manhood and the narrative time of story . . . The beginning, middle and end of *Boyz N the Hood* constitute episodes that mark the young protagonist's incorporation into society.[4]

At the end of the first episode, Tre leaves his mother and friends behind to live with his father, the second episode ends with Doughboy being arrested and the final episodes end with Tre's departure for university after Ricky's and Doughboy's deaths.[5] The key tension is set up with the film's lead-in text that frames the protagonist's dire context: "One out of every twenty-one Black American males will be murdered in their lifetime. Most will die at the hands of another Black male."[6] The film's realism is authenticated by the use of hip-hop.[7] Guerrero contends that *Boyz*'s use of gangsta rap and gangsta rappers in the cast accounts for its success, and that it did well at the box office because it crossed over to white audiences.[8] Black cinema's big challenge is that it operates at the margins. Blaxploitation films of the 1970s and the late 1990s 'hood movies were popular during a slump in the US film market, but even here Black film-makers were expected to make their films cheaply.[9] They were in a precarious position; a film's budget is determined by its crossover power. If a production approaches this budgetary limit, it either does not get financed or its "black point of view, politics, or narrative gets co-opted" or altered to appeal to the sensibilities of wider, white audiences to ensure large profits.[10]

Ice Cube's role in *Boyz* aided its crossover appeal and commercial success.[11] In many respects, Ice Cube's character overshadows Cuba Gooding, Jr.'s Tre. Like Furious Styles (Laurence Fishburne), Doughboy provides key critical insights into the political economy that produced these ghettos. Toward the end of the film when he has avenged Ricky's murder, he reflects upon the racial and class disparities in mainstream news coverage of dramatic events in the world. He tells Tre that the morning news did not make any mention of his brother's death the night before and remarks, "Either they don't know, don't show, or don't care about what's going on in the hood. They had all this foreign shit. They didn't have shit on my brother, man."[12] From Doughboy's perspective, mainstream media are either ignorant or indifferent toward the struggles of poor African Americans.[13] This is an ironic insight because, until this point, Doughboy offers little indication that he thinks about the broader context within which the 'hood's conflicts occur.[14] Doughboy is most active in threatening exchanges with rival groups and he is ready to use his gun when Ricky is harassed. He also avenges Ricky's death without hesitation. The cycle of vengeful violence between gangs therefore seems endless. It is thus significant for Doughboy to offer a critical reflection that links his 'hood's violence to the broader economic and political context that produces the social ills in South Central.

Doughboy's behavior reinforces Singleton's message at the beginning of the film when young Tre and his friends view a crime scene, where posters of former US president Ronald Reagan are visible. Paul Gormley contends that the "focus on Reagan posters, the acousmatic sounds of gunfire, and the bloody crime scene all signal the themes of inner-city and political protest against Reaganite government policies that also lie at the heart of the film."[15] Michelle Alexander argues that de-industrialization and globalization created the economic collapse of Black working-class communities in the 1980s.[16] This can be attributed to Reagan's policies that found favor with citizens after a presidential campaign appealed to white, conservative interests:

> In his campaign for the presidency, Reagan mastered the "excision of the language of race from conservative public discourse" and thus built on the success of earlier conservatives who developed a strategy of exploiting racial hostility or resentment for political gain without making explicit reference to race. Condemning "welfare queens" and "criminal predators," he rode into office with the strong support of disaffected whites – poor and working-class whites who felt betrayed by the Democratic Party's embrace of the civil rights agenda.[17]

The Reagan era's approach to de-industrialization and the outsourcing of manufacturing jobs was thus radicalized.[18] Instead of addressing the causes of the economic collapse of ghettos, an unsympathetic, racialized discourse was used to demonize poor Black communities. Reagan's war on drugs should be read in relation to his economic policies.[19] Dominant media representations of this war on drugs "typically featured black 'crack whores,' and 'gangbangers,' reinforcing already prevalent racial stereotypes of black women as irresponsible, selfish and 'welfare queens,' and black men as 'predators' – part of an inferior and criminal subculture."[20] Entman and Rojecki contend, "Racial representation on television actually does not appear to match crime statistics, with local news overrepresenting Black perpetrators, underrepresenting Black victims, and overrepresenting White victims [sic]."[21] This reinforces Doughboy's interpretation of news media. Furious Styles's lecture to Tre and Ricky and the residents of Compton about gentrification resonates with Alexander's research:

> [W]hy is it that there is a gun shop on almost every corner in this community? Tell you why. For the same reason that there's a liquor store on almost every corner in the black community. Why? They want us to kill ourselves. You go out to Beverly Hills, you don't see that shit. But they want us to kill ourselves. Yeah, the best way you can destroy a people, you take away their ability to reproduce themselves. Who is it that dyin' out here on these streets every night? Y'all. Young brothers like yourselves. You doin' exactly what they want you to do.[22]

Furious suggests that young Black men in his community have internalized the violence that has been acted out upon them by neo-liberal economic policies in a context where class inequalities are racialized. Many of the disparities that were addressed by Civil Rights activists in the earlier generation were continued in the 1980s. *Boyz* thus affords Doughboy and Styles the most meaningful opportunities to address political concerns and helps to authenticate the director's realist project.

However, Ice Cube plays the most significant role here. Michael Eric Dyson contends that

> Singleton's shrewd casting of rapper Ice Cube as a central character allows him to seize symbolic capital from a real-life rap icon, while tailoring the violent excesses of Ice Cube's rap persona into a jarring visual reminder of the cost paid by black males for survival in American society.[23]

Ice Cube's "How to Survive in South Central" features prominently on the film's soundtrack. The song imparts advice on how to survive in South Central in the form of three rules. The first rule is to be found in Ice Cube's first verse:

> Rule number one: get yourself a gun
> A nine in your ass'll be fine
> Keep it in your glove compartment
> cause jackers, yo, they love to start shit
> Now if you're white, you can trust the police
> but if you're black they ain't nothin' but beasts
> Watch out for the kill
> Don't make a false move and keep your hands on the steering wheel[24]

Ice Cube's readiness to embrace gun violence reveals that his aggression is not directed toward the police, but toward "jackers" – in other words, fellow community members. Even though the police are not to be trusted, it would be better for you to be obedient by keeping your hands on the steering wheel. Survival in the 'hood therefore relies on compliance when the police pull you over and a readiness to shoot "jackers" – Black-on-Black violence is therefore acceptable, thereby inadvertently confirming Furious's argument about internalized violence in the 'hood. This internalization is gendered, as rule number two suggests: "Rule number two: don't trust nobody / especially a bitch with a hooker's body / cause it ain't nuttin but a trap / And females'll get you jacked and kidnapped."[25] The misogynist appellation "bitch" is oft repeated by Doughboy in *Boyz*. Ice Cube's advice reduces the Black female body to a set of essentialist and negative character traits, much like racist and sexist discourse on single mothers and "crack whores" demonize Black women. Here, Ice Cube suggests that Black women, whom he equates with sex workers by virtue of their appearance, use their sexuality to harm Black men. bell hooks argues that the "sexist, misogynist, patriarchal ways of thinking and behaving that are glorified in gangsta rap are a reflection of the prevailing values in our society, values created and sustained by white supremacist capitalist patriarchy."[26] The song's values are thus similar to those of the broader hegemonic, misogynist milieu. This may explain why Ice Cube's casting assured the film's crossover. Discussing gangsta rap's contradictions, Michael Quinn asks, "Should Gangsta Rap be valorized for bringing African American rage into the spotlight after the Reagan era or criticized for its glorification of violence and misogyny?"[27] He contends that it should both be lauded and reproached.

Singleton's desire to authenticate his realist representation of the 'hood speaks to the burden of representation placed upon Black artists. Eithne Quinn explains, "Because black Americans, of all racially subordinated groups, have achieved the most in the cultural sphere while at the same time being the most relentlessly typecast in dominant image repertoires, discourses about representational responsibility have accrued an arresting importance."[28] Lee and Singleton have taken on this burden to clear space from which to tell stories from a Black perspective. In *Do the Right Thing* (1989), a precursor to the 'hood genre, Lee employs Public Enemy's Black Nationalist rap song "Fight the Power" to frame his narrative about the marginalized existence of African Americans in Bed-Stuy. The song's counter-hegemonic politics are clear:

> Elvis was a hero to most
> But he never meant shit to me, you see
> Straight up racist that sucker was
> Simple and plain
> Motherfuck him and John Wayne
> Cause I'm Black and I'm proud
> I'm ready and hyped plus I'm amped
> Most of my heroes don't appear on no stamps
> Sample a look back you look and find
> Nothing but rednecks for 400 years if you check[29]

Key signifiers of American nationalism, rocker Elvis Presley and movie cowboy John Wayne, are referenced to critique the racist nature of that nationalism. The cowboy genre is singled out as a symbol of four hundred years of colonialism in which indigenous people, often presented in Westerns as "injins"/"Indians," were systematically exterminated.[30] Likewise, Presley is mentioned to draw attention to arguments about cultural appropriation in rock's crossover to mainstream US audiences.[31] The "proud American century," often signified by Elvis and John Wayne, is blighted by allegations of institutionalized racism, to which Chuck D alludes when he says most of his heroes don't appear on stamps. The song is a sonic interruption in the lives of characters,[32] like Sal (Danny Aiello), who memorialized famous Italian American actors, singers, and sports celebrities on his pizzeria's Wall of Fame, to the annoyance of Buggin' Out (Giancarlo Esposito) who wants Black public figures on Sal's wall. The song's noise is literal and political. It demonstrates Dick Hebdige's discussion of noise in subculture: "Subcultures represent 'noise' . . . interference in the orderly sequence which leads from real events and phenomena to their representation in the media."[33] Public Enemy interrupts hegemonic representations of American patriotism by drawing attention to the fact that, historically, dominant representations of American identity and achievements are racially exclusive. Their interruption in the sequence that leads from real events to its representation in the media draws our attention to the ways in which the media construct our worldview. "Fight the Power" helps to drive the plot to its explosive climax when Radio Raheem is killed by cops. His death results in a riot and Sal's pizzeria is burned down. This raises questions about police brutality and Bed-Stuy residents' anger at not having a sense of ownership of the very neighborhood where they reside.

Like Lee, Public Enemy bear the burden of representation in their critique of racial inequality in the US, as witnessed by Chuck D's claim that they are with the Black community's CNN.[34] Bakari Kitwana contends that the commercial success of 'hood films reveals the "failure of Black intellectuals to make sense of the critical changes in African American life."[35] The Civil Rights movement's gains were rolled back in Black working-class communities. Gangsta rap addresses this failure. In light of the failure of the Civil Rights era to substantially improve the lives of the Black working class, gangsta rappers rejected the burden of representation. Quinn argues that gangsta rappers were aware of this burden of representation, at the very least via media and community critiques of their misogynist lyrics and embrace of violent and nihilist values:

> First, they mobilized the authenticity discourse (representation as depiction) to an unprecedented degree, in order to give expressive shape to materially grounded conditions, experiences, and desires and at the same time to fuel and feed the vast appetite for "black ghetto realness" in the popular-culture marketplace. Second, they reneged on the contract to act as delegates, self-consciously repudiating uplifting images of black life in a gesture of rebellion and dissent.[36]

They rejected the burden of representing images of blackness that countered hegemony, but then they also capitalized on notions of authenticity to meet commercial interest in narrow, fetishized understandings of Black masculinity and life in the 'hood. Gangsta rappers therefore became complicit in the contradictory scenario of the 1990s as described by Patricia Hill Collins:

> The actual ghettoization of poor and working-class African Americans may render them virtually invisible within suburban malls, on soccer fields, and in good public schools, yet mass media created a seemingly authentic Black American culture that glamorized poverty, drugs, violence, and hypersexuality.[37]

Likewise, Greg Tate writes that the

> African American presence in this country has produced a fearsome, seductive, and circumspect body of myths about Black intellectual capacity, athletic ability, sexual appetite, work ethic, family values, and propensity for violence and drug addiction.[38]

Thanks to Hollywood marketing, the narrow representation of Black subjectivity as presented in gangsta rap did more than cross over to white film audiences in the USA; it went global. If global audiences had not been exposed to socially conscious hip-hop by the early 1990s (such as Public Enemy, Afrika Bambaataa, Queen Latifah, or KRS-One), "'hood movies'" use of gangsta rap certainly introduced them to gangsta rappers like Ice Cube, Ice-T, and MC Eiht – thereby assuring their commercial success as rappers and movie stars. The big contradiction in gangsta rap's commercial uptake is that its "wealth has not been able to transform . . . the social reality of substandard housing, medical care, and education that affects over half of all African American children and accounts for as many as one out of three . . . African American males being under the control of the criminal justice system."[39] The use of gangsta rappers and their music in 'hood films, such as *Boyz*, is therefore ironic. This genre's claim to authenticity helps 'hood film-makers to authenticate their narratives. It also helps the film to cross over to wider audiences, thereby securing bigger profits. This is a good return on investment for Hollywood studios, which invested relatively little money in this genre. Gangsta rappers' rejection of the burden of representation effectively absolves them from having to engage with debates about social responsibility or accountability to the communities they claim to represent. In effect, this contradicts Singleton's intention to speak for marginal communities. As my discussion of Spike Lee's use of hip-hop in *Do the Right Thing* suggests, Lee's use of conscious hip-hop does not undermine his intentions.

Saul Williams's poetry in Marc Levin's *Slam* serves a similar function to "Fight the Power" in *Do the Right Thing*. *Slam* does not fall strictly in the 'hood genre, but speaks to key themes addressed in this genre. It also employs hip-hop to critique Black masculinity. Williams plays small-time drug dealer Ray Joshua, who faces a charge of drug possession after his drug supplier is shot. In the scenes before his arrest, we often see Ray at work on his poetry. His poetry saves him from having to choose between two rival prison gangs. In a tense prison yard scene, we see Ray attempting to find a safe spot. Just as a rival gang member walks swiftly up to him, presumably to assault him, Ray breaks out into a performance that speaks to the contradictions of Black-on-Black violence and the internalization of racist interpellation:

> Stealing us was the smartest thing they ever did
> Too bad they don't teach the truth to their kids
> Our influence on them is the reflection they see when they look into their
> minstrel mirror
> and talk about *their* culture
> Their existence is that of a schizophrenic vulture
> They are bound to live an infinite, consecutive, executive life sentence
> So what are you bound to live, nigger?
> So while you out there serving time
> I'll be in synch with the sun
> While you run with the moon
> Life of the womb reflected by guns
> Worship of moons, I am the sun
> And we are public enemies number one
> One, one-one, one
> One, one-one, one[40]

The performance – similar to Williams's "Penny for a Thought"[41] – criticizes the cycle of violence in which Black male characters in this film, *Boyz* and rap songs about "beefs" and territorial disputes, are locked. While Ray's poetry reflects that he possesses critical insights into institutionalized racism that has legitimated cultural appropriation in the form of blackface minstrelsy[42] and the interpellation of Black men as "public enemy number one" (cf. Public Enemy) during the Reagan era, he has yet to realize that the liberation for which he yearns can only take place if he accepts responsibility for his actions. Poetry teacher Lauren Bell (Sonja Sohn) witnesses Ray's performance and helps him to make this realization, as seen in her confrontation with Ray after he visits her when he gets bail. Lauren points out that this burden he is facing is not unique and that she, too, has had to make tough choices in the face of hardship (for example, the loss of her brother and her own humiliating addiction to drugs). Lauren's role is singular because, unlike many 'hood films, it is a female character who plays a key role in guiding the protagonist to redemption. As Dyson reveals, *Boyz* was criticized for suggesting that it is only fathers who can save young men from self-destruction in the 'hood, as seen in Furious's active role in steering Tre away from the violent demise of his friends, Doughboy and Ricky.[43] *Slam* therefore employs a different kind of race and gender politics that seems less interested in crossing over by using gangsta rap, gangsta rappers, or formulaic rites of passage narratives. Instead, it explores notions of individual responsibility while also creating meaningful space for women to drive the plot.

This chapter's explorations of the ways in which hip-hop is employed in *Boyz*, *Do the Right Thing,* and *Slam* reveal competing representations of Black masculinity in popular culture. While Singleton uses gangsta rap to authenticate representations of life in the 'hood, gangsta rap's conservative gender and race politics confirm patriarchal values, thereby contradicting his intentions. The absence of positive representations of women in Ice Cube's lyrics underscores the impression that his work is not authentic, but is merely presenting a set of patriarchal, misogynist values that confirm the status quo just as it, contradictorily, aims to challenge the mainstream. On the other hand, Lee's use of Black Nationalist rappers Public Enemy in *Do the Right Thing* takes on the burden of representation to pose largely unresolved questions about race and belonging in the film. Public Enemy does not contradict Lee's overall agenda. However, Lee has been criticized for sidelining female characters, specifically Mookie's sister, Jade (Joie Lee).[44] Mookie unceremoniously ejects her from the plot when he pushes her out of Sal's pizzeria after he decides that Sal really wants to "hide the salami" when he is being kind to her.[45] An opportunity is lost for this character to drive the plot meaningfully here and in a scene between herself and Buggin' Out. When he asks her if she is down with his call to boycott Sal, she says that she is "down for something positive."[46] But then the plot takes off without her and other female characters, such as Mother Sister (Ruby Dee) and Tina (Rosie Perez). The gender politics in *Boyz* and *Do the Right Thing* remind us that "racism is fundamentally a feminist issue because it is so interconnected with sexist oppression."[47] bell hooks argues that in "the West, the philosophical foundations of racist and sexist ideology are similar."[48] Attempts to address racial politics without acknowledging patriarchy, and its conservative conception of gender roles, are bound to fail. Thus *Slam* offers a more nuanced representation of its protagonist's struggle. As with Lee, Levin's use of hip-hop does not contradict the film's agenda. Instead, it creates room for Sonja Sohn's and Saul Williams's characters to offer more nuanced performances of gendered interaction and to use hip-hop to critique the narrow ways in which Black masculinity has been framed. Ultimately, the different ways in which these films employ socially conscious hip-hop and gangsta rap reveal that hip-hop is not easily boxed in. While certain forms of hip-hop have been co-opted commercially, it is clear that not all hip-hop artists have abandoned its use for social critique and reflection.

Notes

1 Ed Guerrero, *Framing Blackness: The African American Image in Film* (Philadelphia: Temple University Press, 1993); Murray Forman, *The 'Hood Comes First: Race, Space, and Place in Rap and Hip-Hop* (Middletown, CT: Wesleyan University Press, 2002).
2 For a detailed examination of gangsta rap, gender, and race stereotypes and US cultural imperialism, see Adam Haupt, *Stealing Empire: P2P, Intellectual Property and Hip-Hop Subversion* (HSRC Press: Cape Town, 2008).
3 Saul Williams, *Amethyst Rock Star* (American Recording Company, 2001).
4 Manthia Diawara, "Black American Cinema: The New Realism," in Mantha Diawara (ed.), *Black American Cinema* (New York and London: Routledge, 1993), p. 20.
5 *Ibid.*
6 *Boyz N the Hood*, dir. John Singleton (Columbia, 1992).
7 Diawara, "Black American Cinema."
8 Guerrero, *Framing Blackness.*
9 *Ibid.*
10 *Ibid.*, p. 167.
11 *Ibid.*
12 *Boyz N the Hood.*
13 Entman and Rojecki contend that local news depicts US life as "pervaded by violence and danger" and that this approach "heightens Whites' tendency to link these threats to Blacks." They suggest that, instead of an absence of coverage of violence in the 'hood, sensationalized news coverage is racially skewed against African Americans. Thus, instead of an absence of coverage, as Doughboy suggests, sensationalism confirms white prejudices. However, one could argue that Doughboy's view is correct in that journalists do not provide Black working-class perspectives or deeper investigation into the causes of social ills. It is in this sense that they don't "know" or "show" or "care." See Robert M. Entman and Andrew Rojecki, *The Black Image in the White Mind: Media and Race in America* (Chicago and London: University of Chicago Press, 2000), p. 78.
14 For a detailed exploration of African Americans' race and class struggles in Los Angeles, see Josh Sides, *LA City Limits: African American Los Angeles from the Great Depression to the Present* (Berkeley, Los Angeles and London: University of California Press, 2003); Raphael J. Sonenshein, *Politics in Black and White: Race and Power in Los Angeles* (Princeton University Press, 1993).
15 Paul Gormley, *The New Brutality Film: Race and Affect in Contemporary Hollywood Cinema* (Bristol and Portland: Intellect, 2005), p. 83.
16 See Michelle Alexander, *The New Jim Crow: Mass Incarceration in the Age Colorblindness* (London and New York: The New Press, 2010), pp. 49–50.
17 *Ibid.*, p. 47. James Johnson, Walter Farrell and Melvin Oliver contend that Republicans were in power for twenty-one years before the 1992 Los Angeles rebellion (or "riots" as portrayed by the media). Republicans "waged a massive assault on War on Poverty Programs, dismantling some and severely curtailing support for others," resulting in the highest poverty rate in twenty-five years. The authors argue that structural changes in the LA economy were key causes of the 1992 rebellion. Residents of South Central were hit hard by "massive deindustrialization or the loss of manufacturing jobs." See James H. Johnson, Jr., Walter C. Farrell, Jr., and Melvin L. Oliver, "Seeds of the Los Angeles Rebellion of 1992," *International Journal of Urban and Regional Research* 17/1 (1993): 115–117.
18 Alexander, *The New Jim Crow*, pp. 49–50.
19 *Ibid.*
20 *Ibid.*, p. 51.
21 Entman and Rojecki, *The Black Image in the White Mind*, p. 81.
22 *Boyz N the Hood.*
23 Michael Eric Dyson, "Between Apocalypse and Redemption: John Singleton's *Boyz N the Hood*," *Cultural Critique* 21 (1992): 124.
24 Ice Cube in *Boyz N the Hood.*
25 *Ibid.*
26 bell hooks, *Outlaw: Culture: Resisting Representations* (New York and London: Routledge, 1994), p. 116.
27 Michael Quinn, "'Never Shoulda Been Let out the Penitentiary': Gangsta Rap and the Struggle over Racial Identity," *Cultural Critique* 34 (1996): 87.
28 Eithne Quinn, "Black British Cultural Studies and the Rap on Gangsta," *Black Music Research Journal* 20/2 (2000): 198.
29 Public Enemy in *Do the Right Thing*, dir. Spike Lee (Universal, 1989).
30 Andrea Smith, "Sexual Violence and American Indian Genocide," *Journal of Religion & Abuse* 1/2 (1999): 31–52.

31 Kevin J. Greene, "Copyright, Culture, and Black Music: A Legacy of Unequal Protection," *Hastings Communication and Entertainment Law Journal* 21 (1999); Reebee Garofalo, *Rockin' Out: Popular Music in the USA* (Boston: Prentice Hall, 1997).

32 Victoria E. Johnson, "Polyphony and Cultural Expression: Interpreting Musical Traditions in *Do the Right Thing*," *Film Quarterly* 47/2 (1993–94): 18–29.

33 Dick Hebdige, *Subculture: The Meaning of Style* (London and New York: Routledge, 1979), p. 91.

34 Marvin J. Gladney, "The Black Arts Movement and Hip-Hop," *African American Review* 29/2 (1995).

35 Bakari Kitwana, *The Hip-Hop Generation: Young Blacks and the Crisis in African-American Culture* (New York: Basic Civitas, 2002), p. 139.

36 Eithne Quinn, "Black British Cultural Studies and the Rap on Gangsta," *Black Music Research Journal* 20/2 (2000): 202.

37 Patricia Hill Collins, *From Black Power to Hip Hop: Racism, Nationalism, and Feminism* (Philadelphia: Temple University Press, 2006), pp. 3–4.

38 Greg Tate, "Nigs R Us or How Blackfolk Became Fetish Objects," in Greg Tate (ed.), *Everything but the Burden: What White People are Taking from Black Culture* (New York: Broadway Books, 2003), p. 4.

39 *Ibid.*, 12.

40 Williams in *Slam*, dir. Marc Levin (Offline Entertainment Group, 1997).

41 See Williams, *Amethyst Rock Star*; Haupt, *Stealing Empire.*

42 Eric Lott, *Love and Theft: Blackface Minstrelsy and the American Working Class* (New York and Oxford: Oxford University Press, 1993).

43 Dyson, "Between Apocalypse and Redemption."

44 Wahneema Lubiano, "'But Compared to What?' Reading Realism, Representation, and Essentialism in *School Daze, Do the Right Thing*, and Spike Lee Discourse," in Marcellus Blount and George P. Cunningham (eds.), *Representing Black Men* (New York and London: Routledge, 1996).

45 *Do the Right Thing.*

46 *Ibid.*

47 bell hooks, *Feminist Theory from Margin to Center* (Boston: South End Press, 1984), p. 52.

48 *Ibid.*

18 Japanese hip-hop: alternative stories

NORIKO MANABE

In 2013, Major Force, Japan's first hip-hop label, enjoyed its twenty-fifth anniversary. During those years, hip-hop has influenced the musical sensibilities of several generations of Japanese youths. However, in terms of record sales in Japan's music market – the world's largest in terms of recording sales[1] – hip-hop is more on the margins in the early 2010s than it was in the previous decade. With the industry increasingly concentrated on boy bands and idol pop, the only hip-hop albums in Oricon's 100 best-selling chart for 2012 were best-of albums by Ketsumeishi, whose pitched-rap verses sound closer to J-Pop than hip-hop.[2] Condry's ethnography for his 2006 monograph was conducted from the mid 1990s to about 2004,[3] when the poppier elements of hip-hop like m-flo and Rip Slyme were making inroads into the mainstream music industry. Since then, the focus of the hip-hop scene itself has shifted from such pop-friendly groups to harder-edged rappers like Anarchy, Seeda, MSC, Shingo Nishinari, and Dengaryū. While this hardness has always existed in Japanese hip-hop, the severe contraction in the Japanese economy since the mid 2000s[4] has provided an authenticity to hard-edged tales and made them more sympathetic to a larger swath of youth. In this chapter, I will introduce some of the expressions of marginalization that have intensified since the mid 2000s – a shift to hardcore rap, focus on the local, involvement in social movements, neo-nationalism, and moral panics. I begin with a brief discussion of the scene's history and its aesthetic considerations, which are part of the localization process.

Multiple histories, multiple markets

Japan has long been the site of home-grown scenes of African-diasporic musics; its jazz scene dates to the early 1900s.[5] In the 1960s, some youths began imitating the appearance of African American servicemen in the army bases, with their afros and thin suits. These servicemen – many coming through on the way to or from Vietnam – frequented R&B and soul spots in Shinjuku.[6] These spots were succeeded by the disco boom of the 1970s, which established the infrastructure and fan base for dance-oriented Black music; *Soul Train* was rebroadcast in Japan.[7] One group that appeared on that show – the Japanese electronic music band Yellow Magic

Orchestra – recorded what could arguably be the first Japanese rap track: "Rap Phenomena" (1981), a pun on hearing non-existent noises and the growth of rap music. Films like *Wild Style* (released in 1983 in Japan) and *Flashdance* (1983) raised awareness of hip-hop and directly inspired such hip-hop pioneers as DJ Krush and Crazy-A.[8]

In the 1980s, hip-hop developed along two separate trajectories: smart clubs, with performers like Chikada Haruo and Itō Seikō – alumni of the elite Keiō and Waseda universities respectively – and in pedestrianized Yoyogi Park on Sundays (Hokoten), with the likes of b-boy Crazy-A and DJ Krush, both of whom came from rough working-class backgrounds. Rap gained its first commercial successes in Japan in 1994, with Scha Dara Parr's "Konya wa Boogie Back" and East End x Yuri's "Dayone" and "Maicca," in what became known as J-rap.[9] As a counter to this commercialism, rapper ECD organized the Thumpin' Camp concert in Hibiya Open-Air Concert Hall on July 7, 1996, featuring twenty-seven artists then in the underground scene, including King Giddra, Rhymester, Buddha Brand, Muro, and others. The sold-out concert, which was made into a DVD, was a landmark event that is still cited as an inspiration to younger generations of rappers like Infumiai Kumiai and Punpee. Also in the mid 1990s, DJ Krush released a string of solo albums that were released to positive reviews overseas, launching him on an international career. Today, it is the Hokoten side of Japanese hip-hop origins that have come to dominate the scene.

Localizing aesthetics: rapping and DJing

Since the mid nineteenth century, many Japanese songwriters have complained about the difficulties of setting lyrics in the Japanese language to Western idioms. For rappers, the initial challenges included the lack of stress accents,[10] patterns on which American rappers base their flow, and the multi-moraic[11] nature of the Japanese language, which make it difficult to fit a message into a sixteen-pulse line.[12] Furthermore, Itō Seikō noted that the habit of constructing lines according to the seven-and-five morae of Japanese poetry and modern song lyrics tended to leave long, awkward silences at the end of lines, which would be filled by call-and-responses in *minyō* songs. Listening closely to LL Cool J's "I Can't Live Without My Radio" (1985), he found a groove that allowed him to flow in Japanese, using enjambment and putting rests in untraditional points.[13]

In addition, the Japanese literary tradition did not emphasize end-rhymes, as most sentences end with auxiliary verbs like -*desu* and -*masu*, of which there are a fixed number. Nonetheless, rappers felt end-rhymes were a necessary element of the rhythm. Furthermore, the idea of what constituted a rhyme was not firm; in his album *Mess/age* (1989), Itō included a rhyming dictionary, in which many of the rhymes were English phrases in Japanese pronunciation. Japanese rhyming technique took a step forward with King Giddra's 1995 album *Sora kara no chikara*. K Dub Shine, one of King Giddra's rappers, developed a technique akin to newspaper headlines. Mirroring this format, he broke normal Japanese syntax, forming sentence fragments ending with the key word. As this word could be a noun, verb, or adjective, it had an infinite number of rhyming possibilities, which could be fulfilled using Sino-Japanese compounds,[14] English phrases, or Japanese vocabulary. This rhyming scheme was widely adopted among Japanese rappers. Meanwhile, various flow techniques were developed by exaggerating pitch accents or playing with the duration or characteristics of morae.[15]

Since the mid 1990s, some rappers like K Dub Shine have loosened their conception of rhymes to matching vowels (rather than consonants and vowels; K Dub Shine, interview with the author, August 2008). Many have made their verses into more natural-sounding Japanese. In "Sho senpai gata kara no okotoba" (Words from the Elders, 2007), Shingo Nishinari builds rhymes on "nice day" (*nais dee*) by constructing a series of rhymes ending in the conjunction/prepositions -*te* (and, because of, since) and -*de* (emphasis, from, with). The rhymes are in italics:

> Tam*aranaissu nē* ~ *Have a nice day*!
> Demo kane *nai tte*, mama ga *naite*
> Papa ga dete *itte* shitta, jinsei son'nani amaku*nai de*,
> Demo kono ku*rai de* kujike*nai tte* tsutsundaru tte! Dekai *ai de*!

> How unbearable! "Have a nice day!"
> But mama cried, saying there's no money,
> When papa left, I learned that life isn't so rosy.
> But don't be discouraged by such a little thing. I'll wrap you up in much love!

Rappers and fans credit Boss of Tha Blue Herb with popularizing a kind of flow reminiscent of spoken word, whereby he spits out dense textures of words without attempting to fit them exactly into beats and their subdivisions; the rappers of MSC also use metrically complex flow. Several rappers simultaneously operate in the worlds of poetry slams and spoken word (e.g. Suika), and Itō Seikō and Shing02 both have tracks with spoken-word delivery styles. Boss's style of "imperfect" rhythm was also present in earlier rappers (e.g. Rino's verse in DJ Krush's "Kiro" [1995]).

Indeed, these "imperfections" – slight deviations from pitch and beat – are also part of DJ Krush's aesthetic, which are reminiscent of the *wabi-sabi* aesthetic of imperfection in the traditional Japanese arts. Krush has also collaborated with players of traditional Japanese instruments such as *shakuhachi*, *shamisen*, and *taiko*; in order to capture their "flavor," he records them in improvisation rather than in samples. In contrast, Evis Beats takes a parodic approach, sampling distorted *minyō* in Infumiai Kumiai's "Evis Sound," imitating *matsuri* rhythms in their "Oatsui no ga osuki," or taking a theme song from the 1960s *anime, Obake no Q-Tarō*.[16]

Generally speaking, the music used in background tracks encompasses an eclectic mixture of genres, enabled by the existence of record stores with large specialist selections. This creativity and originality is highly prized by Japanese DJs, several of whom have risen to the top at the D.M.C. World DJ competitions in London: DJ Kentarō and DJ Izoh have won the World DJ Championship; DJ Akakabe and DJ Coma, the Battle Championship; and Kireek, the Team Championship five times.[17]

Growth in hardcore and local hip-hop

The journalist Futatsugi Shin cites Shinjuku-based hip-hop crew MSC's debut album *Matador* (2003) as a landmark event that inspired him to become a hip-hop critic.[18] The group's verses about exhausted laborers, criminals, drug deals, and violence against foreigners lent an authenticity to the lyrics not often seen in a scene dominated by middle-class artists at the time. Since then, several rappers who show off their lower-class status with pride have emerged. Many are from regions outside of Tokyo, whose economies have suffered more than the capital since the financial bubble burst in 1990.

Anarchy, a former gang leader from the Mukaijima housing projects in outer Kyoto, gained critical acclaim with his debut album *Rob the World* (2006), full of painful autobiographical stories of growing up without a mother in a drug-infested environment, but also pride in his local milieu and his friends. Also noteworthy is Shingo Nishinari, who has taken as his stage name his home neighborhood – Nishinari, Japan's largest gathering place for day-laborers. At the bottom of the social order, these workers are often old men, abandoned by their families, many living in makeshift homes under shantytown conditions. Alcoholism, gambling, crime, and death are rampant. Shingo had been to college and had a salaried job for eight years when he came back to help the neighborhood. Songs like "Ill Nishinari Blues" and the previously quoted "Words from the Elders" encapsulate scenes from this difficult life, while "U.Y.C." expresses disappointment with the hypocrisy of politicians, teachers, businesses, and society.[19] Farther afield from major cities, Dengaryū, a rapper from a rural town in Yamanashi Prefecture, has gained attention for his criticisms of neglected regional cities ("Ice City") and national energy and entertainment policies ("Straight Outta 138"), in addition to some hopeful songs.[20]

Taking up political causes

Since the triple disaster of earthquake, tsunami, and nuclear accident on March 11, 2011, called "3/11," hip-hoppers have become more active in political commentary. The members of Gagle, from tsunami-battered Sendai, were among the many hip-hoppers who volunteered in the stricken region; they released "Ubugoe" (2011), a song of encouragement, and donated the proceeds to charity.

Hip-hoppers have been at the forefront of the antinuclear movement, performing at demonstrations on top of trucks loaded with sound equipment; these demonstrations have attracted tens of thousands, with 200,000 participating on July 29, 2012. These performers have included reggae pioneer Rankin Taxi; DJ Shinco of Scha Dara Parr; rappers ECD, Akuryō, Rumi, and Deli; and the sound unit i Zoom i Rockers (composed of rapper ATS and music critic Noma Yasumichi, often joined by Akuryō and ECD).[21] In addition to performing pre-written antinuclear songs, this last unit has developed a new participatory style of performance, rapping antinuclear slogans like "Saikadō hantai" (We oppose restarting nuclear reactors) to beats in a call and response with the protesters.[22]

Hip-hoppers have also released antinuclear recordings, many of which make references to music from the African diaspora. Public Enemy's "Don't Believe the Hype" has been reinterpreted by Deli and by DJ Honda, Zeebra, Anarchy, and others, who use the refrain to comment on the slanted nature of news coverage. The media is also criticized by Shing02 and Hunger (of Gagle) in "The Revolution Will Not Be Televised" (2011),[23] in which they take Gil Scott-Heron's original track and premise of the media as a distortive presenter of hegemonic views (by whites about African Americans) and apply it to the Japanese case, where the media has broadcast primarily the official views of the nuclear industry and the government. In "Safe is Dangerous" (2012), Darthreider plays on the homonyms *seifu* (government) and *se-efu* (Japanese pronunciation of "safe"), sampling the word "dangerous" from Peter Tosh's "Stepping Razor" and applying it to several government institutions. The references were sometimes domestic: Scha Dara Parr's "Kaese! Chikyū o" (Return the Earth to Us, 2011) mashes the guitar riff from Tone-Loc's "Wild Thing" with the sung melody of "Kaese! Taiyō o" (Return the Sun to Us), a song from the movie *Godzilla vs. Hedorah* (1971). The original song lists industrial pollutants from the 1970s, to which MCs Bose and Ani add the names of radioisotopes; in between are interspersed samples of Flavor Flav's exclaiming "Don't Believe the Hype!"[24]

As the demonstrations went on, the intertextual references moved to protests themselves. Sakamoto Ryūichi sampled the calls of protesters at the Ōi nuclear power plant, to which Shing02 added a rap, calling for people to demonstrate; the track's title, "Odakias" (2012), is "saikadō" (restart [nuclear reactors]) spelled backwards.[25] In "Baby Cart and Placard" (2012), ECD tips his hat to mothers at demonstrations, with "a baby cart in one hand, a placard in the other...They will surely be the ones that stop nuclear power."[26] In "Straight Outta 138" (2012), his collaboration with Dengaryū, ECD references the refrain from his own anthem of the 2003 antiwar protests. He flips its meaning by taking the key words, *yūkoto kiku* (listen to what one's told), and changing them into *yūkoto kikaseru* (make others listen). The retained words and their translations are underlined:

Yūkoto kikuyō na yatsura ja naizo	We're not the types who <u>do as we're told</u> into
Yūkoto kikaseru ban da, oretachi ga	It's our turn to <u>make them listen to us.</u>

He implores citizens to make their views known – "sign petitions, vote, demonstrate."[27]

Other rappers have also encouraged the youth to vote: with voting participation rates among those in their 20s about 30 percentage points lower than those over 50, their votes amount to only about 9 percent of the total vote, disempowering them in the electorate. Dengaryū, Rhymester, and Akuryō all released songs prior to the Lower House Election in December 2012, encouraging people to think for themselves about the nation's problems.[28] In July 2013, reggae musician Miyake Yōhei ran for a seat in the Upper House; as a campaign tactic, he held "Election Festivals" in front of central train stations across the country, in which he and other musicians – including Dengaryū and K Dub Shine – performed and talked politics. These festivals attracted thousands; many more watched them through simulcasts and video uploads. Although Miyake lost his bid, he raised interest in politics among youth and arguably helped Yamamoto Tarō, an actor fired from his television series after appearing in an antinuclear video, to win his Upper House seat.

Neo-nationalism, race, and Japanese hip-hop

The Japanese hip-hop scene has several successful artists from non-Japanese or mixed ethnicities including Verbal of m-flo (*zainichi*[29] resident Korean), Aoyama Teruma (quarter-Trinidadian), Ilmari of Rip Slyme (half-Finnish), Rino (half-Filipino, quarter-Chinese), and Simi Lab, whose members include Dyypride (half-Ghanaian), Maria (half-Caucasian American), and OMSB (half-African American). In addition, rappers have paid respect to their multi-ethnic neighbors: Norikiyo mentions his Korean and Latin American friends in Sagamihara ("Do My Thing"),[30] and Dengaryū and Stillichimiya's "Yabee ikioi de sugee moriagaru" (2012) contains a line in

Mandarin inviting people to join the revelry.[31] The major record labels typically do not release, or actively recall, recordings with discriminatory content.[32]

On the other hand, Tanaka,[33] Morris,[34] and Thomas[35] have highlighted the neo-nationalist rhetoric and racism (against Koreans and Chinese) behind some Japanese hip-hop. Thomas notes that Zeebra holds up Blacks and the Japanese as both victims oppressed by white America. My observation is that this view is held by a number of hip-hoppers, but this perception of US oppression runs deeper than the Allied Occupation, which Thomas takes as the starting point: it began before World War II, with unfavorable international trade, peace, and immigration treaties in the nineteenth and early twentieth centuries, and continues to the US military's use of bases in Japan and perceived pressure on economic and international policy today. Furthermore, the most vivid memories of Japanese alive at the time is the American firebombing that destroyed sixty-seven civilian cities (in addition to Hiroshima and Nagasaki) and the starvation that was rampant in the last two years of World War II.[36] Most Japanese have heard personal stories of traumatic hardships directly from those then present, and they empathize with these victims. It is these depictions of bombings that occur frequently in hip-hop imagery, e.g. Zeebra's recalling the Hiroshima bomb in "911"; "Atomic Bomb," the name of K Dub Shine's management company; "Yakenohara" ("burnt field," the name given to cities after a bombing), a DJ and rapper's stage name; and the frequent occurrence of bombers in hip-hop gig posters and CD inserts. Nonetheless, many hip-hoppers find the USA–Japan relationship to be unrelated to their choice of hip-hop as a mode of self-expression;[37] Futatsugi finds K Dub Shine and Zeebra to be more concerned with the USA than most other hip-hoppers.[38] Furthermore, seeing one's relatives as victims of the war doesn't necessarily translate into a hostile view of Koreans and Chinese (or Americans). Nonetheless, since the mid 1990s, there has been a revival of neo-nationalists, who harken back to propagandistic beliefs of the 1940s: they believe that Japan's war in the Pacific was justified, deny Japanese atrocities as fabrications, and fear the economic power and cultural influence of the former colonies.

In a 2009 interview, Morris caught Zeebra – Japan's most commercially successful rapper to date and highly influential in the community – making statements denying Japan's wartime atrocities.[39] His King Giddra crewmate K Dub Shine served as music director for *Kyōki no sakura* (2002), a violent film about neo-nationalist, anti-foreigner vigilantes.[40] In an interview with Futatsugi Shin, K Dub made clear his neo-nationalist leanings, saying that all the demands for apologies had made Japan into suckers.[41] Thomas quotes him as saying to a *zainichi* Korean in 2009, "Going way back into history, and saying stuff like 'Japanese people back then were mean' doesn't help anything." Family history may have played a role in both rappers' outlooks: K Dub's father, who lived apart from him and his mother but maintained a relationship with them, was the scion of a family of army officers and a prisoner of war in Siberia during World War II; the father frequently paid his respects to his fallen colleagues at Yasukuni Shrine – a controversial site, as it houses the souls of *all* of the war dead, including war criminals.[42] Morris points out that Zeebra's grandfather, the late real estate mogul Yokoi Hideki,[43] benefited from doing business with the Imperial Army during the war and in the black market after it. Morris criticizes Condry (and global hip-hop studies more generally) for insisting on a postcolonial, progressive lens for Japanese hip-hop and thereby turning a blind eye to right-wing rhetoric.[44]

Neo-nationalist rhetoric is well illustrated in the recordings of Arei Raise. The group came to attention through a song contest at Yasukuni Shrine. Although it did not win, the group's entry, "Kyōji" (Pride, 2007),[45] was included in a compilation CD and sold at Yasukuni Shrine.[46] The song calls the Pacific War a "holy war" that was "noble and grand." The video is shot in Yasukuni itself. A step further is "8.30" (2009),[47] a xenophobic rant fearing that the Chinese would taking over Japan, which asks, "Are we going to turn our backs on the blood and tears of our ancestors?/ We keep repeating the defeat in war." Their records are issued under their label, Great Far East Records – a reference to the wartime pan-Asian "co-prosperity" sphere.

The hip-hop world has attempted to counter racism. When Show-K released "Nihonjin Stand Up!" (2010),[48] a rant against China in the wake of the Senkaku Islands fishing incident, Takuma the Great and Haiiro de Rossi released "We're the Same Asian," calling for peaceful solutions.[49] In 2013, music critic Noma Yasumichi formed the Counter-Racist Action Collective (CRAC, formerly *Shibaki-tai*) to impede demonstrations by the Zaitokukai, an anti-*zainichi* Korean group who have been spewing hate speech at children in ethnic Korean neighborhoods. Rappers ECD, ATS, and Akuryō have been active in this antiracist group; the latter two have performed in antiracist demonstrations.[50] ECD and Illreme have released "The Bridge Anti-Racist Remix" (2013) in reaction to these anti-*zainichi* demonstrations.[51] Journalists like Futatsugi Shin, who has participated in liberal causes through Shirōto no Ran, have ignored Show-K, even though the latter approached him to be interviewed.

Under these circumstances, one might expect to see more engagement with racism by *zainichi* artists themselves than one does. Armstrong noted that *zainichi* rappers in the Kansai generally shied away from addressing their ethnicity; he singled out 02 and Youngi as exceptions who highlighted their Korean identity and rapped about discrimination.[52] When Show-K presented an answer song to "We're All the Same Asian," Haiiro responded without Takuma, later explaining that Takuma – a *zainichi* Taiwanese whose family lived in Chinese districts – had felt it had become too dangerous for him to continue the battle.[53] *Zainichi* reggae artists like Chehon or Pushim are more upfront about their ethnicity, but (quarter-Chinese) brothers of Mighty Crown tend to avoid it in conversation. These actions suggest that it is difficult for multi-ethnic artists (or residents) to start a discussion about race themselves.

Last dance? Japan's entertainment laws and moral panics

Recently, the Japanese hip-hop scene has been under pressure from the Entertainment Business Control and Improvement Law (*fūeihō*). This law was enacted during the Allied Occupation in 1948, over fears that dancehalls were hotbeds of prostitution. The law, which extends to ballroom dancing schools as well as dance clubs, specifies that an establishment that serves drinks and whose customers dance must be properly licensed and close by midnight or 1 a.m.[54]

In reality, clubs that stay open all night have been an important part of the nightlife scene for decades. These all-night clubs, where people enter when the trains have stopped running past midnight and leave when they start running again around 5 a.m., have comprised the primary *genba* (site) in the ecosystem of Japanese hip-hop, as highlighted by Condry.[55] In my experience, these clubs typically peak between 2 and 3:30 a.m. and remain open until 6 or 7 a.m.[56] For decades, the police had turned a blind eye: for the past twenty years, an average of only seven clubs a year had been closed due to violations of the law. As Chikada Haruo rapped in his 1987 single "Hoo! Ei! Ho!," "The *fūeihō* is mere harassment. If you follow it, you'll lose out. Just close the door, and you won't be found out."

The situation changed after a college student died after a fistfight at a club in the Osaka district of Amerika Mura in 2010.[57] Citing local complaints about noise and drunkenness – and acting on suspicions of drug use and wanton behavior – the police cracked down on clubs, closing six in Amerika Mura alone in 2011. Between 2008 and 2013, the number of clubs in the district fell from 134 to 102, and the number of customers from 8.1 million to 5.9 million; once perpetually teeming with people, the district became a shadow of its former self.[58] The crackdown widened to other parts of Osaka, Kyoto, Fukuoka, and Tokyo. Police pressure in Tokyo intensified after an organized crime group beat a man to death at Roppongi club Flower in September 2012, calling attention to their presence in the club scene;[59] at least two Roppongi clubs have been shut down in 2013.

Since 2010, the police have shut down forty-six clubs nationwide (as of October 2013). Many more clubs closed "voluntarily," as club operators claimed that they could not make a profit on shortened hours (Taku Taka-hashi, interviews, July–August 2012). The police also harassed customers at clubs: on February 11, 2012, 150 police stormed into hip-hop club Ike-bukuro Bed and tested people present for drugs; none were found.[60] Even daytime clubs were not immune: in September 2013, the seaside venue Otodama closed following apparent pressure from locals looking to "restore public peace and morals."[61] The law is so controversial that managers of well-known artists have run after me following interviews, asking that I not write about their charges' comments.

The club industry has fought back. The citizens' group Let's Dance has collected 176,000 signatures, including those from well-known musicians and writers representing several generations and genres, for the deletion of dancing from the Entertainment Law. Artists formed the Society to Preserve Clubs and Club Culture (CCCC), led by Zeebra and the rapper Darthreider, among others. These groups, along with representatives of ballroom-dancing and tango clubs, have lobbied with legislators to change the law. In October 2014, the Cabinet approved a bill revising the law to allow dance clubs to operate past midnight, if their lighting exceeded 10 luxes and they received a license from the local public safety committee. Nonetheless, many important venues have closed in the past few years, and it will take time for momentum at clubs to rebuild or for Japan's hip-hop community to find other *genba*.

Conclusion

In a country where the charts are topped by professionally written pop songs sung by large teams of girls not allowed to date,[62] hip-hop offers an alternative of self-written tracks, often expressing real emotions about real life. They may be witty takes by middle-class youth or desperate stories of poverty from the people who have lived it. As the genre has become more hardcore, critics are revising its past to emphasize its lower-class roots, thereby presenting an alternative history of Japanese musical culture.

Hip-hop's reputation as a frank expression has made it an ideal vehicle for protests against government policies and societal injustice. This charac-teristic of frankness has also made it a vehicle for neo-nationalist and racist rhetoric. As of early 2014, Japan sits at a crossroads: on the one hand, most citizens are against the Secrecy Law, which many fear would limit freedom of the press and the right to demonstrate; on the other hand, some citizens agree with the neo-nationalist leanings of the Abe Cabinet and want Japan to remilitarize. Not beholden to any point of view except to keep it real, hip-hop is being used to express the views of both sides. Its directness in a culture that avoids such expression makes it the ideal vehicle for alternative stories.

Discography

Anarchy, *Rob the World* (R-Rated Records, RRR-1004, 2006).

Chikada Haruo (as President BPM), *Heavy* (BPM, BPM 28SL-12, 1987).

Darthreider, *Super Dead* (Da.Me.Records, DMRCD-061, 2012).

Dengaryū, *Just* (Mary Joy Recordings, 2008).

DJ Krush, *Meisō* (Sony Music, SRCS7752, 1995).

Infumiai Kumiai, *Jangaru* (P-Vine, PCD5852, 2003).

Itō Seikō, *Mess/age* (File Records, 23FR031D, 1989).

King Giddra, *Sora kara no chikara* (P-Vine, PCD4768, 1995).

Shingo Nishinari, *Sprout* (Libra Records, LIBCD-008, 2007).

Yellow Magic Orchestra, *BGM* (Alfa Records, 38XA-16, 1981).

Notes

1 "Japan Outranks US in Recorded-Music Sales," *Japan Times*, April 11, 2013. Available at www.japantimes.co.jp/culture/2013/04/11/music/japan-outranks-u-s-in-recorded-music-sales/ (accessed June 1, 2014).

2 CD arubamu nenkan rankingu, Oricon Style. Available at www.oricon.co.jp/rank/ja/y/2012/ (accessed October 23, 2013). Exile, a dance-pop boy band whose dance moves show hip-hop influence, had the number five album for the year. Also included in the Oricon top-100 albums of 2012 was a best-of album by Def Tech, classified as "Jawaiian reggae," and an album by Malaysian R&B singer Che'Nelle.

3 Ian Condry, *Hip-Hop Japan: Rap and the Paths of Cultural Globalization* (Durham, NC: Duke University Press, 2006).

4 Japan's real GDP fell by 1 percent in 2008 and 5.5 percent in 2009.

5 E. Taylor Atkins, *Blue Nippon: Authenticating Jazz in Japan* (Durham, NC: Duke University Press, 2001).

6 Isobe Ryō, "Yankii to hippu hoppu: Souru zoku kara B-Boy to tsuzuku mou hitotsu no yankii no rekishi," in Tarō Igarashi (ed.), *Yankii bunkaron josetsu* (Tokyo: Kawade Shobō Shinsha, 2009). Japanese personal names are presented with family name first as per Japanese convention.

7 Emori Shigeru, *Kuroku odore! Sutoriito dansaazu retsuden* (Tokyo: Ginga Shuppan, 2008).

8 Condry, *Hip-Hop Japan*; Noriko Manabe, "Representing Japan: 'National' Style among Japanese Hip-hop DJs," *Popular Music* 32/1 (2013): 35–50.

9 Condry, *Hip-Hop Japan*.

10 Stress accents mark a syllable by volume, duration, and sometimes pitch.

11 The shortest prosodic unit in the Japanese language is a mora, which is akin to a short syllable. A Japanese mora consists of a single vowel (with or without a consonant), a double consonant, or the nasal "N." Long vowels are pronounced as two morae: e.g. "Tokyo" is pronounced as four morae (To-o-kyo-o) but heard as two syllables (Tō.kyō).

12 Noriko Manabe, "Globalization and Japanese Creativity: Adaptations of Japanese Language to Rap," *Ethnomusicology* 50/1 (2006): 1–36.

13 Itō Seikō, interview with the author, January 7, 2009.

14 Sino-Japanese compounds are derived from the Chinese language. Like Latinate words in English, many of them constitute technical vocabulary that is less used in common speech.

15 Manabe, "Globalization and Japanese Creativity": 1–36.

16 Manabe, "Representing Japan." "Matsuri" is a traditional festival.

17 *Ibid.* The D.M.C. World DJ Championship is the most widely recognized international competition of virtuosic turntabling. It has been held annually in London since 1985.

18 Futatsugi Shin, *Shikujirunayo, Ruudii* (Tokyo: P-Vine, 2013).

19 Andrew Armstrong, "The Japanese 'Ghetto Gangsta': Searching for Prestige in Kansai Hip Hop Performance," Ph.D. Dissertation, Boston University, 2012.

20 Noriko Manabe, "Straight Outta Ichimiya: The Appeal of a Rural Japanese Rapper," *The Asia Pacific Journal* 11/1 (2013). Available at www.japanfocus.org/-Noriko-MANABE/3889 (accessed June 1, 2014).

21 In addition, several techno DJs have performed in antinuclear demonstrations, including DJs Mayuri and Tasaka, among others.

22 Noriko Manabe, "Music in Japanese Antinuclear Demonstrations: The Evolution of a Contentious Performance Model," *The*

Asia-Pacific Journal 11/3 (2013). Available at http://japanfocus.org/-Noriko-MANABE/4015 (accessed June 1, 2014).

23 Shing02 and Hunger, "Kakumei wa terebi ni utsuranai." Available at http://e22.com/notv/.

24 Noriko Manabe, "The Revolution Will Not Be Televised: Music, Musicians, and Anti-Nuclear Protest in Post-Fukushima Japan," paper presented at Inter-Asia Popular Music Studies Group Conference, Taipei, Taiwan, July 15, 2012; see also Noriko Manabe, *The Revolution Will Not Be Televised: Music in the Antinuclear Movement Post-Fukushima Daiichi* (New York: Oxford University Press, forthcoming).

25 Shing02, Sakamoto Ryūichi, and Tokimonsta, "ODAKIAS," SoundCloud, July 1, 2012. Available at http://soundcloud.com/ryuichi_sakamoto/odakias (accessed June 1, 2014).

26 ECD, "Bebii kaa to purakaado," ECD, SoundCloud, December 2011. Available at https://soundcloud.com/ecd-1/ecd (accessed June 1, 2014).

27 Manabe, "Straight Outta Ichimiya."

28 The songs are Dengaryū, "Senkyo ni ikō" (Let's Go Vote, December 2012; available at https://soundcloud.com/dengaryu/senkyo-ni-ikou); Rhymester, "The Choice is Yours" (released as a single, August 2012); and Akuryō, "The Choice is Yours Remix" (unrelated to Rhymester, December 2012). Available at www.youtube.com/watch?v=dwfSK02_aA0).

29 Japan has a large ethnic Korean community, most of whom are descendants of laborers who arrived in Japan in large waves from the 1920s through World War II, when Korea was a Japanese colony. In 1947, the government began regarding residents from the former colonies as foreigners, and the *zainichi* residents lost their Japanese citizenship and their right to vote unless they naturalized. As of 2010, there are 570,000 ethnically Korean residents and another 285,000 ethnic Koreans who have been naturalized as Japanese citizens. In addition, there are *zainichi* Chinese, who have been joined by more recent waves of immigrants; as of 2010, there are 687,000 ethnic Chinese residents, not including those who have been naturalized. While these groups together only account for 1.2 percent of Japan's population, they are visible and established communities.

30 "Do my thing," Norikiyo, Youtube video. Available at www.youtube.com/watch?v=_70Zvs2tOSk (accessed June 1, 2014). See also Futatsugi, *Shikujirunayo*.

31 Manabe, "Straight Outta Ichimiya."

32 King Giddra's single, "Unstoppable"/"FFB"/ "Drive-By" (2002), was pulled from the shelves due to complaints from a gay rights organization regarding "Drive-By"; it was re-released without this song and with edits to "FFB" which was found to be offensive to HIV patients.

33 Tanaka Yuki, "The Songs of Nippon, the Yamato Museum and the Inculcation of Japanese Nationalism," *Asia-Pacific Journal* (2008). Available at www.japanfocus.org/-Yuki-TANAKA/2746 (accessed June 1, 2014).

34 David Morris, "The Sakura of Madness: Japan's Nationalist Hip Hop and the Parallax of Globalized Identity Politics," *Communication, Culture & Critique* 6/3 (2013): 459–480.

35 Dexter Thomas, "Niggas and Japs: Race, Identity, and the Right Wing in Japanese Hip-Hop," paper presented at the Association for Asian Studies Conference, San Diego, March 23, 2013.

36 Mark Selden, "A Forgotten Holocaust: US Bombing Strategy, the Destruction of Japanese Cities and the American Way of War from World War II to Iraq," *Asia-Pacific Journal* (2007). Available at www.japanfocus.org/-mark-selden/2414 (accessed June 1, 2014).

37 Erone, interview with the author, April 2008.

38 K Dub Shine and Futatsugi Shin, "K Dub Shine: Long Interview," *Remix* 215 (2009): 54–61.

39 David Morris, "Zeebra Pt. II: The Correction," Tiny Mix Tapes, September 11, 2009. Available at www.tinymixtapes.com/column/zeebra-pt-ii (accessed June 1, 2014).

40 Morris (2013) interprets the film as morally ambiguous, as the extreme violence of the vigilantes equates them with the *yakuza*. K Dub says the film has a "strong message" (K Dub Shine 2007, pp. 82–83). The title is a multi-layered play on words: *kyōki* is an amalgamation of "murder weapon" and "insanity," while *kyōki no sakura* is a reference to *dōki no sakura* (cadets of the same class, 1944), a wartime military song about two pilots who fully expect to die. Falling *sakura* (cherry blossoms) were a metaphor for young soldiers dying in battle; the metaphor is aligned with the spectacular *sakura* trees at Yasukuni Shrine. See Emiko Ohnuki-Tierney, *Kamikaze, Cherry Blossoms, and Nationalisms: The Militarization of Aesthetics in Japanese History* (University of Chicago Press, 2002).

41 K Dub Shine and Futatsugi, "Long interview," p. 55.

42 K Dub Shine, *Shibuya no don* (Tokyo: Kōdansha, 2007); K Dub Shine and Futatsugi, "Long interview."

43 Yokoi was convicted for negligence in the 1982 fire at his Hotel New Japan, in the high-end business district of Akasaka, which killed thirty-three people (*Los Angeles Times*, May 21, 1987). He was also spectacularly rich, having once owned the Empire State Building. This vast family wealth gave Zeebra a privileged lifestyle and education (in the Keio prep system) until he dropped out.

44 Morris, "Sakura of Madness," 472.

45 Arei Raise, "Kyōji," Youtube video, August 27, 2007. Available at www.youtube.com/watch?v=snDrZKBZx1Y(accessed June 1, 2014).

46 Tanaka, "Songs of Nippon."

47 Arei Raise, "8.30," Youtube video, August 18, 2009. Available at www.youtube.com/watch?v=-77kO26eQGE (accessed June 1, 2014).

48 Show-K, "Nihonjin, Stand Up!!," Youtube video, September 30, 2010. Available at www.youtube.com/watch?v=cB_S2R4VkqY (accessed June 1, 2014).

49 Thomas, "Niggas and Japs"; Futatsugi, *Shikujirunayo*.

50 Manabe, "Music in Japanese Antinuclear Demonstrations."

51 ECD and Illreme, "The Bridge han reishizumu Remix," Youtube video, March 8, 2013. Available at www.youtube.com/watch?v=gYvCwIaw3JM.

52 Armstrong, "The Japanese 'ghetto gangsta.'"

53 Futatsugi, *Shikujirunayo*; Thomas, "Niggas and Japs."

54 "Fūzoku eigyō nado no kisei oyobi gyōmu no tekisei ka nado ni kansuru hōritu," E-Gov. Available at http://law.e-gov.go.jp/htmldata/

S23/S23HO122.html (accessed October 26, 2013).

55 Condry, *Hip-Hop Japan*.

56 Often the same venue hosts several different genres – hip-hop, dub, house, techno, dubstep, electro, etc. – which are segregated into different days.

57 Isobe Ryō (ed.), *Odotte wa ikenai kuni, nihon: Fūeihō mondai to kajō kisei sareru shakai* (Tokyo: Kawade Shobō, 2012), p. 20.

58 "Kurabu gyōkai 'Kisei teppai de 1000 oku en': Keizai kōka de fujō nerau," *Asahi Digital*. Available at www.asahi.com/articles/TKY201310230188.html (accessed October 26, 2013).

59 Jake Adelstein, "What's with the Police Purge on Dance Clubs?," *The Japan Times*, April 7, 2013. Available at www.japantimes.co.jp/news/2013/04/07/national/whats-with-the-police-purge-on-dance-clubs/#.UWBdwKvwJGE (accessed October 26, 2013).

60 "Tōkyō no kurabu ni daikibo na gasa-ire. Shikashi nani mo dezu," *Togetter*. Available at http://togetter.com/li/256312 (accessed October 26, 2013).

61 "Kimaguren keiei, ontama OTODAMA shī STUDIO konka de shūryō," *Natalie*. Available at http://natalie.mu/music/news/97834 (accessed October 26, 2013).

62 The idol-pop group AKB48, consisting of eighty-nine girls from their teens to mid-twenties, had the four best-selling singles of 2013. The girls' contracts forbid them from dating.

19 Council estate of mind: the British rap tradition and London's hip-hop scene

RICHARD BRAMWELL

Alongside the innovative approach to musical production developed by DJs in the Bronx during the 1970s, rap has become one of the most commercially successful exports of American culture. The linguistic practice of rapping can be traced, through forms of Christian worship and "toasting" over popular music in Jamaica, to West African griot culture.[1] This oral tradition migrated from the Caribbean to the USA and the UK in the 1960s, carried by figures such as Clive Campbell and Linton Kwesi Johnson, and has produced the most popular poetic form in the world today. The complex migratory patterns and cultural currents that structure the Black Atlantic diaspora continue to produce important exchanges between the Caribbean, North America, and Great Britain. However, whereas US hip-hop has received considerable scholarly attention, rap in the UK remains relatively under explored.[2]

Dick Hebdige's studies of reggae, Rastafari, and rude-boy cultures were among the earliest scholarly works on the practice of rhythmic rhyming in Black British musical culture.[3] Linton Kwesi Johnson, whose "black English patois" fused "dark political scenarios with the startling effects of dub," produced with Dennis Bovell "some of the most important British reggae recordings of the late 1970s."[4] Johnson's dub poetry worked within the tradition of U Roy, I Roy, and Big Youth that Clive Campbell drew upon in the production of American hip-hop culture. Paul Gilroy identifies how "the close correspondence between the structures of reggae and hip-hop sub-cultures ensured that the latter would be able to usurp the themes of fraternity and solidarity."[5] His discussion of Smiley Culture's 1984 hit "Cockney Translation" and the 1985 London Rap Championships registers a shift in Black British political culture that sought to redefine Britain as a plural community. In the late 1980s the Cookie Crew's singles "Females" and "Got to Keep On" as well as Monie Love's "Monie in the Middle" and "It's a Shame" adopted American hip-hop styles. Rebel MC, whose single "Street Tough" reached number three in the UK charts, contributed to a distinctive reorientation in British music by combining US styles and techniques with his Caribbean cultural resources. UK hip-hop emerged as a vibrant and distinctive scene during the 1990s, with MCs such as Mell "O," Black Twang, and the London Posse's Rodney P and Bionic drawing on styles and influences from Britain, the USA, and the Caribbean. At the beginning of the new millennium a significant shift occurred in British rap music, with the emergence of Grime from UK Garage. Wiley's departure from the Garage crew, Pay As You Go, to form Roll Deep in 2002 was an important part of this development, which roughly coincided with the stagnation, and then decline, of the UK hip-hop scene. In 2003 Dizzee Rascal (a former member of the Roll Deep crew) was awarded the Mercury Music Prize for his album *Boy in da Corner*. Grime's rise – and the string of top ten singles by Black British artists that accompanied it – has made an important contribution to the mainstreaming of Black culture in the UK.

The Deal Real scene

Toward the end of the 1990s and during the first years of the new millennium, Deal Real became a key site within British and European hip-hop culture. This small store, with shutters decorated in "fantastic graffiti,"[6] was located on Noel Street in London's Soho area. Micall Parknsun recollects London's hip-hop scene during this period: "There was a scene where we had the Kung fu, we had Mr Bongos, and... Deal Real, 'cause there was a lot of record shops still going out around the West End."[7] The fortunes of British hip-hop were bound up with independent record stores such as Deal Real. MCs like Micall, who established independent labels, developed an intimate relationship with the production and marketing of their creative work. Through their "hustling," aspiring rap artists were able to gain recognition for themselves within the hip-hop scene:

> We would press 1000 records. A thousand twelve inch record singles, double A sides... and we would basically get like 500 or 300 we would give to a distributor and we would be left with [700] so the distributor would try and get it to, you know, everywhere other than London. You know, abroad. The distributor that we had at the time was Cargo... They would take 300, they would get rid of the 300 and it would work by them taking 300 because we would get a press agent or something like that. And the press agent would get our records reviewed in all the hip-hop magazines across the country from your *Hip-Hop Connection*, which is now gone, *Undercover* magazine, *Blues and Soul*, you know a lot of magazines... So that had done if anything about one quarter of the work for us. Now the rest of the work for us is obviously, like, trying to speak to radio DJs who we know. Choice FM, you know at the time, even Excalibah when he was doing his thing on 1Xtra, we would give them our records and they would play our records and that would be another boost and we would tell them "Oh, you can get them from these shops." So what we would do, we would take our records on a Saturday. We would go to Mr Bongo's, we would go to Deal Real, we'd go to

every shop located, which we know sells UK hip-hop and we would go "Yo, how much do you want? We're selling em – Boop!"[8]

The traffic of entrepreneurial MCs between London's independent record shops led to the development of an influential crowd at Deal Real. The relation that working-class MCs developed with their recorded work also shaped how they came to see themselves as artists. Hustling conveyed a "dream and the whole rapport of actually being an independent record label and actually being hands on running – distributing, even manufacturing your own product – and knowing what's happening. There is no middle guy, you are the middle guy – you are everything."[9]

Excalibah, who DJ'd on the pirate radio station Juice FM while attending college, recalls how spending time listening to music at the record shop provided the opportunity to meet respected figures within London's hip-hop community: "It was the first place I ever met Skinnyman, standing outside there, the first place I met Taskforce. And literally I would just go down there and chill, like either as soon as my lessons were over, or on the weekend I would just go there, hangout, listen to the music."[10] However, it was Excalibah's suggestion to Pete Real to put on an open mic event that led to this small store coming to play a leading role in British hip-hop culture:

> Just loads of heads would pass through, Fallacy, Mud Family, and I suddenly went "All these people are coming down here, why don't we just . . . you know, open the shop 'til ten o' clock and, say, from seven we just have someone on the decks, someone hosting, giveaways." And then it took off. I got Disorda to help me out with the first one. I just ran off a flier in my college break, ran up to Staples, printed it off on blue paper . . . gave it to Disorda, he sent it out to all of his mailing list that he had from his mix tapes and his UK hip-hop underground compilations that he used to put out. And at the first one we had Jehst . . . down from Huddersfield or wherever he was living, Out Da Ville came down from Nottingham, before any of them were really that known. But I was really amazed that Lee Ramsay was there, 'cause I'd seen him on TV when Westwood done a live radio show on TV.[11]

The monthly open mic nights enabled Deal Real to distinguish itself from other London record shops, by attracting artists from across the country. "You'd have people like Cappo . . . who had a twelve inch out, so people were aware of him . . . and he'd be rubbing shoulders with people like Black Twang and Skinnyman who were kind of established. You know Taskforce, the Mud Family."[12] The packed events, with young MCs and DJs smoking and drinking in the small store, crammed together with puffer jackets rubbing against one another, developed the feeling of being part of a hip-hop community: "There was no stage, so it was whoever had the mic and you all just shifted focus to that person. Someone would put their hand up on the other side of the room and you'd all just shift focus over there and the mic would go around."[13] As a result of the open mic sessions the shop began to draw international attention. American rap artists visiting London frequently performed at the in-store events and the French underground music magazine, *Vibrations*, ran an article on pirate radio stations which also highlighted Deal Real as an important hub within the UK hip-hop scene.[14]

Despite its cultural success, the Noel Street store eventually closed as a result of the poor management of the business: "there'd be days or weekends when Pete had gone missing."[15] However, the name Deal Real was resurrected when Vincent Olutayo and his associates, Tony Tagoe and Sef Khama, opened another record shop off London's Carnaby Street. They increased the frequency of the open mic events and began to stock the music of European hip-hop artists. The store grew an international customer base, with weekly open mic events enabling emerging artists to view a range of national and international talent and to develop their own participation in British hip-hop culture. In contrast to the Noel Street store, in which more established rappers gathered, the Carnaby Street Deal Real "became a place of nurturing,"[16] allowing aspiring young rappers to participate in this community. Muneera and Sukina of Poetic Pilgrimage, who attended these open mic nights, recollect the impact of the events on their development as MCs:

> MUNEERA: Every Friday they would do in-stores . . . so they would have an act or a group releasing an album and have probably like a British group and an American group, but beforehand they would have an open mic session. So that would give us the opportunity to view different MCs as well.
> SUKINA: Deal Real, I think, played a big role for us. That influenced me and affected me as an MC? I would probably say yes, Deal Real, definitely.
> MUNEERA: In fact I think Deal Real maybe shaped us more than we think, because there were other people – OK this was a bit later . . . there was this girl . . . I used to watch her and then go home and write lyrics and be like "OK, I'm gonna top her." Or there was like something actively – there was a way that we could be heard, every single week. So I was like, consciously writing because I knew every week there was an opportunity for us to come out . . . It was then that I started thinking about punch lines more, start thinking about 16 bars . . . different metaphors, because people would rate you. And in Deal Real, if people didn't like you they would boo you, so I think that was quite important for us.[17]

The vibrant atmosphere, demanding standards, and the constructive, critical environment provided by the events enabled young MCs to hone their skills.

The development of Deal Real as an international hub also provided opportunities for more established artists to develop their contacts within the subculture and the wider music industry. Micall's memories of the networks formed through Deal Real highlight the significance of spaces such as this to the development of British hip-hop: "It's funny – if I didn't go to Deal Real the day he [Excalibah] invited us lot, I wouldn't have been heard of by the people who put my records out now. . . . You know it was the place where everyone would meet if you were into UK hip-hop, or hip-hop generally."[18] The success of the open mic events led to young British rap artists developing an international audience and traveling to perform in cities across Africa, Australia, Asia, Europe, and North and South America. In 2002 BBC Radio 1Xtra was launched. The playing of rap music on national radio increased the awareness of UK hip-hop among mainstream British audiences. "It was in the public realm more than it was before. It had been an underground subculture and it started to shoot into mainstream consciousness."[19] The open mic events at Deal Real also supported the active participation of young women in hip-hop culture:

> SUKINA: They used to have ladies night as well, which was once a month. But we were always like, "we're not performing at ladies night, we'll rap with the best of the men, we don't need to perform on a women only night, what's that about?" I think we probably did open mic at ladies night and it was nice, but we were like "Huh? No. We'll battle the men" – but not battle in like – we're not battle rappers, but more like lyrically, we can test men, we don't need to just be in a little compound for women.
>
> MUNEERA: But I think one thing that was good about ladies night was it was always ram. Men always supported, or everyone always supported ladies night. It was always ram. And I think it was because there was always – you would have some wayward singers or what have you – but they always had a really good caliber of MC, and DJs as well. Some of the DJs were better than the male DJs that were there.[20]

However, UK hip-hop's strong identification with American hip-hop culture limited the potential of this scene to develop autonomously.[21] The Carnaby Street Deal Real's eventual closure was, as for a large number of independent record shops, connected to the rise of the internet in the production and circulation of digital music. This also had a significant impact on the UK hip-hop scene, which began to stagnate and decline toward the end of the decade.

Grime emerged from a scene in which aspiring MCs, DJs, and producers (who would create and disseminate digital music through computers, consoles, and social networking applications) had little attachment to the vinyl cherished in UK hip-hop culture. Pirate radio stations also played a significant role in the growth of Britain's hip-hop and Grime scenes. Indeed, the British Broadcasting Corporation's launch of Radio 1Xtra, with a remit to play "the best in contemporary black music,"[22] can be seen as a direct response to the success of pirate radio in meeting the needs of an audience that, at the turn of the century, the BBC was not. The recruitment of DJs from local pirate stations to this national network enabled MCs to reach a broader audience, although its impact was limited by 1Xtra's restriction to digital audio broadcasting and the station's unavailability on the FM band. Micall notes how the transition from vinyl to CD and MP3 has changed the way music is valued: "To be honest, I kind of miss that scene 'cause things were, we were selling a lot more music than we are now, 'cause nowadays we are in a digital age and, you know, everything's free. Your music is your business card if anything."[23] Nevertheless, the impact of Deal Real is still felt by artists like Micall, Excalibah, and Poetic Pilgrimage, who continue to work in a scene that has shifted from specialist record shops to the internet. Sukina's experience of organizing events in local community centers enables her to discern the continued influence of the record store open mic nights on Poetic Pilgrimage and the UK hip-hop scene more generally:

> I think now, because I organise Rebel Muzik and seeing what open mic means to up-and-coming artists and how they improve. I've literally seen artists every week come on to my open mic and flourish. I can see what Deal Real did for us as MCs, we definitely did flourish as MCs.[24]

The interaction between Grime and UK hip-hop, especially in the work of artists such as Sway and Klashnekoff, suggests that the mainstreaming of rap music in Britain through the former opens the possibility for a revival of the latter.

Deal Real Records provided a space which facilitated interaction between MCs, DJs, and their audiences prior to the widespread use of the internet. Through this interaction the shop also contributed to the organization of the broader UK hip-hop scene. London's position as a transport hub enabled MCs from across the United Kingdom to travel to a cluster of specialist record shops in order to distribute their music, promote themselves and to engage with other artists. Deal Real came to play a key role in the scene because, like other London record shops, it enabled face-to-face contact, in a central location, between those with common interests in this Black cultural tradition. These factors contributed to the serendipitous suggestion of establishing an open mic night, which in turn intensified the activity around this particular cultural institution. The appropriation of the name by the owners of the new record shop near Carnaby Street highlights the significance that the Noel Street store had gained as a centre within the British hip-hop scene. The events at that record shop had enabled Rodney P to develop his contact with Braintax, owner of the Low Life record label, through which he furthered his music career. The open mic nights also supported emerging artists such as the Colony (who honed their lyrical skills and expanded their social relations with DJs and producers in the wider scene through Deal Real) and Cappo, who broadened his audience and released his second album after performing at the in-store events. Mystro's first single, "Kiss That Arse Goodnight," featured Skinnyman and was produced by Harry Love, one of the lead DJs at the open mic events who himself went on to become an influential producer. The Deal Real brand survived the two record shops and endured well into the new millennium through the nightclub events promoted by Sarah Love, who DJ'd at the store before achieving national recognition through her show on 1Xtra. DJs and producers, as well as MCs, benefited from the interaction that the record shop facilitated between highly motivated cultural entrepreneurs. The social relations formed through Deal Real enabled rap artists from across the United Kingdom to work collaboratively, hone their creative skills, and to cultivate a vibrant hip-hop scene.

Notes

1 Edward Kamau Brathwaite, *History of the Voice* (London: New Beacon Books, 1984); Dick Hebdige, "Reggae, Rastas and Rudies," in *Resistance Through Rituals* (Birmingham: Centre for Contemporary Cultural Studies, University of Birmingham, 1976); Linton Kwesi Johnson, "Jamaican Rebel Music," *Race & Class* 17 (1976): 397–412.
2 For further reading on British hip-hop and Grime see Andy Bennett, "Rappin' on the Tyne: White Hip Hop Culture in Northeast England," *The Sociological Review* 47/1 (1999): 1–24; Richard Bramwell, *UK Hip Hop, Grime and the City: The Aesthetics and Ethics of London's Rap Scenes* (London: Routledge, forthcoming 2014); Todd Dedman, "Agency in UK Hip-hop and Grime Youth subcultures: Peripherals and Purists," *Journal of Youth Studies* 14/5 (2011): 507–522; David Hesmondhalgh and Caspar Melville, "Urban Breakbeat Culture: Repercussions of Hip-Hop in the United Kingdom," in Tony Mitchell (ed.), *Global Noise: Rap and Hip Hop Outside the USA* (Middletown, CT: Wesleyan University Press, 2001), pp. 86–110; John Hutnyk, "The Dialectics of European Hip-Hop: Fun^da^mental and the Deathening Silence," *South Asian Popular Culture* 3/1 (2005): 17–32; Helen Kim, "A 'Desi' Diaspora? The Production of 'Desiness' and London's Asian Urban Music Scene," *Identities: Global Studies in Culture and Power* 19/5 (2012): 557–575; Sophy Smith, *Hip-Hop Turntablism, Creativity and Collaboration* (Farnham: Ashgate, 2013).
3 Dick Hebdige, *Cut 'N' Mix* (London: Routledge, 1993).
4 Iain Chambers, *Urban Rhythms: Pop Music and Popular Culture* (London: Macmillan, 1985).
5 Paul Gilroy, *There Ain't No Black in the Union Jack* (London: Routledge, 2002).
6 Micall Parknsun, interview with the author, August 13, 2013.
7 Parknsun. Micall's name signifies on the English broadcaster Michael Parkinson.
8 Parknsun.
9 *Ibid.*
10 Excalibah, interview with the author, July 2008.
11 *Ibid.*
12 *Ibid.*
13 *Ibid.*
14 "Ondes Libres," in *Vibrations* 21 (2000).
15 Excalibah.
16 *Ibid.*
17 Muneera Rashida and Sukina Abdul Noor, interview with the author, June 2008.
18 Parknsun.
19 Excalibah.
20 Rashida and Abdul Noor.
21 Hesmondhalgh and Melville, "Urban Breakbeat Culture," 86–110.
22 1Xtra Service Licence. Available at www.bbc.co.uk/bbctrust/our_work/services/radio/service_licences.html.
23 Parknsun.
24 Rashida and Abdul Noor.

20 Cuban hip-hop

SUJATHA FERNANDES

Cuban hip-hop has stood out within contemporary global hip-hop movements. Although the elements of DJing, graffiti writing, and b-boying were never so developed as in other places, Cuban rappers developed a unique voice and culture. Being outside the orbit of American commercial culture, Cuban rappers drew on their own traditional instrumentation, lyrical development, and local inspiration. With state sponsorship, they organized yearly festivals that brought hip-hop groups from across Latin America and the world. And with few other forums for talking about problems such as racial inequality, rap music took on a unique role as a voice for young Black people on the island.

The emergence and development of Cuban rap

Cuban hip-hop is shaped by a highly specific set of social and economic conditions, including the demographic restructuring of the urban metropolis and increasing racial inequalities in the post-Soviet period. For the first five years of its evolution in Cuba up until 1992, hip-hop culture was produced and consumed within the specific social context of the local community or neighborhood. At parties, people would play music from CDs that had been brought from the USA, or music recorded from Miami radio, and they would pass on recorded cassettes from hand to hand. There would be b-boy competitions and people would rhyme in private houses, on the streets, or in parks.

The period from 1995 to the present involved the institutionalization and commercialization of Cuban hip-hop culture in several different ways. As the art form developed its own Cuban style, as it became distinctly more complex, and as it began to garner large levels of support among Cuban youth, rap music simultaneously, and on different levels, became intertwined with Cuban state institutions, transnational record companies, and underground hip-hop movements in the USA.

Hip-hop culture emerged in Cuba amid changes in demography: the relocation of large numbers of predominantly Black populations to areas on the outskirts of the city where kinship networks were weakened, and where there were fewer economic opportunities. After the revolutionary government came to power it embarked on a project to provide access to housing for those living in slum areas, or those without houses. In 1970, the government projected to build a large housing complex in Alamar, a suburb on the outskirts of Havana. Unlike in the large-scale relocation programs in the USA, the Cuban government built day care centers, boarding schools, theaters, sports, and healthcare facilities for the new residents of Alamar. However, projects such as Alamar were propeled by the same spirit of modernism that animated projects such as the South Bronx, with little concern for how communities would rebuild their networks and function in a vastly new environment.

The need to rebuild a sense of community and to reforge personal bonds in a new terrain underlay the popularity of hip-hop music for the young, Afro-Cuban residents of Alamar. The relatively relaxed social control compared to Havana was another reason why hip-hop was freer to flourish in Alamar. The location of Alamar outside of Havana also made it easier to gain access to Miami radio stations such as 1040 AM and 99 Jamz FM that played American hip-hop music regularly.

Rap music and hip-hop culture also grew rapidly in other urban areas occupied by mainly Black, working-class communities such as Old Havana, Central Havana, Santos Suárez, and Playa. Until the collapse of the Soviet Union, Black and working-class communities in Cuba were relatively protected from late capitalist processes of economic restructuring. However, the decline of the Soviet Union caused a severe economic crisis, leading the Cuban state to declare a "special period in times of peace" in September, 1990. The Cuban government was forced to adopt policies of austerity in order to increase the competitiveness of the Cuban economy in the global economy, which had negative impacts for Cubans.

Black Cubans were particularly affected by the economic crisis of the special period. Family remittances were an important source of income for many Cubans, and since the majority of Cubans in the diaspora tend to be white, it was white Cuban families who benefited most from remittances. In the tourism sector, Blacks tended to be excluded on the grounds that they did not have the education or proper appearance and attire to interact with tourists. Racial prejudice became increasingly visible and acceptable in the special period.

In a period of increasing racial tensions and inequalities, Afro-Cubans found themselves deprived of a political voice. Drawing on discourses of racial democracy, Castro's revolutionary leadership attempted to eliminate racism by creating a colorblind society, where equality between Blacks and whites would render the need for racial identifications obsolete. While desegregating schools, parks, and recreational facilities and offering housing, education, and healthcare to the Black population, the revolutionary leadership simultaneously closed down Afro-Cuban clubs and the Black press. Rap music has taken on a more politically assertive and radical stance as the voice of Black Cuban youth. Although some older Black Cubans cannot relate to the militant assertion of Black identity in Cuban rap, it is becoming increasingly relevant to Cuba's youth, who did not live through the early period of revolutionary triumph, and are hardest hit by the failure of the institutions established under the revolution to provide racial equality in the special period.

Cuban hip-hop emerged as a local response to experiences of displacement and relocation, as well as impoverishment and discrimination. However, it has grown and developed with the support of state and commercial institutions. The main form of institutional support for Cuban rap came from the Cuban state. In summer 1992, the Asociación Hermanos Saiz (Brothers Saiz Organization, AHS), the youth cultural wing of the official mass organization of Cuban youth, Unión de Jóvenes Comunistas (Communist Youth League, UJC), created a venue for rap in La Piragua, a large open air stage by the Malecón. In 1994, this space ceased to exist. Then, the rap entrepreneur DJ Adalberto created another venue in the "local" of Carlos III and Infanta. Up until this moment there was no real movement of rappers, only individuals improvising or "freestyling." From the local emerged the pioneers of Cuban rap: SBS, Primera Base, Triple A, Al Corte, and Amenaza. An association of rappers called Grupo Uno (Group One), relatively autonomous from AHS, was created by a promoter known as Redolfo Rensoli, and this network went on to organize the first festival of rap in June 1995.

North American rap music is the original source of Cuban rap music, and from the early days Cuban rappers have maintained close ties with rappers in the USA. While in the early 1990s, young Cubans were building antennas out of wire coat hangers to listen to 2 Live Crew and Naughty by Nature on Miami's 99 Jamz, by the time of the first rap festival in 1995, Cubans were hearing African American "conscious" rappers such as Paris and Common. The visits of these African American rappers were crucial to the formation of Cuban hip-hop, particularly through a network known as the "Black August Hip-Hop Collective," in which these artists and others such as dead prez and Talib Kweli participated. Black August concerts held in New York raised money for the Cuban hip-hop movement, including funding for an annual hip-hop concert, attended by American rappers.

Like the African American activists who visited Cuba during the 1960s and 1970s from Stokely Carmichael through to Angela Davis and Assata Shakur, who is currently in exile in Cuba, African American rappers such as Paris, Common, Mos Def, and Talib Kweli spoke a language of Black militancy that was appealing to Cuban youth.

The global market, via multinational record companies, has also been an important avenue of transnational participation in Cuban hip-hop. While hip-hop in the USA started as an urban underground movement, it is now a major commercial product, distributed by the three multinational music labels (or "Major labels"): Sony Music Entertainment, Universal, and Warner Music Group. In the Cuban context, the multinational labels with their promises of videos, discs, and large contracts were tempting to Cuban rappers whose resources were scarce. At times, signing a deal meant leaving the country, such as happened with the Cuban rap group Orishas who signed with the transnational record company EMI and now reside in France.[1]

Cuban rap has been influenced by these diverse networks of African American rap and transnational record companies. Underground groups maintained a politically committed message in their lyrics and distanced themselves from commercial rappers, who sought to integrate popular Cuban rhythms in order to become commercially viable. Although there is no private music industry in Cuba, categories of "underground" and "commercial" have some resonance in the context of Cuba because they reflect real contests over access to resources and diverging ideological positions. For some Cuban rap groups who self-identify as underground, there is hostility toward those groups who attract foreign funding and attention because they are willing to dilute their political stance.

Groups such as Orishas who have enjoyed mainstream success both in Cuba and abroad, were previously part of a group called Amenaza who were central to the evolution of the Cuban hip-hop movement. Although Orishas maintained close ties with Cuban rappers, they were also viewed with a degree of contempt by some artists who felt that Orishas had abandoned their earlier political stance to appeal to commercial interests. In their album *A Lo Cubano* (The Cuban Way), released in 2000, Orishas popularized the pre-revolutionary iconography of Cuban life such as rum, tobacco, and 1930s Chevys and Oldsmobiles. Like the internationally marketed film and album of the Cuban group Buena Vista Social Club, the Orishas represent Cuba as a nostalgic fantasy that has been preserved intact from the 1950s. Given the marketing of Afro-Cuban culture as an export commodity and a fetishized object within the tourist industry, rap musicians themselves seek to exploit local and international markets by reproducing certain representations of blackness that are commercially successful.

Rap musicians and the Cuban state

The Cuban state has had an ambivalent relationship to Cuban rappers, as certain sectors in different levels of state institutions build allegiances to distinct networks and as those in official positions seek to appropriate various transnational agencies toward different political ends. In the early days, state disc companies such as EGREM (Empresa de Grabaciones y Ediciones Musicales/Company for Recordings and Musical Editions) chose to promote commercial sounding rap music as representative of Cuban rap. Initially, commercially oriented rap was promoted by the Cuban state as a way of diluting the radical potential of the genre. The more commercial rap was exploited by the Cuban state for its revenue-earning potential, as part of a larger push to attract foreign funding through Cuban music and arts. The promises of money and promotion by the foreign producers did cause several Cuban rap groups to change their music and become more commercial, or to break up as members disagreed about how to proceed.

Those rap groups who did not sign deals or change their music continued to build the Cuban hip-hop movement through the help of producers Ariel Fernández and Pablo Herrera who brought rap groups from the USA and all over the world for the festivals. Since the early millennium, the Cuban state realized the need to relate more to the "underground" rappers, partly because of the increasing appeal of their radical message to large sectors of Black youth in Cuba. The political leadership began to prioritize the creation of a leadership of rappers loyal to the revolution. In July 2001, the Minister of Culture Abel Prieto held a meeting with leading Cuban rap groups, where he discussed provisions of resources for rappers, such as studio space, airtime, and their own music agency, and he pledged ongoing support for Cuban rap. While initially the Cuban state attempted to sideline the underground rappers by supporting the commercial elements, the state increasingly related to the former, praising them for their rejection of commercialism.

Journalists and cultural critics equated the egalitarian ideals of Cuban rappers with calls for equality and justice between nations made by Cuban leaders such as Fidel Castro in the international arena. In a speech following the September 11 attacks on the World Trade Center in New York, Fidel Castro argued that given the global economic crisis of neo-liberalism, the alternative path being forged by the Cuban nation would provide a solution to the crisis: "The fundamental role has been played and will continue to be played by the immense human capital of our people."[2] The music journalist Elena Oumano associated these sentiments with Cuban rappers, arguing that,

> The government here is a major power in the rest of the world, so when hip-hop is rebelling . . . they're really rebelling against the status quo worldwide, the new world order . . . Cuba itself is kind of the underdog and the rebel in terms of the world scene, it's the last bastion of Marxism, so there's more of an allegiance between the government and hip-hop.[3]

Images of rebellion and resistance in Cuban rap are drawn into broader geopolitical strategies of Black cultural opposition; these are identified with the Cuban revolution and by extension the Cuban government as the lone voice contesting neo-liberalism in a largely capitalist world order.

The image of Cuba as the Black nation rebelling against neo-liberalism was evoked by rappers themselves,[4] partly because it was attractive to them and partly because it could be deployed strategically as a way of gaining official recognition for the genre. Rappers associated the Cuban nation with the condition of "underground," and its connotations of political awareness and rebellion. In their song "Juventud Rebelde (Rebellious Youth)," the name of the official youth newspaper, rappers Alto Voltaje claimed that "Like a cross I go, raising the 'underground' banner for the whole nation." Rappers identified their movement with statements by the political leadership about justice and sovereignty in the international arena. In his post-9/11 speech, Castro had urged the American government to exercise restraint: "We would advise the leaders of the powerful empire to keep their composure, to act calmly, not to be carried away by a fit of rage or hatred and not to start hunting people down, dropping bombs just anywhere."[5] In their song "No More War!," the group Anonimo Consejo drew on this speech, rapping, "No more war, no more deaths, talkin' 'bout something real, this ain't a game. Prepare yourself for what's coming. I know what it is, stay calm, I take action."

Partly as a result of the appropriation of rap music by the Cuban state, rappers succeeded in winning greater visibility in Cuban society. After the 2001 rap festival, a session of the nationally broadcast television talk show *Dialoga Abierto* (Open Dialogue) featured a discussion with several rap promoters and Cuban artists about Cuban rap, showing footage of performances from the rap festival. During the 2001 Cubadisco music festival, attended by producers and recording labels from around the world, rappers and rock musicians were given their own stage in Playa. Magia López and Alexey Rodríguez of the husband–wife rap duo Obsesión were nominated for an award. The increasing visibility of Cuban rap facilitated a shift to an acceptance by some political leaders that racial discrimination existed in Cuban society. In contrast to earlier criticisms of rap music for its racial content, the Cuban state began to praise rap for addressing issues of race.

The state also gave more institutional support to rap music in the early millennium. After the 2000 festival, Grupo Uno was disbanded by AHS, and AHS took over the coordination of the festivals and concerts. Following the 2001 meeting with Prieto, the state created a rap agency in order to group rap artists together and various rappers were selected to enter the agency.

The institutional support given to Cuban underground rappers and the greater profile for their demands for social justice and racial equality came at the cost of a part of their autonomy. Increasing institutionalization of rap music also meant that the state could exercise greater censorship over the activities of rappers. Those in official bureaucratic positions had more control over aspects of the artistic process. Rappers were aware of the control being exerted over the rap movement as it became more integrated into state institutions. One of the responses to this was to make increased use of digital technology and the internet. The underground rap group Los Aldeanos was given little airplay on Cuban radio, but they began to use Youtube and other digital media to build an international following. Rappers also began to produce and distribute their own mixtape CDs. Another response was to migrate abroad in search of more opportunities.

The emergence of new transnational spaces

Since 2005, there has been a large exodus of Cuban rappers to different parts of the world. Orishas was the first to leave Cuba – in 1999, they moved to Paris and signed with the record label EMI. In September 2001, Julio Cardenas from RCA stayed behind after a tour of New York City. Since then, various other rappers have also emigrated from Cuba. Promoter and DJ Ariel Fernández left Cuba in 2005 to live in New York City.

But given the strong connection between rap music and place, what value does Cuban hip-hop have outside of this geographical space? Made in Cuba, and made for Cubans, how can this music speak to a public that does not share its same context? How can Cuban rappers reconnect in the diaspora? It has been difficult for rappers, as new immigrants, to pursue their art, given the demands for everyday survival. They are often separated from their group members, making it necessary to reinvent themselves as solo artists or move into other fields.

In the contemporary moment, it is probably most accurate to speak of Cuban rap as a diasporic movement given that a considerable amount of musical production is taking place outside the geographical boundaries of the island. Cuban rap is no longer physically anchored in Cuba, although many groups continue to reside on the island and the island itself still provides inspiration for much diasporic music.

Further reading

Fernandes, Sujatha, *Close to the Edge: In Search of the Global Hip Hop Generation* (New York: Verso, 2011).

   Cuba Represent! Cuban Arts, State Power, and the Making of New Revolutionary Cultures (Durham, NC: Duke University Press, 2006).

   "Fear of a Black Nation: Local Rappers, Transnational Crossings and State Power in Contemporary Cuba," *Anthropological Quarterly* 76/4 (2003): 575–608.

"Made in Havana City: Rap Music, Space, and Racial Politics," in Anke
Birkenmaier and Esther Whitfield (eds.), *Havana Beyond the Ruins: Cultural
Mappings after 1989* (Durham, NC: Duke University Press, 2011), pp. 173–186.

Fernandez, Ariel, "¿Poesía Urbana? o la Nueva Trova de los Noventa," *El Caimán
Barbudo* 296 (2000): 4–14.

"SBS. ¿Timba con Rap? El hip-hop de la pólemica," *Revista Salsa Cubana* 5/17
(2002): 43–45.

Saunders, Tanya, "Black Thoughts, Black Activism: Cuban Underground Hip-hop
and Afro-Latino Countercultures of Modernity," *Latin American Perspectives* 39
(2012): 42–60.

West-Duran, Alan, "Rap's Diasporic Dialogues: Cuba's Redefinition of Blackness,"
Journal of Popular Music Studies 16/1 (2004): 4–39.

Zurbano, Roberto, "¡El Rap Cubano!: Discursos Hambrientos de Realidad (Siete
Notas de Viaje sobre el Hip-Hop Cubano en los Diez Años del Festival de Rap de
la Habana)," *Boletín de Música Cubana Alternativa* (2004): 1.

Notes

1 EMI was the fourth major label of the "Big Four" before the music branch was sold to Universal Music Group and its publishing sold to a Sony/ATV consortium in November 2011 (after being sold to Citigroup in February 2011).

2 Fidel Castro, September 11, 2011. Available at www.cuba.cu/gobierno/discursos/2001/ing/f110901i.html (accessed 1 June, 2014).

3 Elena Oumano, *Global Hit for Friday*, August 27, 1999.

4 As many white Cubans fled after the revolution, the Cuban government made alliances with both Black revolutionary groups in the US and decolonization struggles in Africa, thus consciously attempting to represent Cuba as a "Black nation."

5 Castro, September 11.

21 Senegalese hip-hop

ALI COLLEEN NEFF

Hip-hop in Senegal manifests the longstanding conversation between African practitioners and the arts of the Black diaspora in a spectrum of practices, modes, and media. The streets of the Senegalese capital of Dakar and its populous *banlieue* (poor, overcrowded migrant suburbs) are thick with hip-hop practices that reflect ideas about Americanness, global resistance, and the politics of style. Evolutionary narratives suggest that African hip-hop began with the initial introduction of rap recordings to the continent, moved subsequently into a long imitation phase, and was eventually adopted by Africans. Through this lens, African innovation represents the endpoint of hip-hop's trajectory, and non-Westerners are its latecomers. Senegalese hip-hop, however, shows that global hip-hop is part of an ongoing poetic, sonic, and stylistic dialogue between Africa and the North Atlantic that unfolds through multiple historical lines and overlapping genealogies. The richness and polyvalence of hip-hop in Senegal is a result of the historical infusion of New World creativity with African poetic and vocal traditions, the transatlantic rhetorics of the Civil Rights, Négritude, and Black Power movements, and the circulation of global popular music throughout the twentieth and twenty-first centuries.

Today, hip-hop is a national discourse in Senegal as young people continue to debate and reinvent hip-hop styles, which they call "Galsen" (from "Senegal"), or "Senerap." The body of Senegalese hip-hop speaks at once to national politics, to international youth solidarity, and to a passion for Sufi Islam, to which 96 percent of the Senegalese population adheres. It is deployed in an assemblage of languages, from the colonial French to Arabic-inflected indigenous languages Wolof and Pulaar to, less often, English. Much of the hip-hop that enters global venues is francophone, while local hip-hop stars most often rap in Wolof, a language suited to rapid-fire cadences. Themes of Pan-Africanism, Third World solidarity, and a global hustle by which Africans can survive and thrive remain common across Senegal's many hip-hop styles, from its foundational sample-based productions of the 1990s to its current 808 chants, dance-pop fusions, and Afro-folk iterations.[1]

A study of hip-hop in Senegal requires attention to the longstanding role of the regional griot, or praise singer, who is part of a family line of musicians. Across Senegambian ethnic groups, griots specialize in drum or kora, dance, and the craft of musical poetry, which they employ to resolve community conflicts, empower or remove leaders, convey news, and to recite the genealogies of their neighbors. Men and women griots have for millennia recited improvised and memorized verses over the rhythms of talking drums for the purposes of life-cycle ritual, diplomacy, and battle. These traditions of eloquence set the stage for contemporary hip-hop styles, which draw on these practices of collaborative ritual music-making, and a number of Senegalese rappers are themselves from griot families.[2] Owing to the legacy of the griots, the calls of the Islamic *muezzins* at prayertime, and the open use of rented ad hoc sound systems for ritual, celebration, and religious oratory, Dakar is a thriving community in sound that quickly integrates new global sounds and styles. Another important influence in the contemporary Senegalese culture is that of Sufi Islam. The devotional poetry and public chants, or *zikr*, of Senegalese Sufism involve improvised, impassioned verse that infuses the poetic practices of the region and nourishes the worldviews and lyrics of many prominent Senegalese rappers.

Given the traditional importance of migration to economic systems of this Sahelian savannah region, most Senegalese people speak a handful of languages. While some formally educated Senegalese speak the colonial French or Arabic learned in Qur'anic school, Wolof is the Senegambian *lingua franca* shared across regional ethnic groups as they meet in the cultural crossroads of Dakar. Non-Wolof Senegambians tend also to speak their own ethnic languages and those of the nations in which they work and trade. The location of the small former British colony of the Gambia within the boundaries of Senegal infuses Senegalese Wolof with English phrases even though it is a lesser-spoken language in this largely francophone part of the African continent. In turn, Senegalese hip-hop has to date been more directly influenced by the cadence, style, and production values of American hip-hop than by its lyrics. The Wolof language, which involves long strings of phonemic prefixes and suffixes which are easily suited to quick syncopation and rhyme, lends itself to improvised verses by which the Senegalese developed their own hip-hop lexicon mixed with English choruses and phrases. The additional influences of French and Islamic hip-hop have added further complexity to Galsen's polyvalent lyrics. Tupac Shakur, Public Enemy, the Fugees, Wu-Tang Clan, Busta Rhymes, 50 Cent, and Wiz Kalifa are among the American acts whose sounds, lyrical themes, and (sometimes) Islamic names resonate with young people in Senegal.

Young Senegalese people witnessed the emerging hip-hop movement in the 1980s when a devastating national drought led them to seek work en masse in Europe and the USA. As they immersed themselves in the international neighborhoods of New York City's outer boroughs and the struggling Parisian *banlieue*, they found polyrhythms, dance, and poetic styles that resonated with their community lives back home. These musical practices, already deeply influenced by the historical creativity of enslaved Senegambian peoples in the new world, spoke both to shared histories and an emerging global hip-hop solidarity.[3] Early Senegalese hip-hop, in turn, incorporated sounds and styles popular in both the USA and in the growing European scene, infused them with themes of African migration and struggle, and breathed regional aesthetics into their sonic structures. The result was a spectrum of hip-hop practices, from streetside freestyle battles, to the incorporation of break-dance moves into traditional dance celebrations, to a thriving recording industry. Each of these represents one of many strains of Senegalese hip-hop that resonates variously with global movements and contributes to discourses on what hip-hop means to young people worldwide.

Even as the thickness of African and American cultural conversation, the efforts of particular Senegalese leaders have helped establish national acts and the whole of African hip-hop on the international hip-hop scene. Senegal's most active early group, Positive Black Soul (PBS), was led by Didier Awadi and Duggy Tee, who remain active in the Senegalese scene today. Afro-French hip-hop pioneer MC Solaar fostered the group as a member of the francophone African diaspora; these kinds of transnational partnerships characterize Senegalese hip-hop's circuits of mobility today. Along with Daara J and Pee Frois (Xuman), PBS pioneered the three-vocalist sound that characterized Senegalese hip-hop in the 1990s: an American-style rapper, a reggae MC whose style is inflected with Jamaican patois, and a chanteur, or singer, who leads the chorus. Women's collective ALIF (Attaque libératoire de l'infanterie féministe) drew from this model in forming the first internationally recognized female African hip-hop crew at the turn of the twenty-first century. This style has largely phased into larger collectives and solo acts in the 2000s as global trends move away from sample-based and roots reggae sounds and into a more heavily synthesized club/electronica aesthetic.

Like its North and West African neighbors, Senegalese music has always engaged with global movements in popular music. Senegalese soldiers returned from the world wars with French, Cuban, Spanish, and American records in hand. These contributed to *mbalax*, the national popular music of Senegal, which fuses Afro-Caribbean instrumentation with vocal riffs drawn from the songs of the griots. While Galsen often draws from the styles and dance-floor orientation of *mbalax* pop, many Senegalese artists define their work in opposition to the genre's mainstream, regional, and gender-participatory orientations. Galsen also overlaps with a longstanding regional reggae scene inspired by Bob Marley and South African artist Lucky Dubé, and current global fashion, to which the Senegalese – traders, performers, craftspeople, and exporters – are keenly attuned. Gokh-Bi System and Fafadi are among artists who identify with Galsen but who heavily use live reggae instrumentation. Fusion artists including rapper Fata and chanteuse Vivian N'Dour mine *mbalax* for hip-hop and R&B inspiration; even as *mbalax* artist Pape Ndiaye Thiopet infuses his *taasú*, or toasting rhymes drawn from women ritual griottes, with hip-hop phrasing and posture.

R&B took early Senegalese root with Smokey Robinson, Marvin Gaye, Michael Jackson, Sadé, and Lionel Ritchie among regional favorites. The booming West African metropolis of Dakar itself is an urban crossroads in which critical young practitioners engage and remake cutting-edge global styles. Senegalese migrants thicken African American networks as workers circulate from home to factory, IT, taxi driving, and informal work in Atlanta, Memphis, Raleigh, and Washington, DC. As a largely Islamic nation with longstanding trade ties with the Arab world, the Senegalese are well versed in global religious and political movements. Writers and film-makers including Miriama Ba and Ousmane Sembené, and intellectuals Léopold Senghor and Cheikh Anta Diop, put European and American intellectual movements into conversation with Afrocentric worldviews and politics. Within this long context of Afro-modernity, Senegalese hip-hop renews the dialogue between critical West African creativity and mass global culture. Sites of hip-hop creativity in Dakar include the Institut Culturel Français, the British Council, and events presented by the US State Department and (independent American event and documentary producers) Nomadic Wax.

For many young nationals, Atlanta-based rapper Akon is the most prominent icon in Senegalese hip-hop. His father, international jazz drummer Mor Thiam, hails from a famous Dakar griot family and emigrated to the USA to work with dance anthropologist Katherine Dunham for various jazz projects. Akon's clear sung tenor and pared-down lyrics appeal to the Senegalese who recognize his griot's style and for whom English is a less-spoken language. They respond, in the wake of mass emigration for young men, to images of mobility and self-sufficiency in his videos. His music translates well to the Senegalese club or street dance, where it is most often deployed next to *mbalax* hits and international pop as young men mimic his tie-and-tailored-cardigan Atlanta street style. Akon's status as a mainstream rapper speaks more toward global migrations of hip-hop and griot culture than it does to the direct influence of hip-hop's germinal Bronx scene of the late 1970s. His work articulates a special facet of the Africa–USA hip-hop conversation that becomes evident through an inclusive notion of hip-hop practice based less on English-language lyrical complexity and more on the notions of Afro-modern musical conversation and community. Akon and his family maintain a household in Dakar, returning regularly to hold free concerts and fund humanitarian work.

Many of Galsen's earliest touring artists hailed from the central Dakar regions of SICAP or "the Plateau," rare middle-class neighborhoods where, in the 1980s and 1990s, young people were more likely to possess the resources of formal education and international mobility than their suburban peers. They were able to rap in French and English, and to obtain educational or artists' visas to tour these regions and further establish their spokespersonship. Today, Fou Malade of Guediawaye, Matador of Pikine, and Gaston of Parcelles are leading artists of the outer Dakar region, while Keur Gi Crew represent the inland region of Kaolak. These artists hail from neighborhoods thick with ritual drumming and speech events and draw from classic proverbs and cadences from "deep Wolof" speech. Often, these artists have a family member or close friend working in the outer neighborhoods of the southern USA or minor European cities, and their sound reflects the club and lyrical aesthetics of those communities. Woman artist Sister Fa, whose cosmopolitan hip-hop is inflected with the buoyant song of her Djola people, hails from the southern Senegalese region of the Casamance; her style has a reggae accent that reflects her community's preferred sound. Galsen artists such as Nix identify more heavily from Akon's US "Dirty South" and reality-based (or "gangsta") hip-hop than the classic 1990s era, and are more likely to record entire songs in English.

The political dimension of Senegalese hip-hop is often cited in world news reports. Awadi helped to lead a youth movement called *Boul Fallé* ("don't care"), along with professional wrestler Tyson, that demanded political answers to an increasingly disenfranchised migrant youth population. Senegalese historians and world journalistic reports credit the 2012 regime change in Senegal, which ushered unpopular president Abdoulaye Wade from his seat, to the hip-hop centered *Y'en a Mare* ("fed up") movement. The World Social Forum was held in Dakar in 2010 and involved a number of Senegalese rappers, many of whom springboarded into participation in the FESMAN World Festival of Black Arts, held in Dakar later that year. Both events offered international exposure to grassroots, Wolof-speaking hip-hop acts who have since started touring internationally. In 2012, rappers Xuman and Keyti initiated a series of TV spots entitled *Journal Rappé*, a hip-hop satire on national and international politics set to music.

Given the traditional ritual and political importance of women musical poets in the Senegambia region, women's participation in Senegalese hip-hop culture has been steady, if not always publicly visible. Senegalese women's collective ALIF staged a feminist intervention into African hip-hop beginning with their work with Awadi's group in the early 2000s. Miryam (ALIF) Diallo and Njaaya (Gueye) continue to work as multimedia solo

Figure 21.1 Senegalese woman rapper Toussa Senerap, leader of women's hip-hop collective
GOTAL, draws her rhymes from traditional women's *taasú* poetry and American Southern hip-hop
alike.

artists and have inspired a number of emerging women artists and collectives, including Sister Coumbis Cissokho (of a Dakar-based Mandé griot
family) and Toussa (Figure 21.1), who participate in an active women's
hip-hop collective called GOTAL. Sister Fa regularly tours the region to
promote awareness of women's rights. Women radio personalities and pop
recording artists infuse their styles with hip-hop. These artists work in conversation with French feminist artists such as Diam's and Americans Missy

Elliot, Lauryn Hill, and Nikki Minaj to imagine space for less visible figures in hip-hop.

The Senegalese hip-hop industry remains largely homegrown. The omnipresence of live music and nationalized TV and radio programs for Senegalese music translate to a low demand for high-quality recordings and officially released CDs. As album sales are further compromised in the bootleg cassette market (often sold to taxi drivers) and the sharing of MP3 catalogues via cellphone sim cards, local artists focus their promotional efforts on hip-hop showcases in which a line-up ranges from three to dozens of artists. One of the challenges to Senegalese hip-hop is the need for production resources for independent artists. Strict national import-substitution policies make foreign equipment scarce and expensive. The lack of access to production software and training contribute to this difficulty. Many artists resort to downloading unlicensed beats from websites or to using very basic software to produce beats. Awadi's Studio Sankara and Gaston's Studio Def Dara are among a handful of Senegalese studios at which upcoming artists can pay to have a song recorded at the rate of US$60 per song; other studios require that their recording artists sign over rights to songs or management in exchange for productions. Many artists work with European and American producers for songs, albums, and videos.

Hip-hop is manifest in a number of registers, from graffiti to dance. The annual Kaay Fecc ("Come Dance") festival evidences Senegalese innovation and play with hip-hop dance forms. The Dakarois smurfing scene, inspired by French versions of American hip-hop dance, has infused club dance styles in the city for two decades. Today, many young Dakarois people practice breakdance in the soft silt of the Dakar beaches and in national group dance competitions, alongside dances taken from bhangra, salsa, and global dancehall bass. Freestyle hip-hop flourishes in the outer Senegalese suburbs of Ginaaw Rail, Thiaroye, and Rufisqe, where young people gather around boom boxes to improvise rhymes in the rapid-fire cadences of Wolof mixed with French, English, and Arabic phrases. Venues like Pikine's Cafeteria host evening-long freestyle battles. Young Senegalese practitioners, already skilled and schooled in the deployment of the poetic word, activate regional culture to converse with hip-hop forms. The monthly Kool Grawoul party at a downtown beach features DJs from around the world, mixing hip-hop from the Dakar plateau with French and Arabic-language rap, Tupac Shakur, *zouk*, *kwaito*, and *mbalax*. Bidew Bou Bess and Carlou D use the hip-hop form to declare their faith in the Sufi Islamic orders of which they are devotees.

As hip-hop practitioners, academics, and fans debate the core aesthetics and boundaries that define the genre as an international cultural formation,

Senegalese hip-hop demonstrates the polyvalence of hip-hop forms. The "72h" hip-hop festival, which was first held at the public obelisk near the hip-hop heavy Medina neighborhood in December 2009, offers a yearly, three-day showcase of Senegalese hip-hop acts. A number of discourses surrounding hip-hop authenticity have arisen in the wake of this event, which is largely influenced by contemporary American styles. Like their global counterparts, young Senegalese activate hip-hop to think through the connectivity of the African diaspora, the politics of the political stage and of the dancefloor, and the creative future of Third World youth. The Senegalese hip-hop community is keenly aware of the importance of its own representation in global discourses. To this end, Senegalese artists and cultural figures such as Keyti are filming documentaries about the scene, and Senegalese national television is heavy with hip-hop programming. The people of Senegal's longstanding cultural investment in thinking critically about national self-representation amid changing global circumstances – beginning with revolutionary president Leopold Senghor's leadership on the Négritude poetic movement in the 1960s – ensures the ongoing development of new forms and discourses in hip-hop. The world of Galsen positions itself at the cutting edge of, never as an echo to, new movements in global Black creativity.

Further reading

Duran, Lucy, "Key to N'Dour: Roots of the Senegalese Star," *Popular Music* 8/3 (1989): 275–284.

Herson, Ben, Magee McLvane, and Chris Moore, *Democracy in Dakar*, documentary film (Nomadic Wax, 2007). Available at http://nomadicwax.com/democracyindakar/.

McLaughlin, Fiona, "'In the Name of God I Will Sing Again, Mawdo Malik the Good': Popular Music and the Senegalese Sufi Tariqas," *Journal of Religion in Africa* 30/2 (2000): 191–207.

Neff, Ali Colleen, "'In One, All': Senegalese Women Freestyle Artists Unify the Global Ghetto," Close to the Edge Dossier, *Social Text Online* (2011). Available at http://socialtextjournal.org/periscope_article/in_one_all_senegalese_women_freestyle_artists_unify_the_global_ghetto/.

Other media resources

Documentary film available at www.youtube.com/watch?v=cKhGLH3DygE.

Keyti, "100% Galsen," in series, *Redefinition: African Hip Hop*, 2012.

NPR Daara J., "Senegalese Hip-Hop." Available at www.npr.org/templates/transcript/transcript.php?storyId=4660446.2005.

Xuman and Keyti, *Journal Rappé*. Available at www.youtube.com/user/jtronline?feature=watch, 2013.

Notes

1 Much contemporary hip-hop in the American and global Souths uses vintage electronic instruments – particularly the Roland TR-808 – to produce a thickly distorted sound that marks their stylistic difference from the more nuanced (and less dance-floor-ready) production values of East Coast hip-hop.

2 For a comprehensive study of contemporary griot culture and hip-hop in Senegal, see Patricia Tang, "The Rapper as Modern Griot: Reclaiming Ancient Traditions," in Eric Charry (ed.), *Hip Hop Africa: New African Music in a Globalizing World*, African Expressive Cultures Series (Bloomington, IN: Indiana University Press, 2012).

3 DJ Awadi Biography, January 13, 2013. Available at www.rfimusique.com/artiste/rap/didier-awadi/biographie.

22 Off the grid: instrumental hip-hop and experimentalism after the golden age

MIKE D'ERRICO

Every Wednesday night, hip-hop heads and electro-ravers make the trek to the east Los Angeles barrio of Lincoln Heights for *Low End Theory*, a club night featuring experimental hip-hop, dubstep, and various forms of emerging "bass" music. Titled after the 1991 A Tribe Called Quest record of the same name, a key album in the fusion of rap and jazz traditions, the venue embodies hip-hop's inherent desire for juxtaposition, coalescence, and convergence. Veterans from 1990s G-Funk bob heads with legends of British house and dubstep, while experimental producers and DJs representing the entirety of Los Angeles pass joints and talk gear, analyzing the quality of the set they just heard, and offering feedback to new talent. Representing a wide diversity of aesthetics, techniques, and geographies, *Low End Theory* epitomizes the changing face of hip-hop in the twenty-first century. At a time in which many producers are establishing their musical chops on digital tools, rather than traditional turntable setups, the basic techniques and processes through which beatmakers work have shifted, influenced by broader trends in digital music and emerging media.

Through analyses of beats by producer-auteurs J Dilla, Madlib, and Flying Lotus, this chapter details three dominant compositional trends that have emerged in what has broadly become known as "experimental hip-hop": side-chain compression, "off-the-grid" rhythmic sequencing, and the use of hardware peripherals to control digital software. While my survey covers three of the more prominent figures surrounding the Los Angeles "beat scene," the compositional trends I discuss have become canonical sonic gestures in not only contemporary instrumental hip-hop music, but various forms of electronic dance music as well. Most noticeably, these techniques have tended to disregard the turntable and the vinyl record as a compositional metaphor, instead choosing to push the limits of hardware samplers and drum machines while simultaneously experimenting with emerging technologies, from digital audio workstations such as Ableton Live to mobile music platforms such as the Apple iPad.

"Experimental" hip-hop

People call it many things: aquacrunk, future blap, lazer bass, wonky, glitch hop.[1] The music is often as vague and capacious as these terms, covering a broad range of electronic dance music styles, not tied down to a single geographic origin, and – as the variety of names suggests – always changing. Throughout this chapter, I use the title "experimental hip-hop" to delineate the production styles under discussion, since this is perhaps the only phrase in circulation that has yet to be completely shot down by the artists and audiences making and consuming the music. While the title has been thrown around throughout the history of the genre, three major factors allowed the style to coalesce into a distinct and recognizable subgenre of hip-hop in the mid to late 2000s: the death of pioneering beatmaker J Dilla,[2] the rise of social media platforms for music, and the emergence of clubs that would eventually become global hubs for "bass music" more broadly.[3]

Two features most clearly distinguish "experimental hip-hop": the intentional lack of a rap element, and the self-conscious foregrounding of production techniques.[4] In this way, the historical roots of the performance aesthetic may be said to begin with solo turntablists such as Grandmaster Flash and Afrika Bambaataa, who – while they also created music for rap groups of which they were a part – defined the core aesthetics of hip-hop composition through the creation of solo mixtapes that showcased the technological capabilities of the turntable.[5] As sampling technologies developed and became more affordable in the late 1980s and early 1990s, hip-hop entered what became known as its "golden age," defined by a solid "boombap" sound that was shaped by the interactions between emerging sampling technologies and traditional turntable practice.[6] Producers such as DJ Premier from Gang Starr, Prince Paul from De La Soul, and producer-auteur DJ Shadow used turntables alongside popular samplers such as the Akai MPC and E-Mu SP-1200 to create instrumental mixtapes with gritty, lo-fi audio qualities (12-bit sample resolution, as opposed to 16-bit CD quality audio) and innovative performance practices that continue to define the sound of "underground," "old-school" hip-hop. In the absence of a rapper, these DJs and beatmakers developed a specific set of values and aesthetics that were shaped by the capabilities and limitations of turntable and sampling technologies, as well as the user's ability to transcend these limitations. In this way, the history of "experimental" hip-hop production emerged from instrumental hip-hop production – defined by the technologies being used, as well as the ability of the producer to expand on these technologies through individual skill and technical manipulation.

However, as the 1990s reached their end, hip-hop witnessed the twilight of its "golden age" as the culture became a global phenomenon, diversifying its scope to encompass the values and ideologies of youth cultures around the world.[7] In this context, the "underground" (re: authentic) hip-hop stance permeated across geographic lines as an ideology of alterity, setting itself in contrast to a mythical "mainstream" that seemed to reflect the perceived uniformity of an emerging globalized world. For producers establishing themselves as instrumental hip-hop musicians during this time – the RZA of the Wu-Tang Clan, J Dilla, and Madlib, for example – the debate over aesthetic "realness" no longer took place between the turntable and the hardware device, but rather between hardware devices such as the MPC, and their digital software equivalents that reside on computer workstations.

Giving up the title "DJ" from their names, this new generation of experimental hip-hop artists have embraced their primary role as sample-based "beatmakers" rather than turntable DJs. As many of their monikers suggest – MF Doom as "Metal Fingers," or Madlib as the "Beat Konducta" – removing the title "DJ" from their alias is a way of asserting their identity as progressive "post-turntable" artists who focus their energies solely on sample-based, instrumental beats. For some, the digital audio workstation represents exactly what is wrong with hip-hop after the "golden age." As Madlib states,

> I don't have no computers, I don't have any big setups people have. I just have a 303 sampler, or SP 12, or whatever I use, and just records. That's all I need. I mean, I buy new things like an MPC, but it's still basically the same. I'll be having no computer setup or 24 tracks and none of that Pro Tools.[8]

On the contrary, artists such as Flying Lotus and other members of the LA "beat scene" have embraced what Simon Reynolds has termed "digital maximalism": a general trend of electronic dance music in the 2010s, in which there are "a hell of a lot of inputs, in terms of influences and sources, and a hell of a lot of outputs, in terms of density, scale, structural convolution, and sheer majesty."[9] In contrast to turntablists such as DJ QBert, DJ Shadow, and other "golden age" artists who helped shape hip-hop production in its early years, beatmakers in the digital age no longer feel the need to assert their skills by "paying dues" to the turntablist tradition. Instead, they have developed entirely new technical practices by either embracing or rejecting emerging digital software. In this way, the first self-consciously "experimental" producers may be seen as a product of a noticeable rift in hip-hop culture more broadly.

Moving off the grid

In the absence of an MC to verbally "flow" over solid, rhythmically consistent beats – combined with more complex sampling and sequencing

capabilities – experimental hip-hop producers have embraced various techniques for "dequantizing" their rhythms. The most influential compositional strategies have come from J Dilla – an MPC virtuoso and Detroit
neo-soul pioneer who made a name for himself working with the likes of
A Tribe Called Quest, Busta Rhymes, and Janet Jackson, before moving to
Los Angeles to focus on solo work. While his early productions continue
to influence the hard "boombap" aesthetic originally made famous in the
early 1990s, it is his solo work post-2000 that has most clearly shaped the
emerging generation of experimental hip-hop producers. With techniques
such as side-chain compression, unquantized sample sequencing, and metric modulation, Dilla's solo beatmaking is shaped less by turntablist techniques and "boombap" rap beats, and more by the seemingly untapped
technological affordances of his primary instrument, the Akai MPC
sampler.

Musically, this shift from a mix-based turntable aesthetic (emphasis on
juxtaposition of disparate musical sources) to a modulation-based digital
sampler aesthetic (emphasis on recombination/reconfiguration of single
musical sources) can be heard in the obsessive focus instrumental hip-hop
artists place on the rhythmic sequencing of single samples. For example, in "Don't Cry," a track off his seminal 2006 album *Donuts*, Dilla
abstains from juxtaposing various samples into a multi-layered loop, instead
rearranging fragments of a single sample into an altogether different groove
(see Figure 22.1).[10]

The primary groove of this track is generated, at least partially, by Dilla's
strategy of presenting the listener with the original, unadulterated sample,
before manipulating it in various ways. "Don't Cry" begins with a slightly
speeded up iteration of the first five bars of the Escorts' "I Can't Stand (To
See You Cry)," followed by a short portion of the first verse. At this point,
Dilla cuts to 1:23 of the Escorts' track, introducing a verse outside of the
falsetto register, as well as the primary material to be chopped. After a single
vocal line in this lower register ("I can't stand to see you cry now, baby"),
Dilla performs his own version of the sample by rearranging the chops with
an Akai MPC sampler (see Figure 22.1(b)).

The stabilizing effect of Dilla's performance – the anacrustic function of
the general loop – is retained because the listener was previously introduced
to the original sample. However, instability is introduced into the original
sample by the sudden fragmentation of Dilla's reworking, ultimately giving
the track its dynamic motion and "flow." In this way, Dilla's performance
in "Don't Cry" epitomizes what Tricia Rose calls an "equilibrium inside the
rupture": the essential double nature of loop-based repetition in hip-hop,
in which processes of cutting, chopping, and slicing are normalized in the
context of a stable and repetitive loop.[11] In other words, while we externally

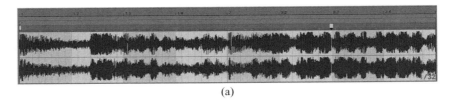

(a)

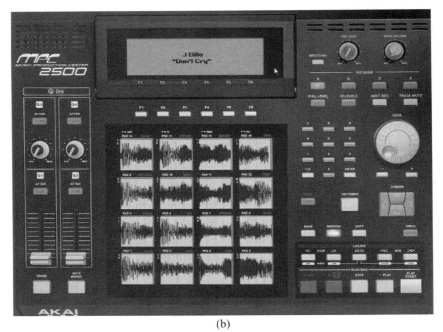

(b)

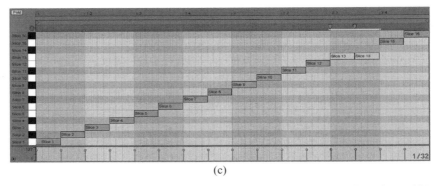

(c)

Figure 22.1 The process of sample chopping in J Dilla's *Donuts*. (a) The Escorts, "I Can't Stand (To See You Cry)" (full sample at 1:23); (b) sample chopped into eighth notes, distributed among the pads of an Akai MPC sampler/drum machine; (c) MIDI piano roll of the "Baby" chop as performed on "Don't Cry."

hear the track as a loop, the altered groove in Dilla's performance allows us to *feel* the "bounce" of the beat as a dynamic process.

Just as his techniques of sample chopping and sequencing allow Dilla to belie a strict rhythmic grid, his emphasis on side-chain compression has proved to be another influential compositional technique. The "ducking," "pumping" effect of side-chain compression – a result of one element of a beat "compressing" the dynamic level of another – has become ubiquitous in experimental hip-hop communities, from the ambient beats of artists such as Teebs, Nosaj Thing, and Shlohmo, to the off-kilter grooves of Samiyam and EPROM.[12] As Jay Hodgson states in his article, "Lateral Dynamics Processing in Experimental Hip-Hop," compression is "as foundational in experimental hip-hop as 'power chords' and 'tapping' once were in heavy metal. Yet they remain conspicuously absent from the lion's share of research on the genre; and, for that matter, they remain unnoticed in research on popular music recording practice at large."[13] Of particular interest to my argument is the way in which side-chain compression shifts the hip-hop production aesthetic from a tight, "boombap" style to a loose, destabilizing groove.

In *Rap Music and the Poetics of Identity*, Adam Krims defines the "hip-hop sublime" as an aural effect of beatmaking invoked through "layers marked by clashing timbral qualities."[14] While Krims's analysis focuses on the sample-layering techniques of "golden age" producers as a way of articulating a destabilizing sonic effect in which "massive, virtually immobile and incompatible layers of sound are selectively and dramatically brought into conflict with each other" at the level of tonality, exploitation of side-chain compression expands this notion by introducing extreme contrasts of frequency, amplitude, and rhythmic dissonance.[15] If Dilla's reconfiguration of single samples into eighth-note fragments can result in an interactive listening process in which microrhythmic gestures collide to create a feeling of forward motion, the exaggeration of compression in the audio signal mirrors this sensation on a dynamic level. By boosting the threshold of the compressor, as well as adjusting the ratio, attack, and release levels, Dilla overuses the internal compressor of the MPC, giving the music an aggressively dynamic ebb and flow akin to Tricia Rose's idea of "working in the red" (Figure 22.2).[16]

As this figure shows, side-chain compression has an aural effect at the microrhythmic level, thus forcing our analysis outside of a strict rhythmic grid. As Anne Danielsen writes,

> most scholars privilege only attack-point rhythm and ignore the potential impact of sound or any other non-timing aspects. The temporal location of

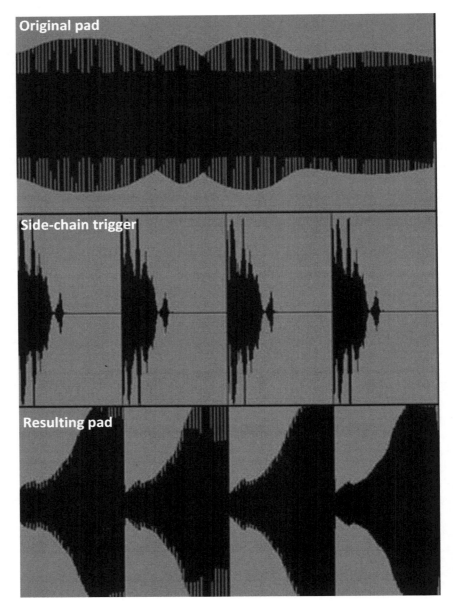

Figure 22.2 Created by Jay Hodgson, this image depicts the perception of rhythmic events in a heavily compressed aural mix. The "original pad" represents an uncompressed sound, whereas the "side-chain trigger" represents a certain instrument (or frequency) in the mix that will compress the original pad. The "resulting pad" reflects the dynamic effect that the side-chain has on the original sound, particularly the decrease in attack amplitude while the kick drum is sounding.

the rhythmic event is identified with its point of attack alone, and relevant durations (or the distances between events) have been conceptualized as the intervals between such attack points, the so-called inter-onset-intervals (IOI).[17]

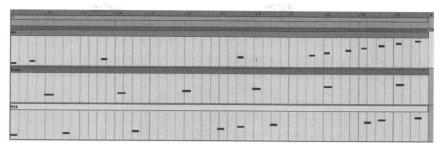

Figure 22.3 Beat deconstruction of "The Payback" done in Ableton Live: basic percussion parts (from low to high: kick, snare, hi-hat) are isolated by converting transient peaks in the original waveform into MIDI piano roll notation. This allows us to see the microrhythmic deviation – from the fixed temporal grid (located at the top of the diagram) – of each part. The irregularity of "attack points" is largely due to the way in which heavy compression deceives the listener's perception of the rhythm. The concept of beat deconstruction was introduced by Patrick Cupo – Dubspot music production school teacher – in the context of a beat by Flying Lotus. His tutorial is available at http://blog.dubspot.com/ableton-live-video-tutorial-beat-deconstruction-flying-lotus/.

Through the use of compression, IOIs and attack points from various elements of the beat (frequency being the most common) constantly vie for sonic space and aural attention, ultimately negating each other through a "ducking" effect (as depicted in Figure 22.2).

For the purposes of this analysis, we may look to the production style of Madlib – one of Dilla's longtime friends and collaborators, and a beatmaker who continues to exploit side-chain compression as a destabilizing sonic force. From the moment the beat drops in "The Payback," bass frequencies momentarily overshadow the rest of the mix. By setting the attack levels fairly low, with release high and threshold very high, Madlib creates a wave-like sonic quality as distinct timbres and frequencies gradually crescendo into the mix, sometimes – in the case of the harsh cymbal crashes on the "and" of beat four – to an extreme degree. This wave-like quality that results from the intense side-chain compression disrupts the listener's sense of solid rhythmic pacing by melting the quantized 4/4 grid, creating the impression that beats are being pushed just a bit ahead or behind the beat (Figure 22.3).

The resulting "feel" of the track is thus circular, as distinct, rhythmically "loose" polyrhythms become normalized through the looping of the beat. When a rhythmically dissonant moment is repeated, what was previously a rupture in the coherence of the groove becomes transitional material, enhancing the effect of the anacrusis and solidifying the stability of the beat. Although holistically stable, the "feel" or "bounce" of the groove is almost overdone – a common effect of what Danielsen calls "the exaggerated rhythmic expressivity of the machine": a wobbly, seasick feeling produced when beatmakers exaggerate the internal capabilities of the digital sampler.[18] Just as time becomes mercurial in Dilla's sample chopping, aural space and rhythmic structure take on a fluid character through Madlib's experimental use of side-chain compression.

New directions

While the previously discussed techniques are, in many ways, products of a general resistance to emerging digital tools, the emphasis many post-"golden age" producers have placed on overcoming the limits of hardware samplers has influenced the general framework and culture of experimental hip-hop production. This general (assumed) resistance to technology is reminiscent of a quote by Brian Eno – which has perhaps detailed the general technological dialectic in hip-hop culture since its inception – as he writes, "even the 'weaknesses' or the limits of tools become part of the vocabulary of culture... what was once thought most undesirable about these tools became their cherished trademark."[19] Yet, in recent years many experimental hip-hop producers have challenged this aesthetic emphasis on technological limitations, embracing emerging digital tools most notably through the use of various touch-based hardware peripherals. Some examples include the creation of iOS apps for digital music production, and the use of the Apple iPad to control Ableton Live and other digital audio workstations, as well as digital vinyl systems such as Serato Scratch Live. Together, these tools exemplify the ways in which shifts in technical practice and performance have reflected broader shifts in the general aesthetic and cultural sensibilities of hip-hop culture.

With the iPad and other digital audio tools, the technical paradigm is no longer simply about manipulating temporal aspects of music, but also spatial characteristics. Whereas the turntable scratch is a singular gesture, either referencing disparate points along a temporal object, i.e. the needle moving forward or backward along a circular vinyl groove, the increasing prevalence of buttons, pads, and other grid-based interfaces reflects a growing aesthetic emphasis within hip-hop production on timbral layers, mashups, and other sorts of sonic architectures. In an article for *Loops*, Matthew Ingram writes about how digital audio workstations like Ableton Live encourage an "interminable layering" and how the graphic interface insidiously inculcates a view of music as "a giant sandwich of vertically arranged elements stacked upon one another." The various controllers used by performers at *Low End Theory* and other experimental hip-hop venues reflect this shift from a circular turntable-based form of production to a grid-based, spatial, and architectural form. The iPad takes this trend a step further, incorporating every interface design form (whether based on a turntable, keyboard, drum machine, or X-Y pad) into the logic of a grid, simultaneously allowing for the juxtaposition of sonic and technical elements.

This highlights another significant shift in the performance practices of hip-hop artists, perhaps best exemplified by the musicians of *Low End Theory*. Whereas traditional turntablism primarily involves the juxtaposition of music as its fundamental logic, the incorporation of the iPad exemplifies a convergence of various media, from music to visual art and video games, the touch-screen device becoming the prime interface for a cloud-based view of information. More and more, new media are asking users to experience data as visual, external, and tangible, a phenomenon shared by the recent popularity of infographics, interactive websites and blogs, the public spread of APIs and other developments in open-source culture, as well as the spread of the "digital humanities" within academia. Trends in digital music software reflect this, as programs such as Max/MSP and Pd present visual interfaces that run solely on the mashing up of buttons, knobs, sliders, and wires of various sorts, in what has become known as "physical computing," or "live coding." The status of being a "button pusher" is no longer a denigrating term for many electronic musicians, but a metaphor for the convergence of a certain video game logic within digital music production, one embraced by many experimental hip-hop musicians.[20]

In this chapter, I have introduced just a few of the trends that have emerged in instrumental hip-hop composition since the advent of widely accessible digital audio production tools in the early 2000s. While many of these techniques are continuing to shape various genres of electronic dance music, the twilight of "golden age" hip-hop aesthetics is all too clear for many critics. In a 2012 *San Francisco Weekly* editorial post, "Instrumental Hip-Hop Sucks. Ban It Forever," Phillip Mlynar rants against the emergence of a new generation of instrumental hip-hop musicians (directly attacking both J Dilla and Madlib):

> Instrumental hip-hop should be banned. It's the banal, meandering stepchild of hip-hop. It's a front-runner for the dubious honor of being the world's most snooze-inducing form of music. And, shockingly, there are still producers and fans who insist on validating it like it's anything but sample-based Chinese water-torture.[21]

At the top of Mlynar's hit list is what he sees as a static, repetitive, and non-teleological structure that inhibits pleasurable listening: "Where is the joy and excitement in listening to three minutes of plodding drum beats overlaid with a short sample that repeats but goes nowhere?"[22] For many hip-hop producers and audiences, it is clear that experimental practices in beatmaking and digital audio production have destabilized the "vinyl is final" standard of "realness" for compositional style. Yet, as experimental hip-hop artists continue to break down generic and stylistic boundaries in electronic dance music culture more broadly, they are also contributing to the inherently dialectical nature of cultural practices in hip-hop. As artists and audiences continue to embrace beatmaking as the so-called "fifth element" of hip-hop culture, scholars must continue to examine the sometimes elusive elements behind the beat that work to define and shape it.[23]

Discography

Daedelus, *Live at Low End Theory* (Alpha Pup Records APR022, 2008).
Dibiase, *Machines Hate Me* (Alpha Pup Records APR030, 2010).
Eprom, *Metahuman* (Rwina Records RWINALP001, 2012).
Flying Lotus, *Cosmogramma* (Warp Records WARPCD195, 2010).
   Los Angeles (Warp Records WARPCD165, 2008).
J Dilla, *Donuts* (Stones Throw Records STH2126, 2006).
Jonwayne, *Bowser* (Alpha Pup Records APR036, 2011).
Knx, *Anthology* (Leaving Records LR026, 2013).
Madlib, *The Beat Konducta, Vols. 1–2: Movie Scenes* (Stones Throw Records STH2133, 2005).
   The Beat Konducta, Vols. 3–4: Beat Konducta in India (Stones Throw Records STH2177, 2007).
   The Beat Konducta, Vols. 5–6: A Tribute to J Dilla (Stones Throw Records STH2205, 2008).
MF Doom. *Metal Fingers Presents: Special Herbs (The Box Set Vols. 0–9)* (Nature Sounds NSD-120, 2006).
Ras G., *Brotha From Anotha Planet* (Brainfeeder BFD002, 2009).
Samiyam, *Sam Baker's Album* (Brainfeeder BFD022, 2011).
Shlohmo, *Bad Vibes* (Friends of Friends FOF109CD, 2011).
Teebs, *Ardour* (Brainfeeder BFD010, 2010).
Various Artists, *TeamSupreme: Collection 1* (Alpha Pup Records APR, 2013).

Notes

1 Laurent Fintoni, "Return of the Boombap," *Red Bull Music Academy,* July 8, 2012. Available at www.redbullmusicacademy.com/magazine/return-of-the-boom-bap (accessed June 1, 2014).

2 Aside from maybe Biggie Smalls and Tupac Shakur, J Dilla is one of the most eulogized artists in hip-hop. The "J Dilla Changed My Life" T-shirt has become a foundational symbol in the experimental hip-hop scene, and the J Dilla Foundation has helped spread Dilla's influence across musical styles and audiences. For an example of one of the many eulogies following Dilla's death, see Tolu Olorunda, "Death, Donuts, and Dilla," *thisisrealmusic,* February 28, 2011. Available at www.stonesthrow.com/news/2011/09/death-donuts-dilla (accessed June 1, 2014).

3 *Ibid.*

4 Whereas Schloss, in *Making Beats: The Art of Sample-Based Hip-Hop* (Middletown, CT: Wesleyan University Press, 2004), views the primary aesthetic binary of hip-hop to occur between "live" and "sampled-based" hip-hop production, I hope to problematize this distinction by introducing specific trends in "experimental hip-hop" that allow for the expansion of who and what gets to be considered "hip-hop" in general.

5 An insightful discussion of the musical practices of early hip-hop culture can be found in David Toop, *Rap Attack 2: African Rap to Global Hip-Hop*, 2nd edn. (London: Serpent's Tail, 1991), and Mark Katz, *Groove Music: The Art and Culture of the Hip-Hop DJ* (New York: Oxford University Press, 2012).

6 For studies that have dealt with the aesthetics of "golden age" hip-hop, see Jon Caramanica,

"Hip-Hop's Raiders of the Lost Archives," *New York Times,* June 26, 2005. Available at www.nytimes.com/2005/06/26/arts/music/26jon.html?_r=0 (accessed June 1, 2014); Wayne Marshall, "Giving Up Hip-Hop's Firstborn: A Quest for the Real After the Death of Sampling," *Callaloo* 29/3 (2006): 868–892; Justin A. Williams, "The Construction of Jazz Rap as High Art in Hip-Hop Music," *The Journal of Musicology* 27/4 (2010): 435–459.

7 For studies on hip-hop culture around the world, see Tony Mitchell (ed.), *Global Noise: Rap and Hip Hop Outside the USA* (Middletown, CT: Wesleyan University Press, 2001); Ian Condry, *Hip-Hop Japan: Rap and the Paths of Cultural Globalization* (Durham, NC: Duke University Press, 2006); and Ian Maxwell, *Phat Beats, Dope Rhymes: Hip Hop Down Under Comin' Upper* (Middletown, CT: Wesleyan University Press, 2003). For studies on cross-cultural hip-hop within the United States, see Raquel Z. Rivera, Wayne Marshall, and Deborah Pacini Hernandez (eds.), *Reggaeton* (Durham, NC: Duke University Press, 2009); and Nitasha Tamar Sharma, *Hip-Hop Desis: South Asian Americans, Blackness, and a Global Race Consciousness* (Durham, NC: Duke University Press, 2010).

8 Adrian Schraeder, "Interview with Madlib," *Urban Smarts,* October 14, 2004. Available at http://urbansmarts.com/interviews/madlib.htm (accessed June 1, 2014).

9 Simon Reynolds, "Maximal Nation: Electronic Music's Evolution Toward the Thrilling Excess of Digital Maximalism," *Pitchfork,* December 6, 2011. Available at http://pitchfork.com/features/articles/8721-maximal-nation/ (accessed June 1, 2014).

10 This process is markedly different from previous sampling practices, which often juxtaposed fragments of disparate samples so as to allow the rapper to inhabit the textural space between them. Much of the work by RZA of the Wu-Tang Clan reflects this practice. See Genius/GZA, *Liquid Swords* (Geffen Records GEFD-24813, CD, 1995).

11 Tricia Rose, *Black Noise: Rap Music and Black Culture in Contemporary America* (Middletown, CT: Wesleyan University Press, 1994), p. 70.

12 In the case of hip-hop, bass frequencies often cause other frequencies to "duck" in and out of the mix. For an in-depth discussion of this technique, see Jay Hodgson, "Lateral Dynamics Processing in Experimental Hip-Hop: Flying Lotus, Madlib, Oh No, J-Dilla and Prefuse 73," *Journal on the Art of Record Production* 5 (2011).

13 *Ibid.*

14 Adam Krims, *Rap Music and the Poetics of Identity* (Cambridge University Press, 2000), p. 73.

15 *Ibid.*

16 Rose, *Black Noise,* p. 75.

17 Anne Danielsen, Introduction, in Anne Danielsen (ed.), *Musical Rhythm in the Age of Digital Reproduction* (Farnham: Ashgate, 2010), p. 9.

18 Danielsen, Introduction, p. 1.

19 Brian Eno, "The Revenge of the Intuitive: Turn Off the Options, and Turn Up the Intimacy," *Wired* January, 1999. Available at www.wired.com/wired/archive/7.01/eno_pr.html (accessed June 1, 2014).

20 For insightful discussions regarding the "button-pushing" debate, see Ed Montano, "How do you Know He's not Playing Pac-Man While He's Supposed to be DJing? Technology, Formats and the Digital Future of DJ Culture," *Popular Music* 29/3 (2010): 408. Also, see electronic dance musician Deadmau5's controversial blog post on the subject, "we all hit play," *United We Fail* blog 2012. Available at http://deadmau5.tumblr.com/post/25690507284/we-all-hit-play (accessed June 1, 2014).

21 Phillip Mlynar, "Instrumental Hip-Hop Sucks. Ban It Forever," *SF Weekly* January 31, 2012. Available at http://blogs.sfweekly.com/shookdown/2012/01/instrumental_hip-hop_sucks_ban.php (accessed June 1, 2014).

22 *Ibid.*

23 As the four hip-hop elements of DJing, MCing, graffiti, and breakdancing are universally acknowledged, a number of elements vie for that "fifth element." "Knowledge" has been the most often celebrated contender, but similar claims have been made about fashion and beatboxing as well. I claim beatmaking as the "fifth element" here as a way of acknowledging the seeming fluidity and ever-changing nature of the culture.

23 Stylized Turkish German as the resistance vernacular of German hip-hop

BRENNA REINHART BYRD

In an investigation of the spread of hip-hop[1] across the globe, we often find that local, non-standard language varieties are intrinsically tied to the projection of an authentic hip-hop identity. These non-prestige language varieties are called resistance vernaculars, because they are often used for critique or rebellion against the structures of society that perpetuate existing power structures.[2] Resistance vernaculars have been integral in the glocalization (local + globalization) of hip-hop. By using local dialects, an authentic hip-hop identity can be expressed that fits within the global understanding of hip-hop as a mode of expression for the politically and socially repressed.[3] Hip-hop's cultural history as rebellion against those in power is an attractive metaphor for those in other countries feeling similarly repressed by their society and searching for a legitimate means of artistic expression. These "connective marginalities" account for the continued popularity of hip-hop in minority communities around the world.[4] The migrant communities in Germany are no different. Not only has hip-hop been extremely popular as a mode of expression for migrant youth, it has been instrumental in the rebranding of a Turkish-German identity that divorces itself from previous images of the Turk as powerless victim. With this new identity came a new language variety, stylized Turkish German (STG), which has come to be used as an index of an aggressive, street-wise Turkish identity as well as real hip-hopper status.

To understand how this came about, we first need to clarify what is meant by a new language variety. Despite codification attempts through standardized spelling and grammar taught in public schooling, all languages are constantly evolving and no two speakers speak exactly alike. Some speakers have the advantage that their native language variety, that is the grammar, pronunciation, vocabulary, etc. that they use regularly, is close to the one taught in school and used in highly formal settings like news broadcasts and political speeches. We call these prestige varieties, because speaking this way carries a social connotation of being educated, professionally successful, and having middle- to upper-class socio-economic status. Although schoolteachers may argue that double negatives like "I ain't got no satisfaction" are illogical and therefore wrong, in many languages around the world, such as Russian and French, they are the proper way to negate a sentence. The grammaticality judgment is rooted in social beliefs, rather than in logic or linguistics, and double negatives are only frowned upon because they exist in low-prestige varieties.

Why then would a group use a language variety that the mainstream society considers incorrect or low class? We use our language to put forth an image of ourselves to those around us, to communicate who we are, where we come from, what groups we belong to, and how we feel, without being fully aware of the linguistic choices we make.

We often refer to different language varieties as dialects if we think that a person is still speaking some version of the same language, i.e. we can understand most of what the person is saying even if the way it is said is unusual.[5] Most dialects are regionally determined, meaning that people usually speak differently in different areas of the world. Dialects with the most distance between them tend to become distinct, such as American English and British English, or completely separate languages, like French and Spanish. Speakers can also be separated by more than physical distance. If a specific language variety is associated with an ethnicity, such as African American Vernacular English (AAVE), it is often referred to as an ethnolect. Ethnolects form when a specific ethnic group becomes separated from others in their everyday lives, through their jobs, religious affiliations, housing, etc. Both ethnicity and race are socially determined categories where the boundaries are often in flux, and hence ethnolects can often change quite rapidly depending on societal attitudes. New ethnolects usually appear where migrant communities form that are not well integrated into the dominant society after a generation or two. It is in this environment that STG arose.

In Germany, Turks are the largest percentage of the population with recent migrant background. Although there are many other migrant groups in Germany, Turkish German has become the new *Leitethnie*, a dominant minority group under whose category other minority ethnicities tend to be subsumed.[6] They form an ethnoclass, where a defining factor of their ethnic label is their socio-economic status as manual laborers whose social mobility is severely restricted by their lack of citizenship.[7] The new migrant communities first formed after the economic boom of the 1950s, when Germany made several agreements with countries such as Turkey, Greece, and Italy to bring in a much-needed workforce. Most migrant laborers in the 1960s had thought their stay in the host country would be temporary. However, encouraged by their employers, who were eager not to spend additional money retraining new employees, two years turned into twenty, their families moved to join them, and soon many of their children grew up having never visited their parents' country of origin. Because neither the migrants nor Germany's government had thought of the situation as permanent, few attempts were made at a smooth integration into society, and distinct migrant communities sprang up inside most of the major cities. Learning German was not a priority at first, especially once Turkish grocery stores, airlines, newspapers, and restaurants were set up in the migrant neighborhoods. With busy work schedules and little disposable income, there were also few opportunities to take language classes. The children of this first generation felt especially isolated, not having a strong identification with their parents' country but maintaining outsider status in the only country they knew. Lack of viable options for social mobility and parents who worked long hours led many migrant youth to spend their afternoons at youth centers together, furthering their isolation from the rest of German society.

Given their isolation, these migrant communities developed not only a unique way of speaking German, but also a form of Turkish that is noticeably different from the Turkish spoken in Turkey. The language of these communities has been under investigation since their initial formation, and many linguists anticipated the formation of a new hybrid Turkish-German language. While such a hybrid never did come about, a Turkish-influenced variety of German, often called *Kanak Sprak* or *Türkdeutsch*, did arise, which has since made headlines as the youth speech of street gangs and tough inner-city kids. This stylized ethnolect is now synonymous with hip-hop language, although this association did not appear until the mid 1990s. But how did the Turkish-German ethnolect become the language of hip-hop? In order to answer this question, we must first look at the history of hip-hop in Germany.

With the international success of the Sugarhill Gang's hit single "Rapper's Delight" (1979), followed closely by groups like Grandmaster Flash and the Furious Five, Treacherous Three, and Kurtis Blow, the sound, dancing style, and fashion gained a dedicated following across Europe. As a result, pop artists borrowed heavily from this music style for hits like Falco's "Rock Me Amadeus" (1985).[8] Yet, when movies like *Wild Style* (1983) and *Beat Street* (1984) were aired on German television, rap and breakdancing enthusiasts were made aware of the cultural history that produced the art forms they so loved.[9] With this knowledge, the hip-hop practices in Germany fell into two camps – those who saw hip-hop as an art form of the repressed and tool for social critique, and those who enjoyed the different aspects of hip-hop on a more superficial level and wished to bleach them of political implications.[10] The language the groups used reflected this decision.

At first, the hip-hop scene was dominated by English-language rap in an effort to stay true to its US roots, while rap-influenced pop appeared in German. The politically savvy and non-ethnic German group Advanced Chemistry switched from English to German, a move that was initially met with resistance by their audience because of its association with the pop rap "sell-outs." Often credited as the first *real* hip-hop group to rap in German, the language switch was required for them to achieve their goal of changing the conversation on racism and social injustice in Germany. Simply put, in order to fight racism with their words, they needed to be understood by the general audience. Although there were over 6.9 million migrants and their descendants living in Germany by 1994, most Germans still clung to the idea of a static, homogeneous national German culture and ethnic make-up that did not include those of recent migrant background.[11] As the rapper Linguist (aka Kofi Yakpo) of Advanced Chemistry complained in the 1992 song "Fremd im eigenen Land" ("Foreign in one's own country"),[12] despite being born in Heidelberg and having a German passport, his Ghanaian heritage prevented his compatriots from accepting him as German. In an interview for the television documentary *Lost in Music: Hip Hop Hooray!*, Linguist discusses the powerful effect that lyrics can have on the lives of their listeners:

> The fact that you can reach so many people . . . I spoke earlier about responsibility . . . is specifically strong at this point, so that you also have to say the right thing. If I introduce a term like *Afro-Deutsche*, in "Fremd im eigenen Land" [Foreign in one's own country] then, if I'm lucky, a hundred thousand Afro-Germans hear it, and will hopefully continue its usage. And no longer refer to themselves as . . . just "something" . . . or *allow* themselves to be referred to as such, above all.[13]

Not only was it important to use German to reach their audience, Advanced Chemistry consciously appropriated hip-hop as a space for the negotiation of identity that was self-defined rather than placed on them by those in power.

Yet while politically active groups like Advanced Chemistry considered rap as a tool to speak out against racism, German-language rap groups that borrowed the sound but not the message were gaining in popularity. Many of the early ethnic German rappers renamed rap as *Deutschrap* ("German Rap"), *Neuer Deutscher Sprechgesang* ("New German Spoken-Song"), or *Neue Deutsche Reimkultur* ("New German Rhyme-Culture"), thereby claiming the music style as their own while divorcing it from the cultural implications of US hip-hop. Furthermore, after Germany's reunification in 1990, *Deutschrap* groups tended to focus on presenting a unified German national pride, which pushed non-ethnic-German groups to the categories of *Multi-Kulti* and "Oriental" music.[14] Distancing themselves from US hip-hop's critique of hegemonic white society allowed *Deutschrap* to be consumed unproblematically by the white German middle-class as well as to deny the oppression of migrants in Germany as a mainstream concern.[15] This led to the phenomenal success of *Die Fantastischen Vier* ("The Fantastic Four"), a group from Stuttgart, whose bright clothes, upbeat party lyrics, and energetic stage presence made them an instant hit. Sony signed them in 1991, releasing the first German-language rap album on a major label.[16] Their financial success did not translate into acceptance within the hip-hop community, however, and they are often used as an example of precisely what is *not* authentic by German hip-hoppers:

> TONI L. (ADVANCED CHEMISTRY): Accept them? Sure, but not as a hip-hop group. They're a hit pop group, but not a hip-hop group.
> TORCH (ADVANCED CHEMISTRY): I mean, it's nothing personal. It's really good pop music. Of all the pop music, it would be the closest thing to hip-hop, in sound.[17]

The quality of the music is not questioned here; in fact it is lauded. However, the message that so many consider integral to hip-hop is lost, and therefore the group is considered only to be a *pop* group. This distinction between hip-hop and mainstream pop music was especially important in the migrant youth communities, who identified strongly with the voices of oppressed minorities in US hip-hop.[18] Many migrant youth felt the music style had been taken away from them unfairly and turned away from hip-hop for a few years as a result.

With the increase in the violent public attacks against Turks and other minorities in the 1990s, many musicians from different genres, including *Deutschrap*, banded together to produce albums speaking out against violence, but not specifically against discrimination. The lack of a public response that contained deeper reflection on the roots of the attacks led many migrant youth back to hip-hop as a tool of social critique, but this time with a different spin. Rather than appeal to German audiences to be more accepting, migrant youth used rap as a call to arms for oppressed minorities to stand up for themselves, even to use violent force if necessary. In 1995, the mega-group Cartel formed from the hip-hop groups Karakan from Nuremberg, Da Crime Posse from Kiel, and Erci E from Berlin. They opened their first concert by defiantly rapping exclusively in Turkish, something unheard of at the time. To say it was well received by the predominantly migrant youth in attendance would be an understatement. Cartel released a self-titled Turkish-language rap album in the same year, urging Turkish Germans to defend themselves against racism and oppression and to be proud of their Turkish heritage. What they did not expect was the song's popularity outside of Germany, as within a few weeks they had replaced Michael Jackson as the number one artist in the Turkish charts.[19] This success paved the way for other Turkish Germans to start rapping in Turkish. At a time when American gangsta rap was rising in popularity with groups like N.W.A. and Public Enemy reaching international audiences, Cartel's success pushed an association of aggressive, macho hip-hop with a pro-Turkish stance into the public sphere.[20] Turkish Germans began to see themselves as the rightful heirs of hip-hop, with parallels drawn between Brooklyn and Berlin's Turkish neighborhood Kreuzberg.[21] Hip-hop had returned to the migrant youth communities, and this time they were not going to let it go without a fight.

As we saw above, language choice is an indication of identity and allegiance. The decision to rap in Turkish coincided with a positive Turkish identity, just as Advanced Chemistry's decision to rap in German reflected their own self-identification as German and desire to be treated as such. But how can a group put forth a positive Turkish identity and yet still be understood (and consumed) by a German-speaking audience? The answer for many was the creation of the STG ethnolect.

In 1995, Feridun Zaimoğlu published a book called *Kanak Sprak*, a collection of fictional first-person narratives in a highly stylized Turkish-German mixture, which reappropriated the derogatory *Kanake* as a term of empowerment for the migrant communities.[22] The title of the book became synonymous with the ethnolect of the migrant communities, and aspects of this ethnolect were the subject of numerous comedic acts and cinematic portrayals of migrants. Zaimoğlu's book, Cartel's aggressive lyrics, and other public representations of Turks at this time, even in the form of exaggerated parody, produced a shift in the standard depiction of migrants in German media. In contrast to previous images of migrants as victims of racism and violence at the hands of Germans,[23] a new, sometimes terrifying image of the Turkish-German street thug emerged. This new Turk was street-wise, cocky, and dangerous – which suited many migrant youths just fine.

Tired of being victims, the agency available from adopting this new persona was attractive, and youth gangs like the Turkish Power Boys chronicled in Tertilt's 1996 anthropological study boasted about their petty theft and intimidation of ethnic Germans.[24] While German comedy acts like *Mundstuhl* poked fun at the small-minded criminal behavior of their ethnic parodies of Turks, the linguistic features[25] they used gained popularity among Turkish-German youth, who enjoyed the association with rebellion and social disobedience.[26] For many, it was the better of two choices: attempt to integrate and still be denied access to mainstream society, or embrace the stereotypes of juvenile delinquency and be slightly feared by mainstream society as a result.

Many hip-hop artists in Germany use STG as part of their repertoire to project a hypermasculine aggressive image deemed appropriate for a German gangsta rapper.[27] This image also extends to some non-migrant hip-hoppers, such as the Berlin rapper Fler (aka Patrick Losensky). Although

instances of grammatical differences from standard German are more prevalent in unrehearsed interviews than in actual rap lyrics, some features like
article and preposition deletion can be seen in many popular rap songs such
as Fler's "Deutscha Bad Boy" and Sido's "Fuffies im Club." The phonological
aspects (the pronunciation) are more widespread and observable in almost
every rapper who identifies as being part of an urban hip-hop scene.[28]

The need for authenticity integral to a hip-hop persona has kept non-
standard vernaculars at the heart of hip-hop movements around the globe.
In some cases, this need has kept minority language varieties not only alive
but thriving, spilling out of their original communities and appearing in
the mouths of those wishing to align themselves with hip-hop's message of
non-conformity. Through hip-hop, STG has gained acceptance as a preferred language style for those wishing to project an urban street-wise image.
Thus, in Germany we find the previously stigmatized features associated
with migrant language have been reappropriated through their association
with hip-hop as the language of agency for urban youth. In this way, STG has
changed from a marginalized ethnolect to a popular resistance vernacular
within German society.

Discography
Advanced Chemistry, *Fremd im eigenen Land* (MCD/MZEE. 12, 1992).
Cartel, *Cartel* (Mercury, CD, 1995).
Die Fantastischen Vier, *Jetzt Geht's Ab* (Sony/Columbia. LP, 1991).
Falco, *3* (GiG Records, LP, 1985).
Fler, *Fremd im Eigenen Land* (Aggro Berlin/Universal, CD, 2008).
Sido, *Maske* (Aggro Berlin, CD, 2004).
The Sugarhill Gang, *Rapper's Delight* (Sugar Hill Records Ltd./Metronome, 12, 1979).

Further reading
Alim, H. Samy, Awad Ibrahim, and Alastair Pennycook (eds.), *Global Linguistic Flows* (New York: Routledge, 2009).
Cheesman, Tom, "Talking 'Kanak': Zaimoğlu contra Leitkultur," *New German Critique* (2004): 82–99.
Hoyler, Michael and Christoph Mager, "'HipHop ist im Haus': Cultural Policy, Community Centres, and the Making of Hip-hop Music in Germany," *Built Environment* 31 (2005): 237–254.
Kallmeyer, Werner and Inken Keim, "Linguistic variation and the construction of social identity in a German-Turkish setting," in Jannis Androutsopoulos and Alexandra Georgakopoulou (eds.), *Discourse Constructions of Youth Identities* (Amsterdam/Philadelphia: Benjamins, 2003), pp. 29–46.
Terkourafi, Marina (ed.), *The Languages of Global Hip Hop* (New York: Continuum International Publishing Group, 2010).

Notes

1 In this chapter I refer to "rap" as the spoken word music style, whereas "hip-hop" is the cultural movement including rapping, breakdancing, graffiti, and DJing.

2 Russell Potter, *Spectacular Vernaculars* (State University of New York Press, 1995).

3 Tony Mitchell, "Doin' Damage in My Native Language: The Use of 'Resistance Vernaculars' in Hip Hop in France, Italy, and Aotearoa/New Zealand," *Popular Music and Society* 24 (2000): 41–54.

4 Halifu Osumare, *The Africanist Aesthetic in Global Hip-Hop: Power Moves* (Basingstoke: Palgrave Macmillan, 2007).

5 The definition of a dialect is not straightforward, however. There are language varieties that are called dialects, such as Mandarin and Cantonese, which are not mutually intelligible (the speakers cannot understand each other). However, there are separate languages like Norwegian and Swedish that are so close that many speakers can carry on conversations with each other unaided by translation tools. The definition of language vs. dialect is usually a political one, reflecting either the attitudes of those who speak it or of those in power. As a Chinese student of mine told me, the desire to think of all Chinese as belonging to one unified country is more important than a linguistic distinction. This is yet another example of how even the definition of language is tied up with identity.

6 İnci Dirim and Peter Auer, *Türkisch sprechen nicht nur die Türken* (Berlin: Walter de Gruyter, 2004), p. 1.

7 Up until 2001, citizenship eligibility was governed by the law of *jus sanguinis* (citizenship by blood). This meant that many who were born and raised in Germany, spoke German, and considered Germany to be their home were denied political representation and access to jobs that might have changed their socio-economic status, thereby perpetuating the ethnoclass.

8 Verlan and Loh make the argument that although similar styles of spoken word set to music might have existed in German previously, hip-hop was decidedly a different animal. Otherwise one could stretch the argument to claim that medieval monks were the first to rap in German. Sascha Verlan and Hannes Loh, *25 Jahre HipHop in Deutschland* (Höfen, Austria: Hannibal, 2006), p. 134.

9 Dietmar Elflein, "From Krauts with Attitudes to Turks with Attitudes: Some Aspects of Hip-hop history in Germany," *Popular Music* 17 (1998): 255–265.

10 Daniel Bax and Thomas Winkler, "Sprache der Ausgrenzung," *Die tageszeitung* (2002). Available at www.taz.de/1/archiv/archiv/?dig=2002/10/11/a0200.

11 Elflein, "From Krauts with attitudes," 225.

12 Advanced Chemistry, *Fremd im eigenen Land* (MCD/MZEE. 12, 1992).

13 *Lost in Music: Hip Hop Hooray!* documentary, first aired on ZDF March 1993, re-aired on October 17, 2008 (all translations are my own unless otherwise noted).

14 Elflein, "From Krauts with attitudes," 258; Sabine von Dirke, "Hip-Hop Made in Germany: From Old School to the Kanaksta Movement," in Agnes C. Mueller (ed.), *German Pop Culture: How "American" is it?* (Ann Arbor: University of Michigan Press, 2004), pp. 96–112.

15 While some artists did use hip-hop as well as other music styles to speak out against *violence* toward non-Germans, such as in the release of the 1992 "No More Ugly Germans" compilation, the more subtle institutionalized racism and exclusion of certain groups from mainstream German culture was not a subject of concern.

16 Caroline Diessel, "Bridging East and West on the 'Orient Express': Oriental Hip-Hop in the Turkish Diaspora of Berlin," *Journal of Popular Music Studies* 13 (2001): 165–187; Günther Jacob, *Agit-Pop: Schwarze Musik und weiße Hörer. Texte zu Rassismus und Nationalismus, HipHop und Raggamuffin* (Edition ID-Archiv, 1993), pp. 212–216.

17 "Lost in Music," ZDF.

18 Ayse S. Caglar, "Popular Culture, Marginality and Institutional Incorporation: German-Turkish Rap and Turkish Pop in Berlin," *Cultural Dynamics* 10 (1998): 243–261.

19 Verlan and Loh, *25 Jahre*, pp. 227–228.

20 Diessel, "Bridging East and West," 182.

21 Caglar, "Popular Culture," 247–248.

22 Feridun Zaimoğlu, *Kanak Sprak. 24 Mißtöne vom Rande der Gesellschaft* (Hamburg: Rotbuch Verlag, 1995).

23 See films like Fassbinder's 1974 *Angst essen Seele Auf* (*Ali: Fear Eats the Soul*) and Sanders-Brahms's 1975 *Shirins Hochzeit* (*Shirin's Wedding*), as well as Wallraff's 1985 journalistic exposé *Ganz Unten* (*Lowest of the Low*).

24 Hermann Tertilt, *Turkish Power Boys: Ethnographie einer Jugendbande* (Frankfurt: Suhrkamp, 1996); recordings online: hermann.tertilt.info/tpb/.

25 These linguistic features include phonological variants such as rolled /r/, the coronalization of [ç] (voiceless palatal fricative)

to [ʃ] (voiceless alveo-palatal fricative), a specialized vocabulary (*Alter* "dude," *korrekt* "cool," *weissu* "y'know"), and reduced syntax (such as deletion of prepositions and articles).

26 Jannis Androutsopoulos, "From the Streets to the Screens and Back again: On the Mediated Diffusion of Variation Patterns in Contemporary German," *LAUD* (2001).

27 Verlan and Loh, *25 Jahre*, pp. 22–25.

28 The coronalization of [ç] to [ʃ] in *ich* "I," *mich* "me," and *dich* "you" are common examples.

24 "Bringin' '88 Back": historicizing rap music's greatest year

LOREN KAJIKAWA

Pop music fans and critics often enjoy crafting and debating "best of" lists. In hip-hop circles, this practice often involves naming what one believes to be the top rappers, producers, or albums of all time. With close to forty years of recorded music history to consider, such discussions have also turned toward defining the genre's best era or year, and hip-hop heads have long debated whether 1988, 1993, or some other year represents hip-hop's finest.

As the first generation of fans raised on rap enters middle age, it would be wise to regard current nostalgia for hip-hop's golden past skeptically, and it is easy to dismiss such backward-looking judgments as romantic indulgences. The diversity of rap music audiences with respect to age, class, ethnicity, and musical preference makes it difficult – perhaps even impossible – to imagine agreement on such matters of taste. Yet the controversial nature of "best of" claims can provoke thought, channel emotions, and force confrontation with deeply held values and allegiances. As interested parties debate the reasons why one would place this over that, or include that and not this, new ways of looking and listening become available. At their best, impossible claims of supremacy begin conversations rather than end them.

It is in this spirit that I consider the proposition that 1988 represents rap music's finest year. Critics and fans hail '88 with such superlatives as "the dawn of rap's golden era" and "rap's greatest year."[1] Taking these claims seriously, this chapter describes the historical circumstances and musical developments that make 1988 a pivotal year for hip-hop music. From the perspective of artists, producers, journalists, and record labels, the music recorded and released in 1988 documents a time of artistic innovation, thematic diversity, and cultural relevancy that continues to inspire musicians and fans.

Rap music proves its staying power

In the wake of the genre's first big hit a decade earlier – The Sugarhill Gang's "Rapper's Delight" (1979) – observers ranging from industry insiders to casual fans expected the rap "fad" to run its course and vanish.[2] By 1988, however, hip-hop music had become one of the fastest growing sectors of the recording industry. Although one could argue that more high-quality rap albums were produced in later years, 1988 has been hailed as a historic year due in part to the diversity of new themes and styles introduced over this twelve-month period.[3] The recordings released in 1988 run the spectrum from the lighthearted pop rap of DJ Jazzy Jeff and the Fresh Prince to the violent, sexually explicit street tales of Niggaz Wit Attitudes (N.W.A.). The year featured albums by established acts, such as Run-D.M.C.'s *Tougher than Leather* and Ice-T's *Power*, as well as debut efforts from upstarts, such as EPMD's *Strictly Business*, Ultramagnetic MCs' *Critical Beatdown*, and the Jungle Brothers' *Straight Out the Jungle*. Moving in multiple directions at once, the genre made significant inroads into the mainstream without being confined to a single center.

This diversity reflected the creative energies of young artists hoping to make a name for themselves in the genre, but it also depended on behind-the-scenes work by promoters, managers, and independent record labels that had established an infrastructure capable of producing and distributing an increasingly high volume of products. Despite steadily growing profits in the early 1980s, major record labels preferred to keep rap at a distance, working out distribution deals with smaller labels that took responsibility for artists' development. Important examples of these pairings include Def Jam (CBS and Columbia), Jive (RCA), and Tommy Boy (Warner Bros.). Many of these partnerships were first cultivated in the mid 1980s, and the unprecedented bounty of rap albums released in 1988 represents the fruits of their efforts.[4] Some of the most influential music of the year, however, came from outside the major label system. In Los Angeles, rapper Eazy-E and manager Jerry Heller, who had formed their own independent label, Ruthless Records, were unable to find a major willing to market and distribute their music. Ruthless joined forces instead with a new, relatively unknown distributor, Priority Records, who helped introduce the nation to a brand of sensationalized "gangsta rap" that would eventually change the direction of the recording industry.[5]

Recognizing the creative explosion and financial impact of rap music, the National Association of Recording Arts and Sciences (NARAS) announced in June of 1988 the creation of a new Grammy Award category for Best Rap Performance.[6] Nominees for the first award included DJ Jazzy Jeff and the Fresh Prince for "Parents Just Don't Understand," J.J. Fad for "Supersonic," Kool Moe Dee for "Wild Wild West," LL Cool J for "Going Back to Cali," and Salt-N-Pepa for "Push It." The award went to DJ Jazzy Jeff and the Fresh Prince, whose humorous lyrics about everyday family life and accompanying slapstick video helped broaden rap's appeal to a wider and whiter youth demographic. Released on March 29, the Philadelphia-based duo's album *He's the DJ, I'm The Rapper* (Jive) included family-friendly songs that made overt references to pop cultural phenomena, such as video games, horror films, and back to school shopping.

Although their success expanded rap's mainstream appeal and opened the door to subsequent "pop rap" acts, such as MC Hammer, Vanilla Ice, and Tone Loc, there was another side to the duo's music that often goes overlooked: by highlighting the turntable skills of DJ Jazzy Jeff, the album re-emphasized the importance of one of hip-hop's core elements. Today, the Fresh Prince (aka Will Smith) is the greater celebrity, but the future television and film actor began his career in the shadow of famous DJ Jazzy Jeff. In the mid to late 1980s, Philadelphia boasted many of the nation's most innovative DJs, including Jazzy Jeff, Cash Money, Spinbad, and others.[7] Jeff won numerous battles, such as the 1986 New Music Seminar's Battle for World Supremacy, and the title and cover art for *He's the DJ, I'm the Rapper* reminds listeners of his primacy. Jeff appears on the front cover with the words "He's the DJ," while the album must be turned over to see the Fresh Prince and the words "I'm the Rapper." By highlighting the role of the DJ in the group, the album harkened back to hip-hop's origins as a DJ-centered activity. A significant number of songs, such as the album's title track, testified to Jazzy Jeff's turntable skills. *He's the DJ, I'm the Rapper* finds Jeff working with a number of breakbeats from hip-hop's early years, such as John Davis's "I Can't Stop" (1976) and T-Connection's "Groove to Get Down" (1977).[8] Cutting and looping these records with precision, Jeff lays down a steady groove to support the Fresh Prince's fast-paced flow. At times, the Fresh Prince drops out of the mix or calls attention to Jazzy Jeff as he deploys an arsenal of scratch techniques, including the "transformer" that he helped to invent and popularize.[9] Poised at a moment when digital sampling was fast becoming the standard method of rap music production, 1988 represents a transitional period when albums featured a self-conscious mixture of digital techniques and virtuosic in-studio turntable work. This musical experimentation led to a high point for "DJ tracks," the colloquial term describing songs that highlight the unique skills of the hip-hop DJ. Other DJ tracks released in 1988 include Eric B and Rakim's "Eric B Never Scared," Public Enemy's "Terminator X to the Edge of Panic," and EPMD's "D.J. K LaBoss," to name only a few.

The art of rhyme

Not all artists in 1988 devised such a successful formula for reaching a broad audience. While DJ Jazzy Jeff and the Fresh Prince delivered rap music with a pop sensibility, others attempted to advance their craft with less concern for reaching the uninitiated. Eric B and Rakim's *Follow the Leader*, released on

July 25, cemented Rakim's reputation as one of the most innovative MCs in rap. His clear staccato delivery, rhythmic agility, and dense wordplay contrasted with other MCs who often yelled and strained their voices in a considerable show of effort. Rakim's flow featured a virtuosic mixture of expansive diction and multiple-word rhyming tempered by a cool economy of means.[10] His lyrics made use of extended metaphors and a conceptual approach that reflected the MC's growth as a songwriter. "Microphone Fiend," for example, self-consciously calls attention to the craft of rapping itself. The song opens with a metaphor comparing the microphone to a similarly shaped ice cream cone, explaining that his devotion to rapping began at an early age when most children are preoccupied with less serious pursuits. He continues to expand on this theme throughout the song, comparing his hunger to be the best MC to a cigarette smoker's "fiend for nicotine" and a heroin junkie's need for a fix.

The proof of Rakim's devotion to the art of rhyme can be heard, not only in the poetic imagery of his lyrics, but also in the complex nature of his flow. For example, he does not simply assert that his words are "fitted like pieces of puzzles, complicated": he structures his lines so that the word "complicated" lands satisfyingly on a strong beat, completing a multi-syllabic rhyme begun in the previous line with the words "orientated" and "originated." As the verse unfolds, Rakim develops the song's theme while deploying a barrage of multiple-word rhymes (e.g. "to the lab," "mic to grab," "then I add," "rhymes I had"). His rhythmic delivery mixes dramatic pauses with rapid-fire sixteenth-note phrases, creating a variety of cadential patterns that unfold over several lines. In this way, Rakim's flow differed markedly from those found in recordings released just two years prior in which MCs predictably rhymed words and completed rhythmic cadences on the fourth beat of each measure. By self-consciously taking his lyrical skills to a higher level, Rakim and other MCs who released albums in 1988, such as Big Daddy Kane, the Ultramagnetic MCs, and Chuck D of Public Enemy, asserted the importance of craft and made older or less gifted MCs sound stale.

Making beats

In addition to emphasizing lyrical prowess, "Microphone Fiend," whose beat includes a prominent sample of Average White Band's "School Boy Crush" (1975), exemplified the growing use of digital technology in rap music production. In the period from 1983 to 1986 many rap producers and engineers had teamed up with hip-hop DJs, using a mixture of digital drum machine sounds and turntable scratching to craft musical tracks for

MCs to rap over. As digital sampling and sequencing devices became more readily available, however, DJs discovered that they could invest this new technology with the spirit of older hip-hop practices, such as cutting and looping breaks. Many DJs took this opportunity to move into a role as producers (i.e. beatmakers) themselves.[11] At the same time, the growth of battle events such as the New Music Seminar's Battle for World Supremacy and the D.M.C. World Championships fostered the development of hip-hop DJing (also known as turntablism) into an independent art form removed from rap.[12] By 1991, the DJ track would all but disappear from rap albums.

Marley Marl, a DJ and leader of Queensbridge's Juice Crew who had produced many of the tracks on Eric B and Rakim's first album *Paid in Full* (1987), was at the center of the digital revolution. Although the first digital sample in rap dates back to Afrika Bambaataa's 1982 hit "Planet Rock," the high cost of computer music interfaces and their low memory capacities limited their usefulness to rap producers.[13] By 1984, however, sampling devices had become more accessible, leading Marley Marl to an important discovery: rather than relying on the stock sounds that came pre-programmed with drum machines, such as the Roland TR-808 or Oberheim DMX, he could sample the snare, kick, hi-hat, and other sounds directly from pre-existing records and rearrange them to create the rhythmic foundation for his songs.[14] As the memory capacity of digital sampling equipment grew, producers realized they could sample more than individual drum sounds and began turning their attention to entire breakbeats. By the mid 1980s, more affordable, higher-capacity digital samplers, such as E-mu Systems' Emulator and SP-12 (later replaced by the SP-1200) models were becoming commonplace. The year 1988 witnessed the advent of the Akai MPC-60, whose touch-sensitive trigger pads allowed producers to approach beatmaking with renewed tactile sensitivity.[15]

This new machinery freed rap from the rhythmic rigidity of previous drum machines, beginning an era in which sample-based production became the industry norm. The year 1988 represents a pivotal point in the adoption of these technologies and techniques to achieve a diversity of results. Marley Marl himself produced Biz Markie's *Goin' Off* (February 23), Big Daddy Kane's *Long Live the Kane* (June 21), and his own compilation album *In Control, Volume I* (September 1). Layering samples culled mainly from 1960s and 1970s soul recordings by Bobby Byrd, the Meters, Lyn Collins, and others, Marl crafted musical tracks that combined the "live" feel of early DJ-centered hip-hop with a set of functions (e.g. chopping, looping, and layering) that were enabled by sampling technology.

EPMD's *Strictly Business,* one of the most innovative early attempts at using sampling technology to make beats, employed relatively long passages from its pre-recorded sources. Released on June 7, 1988, the album drew from music by Kool and the Gang, Syl Johnson, James Brown, Steve Miller, Aretha Franklin, and other artists popular with hip-hop's first DJs and dancers. The song "You Gots To Chill," for example, connected a loop of Zapp's "More Bounce to the Ounce" to a sample of Kool and the Gang's "Jungle Boogie," creating an electric funk groove for MCs Parish Smith and Erick Sermon to rap over. Other beats on *Strictly Business*, including "It's My Thing," "Let the Funk Flow," and "Strictly Business," followed a similar formula, sampling and looping excerpts that were long enough to be recognizable but rearranging them in a way that imbued the pre-recorded material with new vitality. This aesthetic approach was enabled by the grey areas of copyright law: producers simply used whatever samples they wished, leaving their record companies to settle any resulting claims of copyright infringement out of court. This freedom allowed for a short-lived "golden age of hip-hop sampling" in which producers could make beats without worrying about the prohibitively expensive sample-clearance fees that have since become standard in the music industry.[16]

No group took greater advantage of these liberties than Public Enemy's production team: the aptly named Bomb Squad. For *It Takes a Nation of Millions to Hold us Back*, which was released on June 28, 1988, Public Enemy adopted an approach to production that member Chuck D once described as "loops on top of loops on top of loops."[17] The Bomb Squad's contribution to the growth and expansion of sampling practices was as much conceptual as it was technical. In addition to sampling drum sounds and classic breakbeats that already had been popular with hip-hop DJs and dancers, the group adapted Marley Marl's insights to work with a diverse selection of sounds, including the voices of Malcolm X and Louis Farrakhan, air raid sirens, and bits of noisy sound from various records that producers had yet to exploit. In this way, Public Enemy applied hip-hop's logic of looping to new kinds of source material, an approach Bomb Squad producer Hank Shocklee once aptly described as "organized noise."[18] Due in large part to Public Enemy's influence, after 1988 breaks were no longer limited to the types of instrumental passages that had been played by hip-hop's first DJs; they could be any pre-recorded sound a producer conceived of and treated like a break.[19]

Bigger than rap: politics and pedagogy

In addition to helping change how producers approached beatmaking, Public Enemy's *It Takes a Nation of Millions to Hold us Back* also took rap to another level of sociopolitical engagement. Coming of age in a post-Civil Rights world colored by everyday racism and ongoing inequality, the group conceived of itself as rap music's rebels, responding to a decade in which several racially charged acts of violence – from Michael Stewart's 1983 death at the hands of white NYPD officers to the 1986 white mob beatings of Black teenagers in Howard Beach – dominated the headlines of New York's newspapers.

Responding to their sense that Black youth were locked in a struggle for survival, *It Takes a Nation of Millions to Hold us Back* brought a heightened sense of urgency to the genre. Song titles such as "Bring the Noise," "Louder Than a Bomb," and "Prophets of Rage," give a sense of the group's attempt to strike back at Black America's enemies. Their dense sonic collages amplified the militant rhetoric of Chuck D's lyrics, which were peppered with references to the Nation of Islam and Black Power. Their sartorial style and album imagery evoked the Black Panthers and contemporary street fashion. Backed by the marketing team and creative forces at Def Jam Records, everything about Public Enemy – from their logo featuring a black silhouette caught in a sniper's crosshairs to their stoic and determined looking publicity photos – complemented their revolutionary lyrics and sound. By adopting such a holistic approach to their work, Public Enemy widened the space for political critique in popular music. The music video for "Black Steel in the Hour of Chaos," for example, portrays Chuck D as an inmate instigating a prison rebellion. Coupled with the song's anti-government lyrics and the decision to cast the prison warden and nearly all of the correctional officers as white, the video symbolizes a white controlled society in which Black bodies are subject to systematic abuse. Although *It Takes a Nation of Millions to Hold us Back* touched on a number of specific issues, including drug abuse, mass incarceration, and the US military's reliance on young people of color, Public Enemy's most significant contribution may have been the manner in which the group itself became a symbol of contemporary Black resistance.[20]

Public Enemy, however, was not the only group to reflect a growing political consciousness among rap artists. A month earlier on May 10, Boogie Down Productions (BDP) released *By All Means Necessary.* The album's title and cover art parodies a famous poster of Malcolm X holding a rifle and peering out from behind a window curtain. The caption on the original poster read, "LIBERATE OUR MINDS... BY ANY MEANS NECESSARY," and comes from a speech Malcolm X gave toward the end of his life. BDP's album cover features MC KRS-One in a similar pose by the window holding a Uzi.

Despite this imagery of KRS-One brandishing a machine-gun, however, BDP was in the midst of transforming itself into rap music's leading preachers of non-violence. In the months following the release of their first album, *Criminal Minded* (1987), the group's DJ Scott LaRock was shot and killed. Rather than disband, KRS-One decided to continue the group, and on *By All Means Necessary* he refers to his DJ repeatedly, often as if he was still alive and an active member of BDP. In addition to immortalizing Scott LaRock, KRS-One decided to eschew violent street narratives such as "9mm Goes Bang," one of the most popular tracks on *Criminal Minded*. He poured his energies instead into casting himself as hip-hop's leading teacher and scholar. Tracks like "My Philosophy," "Ya Slippin'," and "Part Time Suckers" extol BDP and KRS-One's command of knowledge and their commitment to righteous living, while "Stop The Violence" urged the hip-hop community to take a stand against senseless killing. This self-reflexive critique and call for greater responsibility, however, was matched by an equally sharp analysis of the institutional inequality and oppressive forces bearing down on the Black community. "Stop the Violence," for example, also included a critique of the US government's apathy toward the plight of the poor, and the album's darkest track, "Illegal Business," tells the tale of a small-time drug dealer extorted by corrupt police officers. Threatened with the loss of his life, the dealer agrees to pay bribes in order to stay in business. KRS-One's parable reflects widespread mistrust of the police force bred by a history of entrapment, surveillance, and repression, of which US President Ronald Reagan's War on Drugs was only the most recent manifestation.

N.W.A. puts Compton on the map

The most cogent rap response to life in de-industrialized inner city neighborhoods, however, did not come from New York City. It came from Niggaz Wit Attitudes (N.W.A.), a group whose album *Straight Outta Compton* (August 8) put Southern California on rap's map. N.W.A. shocked many on the East Coast with its rapid rise to popularity and became one of the first rap groups from the West Coast to be taken seriously by fans at the national level. Backed by musical tracks that blended the sample-based techniques of East Coast producers with instrumental parts played by studio musicians, N.W.A. crafted a distinctive West Coast sound whose booming beats and explicit lyrics evoked the harsh and unpredictable realities facing Black and Latino youth in Los Angeles's urban ghettos.

N.W.A.'s core members – Eazy-E, MC Ren, DJ Yella, Dr. Dre, and Ice Cube – grew up in Los Angeles's Compton and South Central neighborhoods. Their music was inspired by the crime and violence connected to the underground drug trade, which had flourished in the void created by massive lay-offs and high rates of unemployment that had hit the Southland's Black communities particularly hard. The rise of gangs that fought bitterly for control of the lucrative drug economy was met with a heavy-handed response from the Los Angeles Police Department (LAPD).

Despite being chemically identical to powder cocaine, which was associated with wealthy white users, the news media and law enforcement agencies had exaggerated the dangerous effects of smoking "crack" cocaine. In this context of public panic of the crack "epidemic," the US Congress passed the Anti-Drug Abuse Act of 1986, which allowed crack possession to be punished at a rate one hundred times greater than that for powder cocaine and stipulated new mandatory minimum sentencing guidelines for drug crimes that previously would not have resulted in imprisonment.[21] These measures disproportionately affected African Americans who lived in communities where street dealers made easy prey for law enforcement. Moreover, the LAPD response to the drug and gang problem was particularly aggressive. With draconian names, such as "C.R.A.S.H." (Community Resources Against Street Hoodlums) and "Operation Hammer," the LAPD's activities included round-ups of suspected gang members and destructive search and seizure missions whose purposes were not only to find contraband, but also to intimidate. The War on Drugs provided a pretext for the LAPD to adopt paramilitary equipment such as the batter ram, a small tank whose purpose was to break down the doors and walls of suspected crack houses in dramatic fashion.[22]

Through their music, N.W.A. found a way to shed light on these and other issues from the perspective of those living in the neighborhoods where the LAPD was most active. Rather than critique these problems from a third person perspective, N.W.A. adopted the first-person personas of gangsters themselves. In the segregated Los Angeles environment where Black youth were often viewed suspiciously as an unwelcome presence and inner city communities such as Compton and South Central became virtual no-go zones for affluent white citizens, N.W.A. offered listeners a voyeuristic tour of the devastation and mayhem. On songs like "Straight Outta Compton" and "Gangsta Gangsta" group members Ice Cube, MC Ren, and Eazy-E bragged about their merciless attitudes and penchant for violence. Using the media-induced panic over gangs and drugs to their advantage, the group made their infamy pay.[23] What is more, by taking on the role of the "bad guy," they captured public attention and put themselves in a position where they could respond irreverently to authority.[24] "Fuck The Police," which earned Ruthless Records and its distributor Priority Records a warning letter from the FBI, featured N.W.A. members taking the stand in a mock courtroom to testify against the LAPD's widespread racial profiling and use of excessive force.

Conclusion: rap comes full circle

If *Straight Outta Compton* critiqued the criminalization of Black youth by embodying gang stereotypes in dramatic fashion, then *Straight out the Jungle* by New York City-based group the Jungle Brothers sought to portray hip-hop culture and Black life in the most uplifting terms. Released on November 8, the album brought a Black bohemianism to 1988 that contrasted markedly with the roughneck aggressiveness of N.W.A. Celebrating Black pride and African American heritage, the jungle proved a fertile space. In the album's title track, for example, MCs Mike Gee and Afrika Baby Bam refer to "the jungle" as the origin of authentic, pure Africanness as well as a metaphor for the Black experience in white America. Whereas Public Enemy and BDP mined the Black Power imagery and rhetoric of militant leaders such as Malcolm X, the Jungle Brothers concentrated on the cultural nationalist legacy of the 1960s and 1970s, adding their voices to a resurgence of Afrocentrism in the late 1980s and 1990s. As if seeking to use rap music to rebuild a connection to Africa, the album's title track "Straight Out the Jungle" was built from a mixture of samples including African American soul artist James Brown and Cameroonian saxophonist Manu Dibango.

The Jungle Brothers' playful Afrocentricity initiated the Native Tongues movement, a collective of like-minded artists that would grow to include, among others, A Tribe Called Quest, De La Soul, and Queen Latifah – all of whom would release historic albums the following year. The Native Tongues embraced rap music as an alternative cultural space, blending the artistic experimentation of 1960s freedom jazz with the counter-cultural tendencies of one of early hip-hop's most influential DJs: Afrika Bambaataa, founder and leader of the Universal Zulu Nation.

Finally, it is important to acknowledge another reason that makes 1988 special: the year marks a time when female artists emerged better represented and more central to the industry than at any time before, and possibly ever since. Although women, such as Sha Rock of the Funky Four Plus One, have been a part of hip-hop music since its early days, 1988 and 1989 witnessed unprecedented stylistic diversity and thematic development in the work of numerous talented female rappers, including Salt-N-Pepa, MC Lyte, Queen Latifah, and Monie Love. Ranging from the proactive, dance-floor sensuality of Salt-N-Pepa's "Push It" to the virtuosic lyrical flow of Queen Latifah and Monie Love's "Ladies First," women proved that they could deliver funky rhymes and empowering lyrics that rivaled those of their male counterparts.

The diversity of the artists, viewpoints, and sounds expressed in the music of 1988 represents a moment of transformation and growth for the rap genre, prefiguring many of the stylistic categories used to describe hip-hop and rap music today. Contemporary listeners often invoke "gangsta rap," "conscious hip-hop," or "pop rap," categories that have clear connections to 1988 releases by N.W.A., Public Enemy, and DJ Jazzy Jeff and the Fresh Prince respectively. Although it can be enlightening to view 1988 as prologue for future developments and artists, such retroactive assessments run the risk of muting the sense of experimentation and excitement that animated this particularly creative twelve-month period. One of the remarkable things about 1988, as Mike Gee of the Jungle Brothers points out, is that "there was a sense of inclusiveness in hip-hop that doesn't exist today. Today, you'd get laughed at [for liking both N.W.A. and the Fresh Prince], but then it was like, 'look what's possible!'"[25]

Whether or not we accept Mike Gee's implication that hip-hop music has become less inclusive and more narrow-minded than it used to be, 1988 remains an important and pivotal year for rap. Yet how we evaluate claims about it or some other year being rap's greatest depends largely on where we stand. A DJ, for example, might look back fondly on 1988 in part because of the prominent role that DJs played in the albums that were released that year. Indeed, one explanation for why the year is held in such high esteem is the variety of angles from which judgments of excellence can be made. The year 1988 is an important one for rappers who cultivated increasing lyrical sophistication and heightened rhythmic sensibilities. For producers, it signaled the widespread adoption of newly available technologies to transform how beats were made and consequently how they sounded. And it provided rappers with an opportunity to step more assuredly than ever before into roles as spokespeople for their generation. For Black youth and other members of the hip-hop generation in New York, Los Angeles, and beyond, rap music grew into a multi-faceted site where musicians and their fans could make sense of the world they had inherited and find their place within it. In some instances rap provided a canvas for direct political critique, but in others it also served more broadly as a testament to the creativity and intelligence of those from whom few outside America's ghettos expected anything good to come. As a form of self-expression, rap captured the restless energy, desire to be seen and heard, and the humanity of artists that had few other outlets. Resisting the nostalgia that prompts some to declare 1988 the beginning of a "golden age" when music was simply better than it is today, we can acknowledge that the music released that year was indeed great, but it was also transformative, daring, and timely.

Selected albums released in 1988
2 Live Crew, *Move Somthin'* (Luke Skyywalker Records XR-101).
Audio Two, *What More Can I Say?* (First Priority Music, Atlantic 7 90907–1).
Bass Patrol, *Rock This Planet* (Joey Boy Records JB-5020).
Big Daddy Kane, *Long Live the Kane* (Cold Chillin' 9 25731–2).
Biz Markie, *Goin' Off* (Cold Chillin' 9 25675–2).

Boogie Down Productions, *By All Means Necessary* (Jive 1097–1-J).

DJ Cash Money and Marvelous, *Where's the Party At?* (Sleeping Bag Records
TLX-42016).

DJ Jazzy Jeff and the Fresh Prince, *He's the DJ, I'm the Rapper* (Jive 1091–1-J).

Doug E. Fresh and The Get Fresh Crew, *The World's Greatest Entertainer* (Reality
F-9658).

Eazy-E, *Eazy-Duz-It* (Ruthless Records, Priority Records SL57100).

Eric B and Rakim, *Follow the Leader* (UNI Records UNI-3).

EPMD, *Strictly Business* (Fresh Records LPRE-82006).

Ice-T, *Power* (Sire 9 25765–1).

Jungle Brothers, *Straight Out the Jungle* (Warlock Records WAR-2704).

JVC FORCE, *Doin' Damage* (B-Boy Records BB 20–1000).

Kid 'N Play, *2 Hype* (Select Records SEL 21628).

King Tee, *Act a Fool* (Capitol Records C1 90544).

Lakim Shabazz, *Pure Righteousness* (Tuff City TUF LP 5557).

Marley Marl, *In Control Volume 1* (Cold Chillin' 92 57831).

Masters of Ceremony, *Dynamite* (4th and Broadway BWAY-4010).

MC Lyte, *Lyte as a Rock* (First Priority Music, Atlantic 7 90905–1).

MC Shan, *Born To Be Wild* (Cold Chillin' 9 25797–2).

MC Shy D, *Comin' Correct in 88* (Luke Skyywalker Records XR-1005).

N.W.A., *Straight Outta Compton* (Ruthless Records, Priority Records SL 57102).

Public Enemy, *It Takes a Nation of Millions to Hold us Back* (Def Jam Recordings 527
358–1).

Rob Base and DJ E-Z Rock, *It Takes Two* (Profile Records PRO-1267).

Rodney O & Joe Cooley, *Me and Joe* (Egyptian Empire Records DMSR 00777).

Run-DMC, *Tougher Than Leather* (Profile Records PRO-1265).

Salt-N-Pepa, *A Salt with a Deadly Pepa* (Next Plateau Records Inc. PL 1011).

Schoolly D, *Smoke Some Kill* (Jive 1101–1-J).

Sir Mix-A-Lot, *Swass* (Nastymix Records NMR 70123–1).

Slick Rick, *The Great Adventures of Slick Rick* (Def Jam Recordings C 40513, FC
40513).

Stetsasonic, *In Full Gear* (Tommy Boy TBLP 1017).

Super Lover Cee and Casanova Rud, *Girls I Got 'Em Locked* (Elektra, DNA
International Records 9–60807–1).

The 45 King, *Master of the Game* (Tuff City TUF LP 5553).

Too $hort, *Life is . . . Too $hort* (Dangerous Music 1149–1-J).

Tuff Crew, *Danger Zone* (Soo Deff Records, Warlock Records WAR-2705).

Ultramagnetic MCs, *Critical Beatdown* (Next Plateau Records Inc. PLCD 1013).

Further reading

Chang, Jeff, *Can't Stop Won't Stop: A History of the Hip-Hop Generation* (New York:
St Martin's Press, 2005).

Charnas, Dan, *The Big Payback: The History of the Business of Hip-Hop* (New York:
New American Library, 2010).

Forman, Murray, *The 'Hood Comes First: Race, Space, and Place in Rap and Hip-Hop,
Music/Culture* (Middletown, CT: Wesleyan University Press, 2002).

Katz, Mark, *Groove Music: The Art and Culture of the Hip-Hop DJ* (New York: Oxford University Press, 2012).

Rose, Tricia, *Black Noise: Rap Music and Black Culture in Contemporary America* (Middletown, CT: Wesleyan University Press, 1994).

Wang, Oliver, *Classic Material: The Hip-Hop Album Guide* (Toronto: ECW Press, 2003).

Notes

1 Charise Cheney, *Brothers Gonna Work It Out: Sexual Politics in the Golden Age of Rap Nationalism* (New York University Press, 2005); "Hip-Hop's Greatest Year: Fifteen Albums That Made Rap Explode," *Rolling Stone*, February 12, 2008.

2 Dan Charnas, *The Big Payback: The History of the Business of Hip-Hop* (New York: New American Library, 2010), pp. 42–61.

3 Fans and critics also tend to name 1993 as hip-hop and rap music's best year, citing classic albums such as Snoop Doggy Dogg's *Doggystyle*, A Tribe Called Quest's *Midnight Marauders*, and Wu-Tang Clan's *Enter the Wu-Tang 36 Chambers*. Not only was the amount of music released in 1993 greater than in 1988, but 1993 also marks the year when radio and music television fully embraced hardcore hip-hop and rap music as mainstream, youth-oriented pop. Supporters of 1988 can counter, however, that the diversity of styles and perspectives that make 1993 such a special year can be traced back to 1988.

4 Charnas, *The Big Payback*, pp. 147–171.

5 Jerry Heller, *Ruthless: A Memoir* (New York: Gallery, 2007), pp. 128–140.

6 Murray Forman, *The 'Hood Comes First: Race, Space, and Place in Hip-Hop and Rap Music* (Middletown, CT: Wesleyan University Press, 2002), p. 171.

7 Mark Katz, *Groove Music: The Art and Culture of the Hip-Hop DJ* (New York: Oxford University Press, 2012), pp. 101–108.

8 John Davis and The Monster Orchestra, "I Can't Stop" b/w "I Get a Kick" (Sam Records S-12451, 1976); T-Connection, "Let Yourself Go" b/w "Groove to Get Down" (TK Disco 82, 1977).

9 Katz, *Groove Music*, pp. 114–117.

10 "Flow" is a colloquial term describing an MC's characteristic combination of rhyme scheme and rhythmic delivery.

11 Joseph Schloss, *Making Beats: The Art of Sample-Based Hip-Hop* (Middletown, CT: Wesleyan University Press, 2004), pp. 25–62.

12 Katz, *Groove Music*, pp. 100–126.

13 Robert Fink, "The Story of ORCH5, or the Classical Ghost in the Hip-hop Machine," *Popular Music* 24/3 (2005): 339–356.

14 Tricia Rose, *Black Noise: Rap Music and Black Culture in Contemporary America* (Middletown, CT: Wesleyan University Press, 1994), p. 109.

15 Oliver Wang, "Beat-making," in Charles Hiroshi Garrett (ed.), *Grove Dictionary of American Music*, 2nd edn. (Oxford University Press, 2013).

16 Kembrew McLeod and Peter DiCola, *Creative License: The Law and Culture of Digital Sampling* (Durham, NC: Duke University Press, 2011), pp. 19–35.

17 Mark Dery, "Public Enemy: Confrontation," *Keyboard Magazine*. September 1990, pp. 81–96.

18 *Ibid.*, p. 83.

19 Schloss, *Making Beats*, pp. 38–40.

20 Jeff Chang, *Can't Stop Won't Stop: A History of the Hip-Hop Generation* (New York: St. Martin's Press, 2005), pp. 231–262.

21 Michelle Alexander, *The New Jim Crow: Mass Incarceration in the Age of Colorblindness* (New York: The New Press, 2012), pp. 53–54.

22 The LAPD's batter ram was immortalized in a rap song: Toddy Tee, "Batterram" (Evejim Records 1979, 1985).

23 Eithne Quinn, *Nuthin' But a "G" Thang: The Culture and Commerce of Gangsta Rap, Popular Cultures, Everyday Lives* (New York: Columbia University Press, 2005), p. 169.

24 Robin D. G. Kelley, *Race Rebels: Culture, Politics, and the Black Working Class* (New York: The Free Press, 1994), pp. 202–203.

25 Mike Gee as quoted in "Hip-Hop's Greatest Year."

25 "Where ya at?" Hip-hop's political locations in the Obama era

MICHAEL P. JEFFRIES

Whenever a major album is released, millions of self-appointed music reviewers flock to social media to share their thoughts. Everyday consumers, celebrities, and even politicians had plenty to say about Jay-Z's highly anticipated 2013 LP, *Magna Carta Holy Grail*. One elected official took it upon himself to release a barrage of thoughts on Twitter about the record from start to finish, most of which were positive. "ONLY #JayZ can pull off a #hiphop ode to Kurt Cobain and REM. Not just an ode... But lyrical references! Pretty sick," he typed.[1] The reviewer in question was not Barack or Michelle Obama. It was not Corey Booker, Harold Ford Jr., Kendrick Meek, or Kwame Kilpatrick, four Democratic Black male public figures born in the post-Civil Rights era, and once thought to be the vanguard of a new wave of hip-hop generation politicians.[2] The self-styled hip-hop journalist was Congressman Trey Radel, a thirty-seven-year-old white male Republican and former conservative media mogul, from Florida's 19th congressional district.

Imani Perry establishes hip-hop's "political location" as one defined by blackness, despite hip-hop's multiracial history.[3] This means not only that hip-hop is comprised of artistic features that grow from Black Atlantic cultural exchanges, but that when hip-hop is politicized it is heavily racialized and a form of blackness is implicated. Scholars have long argued that mainstream white America has a love/hate relationship with hip-hop.[4] There is a precarious balance in the cultural realm between the gradual commoditization and absorption of hip-hop aesthetics into the mainstream, and a constant strain of revulsion directed at lawless, disrespectful "thug" rappers and those who follow them.[5] Black vernacular virtuosity and projections of hypermasculine danger have always been popular with white consumers and the culture industry, so the most purportedly dangerous rappers are often the most saleable. This was never more clear than during the commercial explosion of hip-hop during the 1990s and early 2000s, as previously fearsome rappers like Ice Cube and Ice-T became movie stars, and hip-hop soundtracks made their way into fast food commercials and television cartoons.

But this balance between revelry and revulsion has not historically existed in the realm of electoral politics, including during hip-hop's late twentieth-century ascent to mainstream prominence. Through the Bill Clinton (1992–2000) and George W. Bush (2000–2008) presidential years, there was no sign that hip-hop would eventually find its way into legislative halls and on to campaign trails. And for the most part, the most visible hip-hop acts expressed little interest in such inclusion. If anything, prior to the 2008 election of Barack Obama, relations between hip-hop's commercial vanguard and the political establishment were growing more contentious, as George W. Bush became a favorite target among dissenting rap stars. For example, Common inserted a jab at Bush during an unapologetically radical spoken word performance at HBO's Def Poetry Jam. Kanye West famously asserted, "George Bush doesn't care about black people," during a live telethon for Hurricane Katrina victims. Even 50 Cent, who previously (and cryptically) noted that he saw a great deal of himself in Bush, was sour on Bush by 2007, explaining "George Bush has a talent: He has less compassion than the average human. By all means, I don't aspire to be like George Bush."[6] From "conscious" rappers like Common, to gangsta anti-heroes like 50 Cent, hip-hop was overwhelmingly hostile toward the American political establishment in the early twenty-first century. Politicians either tuned rappers out or used them to score political points with conservative constituents via thinly coded racist appeals.

All of this changed dramatically as President Obama made the transition from Illinois State Senator to Democratic candidate for president in 2007. The early years of the Obama era were rife with enthusiasm among prominent hip-hop figures. But even at the height of Obama-mania, hip-hoppers' commentary and disposition toward mainstream politics was multi-faceted. Obama remains a figure frequently invoked by rappers in various contexts, but as disappointment with the Obama administration and the political process has grown since 2008, a stream of critical and politically radical commentary has emerged. These dynamic crosscurrents of Obama discourse in hip-hop force us to reconsider hip-hop's political location. Hip-hop cultures can no longer be described purely in terms of counter-hegemonic Blackness. But even as they flow into electoral politics and other elements of the mainstream, hip-hop discourses retain their brew of social critique and irreverent imagination.

Hip-hop's place in Obama era politics

After a brief flirtation with Hillary Clinton as hip-hop celebrities' candidate of choice during the early stages of the 2008 presidential election, a gaggle of highly visible hip-hop stars threw themselves behind upstart candidate Barack Obama. In part, rappers' embrace of Obama was driven by the Senator's trendiness and charisma. Obama was an easy lyrical reference point that rappers knew would resonate with audiences. As Obama's national election prospects grew, hip-hop acts increasingly commented on the substantive meaning of his campaign. Talib Kweli cast Obama as "someone speaking my own language amidst a sea of double talk,"[7] and Common suggested, "He represents what hip-hop is about. Hip-hop is about progress, the struggle."[8]

Rappers' early injection into Obama-related discussion is noteworthy because they forced Obama to recognize and address hip-hop as a salient cultural force. Obama did not campaign in 2008 as a hip-hop candidate, but he was keenly aware that hip-hop celebrities had the ears of young voters. Two-thirds of voters aged eighteen to twenty-nine voted for Obama in 2008, and this core demographic identified with the sleek visual and communicative aesthetics of the Obama brand, which included a massive internet presence and a street art inspired campaign poster designed by Shepard Fairey. Obama could not ignore hip-hop, so he carefully incorporated it into his public image.

The character of this incorporation constitutes one of the major arguments of this chapter – Obama's strategic engagement established a new political location for hip-hop, setting a course that subsequent politicians have followed. Rather than distancing himself from the most recognizable signs and performers of hip-hop culture, and keeping hip-hop outside the borders of mainstream politics, Obama repeatedly demonstrates hip-hop literacy and affinity for rap music. These demonstrations take multiple forms, including direct and indirect references, connections to hip-hop celebrities, and light-hearted, hip-hop music-infused public appearances. Simultaneously, President Obama leaves himself the rhetorical wiggle room to distance himself from hip-hop when necessary. The president draws upon old tropes of hip-hop-driven moral panic, maintaining his status as a moderate, and defending himself from opponents who might use Obama's hip-hop associations to cast him as an angry and dangerous Black radical. In other words, hip-hop's new political locations have not replaced the old; they exist alongside one another, and Obama operates in multiple spaces.

Obama has consistently drawn on hip-hop in public. The 2008 election season saw Obama dance to Beyoncé and Jay-Z's "Crazy in Love" on Ellen Degeneres's talk show, give a subtle acknowledgment to Jay-Z by brushing off his shoulders during a campaign event, and confirm that Ludacris's music was on his iPod.[9] In 2009, he shouted "Hallelujah, Holla Back!" during a commencement speech at Notre Dame University, a catch phrase that only the hip-hop literate would recognize as the signature call of John Brown, winner of VH1's "The (White) Rapper Reality Show." At the 2011 White House Correspondents dinner, the president playfully mentioned 2pac, Notorious B.I.G., Lil' Jon, and Ol' Dirty Bastard. At the 2012 dinner, he joked about singing Young Jeezy, a clear reference to the most popular Obama-rap song, Jeezy's "My President," and at the 2013 dinner, Obama strolled on to the stage with DJ Khaled's "All I Do Is Win" playing in the background. Finally, the official Obama Tumblr page invoked the image and branding of rap pioneers Run D.M.C. during an advertising blitz for the Democratic National Convention in 2012. The webpage featured a black and white depiction of Bill Clinton, Joe Biden, and Barack Obama with the words "Run DNC" beneath their faces, written in a font and style that rap fans would immediately associate with the iconic rap group.

The common thread tying these instances together is their hip, light-hearted tone. They are specifically designed to appeal to and tickle constituents who not only understand the references, but understand Obama's signifying upon them as a sign that he is not merely knowledgeable, but clever and fun. This is not about content. There is no explicitly ideological message embedded in these tactics, and there is no forthright commentary about hip-hop. But the frequency with which hip-hop images, ideas, and performers are cast in a positive light within the political mainstream would have been unimaginable a decade ago.

After 2008, Obama's peers recognized that this sort of limited affiliation with hip-hop does not necessarily endanger one's chances of winning an election. Given the voter demographics, policy, and rhetoric of both parties, we might expect Democrats to continue to utilize hip-hop as a means to brand their candidates and communicate their messages. But as evidenced by Congressman Radel's Jay-Z album review, conservative Republicans have found a place for hip-hop in their self-styling. Radel is not a nationally recognizable symbol of the party, but Florida Senator Marco Rubio is, so much so that he is one of a handful of candidates with his eye on the 2016 GOP nomination for president. In a 2012 interview with *GQ*, Rubio talked extensively about his appreciation for hip-hop, calling Public Enemy "dominant," and listing "Straight Outta Compton," by N.W.A., "Killuminati," by 2pac, and "Lose Yourself," by Eminem as his three favorite songs.[10] This is mind-blowing: a Republican presidential hopeful *praising* Public Enemy, N.W.A., and Tupac, three of the most iconic hip-hop scapegoats and symbols of Black danger and criminality.

Of course, Rubio does not follow up his commentary with a strong critique of the policies and discourse that continue to lock poor people of color behind bars and cast them as social pariahs. Then again, neither does Obama. For all the subtext and implicit incorporation of hip-hop into his brand and public persona, the President's explicit commentary about hip-hop is conflicted and ambivalent at best. For example, he affirms that we need to take hip-hop seriously, because it is "reflective of the culture of the inner city, with its problems, but also its potential, its energy, its challenges to the status quo."[11] But there is no causality in this statement; no indication that the problematic culture of the inner city is the direct result of institutional racism and governmental neglect, as manifest in employment and housing discrimination, the proliferation of firearms, the abandonment of public education, the War on Drugs, racial profiling, and mass incarceration. Rather than publicly make such arguments about the roots of Black American suffering, Obama has repeatedly argued for an increased sense of personal responsibility, especially as it pertains to Black fathers and child socialization.[12] Such calls may be well intentioned, but when emphasis is placed on cultural and personal choice instead of racism as a political force that restricts choice, victim blaming prevents problem solving.

On other occasions, statements by Obama and his surrogates align even more closely with conservative moral panic about hip-hop. When Ludacris released the song "Politics (Obama is Here)" during the campaign season in 2008, the Obama team was compelled to condemn its lyrics, which featured several impolite insults directed at Hillary Clinton, George W. Bush, and John McCain. But campaign spokesman Bill Burton's statement addressed more than just the song. He explained,

> rap lyrics today too often perpetuate misogyny, materialism and degrading images that [Obama] doesn't want his daughters or any children exposed to. This song is not only outrageously offensive to Senator Clinton, Senator McCain and President Bush, it is offensive to all of us who are trying to raise our children with the values we hold dear.[13]

At issue here is not merely the condemnation, but the emphasis on children's welfare, which echoes the concerns of Tipper Gore and the PMRC from the late 1980s and early 1990s. Casting rap as a threat to children, and therefore all that is innocent and pure in our society, moves beyond rejecting the song's message, stoking antagonism toward hip-hop and scoring points with moderates and conservatives.

Arguments about the damage done by hip-hop cannot be reduced to the absurd notion that the music turns Black children into deadbeats and criminals. But first lady Michelle Obama has implied that fantasies about the rap lifestyle are incompatible with more respectable and realistic notions of success. She laments, "Instead of dreaming of being a teacher or a lawyer or a business leader, [today's young Black people] fantasiz[e] about being a baller or a rapper."[14] This is just one version of the notion that there is something about the hip-hop "attitude" that "keeps Blacks down."[15] A slightly more sophisticated version of this belief suggests there is a clear association between hip-hop style and/or self-presentation, and Black deviance. In other words, looking like a rapper is not respectable, so you cannot expect to be treated with respect.

Many commentators stop short of the claim that this form of racial profiling according to dress is perfectly appropriate. But several politicians and commentators urge men of color to recognize the fact that they are judged by what they wear, and should, therefore, choose a politics of respectability strategy – one that includes more formal and conservative dress – to protect themselves from mistreatment.[16] In an interview with famed hip-hop DJ and MTV host Sway, Obama condemned any and all discrimination on the basis of race, gender, and sexual orientation. He also said that legislation mandating that young people pull up their pants was a waste of time. However, he defended employers' right to set standards of respectability in the workplace, implying that sagging pants were not usually up to such standards. He added that "brothers should pull up their pants" as a sign of respect for their mothers, grandmothers, and others who do not want to see their underwear.[17]

Obama's interview with Sway is not explicitly about hip-hop, but Sway is a hip-hop DJ and celebrity, and Obama is talking about sagging pants (a clothing style with clear roots in American hip-hop), and Obama directly addresses young Black men as "brothers." So there is no question about the set of messages being delivered to young Black men about the perils of hip-hop style. Hip-hop remains central to a larger discourse about respectability that overshadows the structural reasons for crime and antisocial behaviors in impoverished Black communities. Philadelphia Mayor Michael Nutter, who is Black, gave an impassioned speech that illustrates these connections after a string of cowardly crimes and assaults by Black teenagers in Philadelphia. Nutter plainly stated that if they wanted to avoid racial profiling by police, business owners, and everyday citizens, young people should "stop acting like fools." He continued:

> And another thing. Take those doggone hoodies down, especially in the summer. Pull your pants up and buy a belt, because no one wants to see your underwear or the crack of your butt. Nobody. Buy a belt. Buy a belt. Nobody wants to see your underwear. Comb your hair – and get some grooming skills. Comb your hair. Running round here with your hair all over the place. Learn some manners.[18]

Nutter's injection of hoodies into this discussion of young Black men and the politics of respectability calls to mind one of the most famous cases of racial profiling and violence against Black men in the last quarter century, the murder of seventeen-year-old Trayvon Martin in Sanford, Florida. Hip-hop was not directly implicated or discussed as the Martin murder story took shape, but again, the image of the threatening young Black male is embedded in a discourse heavily reliant on hip-hop themes and imagery. It goes without saying that a hoodie is not universally understood as a symbol of criminality, or of anything, really. It is just as likely to be worn by someone camping in a nature preserve as it is by someone doing calisthenics at a football practice. But the hooded sweatshirt has been a staple of hip-hop style for decades; as the Notorious B.I.G. explains in his deeply moving portrayal of inner city depression, "Suicidal Thoughts" (1993), "It don't make sense, going to Heaven with the goodie-goodies/ Dressed in white – I like black Timbs and black hoodies." So the racist implicit association that stains young Black men with the mark of the criminal is interwoven with this widely recognizable garment.

Racist implicit association between hip-hop style and young Black male criminality came full circle during the Trayvon Martin controversy. Bigoted conservative groups were convinced that the innocent image of Martin most frequently used by the media was an image from far earlier in Martin's life; a wild distortion of the powerful, dangerous Black monster that George Zimmerman stalked, fought with, and shot. Such beliefs were totally false, but in place of the heavily circulated image of Martin smiling for the camera, an image of rapper the Game, a man more than thirty years of age, with a portfolio of scowling publicity photos, was circulated as the "real" Trayvon Martin.[19]

The link between these invocations of Black male hip-hop danger and President Obama is not causal. It is not the president's fault that racist stereotypes about Black male hip-hop criminality are so deeply embedded in the American imagination that to many there is no difference between Trayvon Martin and the embellished, corporately funded, gangsta rap persona of the Game. But the point is that hip-hop remains heavily politicized, and it remains tied to its old political location, as the eye of a storm of moral panic threatening wholesome mainstream America. Though Obama embraces light-hearted hip-hop imagery and signification that endears him to younger audiences, he also travels along the same discursive paths that posit fears of sagging pants and hoodies as justifications for institutional racism and violence against innocent Black men. The president's unwillingness to explicitly disrupt those patterns allows the stereotypes and racism to keep circulating with horrible material effects on people's lives. Prominent rappers have plenty to say on these and other facets of the Obama era.

Obama's place in modern hip-hop

Just as hip-hop's location within mainstream politics cannot be painted with one broad stroke, Obama occupies multiple locations within hip-hop. Several prominent hip-hop celebrities have constructed what is best described as an ambivalent stance toward the president and the political process. Meanwhile, Jay-Z, the star with perhaps the greatest gravitational pull in the hip-hop universe, has separated himself with an unprecedented level of consistent positive engagement with Obama. And finally, there is a visible and vocal contingent of hip-hop stars who are explicitly critical of the Obama administration and mainstream politics more broadly.

Young Jeezy's aforementioned smash hit "My President" is by far the most recognizable hip-hop connection to Obama, and it is often interpreted as an endorsement. But a closer reading reveals that the song is steeped in ambivalence and trepidation, despite its celebratory tone. Nas's contribution to Jeezy's track is especially poignant, as he laments that "no President ever did shit for me," and warns Obama not to let ego and the compromise-laden culture of American politics ruin his chance to fight for justice. After Obama's first term, Nas expressed continued support for the president, but qualified it, explaining,

> I've been disappointed by politics since the day I was born. The historic part of him being elected president was got, and everyone was happy about that, and I'm glad I lived to see it. The flipside is, after we get over that, it's back to the politics, and it's something which doesn't have time for people.[20]

Hip-hop mogul and 2008 presidential inauguration attendee Sean "P Diddy" Combs expressed sentiment similar to Nas's in 2011, explaining, "I love the president like most of us. I just want the president to do better."[21] Given the disasters that have befallen American workers and people of color, such disappointment is certainly justified. But the troubles of the first four years did not lead to full-scale revolt against Obama because alternative options proved so dissatisfying. As rapper and producer Kendrick Lamar explained just prior to the 2012 election, "I think I'm going to go ahead [and vote for Barack Obama], just because I can*not* see Mitt Romney [winning]. I'll be on food stamps my whole life! I just don't feel like he's got a good heart at all."[22]

If hip-hop stars like Nas, Kendrick Lamar, and P Diddy are somewhere in the middle of the spectrum of support for Obama, Jay-Z sits at one of the extremes, with an overwhelmingly positive orientation toward the president. P Diddy's "Vote or Die" voter registration campaign in 2008 was a landmark effort, but it was, officially speaking, non-partisan. During the 2008 election cycle, Jay was unapologetically supportive of Obama, but cautious not to allow his involvement to damage Obama's reputation. "I didn't want the association with rappers and gangsta rappers to hinder anything that [Obama] was doing," he said. "I came when I was needed; I didn't make any comments in the press, go too far or put my picture with Obama on MySpace, Twitter, none of that."[23] But as hip-hop's location within mainstream politics shifts, Jay-Z has taken a stand and aligned himself with Obama, for better or worse. Jay has hosted upscale fundraisers for the president, produced an advertisement for the 2012 campaign, performed an anti-Romney version of his hit song "99 Problems," and attended inaugural ceremonies and parties.

Despite a momentary flap with the White House over a vacation to Cuba, the depth of Jay-Z's identification with Obama is troubling at times, especially as it pertains to the rapper's notions of political responsibility and accountability. In 2013, Jay described his mere presence as "charity," which he admitted sounds arrogant. He continued, "Just who I am, just like Obama is. Obama provides hope. Whether he does anything, that hope that he provides for a nation and outside of America is enough."[24] Musicians and actors are not contractually obligated to be political spokespeople or advance social justice. But the trouble here is the conflation between Jay-Z's role and the president's. Obama serves at the discretion of the citizenry, and by definition he is accountable to them. His chief purpose is not to embody charity or "hope," it is to keep the gears of democracy turning. This is the concern raised by hip-hop pioneer Russell Simmons in direct response to Jay-Z's dismissal of Occupy Wall Street:

> You're rich and I'm rich. But, today it's close to impossible to be you or me and get out of Marcy Projects or Hollis, Queens without changing our government to have our politicians work for the people who elect them and not the special interests and corporations that pay them. Because we know that these special interests are nothing special at all. In fact, they spend millions of dollars destroying the fabric of the black community and make billions of dollars in return.[25]

Simmons's embrace of Occupy Wall Street is one of the more public suggestions by hip-hop stars that the government and Obama no longer serve the people's interests. Other rappers echo these sentiments with far more aggressive condemnations of Obama, and more insistence that the solution to seemingly intractable social problems lies beyond mainstream politics. Self-described revolutionary hip-hop group dead prez laughed off Obama's 2009 economic stimulus plan as inconsequential, as it only stimulates corporations that profit from Black debasement, and will never improve the economic standing of working-class and poor people of color. Dead prez also suggested that Obama was no better than his predecessor, George W. Bush, so far as social justice was concerned.[26]

Atlanta rapper Killer Mike offers similar analysis on his critically acclaimed track "Reagan" (2012), a song that mercilessly dissects the Reagan era and describes the US government as a thin veil for oligarchy. Though the song goes into painstaking details about the plagues unleashed during the Reagan administration, especially the War on Drugs and rise of mass incarceration, there is a clear connection between Reagan and those who replaced him in the White House. The Bushes, Bill Clinton, and Obama are all "Just [sic] employee[s] of the country's real masters," the corporations that profit from the expansion of the military and prison state. In describing the song and his political orientation, Killer Mike is uneasy with the notion that he is a "political" rapper for the same reasons Nas is suspicious of politics: politics is not about people. Mike elaborates:

> A lot of people try to peg me as a political rapper and I'm not. I'm a social commentator and at times people have politicized the things I say, but I don't care too much for any political party. I care about people. Under Reagan, drugs were allowed to flood our community and wipe out two to three generations of people that could have kept my community growing, and I take exception to that.[27]

Lupe Fiasco's widely publicized Twitter dialog with comedian D. L. Hughley six weeks before the 2012 election is emblematic of this spirit. Lupe's music, especially his LPs *Food and Liquor* (2006) and *The Cool* (2007), earned him significant critical acclaim, including multiple Grammy nominations, and respect as a sharp and socially astute entertainer. Lupe announced that he did not vote in 2008 and would abstain from the 2012 election because, "Obama need swing states and white people not radical rappers kissing his ass to win this election." In response, Hughley chastised Lupe for misleading young Black men and possibly suppressing their vote. "Young black men are going to listen to him," Hughley explained. "They are the ones who have decisions made for them, [decisions] that they are not even involved in, which is silly to me. You can't go through life and not be a participant, and hope things work out for your benefit." Convincing Lupe to change his stance was out of the question, but the rapper did reply to Hughley with an alternative plan, "I vote for Grace Lee Boggs . . . put her on the ballot and i'd finance the campaign my d*mn self @realdlhughley do u even know who she is???" He continued, "Better yet @RealDLHughley you put up 50k and I'll put up 50k and let's flesh out some programs for rural & inner city youths our d*mn selves."[28] The possibility that hip-hop might turn increasingly toward "do it yourself" or alternative forms of political action is one of many worth considering as the Obama era winds down.

Where ya at?

It is easy to forget that hip-hop is only forty years old, considering the political maturity of its artists and the political weight hip-hop cultures carry in the discursive realm. While some artists have chosen an ethic of conspicuous consumption and mass appeal rather than politicizing their careers, a remarkable number of hip-hop artists demonstrate stunning political maturity and bravery, openly challenging police and politicians to fulfill their mission to protect and serve the people. The social analysis woven through hip-hop performances of eras past has proven tragically prophetic. Rap songs from the 1980s about the abuses of corporate power, the deterioration of poor Black and Brown neighborhoods, and the growth of the surveillance state would comprise an awfully compelling soundtrack to America's contemporary social troubles.

Obama uses hip-hop performances and representations to appeal to multiple audiences, including those who are still seduced by a form of conservatism grounded in damaging race and class bigotry. It is tempting to look at the current landscape and conclude that hip-hop-fueled moral panic appeals will soon disappear, not only due to demographic shifts in the electorate, but because hip-hop styles and sensibilities suffuse across all forms of consumer culture. It is equally tempting to look at the Obama model and conservatives' attempt to copy it, and predict that hip-hop will be further incorporated into mainstream politics in the current election cycles. But such predictions are faulty, because they rely on a static, monolithic notion of hip-hop culture. The unpredictability of hip-hop's future political locations is not a sign of weakness or insignificance. It is testament to the power of hip-hop as a form of communication and cultural toolkit for examining and shaping the world.

Notes

1 Brian Ries, "Rep Trey Radel Reviews New Jay-Z," *The Daily Beast*, July 16, 2013. Available at www.thedailybeast.com/articles/2013/07/16/rep-trey-radel-reviews-new-jay-z-album.html.
2 "Where Have All the Hip Hop Politicians Gone?" *National Public Radio*, January 10, 2013. Available at www.npr.org/2013/01/10/169047496/where-have-all-the-hip-hop-politicians-gone.
3 Imani Perry, *Prophets of the Hood: Politics and Poetics in Hip Hop* (Durham, NC: Duke University Press, 2004) pp. 10, 26–27. Perry cites Houston Baker's *Black Studies, Rap, and the Academy* (University of Chicago Press, 1993) as an influence.
4 Todd Boyd, *Young, Black, Rich, and Famous: The Rise of the NBA, the Hip Hop Invasion, and the Transformation of American Culture* (New York: Doubleday, 2003); Nelson George, *Hip Hop America* (New York: Viking, 1998); Imani Perry, *Prophets of the Hood: Politics and Poetics in Hip Hop* (Durham, NC: Duke University Press, 2004); Tricia Rose, *Black Noise: Rap Music and Black Culture in Contemporary America* (Middletown, CT: Wesleyan University Press, 1994).
5 Rose, *Black Noise*.
6 Roman Wolfe, "Rapper 50 Cent Disses President George Bush," July 18, 2007, *Allhiphop.com*. Available at http://allhiphop.

com/2007/07/18/rapper-50-cent-disses-president-george-bush/.

7 Talib Kweli, "Open Letter to President Barack Obama," *Rap Genius*. Available at http://news.rapgenius.com/Talib-kweli-open-letter-to-president-barack-obama-2008-lyrics.

8 As quoted in Peter Hamby, "Barack Obama Gets Name-Dropped in Hip-Hop," *CNN*, August 17, 2007. Available at www.cnn.com/2007/POLITICS/08/17/obama.hip.hop/.

9 Several hip-hop stars, including Common, and will.i.am, played active, if unofficial, roles in Obama's 2008 campaign. Jay-Z actively campaigned for and with Obama during the 2012 presidential election.

10 Mark Lotto, "Can Marco Rubio, Florida's Young Hip Hop-Loving Cuban Senator, Save the GOP?," *GQ*, November 19, 2012. Available at www.gq.com/news-politics/blogs/death-race/2012/11/can-marco-rubio-floridas-young-hip-loving-cuban-senator-save-the-gop.html.

11 Jeff Chang, "It's Obama Time: The *Vibe* Cover Story," *Vibe Magazine*, September 2007. Available at http://cantstopwontstop.com/reader/its-obama-time-the-vibe-cover-story/.

12 Two examples of this trend are Obama's remarks on Father's Day, June 15, 2008, at the Apostolic Church of God in Chicago, and his speech on urban gun violence at Chicago's Hyde Park Academy on February 15, 2013. The transcript of the Father's Day remarks are available at www.politico.com/news/stories/0608/11094.html, and the Hyde Park Academy speech is available at www.nbcchicago.com/blogs/ward-room/president-obama-speech-chicago-191471731.html.

13 Alexander Mooney, "Obama Camp Says Ludacris Should be 'Ashamed,'" *CNN*, July 30, 2008. Available at http://politicalticker.blogs.cnn.com/2008/07/30/obama-camp-says-ludacris-should-be-ashamed/.

14 "Remarks by the First Lady at Bowie State University Commencement Ceremony," Whitehouse.gov, May 17, 2013. Available at www.whitehouse.gov/the-press-office/2013/05/17/remarks-first-lady-bowie-state-university-commencement-ceremony.

15 John H. McWhorter, "How Hip-Hop Holds Blacks Back," *City Journal*, Summer 2013. Available at www.city-journal.org/html/13_3_how_hip_hop.html.

16 Ann Oldenburg, "Geraldo Rivera Blames Hoodie for Trayvon Martin's Death," *USA Today*, March 25, 2012. Available at http://content.usatoday.com/communities/entertainment/post/2012/03/geraldo-rivera-blames-hoodie-for-trayvon-martins-death/.

17 Chris Harris, "Barack Obama Weighs in on Sagging-Pants Ordinances: 'Brothers Should Pull Up Their Pants,'" *MTV News*, November 3, 2008. Available at www.mtv.com/news/articles/1598462/barack-obama-weighs-on-sagging-pants-ordinances.jhtml.

18 "Mayor Nutter Addresses Recent Problem with Youth Violence at Church in West Philadelphia," *CBS Philly*, August 7, 2011. Available at http://philadelphia.cbslocal.com/2011/08/07/mayor-nutter-addresses-recent-problem-with-youth-violence-at-church-in-west-philadelphia/. The full transcript of Nutter's speech is available at http://www.americanrhetoric.com/speeches/michaelnuttermountcarmelbaptist.htm.

19 Jonathan Capehart, "Fake Photo of Trayvon Martin Still Making the Rounds," *Washington Post*, July 2, 2013. Available at www.washingtonpost.com/blogs/post-partisan/wp/2013/07/02/fake-photo-of-trayvon-martin-still-making-the-rounds/.

20 As quoted in Erik Nielson, "How Hip-Hop Fell Out of Love with Obama," *The Guardian*, August 23, 2012. Available at www.guardian.co.uk/music/2012/aug/23/why-hip-hop-deserting-obama.

21 *Ibid.*

22 James Montgomery, "Kendrick Lamar Hopes Young Voters Don't Just 'Sit Back' On Election Day," *MTV News*, November 3, 2012. Available at www.mtv.com/news/articles/1696705/election-2012-kendrick-lamar-voting.jhtml.

23 As quoted in Nielson, "How Hip-Hop Fell out of Love."

24 Anush Elbakyan, "Jay Z Says 'My Presence is Charity,' Compares Himself to Obama," *Boston Globe*, July 29, 2013. Available at www.boston.com/news/source/2013/07/jay_z_says_my_presence_is_charity_compares_himself_to_obama.html.

25 Cavan Sieczkowski, "Russell Simmons on Jay-Z Occupy Wall Street Diss: 'Right 99 Times, But This Ain't One,'" *Huffington Post*, September 12, 2012. Available at www.huffingtonpost.com/2012/09/12/russell-simmons-jay-z-occupy-wall-street-response_n_1876907.html.

26 "Dead Prez Scoff at Obama's Stimulus Plan," *Hip Hop Wired*, July 3, 2009. Available at http://hiphopwired.com/2009/07/03/dead-prez-scoff-at-obamas-stimuls-plan/; "Dead Prez: Barack Obama No Better Than George W. Bush," Overground Online, February 24, 2011. Available at www.overgroundonline.com/news-5023/dead-prez-barack-obama-no-better-than-george-w-bush.html.

27 Luke McCormick, "Hear Killer Mike's Fiery 'R.A.P. Music': The Rapper Runs Us Through His New LP," *Spin*, May 7, 2012. Available at http://m.spin.com/articles/hear-killer-mikes-fiery-rap-music-mc-runs-us-through-his-new-lp/.

28 "Lupe Fires Back and Offers Challenge to D.L. Hughley," *Reason 4 Rhymes*, September 18, 2002. Available at www.reason4rhymes.com/2012/09/hip-hop-news/lupe-fires-back-at-d-l-hughley/.

Select bibliography

Books and articles

Adams, Kyle, "Aspects of the Music/Text Relationship in Rap," *Music Theory Online* 14/2 (2008). Available at www.mtosmt.org/issues/mto.08.14.2/mto.08.14.2 .adams.html.

  "On the Metrical Techniques of Flow in Rap Music," *Music Theory Online* 15/5 (2009). Available at www.mtosmt.org/issues/mto.09.15.5/mto.09.15.5.adams .html.

Alexander, Michelle, *The New Jim Crow: Mass Incarceration in the Age of Colorblindness* (New York: The New Press, 2012).

Alim, H. Samy, *Roc the Mic Right: The Language of Hip-Hop Culture* (London: Routledge, 2006).

Anderson, Elijah, *Streetwise: Race, Class, and Change in an Urban Community* (University of Chicago Press, 1992).

Armstrong, Andrew, "The Japanese 'Ghetto Gangsta': Searching for Prestige in Kansai Hip Hop Performance," Ph.D. dissertation, Boston University, 2012.

Armstrong, Edward G., "Eminem's Construction of Authenticity," *Popular Music and Society* 2713 (2004): 335–355.

Bailey, Julius (ed.), *Jay-Z: Essays on Hip Hop's Philosopher King* (Jefferson, NC: McFarland Press, 2011).

Baker, Houston A., *Black Studies, Rap, and the Academy* (University of Chicago Press, 1993).

Ball, Jared A., *I Mix What I Like! A Mixtape Manifesto* (Oakland, CA: AK Press, 2011).

Banes, Sally, "Physical Graffiti: Breaking is Hard to Do," *The Village Voice*, April 22–28, 1981.

Banks, Daniel, *Say Word! Voices from Hip Hop Theater* (Ann Arbor: University of Michigan Press, 2011).

Baraka, Amiri, *Blues People: Negro Music in White America* (New York: William Morrow, 1963).

Bass, Holly, "Blowing Up the Set: What Happens When the Pulse of Hip-hop Shakes Up the Traditional Stage," *American Theater*, November 1999.

Bayley, Amanda, *Recorded Music: Performance, Culture and Technology* (Cambridge University Press, 2010).

Bennett, Andy, "Rappin' on the Tyne: White Hip Hop Culture in Northeast England – an Ethnographic Study," *Sociological Review* 47/1 (1999): 1–24.

Boone, Christine, "Mashing: Toward a Typology of Recycled Music," *Music Theory Online* 19/3 (2013). Available at http://mtosmt.org/issues/mto.13.19.3/mto .13.19.3.boone.php.

Boyd, Todd, *The New H.N.I.C.: The Death of Civil Rights and the Reign of Hip Hop* (New York University Press, 2002).

Brewster, Bill and Frank Broughton, *Last Night a DJ Saved My Life: The History of the Disc Jockey* (New York: Headline Publishing, 2006).

Bynoe, Yvonne, *Stand and Deliver: Political Activism, Leadership, and Hip-hop Culture* (New York: Soft Skull Press, 2004).

Caro, Robert A., *The Power Broker: Robert Moses and the Fall of New York* (New York: Vintage, 1975).

Castleman, Craig, *Getting Up: Subway Graffiti in New York* (Boston: MIT Press, 1982).

Chalfant, Henry and James Prigoff, *Spraycan Art* (London: Thames & Hudson, 1987).

Chang, Jeff, *Can't Stop Won't Stop: A History of the Hip-Hop Generation* (New York: St. Martin's Press, 2005).

Chang, Jeff (ed.), *Total Chaos: The Art and Aesthetics of Hip-Hop* (New York: Basic Civitas, 2006).

Charnas, Dan, *The Big Payback: The History of the Business of Hip-Hop* (New York: New American Library, 2010).

Cheney, Charise, *Brothers Gonna Work It Out: Sexual Politics in the Golden Age of Rap Nationalism* (New York University Press, 2005).

Clay, Andreana, *The Hip-Hop Generation Fights Back: Youth, Activism, and Post-Civil Rights Politics* (New York University Press, 2012).

Cobb, William Jelani, *To the Break of Dawn: A Freestyle on the Hip-Hop Aesthetic* (New York University Press, 2007).

Cohen, Sara, "Ethnography and Popular Music Studies," *Popular Music* 12/2 (1993): 123–138.

Condry, Ian, *Hip-Hop Japan: Rap and the Paths of Cultural Globalization* (Durham, NC: Duke University Press, 2006).

Cooper, Martha and Henry Chalfant, *Subway Art* (London: Thames & Hudson, 1984).

Cooper, Martha and Nika Kramer, *We B*Girlz* (New York: powerHouse Books, 2005).

Cook, Miriam and Bruce B. Lawrence, *Muslim Networks from Hajj to Hip Hop* (Durham, NC: University of North Carolina Press, 2005).

Cross, Brian, *It's Not About a Salary: Rap, Race and Resistance in Los Angeles* (London: Verso Press, 1993).

Danielsen, Anne (ed.), *Musical Rhythm in the Age of Digital Reproduction* (Farnham: Ashgate, 2010).

Davis, Eisa, "Hip-hop Theater: The New Underground," *The Source*, March 2000, pp. 172–176.

DeFrantz, Thomas, "The Black Beat Made Visible: Hip Hop Dance and Body Power," in André Lepecki (ed.), *Of the Presence of the Body: Essays on Dance and Performance Theory* (Middletown, CT: Wesleyan University Press, 2004), pp. 64–81.

Denzin, Norman K., *Interpretive Ethnography: Ethnographic Practice for the 21st Century* (Thousand Oaks, CA: Sage, 1997).

Dery, Mark, "Public Enemy: Confrontation," *Keyboard Magazine*, September 1990, pp. 81–96.

Dimitriadis, Greg, "Hip-hop to Rap: Some Implications of an Historically Situated Approach to Performance," *Text and Performance Quarterly* 19 (1999): 355–369.

Donalson, Melvin, *Hip Hop in American Cinema* (New York: Peter Lang Publishing, 2007).

Dyson, Michael Eric, *Between God and Gangsta Rap* (New York and London: Oxford University Press, 1997).

   Holler If You Hear Me: Searching for Tupac Shakur (New York: Basic Civitas, 2001).

   Open Mic: Reflections on Philosophy, Race, Sex, Culture and Religion (New York: Basic Civitas, 2003).

   Race Rules (New York: Vintage Books, 1997).

   "Rap Culture, the Church, and American Society," *Black Sacred Music: A Journal of Theomusicology* 6/1 (1992): 268–273.

Eisenberg, Evan, *The Recording Angel: Music, Records and Culture from Aristotle to Zappa*, 2nd edn. (New Haven, CT: Yale University Press, 2005).

Emerson, Rana, "'Where My Girls at': Negotiating Black Womanhood in Music Videos," *Gender & Society* 16 (2002): 115–135.

Euell, Kim and Robert Alexander (eds.), *Plays from the Boom Box Galaxy: Theater from the Hip-hop Generation* (New York: Theatre Communications Group, 2009).

Fernandes, Sujatha, *Cuba Represent! Cuban Arts, State Power, and the Making of New Revolutionary Cultures* (Durham, NC: Duke University Press, 2006).

Fink, Robert, "The Story of ORCH5, or the Classical Ghost in the Hip-hop Machine," *Popular Music* 24/3 (October 2005): 339–356.

Fintoni, Lauren, "Return of the Boombap," *Red Bull Music Academy*, July 8, 2012. Available at www.redbullmusicacademy.com/magazine/return-of-the-boom-bap.

Flores, Juan, *From Bomba to Hip-Hop* (New York: Columbia University Press, 2000).

Floyd, Samuel A., Jr., *The Power of Black Music* (Oxford University Press, 1995).

Fogarty, Mary Elizabeth, "Dance to the Drummer's Beat: Competing Tastes in International B-Boy/B-Girl Culture," Dissertation University of Edinburgh, 2011.

   "'Each One Teach One': B-Boying and Ageing," in Paul Hodkinson and Andy Bennett (eds.), *Ageing and Youth Cultures: Music, Style, and Identity* (London: Bloomsbury Academic, 2012).

   "Whatever Happened to Breakdancing? Transnational B-boy/B-girl Networks, Underground Video Magazines and Imagined *Affinities*," Master's Thesis, Brook University, 2006.

Forman, Murray, *The 'Hood Comes First: Race, Space, and Place in Rap and Hip-Hop* (Middletown, CT: Wesleyan University Press, 2002).

Forman, Murray and Mark Anthony Neal (eds.), *That's the Joint! The Hip-Hop Studies Reader*, 2nd edn. (New York and London: Routledge, 2011).

Fricke, Jim and Charlie Ahearn (eds.), *Yes, Yes Y'all: The Experience Music Project Oral History of Hip-Hop's First Decade* (Cambridge, MA: Da Capo Press, 2002).

Gastman, Roger and Caleb Neelon, *The History of American Graffiti* (New York: HarperCollins, 2010).

Gaunt, Kyra Danielle, *The Games Black Girls Play: Learning the Ropes from Double-Dutch to Hip-Hop* (New York University Press, 2006).

George, Nelson, *Hip Hop America* (New York: Viking Press, 1998).

Gilroy, Paul, *The Black Atlantic: Modernity and Double Consciousness* (Cambridge, MA: Harvard University Press, 1993).

Gooch, Cheryl R., "Rappin for the Lord: The Uses of Gospel Rap and Contemporary Music in Black Religious Communities," in D. A. Stout and Judith M. Buddenbaum (eds.), *Religion and Mass Media: Audiences and Adaptations* (Thousand Oaks, CA: Sage Publications, 1996).

Gosa, Travis L., "Counterknowledge, Racial Paranoia, and the Cultic Milieu: Decoding Hip-hop Conspiracy Theory," *Poetics* 39/3 (2011): 187–204.

Gosa, Travis L. and Tristan Fields, "Is Hip-Hop Education Another Hustle? The (Ir)Responsible Use of Hip-Hop as Pedagogy," in Brad J. Porfilio and Michael Viola (eds.), *Hip-Hop(e): The Cultural Practice and Critical Pedagogy of International Hip-Hop* (New York: Peter Lang, 2012), pp. 195– 210.

Greenwald, Jeff, "Hip-Hop Drumming: The Rhyme May Define, but the Groove Makes You Move," *Black Music Research Journal* 22/2 (2002): 259–271.

Hager, Steven, *Hip-hop: The Illustrated History of Breakdancing, Rap Music, and Graffiti* (New York: St. Martin's Press, 1984).

Hanchard, Michael, *Party Politics: Horizons in Black Political Thought* (New York: Oxford University Press, 2006).

Harkness, Geoff, "Gangs and Gangsta Rap in Chicago: A Microscenes Perspective," *Poetics* 41/2 (2013): 151–176.

"The Spirit of Rapitalism: Artistic Labor Practices in Chicago's Hip Hop Underground," *Journal of Workplace Rights* 16 (2012): 251–270.

"True School: Situational Authenticity in Chicago's Hip Hop Underground," *Cultural Sociology* 6 (2012): 283–298.

Harrison, Anthony Kwame, "'Cheaper Than a CD, Plus We Really Mean It': Bay Area Underground Hip Hop Tapes as Subcultural Artefacts," *Popular Music* 25/2 (2006): 283–301.

Hip Hop Underground: The Integrity and Ethics of Racial Identification (Philadelphia: Temple University Press, 2009).

Heller, Jerry, *Ruthless: A Memoir* (New York: Gallery, 2007).

Hess, Mickey (ed.), *Icons of Hip-Hop: An Encyclopedia of the Movement, Music, and Culture* (Santa Barbara, CA: ABC-CLO, 2007).

Hoch, Danny, "Here We Go Yo! A Hip-hop Arts Manifesto," *American Theater* 21/10 (2004).

Hodgson, Jay, "Lateral Dynamics Processing in Experimental Hip-Hop: Flying Lotus, Madlib, Oh No, J-Dilla and Prefuse 73," *Journal on the Art of Record Production* 5 (2011).

hooks, bell, *Black Looks: Race and Representation* (Boston: South End Press, 1992).

Hunter, Margaret, "Shake it, Baby, Shake it: Consumption and the New Gender Relation Hip-hop," *Sociological Perspectives* 54 (2001): 15–36.

Huntington, Carla Stalling, *Hip Hop Dance: Meanings and Messages* (Jefferson, NC: MacFarland Press, 2007).

Ibrahim, Awad, H. Samy Alim, and Alastair Pennycook (eds.), *Global Linguistic Flows: Hip Hop Cultures, Youth Identities, and the Politics of Language* (New York: Routledge, 2009).

Isobe, Ryō, "Yankii to hippu hoppu: Souru zoku kara B-Boy to tsuzuku mou hitotsu no yankii no rekishi," in Takeo Igarashi (ed.), *Yankii bunkaron josetsu* (Tokyo: Kawade Shobō Shinsha, 2009).

Isobe, Ryō (ed.), *Odotte wa ikenai kuni, nihon: Fūeihō mondai to kajō kisei sareru shakai* (Tokyo: Kawade Shobō, 2012).

Jackson, John L., Jr., *Real Black: Adventures of Racial Sincerity* (University of Chicago Press, 2005).

Jeffries, Michael, *Thug Life: Race, Gender, and the Meaning of Hip-Hop* (University of Chicago Press, 2011).

Johnson, Imani Kai, "B-Boying and Battling in a Global Context: The Discursive Life of Difference in Hip Hop Dance," *Alif: Journal of Comparative Poetics* 31 (2011): 173–195.

"From Blues Women to B-Girls: Performing Badass Femininity," *Women & Performance: A Journal of Feminist Theory*, special issue "All Hail the Queenz: A Queer Feminist Recalibration of Hip-hop Scholarship" 24/1 (2014), pp. 15–28.

"Dark Matter in B-Boying Cyphers: Race and Global Connection in Hip Hop", Ph.D. dissertation, University of Southern California, 2009.

Katz, Mark, *Capturing Sound: How Technology Has Changed Music* (Berkeley: University of California Press, 2010).

Groove Music: The Art and Culture of the Hip-Hop DJ (New York: Oxford University Press, 2012).

Kautny, Oliver, "'. . . when I'm not put on this list . . .' Kanonisierungsprozesse im HipHop am Beispiel Eminem," in Dietrich Helms and Thomas Phelps (eds.), *No Time for Losers. Charts, Listen und andere Kanonisierungen in der populären Musik* (Bielefeld: Transcript, 2008), pp. 145–160.

Kautny, Oliver and Adam Krims (eds.), *Sampling im HipHop*, in *Samples* 9 (2010). Available at http://aspm.ni.lo-net2.de/samples/9Inhalt.html.

Kaya, Ayhan, "*Sicher in Kreuzberg.*" *Constructing Diasporas: Turkish Hip-hop Youth in Berlin* (Bielefeld: Transcript, 2001).

Kelley, Robin D. G., *Race Rebels: Culture, Politics, and the Black Working Class* (New York: The Free Press, 1994).

Yo' Mama's Dysfunctional! Fighting the Culture Wars in Urban America (Boston: Beacon Press, 1997).

Keyes, Cheryl L., "Empowering Self, Making Choices, Creating Spaces: Black Female Identity via Rap Music Performance," *The Journal of American Folklore* 113 (2000): 255–269.

Rap Music and Street Consciousness: Music in American Life (Chicago: University of Illinois Press, 2002).

"Verbal Art Performance in Rap Music: The Conversation of the 80's," *Folklore Forum* 17/2 (1984): 143–152.

Kitwana, Bakari, *The Hip-Hop Generation: Young Blacks and the Crisis in African American Culture* (New York: Basic Civitas, 2002).

Why White Kids Love Hip-hop (New York: Basic Civitas, 2005).

Knight, Michael Muhammad, *The Five Percenters: Islam, Hip-Hop, and the Gods of New York* (London: One World Books, 2007).

Krims, Adam, "The Hip-Hop Sublime as a Form of Commodification," in Regula Burckhardt Qureshi (ed.), *Music and Marx: Ideas, Practice, Politics* (New York and London: Routledge, 2002), pp. 63–80.

 Music and Urban Geography (London: Routledge, 2007).

 Rap Music and the Poetics of Identity (Cambridge University Press, 2000).

KRS-One, *The Gospel of Hip-Hop: First Instrument* (Brooklyn, NY: powerHouse Books, 2009).

Kugelberg, Johan, Joe Conzo, and Afrika Bambaataa, *Born in the Bronx: A Visual Record of the Early Days of Hip-Hop* (New York: Rizzoli, 2007).

LaBoskey, Sara, "Getting off: Portrayals of Masculinity in Hip Hop Dance in Film," *Dance Research Journal* 33 (2001): 112–120.

Lee, Jooyoung, "Open Mic: Professionalizing the Rap Career", *Ethnography* 10/4 (2009): 475–495.

Lewis, Ladel, "White Thugs & Black Bodies: A Comparison of the Portrayal of African-American Women in Hip Hop Videos," *The Hilltop Review* 4 (2011): 1–17.

Livingston, Samuel Thomas, "The Ideological and Philosophical Influence of the Nation of Islam on Hip-Hop Culture," Ph.D. dissertation, Temple University, 1998.

Manabe, Noriko, "Globalization and Japanese Creativity: Adaptations of Japanese Language to Rap," *Ethnomusicology* 50/1 (2006): 1–36.

 "Music in Japanese Antinuclear Demonstrations: The Evolution of a Contentious Performance Model," *The Asia-Pacific Journal* 11/3 (2013). Available at http:// japanfocus.org/-Noriko-MANABE/4015.

 "Representing Japan: 'National' Style among Japanese Hip-hop DJs," *Popular Music* 32/1 (2013): 35–50.

 "Straight Outta Ichimiya: The Appeal of a Rural Japanese Rapper," *The Asia Pacific Journal* 11/1 (2013). Available at www.japanfocus.org/-Noriko-MANABE/3889.

 The Revolution Will Not Be Televised: Music and Musicians in the Antinuclear Movement post-Fukushima (New York: Oxford University Press, forthcoming).

Maxwell, Ian, *Phat Beats, Dope Rhymes: Hip Hop Down Under Comin' Upper* (Middletown, CT: Wesleyan University Press, 2003).

McLeod, Kembrew, "Authenticity within Hip Hop and Other Cultures Threatened with Assimilation," *Journal of Communication* 49/4 (1999): 134–150.

McLeod, Kembrew and Peter DiCola, *Creative License: The Law and Culture of Digital Sampling* (Durham, NC: Duke University Press, 2011).

McQuillar, Tayannah Lee, and J. Brother, *When Rap Music Had a Conscience: The Artists, Organizations, and Historic Events That Inspired and Influenced the "Golden Age" of Hip-Hop from 1987 to 1996* (New York: Thunder's Mouth Press, 2007).

McWhorter, John, *All About the Beat: Why Hip-Hop Can't Save Black America* (New York: Gotham Books, 2008).

Miller, Ivor, *Aerosol Kingdom: Subway Painters of New York City* (University Press of Mississippi, 2002, repr. 2010).

Miller-Young, Mireille, "Hip Hop Honeys and da Hustlaz: Black Sexualities in the New Hip Hop Pornography," *Meridians: Feminism, Race, Transnationalism* 8 (2008): 261–292.

Mitchell, Tony (ed.), *Global Noise: Rap and Hip Hop Outside the USA* (Middletown, CT: Wesleyan University Press, 2001).

Miyakawa, Felicia, *Five Percenter Rap: God Hop's Music, Message, and Black Muslim Mission* (Bloomington, IN: Indiana University Press, 2005).

Montano, Ed, "'How do you Know He's not Playing Pac-Man while He's Supposed to be DJing?' Technology, formats and the Digital Future of DJ Culture," *Popular Music* 29/3 (2010): 397–416.

Morgan, Joan, *When Chickenheads Come Home to Roost: A Hip Hop Feminist Breaks it Down* (New York: Simon and Schuster, 1999).

Morgan, Marcyliena, *The Real Hiphop: Battling for Knowledge, Power, and Respect in the LA Underground* (Durham, NC: Duke University Press, 2009).

Morris, David Z., "The Sakura of Madness: Japan's Nationalist Hip Hop and the Parallax of Globalized Identity Politics," *Communication, Culture & Critique* 6/3 (2013): 459–480.

Mukherjee, Roopali, "The Ghetto Fabulous Aesthetic in Contemporary Black Culture" *Cultural Studies* 20 (2006): 599–629.

Neff, Ali Colleen, *Let the World Listen Right: The Mississippi Delta Hip-hop Story* (Jackson, MS: University Press of Mississippi, 2009).

Negus, Keith, "The Music Business and Rap: Between the Street and the Executive Suite," *Cultural Studies* 13 (1999): 488–508.

Ness, Alien, *The Art of Battle: Understanding Judged BBoy Battles*. Alien Ness.

Nielson, Erik, "'Here Come the Cops': Policing the Resistance in Rap Music," *International Journal of Cultural Studies* 15 (2012): 349–363.

Ogbar, Jeffrey Ogbonna Green, *Hip-Hop Revolution: The Culture and Politics of Rap* (Lawrence, KS: University Press of Kansas, 2007).

O'Hara, Robert and Harry Elam, *The Fire This Time: African American Plays of the 21st Century* (New York: Theatre Communications Group, 2002).

Osumare, Halifu, *The Africanist Aesthetic in Global Hip-Hop: Power Moves* (New York: Palgrave Macmillan, 2007).

Pabon, Jessica, "Be About It: Graffiteras Performing Feminist Community," *TDR/The Drama Review* 57/3 (2013): 88–116.

Perkins, William Eric (ed.), *Droppin' Science: Critical Essays on Rap Music and Hip-Hop Culture* (Philadelphia: Temple University Press, 1996).

Perkinson, James, *Shamanism, Racism, and Hip-Hop Culture: Essays on White Supremacy and Black Subversion* (Basingstoke: Palgrave Macmillan, 2006).

Perry, Imani, *Prophets of the Hood: Politics and Poetics in Hip Hop* (Durham, NC: Duke University Press, 2004).

Persley, Nicole Hodges, *Remixing Blackness: Sampling Race and Gender in Hip-hop Theater and Performance* (Ann Arbor: University of Michigan Press, forthcoming).

Petchauer, Emery, *Hip-hop Culture in College Students' Lives: Elements, Embodiment, and Higher Edutainment* (New York: Routledge, 2012).

Peterson, Richard A. and Andy Bennett, "Introducing Music Scenes," in A. Bennett and R. A. Peterson, *Music Scenes: Local, Translocal, Virtual* (Nashville, TN: Vanderbilt University Press, 2004), pp. 1–15.

Pfleiderer, Martin, *Rhythmus. Psychologische, theoretische und stilanalytische Aspekte populärer Musik* (Bielefeld: Transcript, 2006).

Phillips, Susan, "Crip Walk, Villain Dance, Pueblo Stroll: The Embodiment of Writing in African American Gang Dance," *Anthropological Quarterly* 82/1 (2009): 69–97.

Pinn, Anthony (ed.), *Noise and Spirit: The Religious and Spiritual Sensibilities of Rap Music* (New York University Press, 2003).

Pollard, Deborah Smith, *When the Church Becomes Your Party: Contemporary Gospel Music* (Wayne State University Press, 2008).

Quinn, Eithne, *Nuthin' but a "G" Thang: The Culture and Commerce of Gangsta Rap, Popular Cultures, Everyday Lives* (New York: Columbia University Press, 2005).

Rabaka, Reiland, *Hip Hop's Inheritance: From the Harlem Renaissance to the Hip Hop Feminist Movement* (Lanham, MD: Lexington Books, 2011).

Ramsey, Guthrie, *Race Music* (Berkeley and Los Angeles: University of California Press, 2003).

Reed, Teresa L., *The Holy Profane: Religion in Black Popular Music* (Lexington, KY: The University Press of Kentucky, 2003).

Reynolds, Simon, "Maximal Nation: Electronic Music's Evolution Toward the Thrilling Excess of Digital Maximalism," *Pitchfork,* December 6, 2011. Available at http://pitchfork.com/features/articles/8721-maximal-nation/.

Rivera, Raquel Z., *New York Ricans from the Hip Hop Zone* (New York: Palgrave Macmillan, 2003).

Roberts, Robin, "'Ladies first': Queen Latifah's Afrocentric feminist music video," *African American Review* 28 (1994): 245–257.

Robitzky, Niels, *Von Swipe Zu Storm: Breakdance in Deutschland* (Hamburg: Backspin, 2000).

Rodriquez, Jason, "Color-Blind Ideology and Cultural Appropriation in Hip-Hop," *Journal of Contemporary Ethnography* 35/6 (2006): 645–668.

Rose, Tricia, *Black Noise: Rap Music and Black Culture in Contemporary America* (Middletown, CT: Wesleyan University Press, 1994).
  The Hip Hop Wars: What We Talk about When We Talk about Hip Hop (New York: Basic Civitas, 2008).

Royster, Philip M., "The Rapper as Shaman for a Band of Dancers of the Spirit: 'U Can't Touch This,'" *Black Sacred Music: A Journal of Theomusicology* 5/1 (1991): 61–67.

Schloss, Joseph G., *Foundation: B-Boys, B-Girls, and Hip-Hop Culture in New York* (New York: Oxford University Press, 2009).
  Making Beats: The Art of Sample-Based Hip-Hop (Middletown, CT: Wesleyan University Press, 2004).

Sewell, Amanda, "A Typology of Sampling in Hip-Hop," Ph.D. dissertation, Indiana University, 2013.

Shapiro, Roberta, "The Aesthetics of Institutionalization: Breakdancing in France," *The Journal of Arts Management, Law, and Society* 33/4 (2004): 316–335.

Sharpley-Whiting, Tracy, *Pimps Up Hoes Down: Hip Hop's Hold on Young Black Women* (New York University Press, 2008).

Simmons, Danny, *Russell Simmons Def Poetry Jam on Broadway and More* (New York: Atria Books, 2005).

Sinnreich, Aram, *Mashed Up: Music, Technology, and the Rise of Configurable Culture* (Amherst and Boston: University of Massachusetts Press, 2010).

Smith, Efrem and Phil Jackson, *The Hip Hop Church: Connecting with the Movement Shaping our Culture* (Downers Grove, IL: InterVarsity Press, 2006).

Sokol, Monika, "Verbal Duelling. Ein universeller Sprachspieltypus und seine Metamorphosen im US-amerikanischen, französischen und deutschen Rap," in Eva Kimminich (ed.), *Rap: More than Words* (Frankfurt: Peter Lang, 2004), pp. 113–160.

Sorett, Josef, "Beats, Rhyme and Bible: An Introduction to Gospel Hip Hop," *African American Pulpit* 10 (2006–2007): 12–16.

"'Believe Me, This Pimp Game is Very Religious': Toward a Religious History of Hip Hop," *Culture and Religion* 10/1 (2009): 11–22.

Spady, James, *Nation Conscious Rap: The Hip-Hop Vision* (PC International Press, 1991).

Spady, James G., H. Samy Alim, and Samir Meghelli (eds.), *The Global Cipha: Hip Hop Culture and Consciousness* (Philadelphia: Black History Museum Publishers, 2006).

Spence, Lester K., *Blues and Evil* (Knoxville, TN: University of Tennessee Press, 1993).

Stare in the Darkness: The Limits of Hip-Hop and Black Politics (Minneapolis: University of Minnesota Press, 2011).

Spencer, Jon Michael, *Theological Music: Introduction to Theomusicology* (New York: Greenwood Press, 1991).

Stephens, Dionne, and April Few, "Hip Hop Honey or Video Ho: African American Preadolescents' Understanding of Female Sexual Scripts in Hip Hop culture," *Sexuality & Culture* 11 (2007): 48–69.

Stephens, Dionne, and Layli Phillips, "Freaks, Gold Diggers, Divas, and Dykes: The Sociohistorical Development of Adolescent African American Women's Sexual Scripts," *Sexuality & Culture* 7 (2003): 3–49.

Stoute, Steve and Mim Eichler Rivas, *The Tanning of America: How Hip-Hop Created a Culture That Rewrote the Rules of the New Economy* (New York: Gotham Books, 2011).

Sylvan, Robin, *Traces of the Spirit: The Religious Dimensions of Popular Music* (New York and London: New York University Press, 2002).

Tate, Greg, *Everything but the Burden: What White People are Taking from Black Culture* (New York: Broadway Books, 2003).

Terkourafi, Marina (ed.), *The Languages of Global Hip Hop* (New York: Continuum International Publishing Group, 2010).

Toop, David, *Rap Attack 2: African Rap to Global Hip-Hop*, 2nd edn. (New York: Serpent's Tail, 1991).

Van DeBurg, William, *Hoodlum: African-American Blacks Villains and Social Bandits in American Life* (University of Chicago Press, 2004).

Wald, Elijah, *The Dozens: A History of Rap's Mama* (New York: Oxford University Press, 2012).

Walser, Robert, "Rhythm, Rhyme, and Rhetoric in the Music of Public Enemy," *Ethnomusicology* 39/2 (1995): 193–217.

Hip Hop Matters: Politics, Pop Culture, and the Struggle for the Soul of a Movement (Boston: Beacon Press, 2005).

Ward, L. Monique, Edwina Hansbrough, and Eboni Walker, "Contributions of Music Video Exposure to Black Adolescents' Gender and Sexual Schemas," *Journal of Adolescent Research* 20 (2005): 143–166.

Watkins, S. Craig, *Representing: Hip Hop Culture and the Production of Black Cinema* (University of Chicago Press, 1998).

Weitzer, Ronald and Charis Kubrin, "Misogyny in Rap Music: A Content Analysis of Prevalence and Meanings," *Men and Masculinities* 12 (2009): 3–29.

Williams, Erik J., "Only God Can Judge Us, Only God Can Save Us: The Hip-Hop Soul of Thugology," *Black Arts Quarterly: Hip Hop Culture: Language, Literature, Literacy and the Lives of Black Youth* 6/2 (2001): 42–45.

Williams, Justin A., "Beats and Flows: A Response to Kyle Adams," *Music Theory Online* 15/2 (2009). Available at www.mtosmt.org/issues/mto.09.15.2/mto. 09.15.2.williams.html.

Rhymin' and Stealin': Musical Borrowing in Hip-Hop (Ann Arbor: University of Michigan Press, 2013).

Wilson, Olly, "The Significance of the Relationship between Afro-American Music and West African Music," *The Black Perspective in Music* 2/1 (1974): 3–22.

Wilson, William Julius, *The Truly Disadvantaged: The Inner City, the Underclass, and Public Policy* (University of Chicago Press, 1987).

When Work Disappears: The World of the New Urban Poor (New York: Vintage, 1996).

Wimsatt, William "Upski," *Bomb the Suburbs*, 2nd edn. (Chicago: The Subway and Elevated Press Company, 1994).

Witten, Andrew and Michael White, *Dondi, Style Master General: The Life of Graffiti Artist Dondi White* (New York: Reagan Books, 2001).

Zanfagna, Christina, "Building 'Zyon' in Babylon: Holy Hip Hop and Geographies of Conversion," *Black Music Research Journal* 31/2 (2010): 145–162.

"The Multiringed Cosmos of Krumping: Hip-Hop Dance at the Intersections of Battle, Media, and Spirit," in Julie Malnig (ed.) *Ballroom, Boogie, Shimmy Sham, Shake: A Social and Popular Dance Reader* (Urbana: University of Illinois Press, 2008), pp. 337–353.

"Under the Blasphemous W(RAP): Locating the 'Spirit' in Hip-Hop," *Pacific Review of Ethnomusicology* 12 (2006). Available at www.pacificreviewofethnomusicology.org.

Plays

Abdoh, Reza, *The Hip-hop Waltz of Eurydice* (Baltimore: Johns Hopkins University Press, 1991).

Alexander, Robert, *A Preface to the Alien Garden* (New York: Broadway Play
    Publishing, 1996).

Bass, Holly, *Moneymaker: An Endurance Performance by Holly Bass* (Washington,
    DC: Corcoran Gallery, February 11, 2012).

Bautista, Kilusan, *Universal Self* (2011).

Compagnie, Kafig, *Boxe, Boxe* (2005).

Davis, Abiola and Antoy Grant, *Goddess City* (2008).

Davis, Eisa, *Angela's Mixtape* (2009).

Diaz, Kristoffer, *Welcome to Arroyo's* (New York: Dramatists Play Services, 2010).

Forbes, Kamilah, *Rhyme Deferred*, in Robert Alexander and Harry Elam's *The Fire
    This Time: African American Plays for the 21st Century* (New York: Theatre
    Communications Group, 2002).

Glover, Savion and George C. Wolfe, *Bring in Da Noise, Bring in Da Funk* (1996).

Hernandez-Kolski, Joe, *You Wanna Piece of Me?* (2006).

Hinds, Rickerby, *Daze to Come* (1989).
    Dreamscape (2012).

Hoch, Danny, *Jails, Hospitals and Hip-hop* (New York: Villard, 1998).
    Some People (New York: Villard, 1998).
    Till the Break of Dawn (2007).

Israel, Baba, *Boom Bap Meditations* (2008).

Jones, Rhodessa, *The Medea Project* (1989). Available at www.themedeaproject
    .weebly.com (accessed May 30, 2013).

Jones, Sarah, *Bridge and Tunnel: A Trip through American Identity in Eight Voices*
    (New York: Three Rivers Press, 2006).
    "Your Revolution (1997).

Jonzi D, "Lyrical Fearta" (2001).

Joseph, Marc Bamuthi, *The Break/s: A Mixtape for the Stage* (2009).
    Red, Black, and Green: A Blues (2013).
    Word Becomes Flesh (2010).

Kreidler, Todd, *Holler if you Hear Me* (2014).

de Leon, Aya, *Thieves in the Temple* (2004).

Miranda, Lin-Manuel, *In the Heights* (New York: Applause Theater, 2013).

Pabon, Jorge and Steffan 'Mr. Wiggles' Clemente, *Jam on the Groove* (1995).
    "*So What Happen Now?*" (1990).

Power, Will, *Fetch Clay, Make Man* (2013).
    Flow (2003).

Reid, Benji, *13 Mics* (2005).

Sax, Matt, *Clay* (2007).

Sax, Matt and E. Rosen, *Venice* (2010).

Simmons, Russell, *Def Poetry Jam on Broadway and More* (New York: Atria Books,
    2005).

Universes, *Slanguage*, in Robert O'Hara and Harry Elam, Jr., *The Fire This Time:
    African American Plays for the 21st Century* (New York: Theatre
    Communications Group, 2002).

Walidah, Hanifah, *Straight Folks' Guide to Gay Black Folk* (2003).

Filmography

8 Mile, dir. Curtis Hanson (Universal Pictures, 2002).

Akira's Hip Hop Shop, dir. Joseph Doughrity (Daydreamer Pictures, Lightspeed Entertainment, 2007).

All the Ladies Say, dir. Ana "Rokafella" Garcia-Dionosio (Full Circle Productions, 2009).

Beat Street, dir. Stan Lathan (Orion Pictures Corp., 1984).

Black and White, dir. James Toback (Bigel/Mailer Films, Palm Pictures, 1999).

Bouncing Cats, dir. Nabil Elderkin (Red Bull Media House, 2010). Available at www.youtube.com/watch?v=RrQpIGW7jVw (accessed September 15, 2013).

Boyz N the Hood, dir. John Singleton (Columbia Pictures, 1991).

Breakin', dir. Joel Silberg (MGM, 1984).

Breakin' 2: Electric Boogaloo, dir. Sam Firstenberg (MGM, 1984).

Brown Sugar, dir. Rick Famuyiwa (Fox Searchlight, 2002).

Bulworth, dir. Warren Beatty (Twentieth Century Fox, 1998).

CB4, dir. Tamra Davis (Universal Pictures, 1993).

Check Your Body at the Door, dir. Sally Sommers (2012).

Class Act, dir. Randall Miller (Warner Bros., 1992).

Cool as Ice, dir. David Kellogg (Alive Films, Capella, Koppelmann/Bandier-Carnegie Pictures, 1991).

A Day in the Life, dir. Sticky Fingaz (Major Independents, 2009).

Death of a Dynasty, dir. Damon Dash (Dash Films, Entertainment Funding Group, Intrinsic Value Films, 2003).

Diamond Dawgs, dir. Chris Rogers (ScreenMagic Films, 2009).

Do the Right Thing, dir. Spike Lee (40 Acres & A Mule Filmworks, 1989).

Everything Remains Raw: Hip Hop's Folkloric Lineage, dir. Moncell "Ill Kosby" Durden (forthcoming).

Exit Through the Gift Shop (A Banksy film, 2010).

Fear of a Black Hat, dir. Rusty Cundieff (Incorporated Television Company, Oakwood Productions, 1993).

Feel the Noise, dir. Alejandro Chomski (Sony Pictures, 2007).

Flashdance, dir. Adrian Lyne (Paramount Pictures, 1983).

Freshest Kids: A History of the B-boy, dir. Baba Israel (QD3 Entertainment Inc., 2002).

From Mambo to Hip Hop: A South Bronx Tale, dir. Henry Chalfant (City Lore Productions, 2006).

Get Rich or Die Tryin', dir. Jim Sheridan (Cent Productions Inc., Paramount Pictures, MTV Films, 2005).

Go For It, dir. Carmen Marron (Sparkhope Productions, 2011).

Graffiti Rock and Other Hip Hop Delights (CB Communication Inc., 2002).

Hip Hop 4 Life, dir. David Velo Stewart (Velocity Productions Ltd., 2001).

History and Concept of Hip-hop Dance: The Street Culture that Became a Global Expression, dir. Moncell Durden (Dancetime Productions, 2010).

Honey, dir. Bille Woodruff (Universal Pictures, Marc Platt Productions, NuAmerica Entertainment, 2003).

House of Trés (Alive TV no. 603, 1990).

House Party, dir. Reginald Hudlin (The Hudlin Brothers, Jackson/McHenry Company, New Line Cinema, 1990).

House Party 2, dir. Doug McHenry and George Jackson (The Hudlin Brothers, Jackson/McHenry Company, New Line Cinema, 1991).

House Party 3, dir. Eric Meza (The Hudlin Brothers, Jackson/McHenry Company, New Line Cinema, 1994).

How She Move, dir. Ian Iqbal Rashid (Sienna Films, Celluloid Creams, MTV Films, 2007).

Hustle and Flow, dir. Craig Brewer (Crunk Pictures, Homegrown Pictures, MTV Films, 2005).

Inside the Circle, dir. Marcy Garriott (La Sonrisa Productions Inc., 2007).

The Janky Promoters, dir. Marcus Raboy (Cube Vision, Dimension Films, 2009).

Juice, dir. Ernest R. Dickerson (Island World, 1992).

Just Another Day, dir. Peter Spirer (Rugged Entertainment, Secret Society Films, 2009).

Kings of Broadway: The History of New York Subway Graffiti, dir. Chris Pape (Broadway Style Productions, 1998).

Krush Groove, dir. Michael Schultz (Crystalite Productions, Film Development Fund, Visual Eye Productions, 1985).

Know Thy Enemy, dir. Lee Cipolla (Future Films, 2009).

Let It Shine, dir. Paul Hoen (G Wave Productions, 2012).

Maestro, dir. Josell Ramos (Sanctuary, 2005).

Malibu's Most Wanted, dir. John Whitesell (Warner Bros., Karz Entertainment, Big Ticket Productions, 2003).

Marci X, dir. Richard Benjamin (Paramount Pictures, Scott Rudin Productions, Munich Film Partners New Century & Company, 2003).

Murda Musik, dir. Lawrence Page (1999).

Notorious, dir. George Tillman, Jr. (Fox Searchlight Pictures, Voletta Wallace Films, Bystorm Films, 2009).

Out of Sync, dir. Debbie Allen (Black Entertainment Television, United Image Entertainment, 1995).

Planet B-Boy, dir. Benson Lee (Arts Alliance America, 2008).

Play'd: A Hip Hop Story, dir. Oz Scott (Stu Segal Productions, 2002).

Rize, dir. David LaChapelle (Lions Gate, 2005).

Reck'n Shop: Live From Brooklyn (Alive TV no. 805, 1992).

Redder Than Red: The Story of B-Girl Bubbles, dir. Martha Cooper and Nika Kramer (We B*Girlz Productionz!, 2005).

Rock Dance History: The Untold Story of Up-Rockin', dir. Jorge "Popmaster Fabel" Pabon (forthcoming).

Save the Last Dance, dir. Thomas Carter (Cort/Madden Productions, MTV Films, 2001).

Slam, dir. Marc Levin (Off Line Entertainment Group, 1998).

Stations of the Elevated, dir. produced by Manfred Kirchheimer (Xenon Entertainment, 1979).

Step Off, dir. Austin LaRon (Lion's Gate, 2011).

Step Up, dir. Anne Fletcher (Summit Entertainment, Touchstone Pictures, Offspring Entertainment, 2006).

Step Up 2: The Streets, dir. John M. Chu (Summit Entertainment, Touchstone Pictures, Offspring Entertainment, 2008).

Step Up 3D, dir. John M. Chu (Summit Entertainment, Touchstone Pictures, Offspring Entertainment, 2010).

Style Wars, dir. Tony Silver and Henry Chalfant (Public Art Films, 1983).

Thicker Than Water, dir. Richard Cummings, Jr. (First Write Productions, Hoo-Bangin', Marsmedia, Priority Films, 1999).

Tougher Than Leather, dir. Rick Rubin (Def Pictures, 1988).

Turn It Up, dir. Robert Adetuyi (MadGuy Films, New Line Cinema, Paris Brothers, 2000).

Underground Dance Masters: Final History of a Forgotten Era, dir. Thomas Guzman-Sanchez (Clockman Vision, 2008).

Video Girl, dir. Ty Hodges (Dan Garcia Productions, Datari Turner Productions, Most Wanted Films, 2011).

Whiteboyz, dir. Marc Levin (Bac Films, Canal+, Fox Searchlight Pictures, Off Line Entertainment Group, 1999).

Wild Style, dir. Charlie Ahearn (Rhino Theatrical, 1983).

You Got Served, dir. Chris Stokes (Screen Gems, Ultimate Group Films, The (TUG), Melee Entertainment, Gotta Dance Inc., 2004).

You Got Served: Beat the World, dir. Robert Adetuyi (Telefilm Canada, The Harold Greenberg Fund, Inner City Films, Ontario Media Development Corporation, Shotz Fiction Film, 2011).

Index

Cambridge Companions to Music

The Cambridge Companion to Schumann
Edited by Beate Perrey

The Cambridge Companion to Shostakovich
Edited by Pauline Fairclough and David Fanning

The Cambridge Companion to Sibelius
Edited by Daniel M. Grimley

The Cambridge Companion to Richard Strauss
Edited by Charles Youmans

The Cambridge Companion to Michael Tippett
Edited by Kenneth Gloag and Nicholas Jones

The Cambridge Companion to Vaughan Williams
Edited by Alain Frogley and Aiden J. Thomson

The Cambridge Companion to Verdi
Edited by Scott L. Balthazar

Instruments

The Cambridge Companion to Brass Instruments
Edited by Trevor Herbert and John Wallace

The Cambridge Companion to the Cello
Edited by Robin Stowell

The Cambridge Companion to the Clarinet
Edited by Colin Lawson

The Cambridge Companion to the Guitar
Edited by Victor Coelho

The Cambridge Companion to the Organ
Edited by Nicholas Thistlethwaite and Geoffrey Webber

The Cambridge Companion to the Piano
Edited by David Rowland

The Cambridge Companion to the Recorder
Edited by John Mansfield Thomson

The Cambridge Companion to the Saxophone
Edited by Richard Ingham

The Cambridge Companion to Singing
Edited by John Potter

The Cambridge Companion to the Violin
Edited by Robin Stowell